19.45

D0385928

UNCOVERING SOVIET DISASTERS

UNCOVERING SOVIET DISASTERS

EXPLORING THE LIMITS OF *GLASNOST*

JAMES E. OBERG

RANDOM HOUSE
NEW YORK

This book represents the private research, analysis, and conclusions of the author
alone, and cannot be construed to reflect the opinions of any corporation, association,
or federal agency or administration.

Grateful acknowledgment is made to the following for permission to reprint previously
published material:

James Publishing: Excerpts from *Conquered: New Shape in the Sky* by Sir George
Edwards.

Little, Brown and Company: Excerpt from *Khrushchev Remembers: The Last Testament*
by Crankshaw, Schector and Talbot. Copyright © 1974 by Little, Brown and Company.
By permission of Little, Brown and Company.

Library of Congress Cataloging-in-Publication Data

Oberg, James E., 1944–
    Uncovering Soviet disasters.

    Includes index.
    1. Disasters in the press—Soviet Union.
2. Disasters—Soviet Union.   3. Government and
the press—Soviet Union.   I. Title.
PN5277.D58O24   1988   302.2'34'0947   87-42658
ISBN 0-394-56095-7

301.2430947
012

To Grigoriy Nelyubov and
the other unremembered victims

All that man can do for humanity is to
further the *truth*, whether it be
sweet or bitter.

—Franz Boas (1858–1942)
father of American anthropology

CONTENTS

INTRODUCTION

It is a basic tenet of Soviet propaganda: Nothing bad of the sort you see in the newsreels about the United States or anywhere else could ever happen in the Soviet Union.

—*Vladimir Bukovsky, Soviet dissident*

In early 1986 I asked cosmonaut Oleg Atkov about the nature of the serious illness of another Russian spaceman that had forced the premature termination of a Soviet space mission the previous fall. His congenial and cooperative manner abruptly changed.

"Don't they still teach the Hippocratic oath in American medical schools?" he demanded haughtily. "And doesn't it still teach the confidentiality of doctor-patient relationships?" There was no use in arguing since he wasn't going to answer.

His sermon delivered, Atkov reverted to congeniality and sat back to await my next—and different—question. As a cardiologist who had been a member of the three-man space team that spent eight months in space in 1984, he had plenty of other, more positive subjects to discuss.

A year after that spectacular space success, the Soviets suffered an embarrassment when another three-man crew had to rush back to Earth after the commander, a thirty-two-year-old prematurely balding Ukrainian jet pilot named Vladimir Vasyutin, fell gravely ill. The Soviets released few specifics about his problem, and Atkov's later rebuff to me showed they hadn't relaxed their secrecy.

It was late October 1985. Two months into a planned record-breaking orbital mission, Vasyutin's life had been threatened by "an infectious inflammation" which could not be properly treated aboard the space station. No official mention was made by Soviet spokesmen during this period, although the TASS news agency took the subtle step of no longer ending its routine progress reports with the words "The cosmonauts feel well" (this hint was noticed only in hindsight). Unknown to almost the entire planet, the stricken cosmonaut had passed the last several weeks in severe pain, fighting a high fever, usually confined to his sleeping bag. His conversations with earthside doctors were conducted over a voice-scrambled radio link, and for a while Western listeners thought that military activities were being concealed by such communications security. Ultimately he became so incapacitated that he was relieved of command of the mission (his flight engineer piloted the Soyuz spacecraft for the return journey).

Back on Earth, Vasyutin spent a month in a Moscow medical institute before being released. His crewmates spent the same period in medical isolation near the landing zone.

Western interest in the extraordinary case (the first-ever confessed medevac from orbit) centered on avoiding a similar incident aboard future American space stations. What had been the source of Vasyutin's infection? What had been its course and its symptoms? What treatments were tried in space, and why were they ineffective? What changes to medical protocol and in-orbit supplies were now being implemented to forestall future recurrences? All these questions were asked by American doctors in order to improve astronauts' chances if the U.S. space travelers were faced with a similar threat.

Although the Soviets never officially disclosed anything, enough information leaked out through face-to-face private meetings that American doctors soon had a pretty good idea of what happened. "If you had the same thing on Earth, you would not want to talk about it," a Soviet doctor advised one American colleague delicately. The Soviet cosmonaut had probably suffered a serious bout with prostatitis which he had carried into space with him (normal preflight screening would not have detected it). Left untreated, such an infection could have developed into blood poisoning, leading to death.

On Earth prostatitis is fought with powerful antibiotics not normally part of a space station's medical cabinet. It turned out that NASA medical contingency plans aboard the Skylab space station in 1973–1974 had called for both antibiotic treatment and "prostate massage" by another crewman's finger, via the affected astronaut's rectum. Conventional prudery could well have contributed to the Soviets' decision not to tell the whole truth about Vasyutin's malady; it may have been deemed demeaning to the glorious image of Soviet hero-cosmonauts. *Glasnost* had reached a limit.

Russian secretiveness goes back centuries and may reflect a deep-seated inferiority complex vis-à-vis foreigners. Revelation of failures and weaknesses would provide "aid and comfort to the enemy." As a result, unpleasant facts were routinely ignored, modified, or denied.

The Soviet state developed in a perpetual psychological state of siege, partially because of actual circumstance and partially as useful gimmick to keep the population in line, all of which developed into a peculiar attitude toward what the population should be allowed to know.

"While the Western concept of truth is based on philosophical and empirical observations," noted Jiri Kotas, chairman of the Czechoslovak Federal Council in Exile, "the Soviet view of things is utilitarian and relativistic in the extreme." What this meant in practice was spelled out by N. G. Palgunov, once the director general of TASS: "News should not be merely concerned with reporting such and such a fact or event. News or information must pursue a definite goal: It must serve and support the decisions related to fundamental duties facing our Soviet society, our Soviet people marching on the road of gradual transition from socialism to communism."

To implement this policy, the Soviet news media have developed a detailed catalog of "don't tells," a listing of the kinds of information which the Soviet people must not be given. Soviet nuclear scientist Mikhail Klochko, who defected to Canada in 1961, recalled seeing in the late 1940s a book, hundreds of pages long, entitled *An Enumeration of Information Prohibited for Publication in the News Media:* "It includes epidemics, accidents in mines, factories, and testing grounds; transport crashes of various kinds; and any natural disaster in the USSR, earthquakes included."

Even decades later the official restrictions were apparently just as thorough. Journalist Robert Kaiser obtained a partial list of the censor's forbidden topics in the early 1970s. Some items were:

- Information about the organs of Soviet censorship which discloses the character, organization, and method of their work
- The amount of crime, the number of people engaged in criminal behavior, the number arrested, the number convicted
- Information about the existence of correctional labor camps
- Facts about the physical condition, illnesses, and death rates of all prisoners in all localities
- Reports about the victims of accidents, wrecks, and fires
- Information about the consequences of catastrophic earthquakes, tidal waves, floods, and other natural calamities
- Information suggesting a low moral-political condition of the armed forces, unsatisfactory military discipline, abnormal relations among soldiers or between them and the population
- Information about occupational injuries

Even under *glasnost* in the late 1980s, serious restrictions remain. What news is fit to print is still explicitly spelled out. Late in 1985 London's *Sunday Times* obtained a bootleg copy of a confidential twenty-five-page guidance manual for Soviet newspapers. "Only 350 copies are issued" by the TASS publishing house, boasted reporter Louise Branson, hinting that the wonders of photocopying were yet another technological enemy of Soviet secrecy.

Mikhail Gorbachev, wrote Bronson from Moscow, "has indicated he wants to liven up the notoriously dull media and make it [*sic*] more critical—but that is unlikely to mean liberalization. The manual is a sharp reminder that the basic tenets of the state-run press are very different from the valued independence of the Western media." The clearly stated purpose of the Soviet newspapers is "to propagandize the Soviet communist way of life, showing its best points and most shining examples . . . with the emphasis on reinforcing the decisions of the five-yearly Communist Party Congress."

Specifically, the manual asserts that "it is a newspaper's duty to tell of the joy of freely given labor and the care with which Soviet man is strengthening the country's economic might." As for problems, "those should show complex and unresolved difficulties in productivity, ideology, social life, business and human relations, indicating the way to set the situation right." Regarding military duty, reports "must show the character-forming experience of the armed services."

Despite these regulations, in case after case in the 1983–1987 period, the Soviet news media and Soviet officials have achieved unprecedented levels of "openness" about various hitherto obscure aspects of Soviet society, including disasters. This policy, enunciated as a goal of the Gorbachev "renewal" and "restructuring" programs, seems more than a veneer or chrome trim. It has already brought about some remarkable revelations in some limited areas.

Once (and if) this trend matures, we can settle down to the serious business of learning from each other's mistakes as well as from our own. As this book will illustrate, in case after case in the long, terrible history of Soviet disasters, we—too late— see examples of tragic accidents which were repeated in the West. Soviet secrecy had Western victims, it may be argued in those cases.

An equally powerful justification for understanding Soviet disasters is the need for a proper evaluation of the effectiveness and reliability of the USSR's science and technology for military, commercial, economic, and diplomatic purposes.

Some accidents seem to have nothing to teach except respect for the truth. That is more than sufficient reason to include them here. If it is traditional for Soviet citizens to trust their government and accept official assurances at face value, exactly the opposite is true in the West. To seek to penetrate Soviet cover-ups is thus an expression of classic Western attitudes toward government (mis)handling of information.

Lastly, a fair-minded chronology of disasters suffered by the Soviet people can serve as a needed antidote to myths, both in the Soviet Union and abroad, that the USSR is somehow immune from history, exempt from the trappings of late-twentieth-century technological civilization.

The obnoxious way that the Soviet media highlight Western disasters while hypocritically denouncing occasionally inaccurate or exaggerated Western treatment of Soviet disasters needs to be condemned. Whatever the provocation, we must not replicate such self-righteous glorification in the misfortunes of "our enemies."

Real people suffer, often hideously. Real families are enveloped in grief that, as we know from our own experiences, fades only gradually, if at all, over decades. These Soviet victims are not to blame; they do not deserve their fates. They deserve, and, with more of their government's openness, would receive, our sympathy and compassion. Investigating these Soviet disasters is done not to gloat over, but to humanize, their victims.

The purpose of this book is to restore a balance to an existing and clearly unbalanced body of literature, which ranges from official Soviet "success stories," by the Soviets or by sycophantic admirers, to the most rabid of the anti-Soviet "dirty linen" collections. Cataloging and analyzing these disasters will make this appear to be a superficially "unbalanced" book. Standing alone, it undeniably stresses trends and patterns that can be accused of being "slanted." The only response is to ask if the factual material is accurate, if the analysis is fair-minded, and if the open questions (of which there must remain very many) are phrased dispassionately.

Investigations of Soviet disasters can even encourage Moscow's openness, as numerous examples in this book will illustrate. The publication of data in the West sometimes leads to the official release of further information on the disaster in question. The events with military significance, such as the Kyshtym nuclear disaster of 1958 or the Nedelin catastrophe at the launchpad in 1960, remain scrupulously exempt. But there have been remarkable recent revelations.

Ultimately this book must serve as a tool for understanding, to satisfy genuine curiosity. For all the good reasons we can conjure up to rationalize it, the bottom line for most of us is that we want to reveal Soviet disasters mainly because the Soviets try so doggedly to conceal them. The cover-ups, evasions, and denials whet the appetite of investigators for the primeval thrill of the hunt, the pursuit of a clever, elusive prey: the truth.

UNCOVERING SOVIET DISASTERS

1

ANTHRAX
IN SVERDLOVSK

It is likely that anthrax will be virtually eradicated in the
USSR within the next five years.

—*Soviet expert, 1958,*
quoted in New Scientist

In the predawn hours of April 3, 1979, a loud explosion shook
the southern suburbs of Sverdlovsk, a large city in the Ural
Mountains. Over the following days and weeks, panic took hold
of the city's population in the face of a deadly epidemic of
uncertain origin. Some rumors blamed the widespread disease
on the mysterious explosion.

By late May stories of some sort of medical disaster in the
Urals were all over the streets in Moscow. Rumors multiplied,
and fear spread. Soviet officials wrapped details of the event in
deep secrecy behind a superficial and suspicious cover story
about "bad meat from infected livestock." American analysts
perceived threatening forms in the resultant dark shadows and

concluded that the Russians were cheating on a germ warfare treaty. The Soviets in turn acted convinced that the United States was deliberately smearing "Mother Russia" in order to lay groundwork for its own intended treaty violations.

Behind the international tensions and suspicions lay a genuine human disaster. Many men and women had died in Sverdlovsk. The lowest estimates say there were only several dozen fatalities; others claim as many as 1,000 or more people lost their lives. The medical diagnosis was anthrax, a virulent disease of livestock for the most part long eradicated in the West. Why it had struck the population of Sverdlovsk was a mystery. It might have been merely bad hygiene, or it might have been an accident at an illegal bacteriological weapons facility thought to be located in southwestern Sverdlovsk.

The quickly spreading reports became distorted and nebulous. One early account which reached the West put the disaster in Novosibirsk, almost 1,000 miles to the east. Another had it occurring in June, two months afterward. The strain of anthrax bacilli was referred to by various military-sounding code names.

It took a year for a single coherent hypothesis to crystallize. By early 1980 the American government was deeply concerned with a scenario it had developed. This account, as portrayed in a Defense Intelligence Agency (DIA) report, was particularly ominous:

> During early April 1979, an accidental release of anthrax occurred in Sverdlovsk that caused many casualties and most probably a very high death rate among Soviet citizens who were exposed. The Soviet government at that time [1980] admitted only to some public health problems, which it said were caused by the illegal sale of anthrax-contaminated meat. They have never acknowledged the existence of the Sverdlovsk facility [allegedly for germ warfare] and, of course, have never revealed the nature of the work conducted there. The U.S. government has requested an explanation of what happened in Sverdlovsk on numerous occasions but the Soviets persist in blaming contaminated meat for the anthrax epidemic.
>
> Our analysis shows that the following events occurred. Early in April 1979, an accidental release of anthrax occurred within the Microbiology and Virology Institute in Sverdlovsk.

The Institute is a military facility located in the southwestern outskirts of the city. While bulk quantities of anthrax spores in dry form were probably being prepared, a pressurized system probably exploded. As much as 22 pounds (10 kg) of dry anthrax spores were released from the Institute. The bacterial aerosol contaminated an area with a radius of at least 2–3 miles.

Within two weeks, which is within the time frame expected for the disease to develop, a significant number of deaths occurred. Residents and workers within the contaminated area contracted pulmonary anthrax through inhalation. In addition it is possible that some may have contracted anthrax by skin contact and, over time, a number may have contracted anthrax by consumption of food contaminated by the fall-out of spores.

Initial disinfection and decontamination procedures were largely ineffective. Mass immunizations with the Soviet anthrax vaccine were partially effective at best. It has been reported that hundreds of Soviet citizens died from inhalation anthrax within seven to ten days of the outbreak despite heroic attempts by Soviet doctors to save their lives. Vaccinations and antibiotic treatment were administered too late as an initial response.

It has also been reported that in subsequent weeks, there may have been 1,000 or more cases. These figures are about 100 or more times the annual incidence of inhalation and intestinal anthrax throughout the USSR in recent years. Containment procedures were effective in confining the problem to the southwest area of Sverdlovsk city. Strict censorship served to neutralize early panic and limit the fears of the Sverdlovsk population. Containment procedures continued into July 1979. Some inspection procedures were conducted until the Fall of 1979.

Further details were released to support the Pentagon's case. Supposedly, the extraordinary Soviet attempts to "clean up" wide areas of the city were inconsistent with the official explanation. There reportedly were early military casualties immediately after the accident, followed by heavy military involvement in the cleanup and total military control within two weeks; there was rooftop spraying of decontaminating solutions from aircraft, as part of aerial spraying activity over an area of three by four miles. There was heavy disinfection (reportedly with steam and hypochlorate solution; the "steam" may actually have been vaporized formaldehyde, a classic disinfection technique) around the military facility. These were interpreted as clear attempts to decontaminate surfaces affected by an infectious aerosol, and such activities allegedly were not consistent with public health control measures for dealing with anthrax acquired by eating bad meat. Concluded the DIA: "Collectively, these events are a very strong contradiction of the Soviet position which claimed the anthrax outbreak was just a minor public health problem resulting from the sale of contaminated meat."

So what really happened in Sverdlovsk in April 1979? Was the U.S. government's conclusion justified, or were the Soviet explanations authentic?

The major diplomatic issue of arms control treaty verification has become intimately intertwined with the Sverdlovsk mystery. Shortly after the United States unilaterally destroyed its biological warfare materials, an international treaty specifically banning such weapons was signed. The Biological and Toxin Weapons Convention of 1972 made it illegal for any nation to "develop, produce, stockpile, or otherwise acquire or retain" or transfer biological or toxin agents or weapons. However, countries could still possess tiny quantities of agents necessary for "prophylactic, protective, or other peaceful purposes."

One key shortcoming of this treaty was and still is its lack of reliable verification procedures. The technology of germ warfare makes such a treaty impossible in practice to police. The amount of materials sufficient to violate the treaty are much less than the amount likely to be detected by existing national intelligence resources. So the treaty was based on trust, and the real damage of the 1979 "Sverdlovsk incident" was that this trust was destroyed.

An attempt at a chronology follows:

The American DIA interpretations pinpointed the origin of the anthrax outbreak in the Chkalovskiy (sometimes misspelled "Chakalov") district of the city. There a facility, named Compound 19 by the Soviets, had attracted the interest of U.S. intelligence agencies long before this incident because of its peculiar features, which included buildings with special venting systems, animal pens, smokestacks, refrigeration facilities, and nearby concrete bunkers suitable for munitions storage (such as explosive shells for spores dissemination in combat). It was surrounded by double barbed-wire fences which had narrow, heavily guarded gates. In terms of its physical layout, it looked very much like Fort Detrick, an American facility in Maryland which had served as a development area for biological weapons. None of the official Soviet explanations for the outbreak even touched on the nature of this facility.

At the time of the initial explosion, according to the DIA scenario, there was a wind from the north, and the spores were carried away from the city itself and into a small suburb named Kashino.

Several days after the mysterious explosion, according to secondhand accounts, seven or eight persons were admitted to a neighborhood hospital. Their symptoms included high fever (above 107 degrees), bluish ears and lips, choking, and other breathing difficulties. Within a few hours they all were dead. Autopsies revealed a consistent pattern of severe pulmonary edema, along with serious toxemia (blood poisoning). The DIA stated that the "first casualties were a fairly large number of male [military] reservists at the military installation." More cases came in by the hour, and within several days the death toll had risen to several dozen. Some accounts claim many victims were dying every day for more than a month, while others are much more restrained.

A nine-story hospital was commandeered by military medical forces and devoted exclusively to anthrax victims. Special army nurses wearing protective clothing were flown in from other installations. Everyone in the area of the explosion was vaccinated twice. Hospital workers were vaccinated and then were given daily doses of tetracycline, presumably orally (penicillin in high doses, by intramuscular injection, is the drug of choice in the West for such treatment).

Workers in a ceramics factory across the street and downwind of the compound were supposedly exposed when ventilators sucked in the fatal bacilli; within days many had died. The ceramics factory was closed briefly, according to reconnaissance satellite photography, and secondhand reports allege this was to decontaminate it with chloramine, a disinfecting chemical. However, a meat factory next door remained open.

The DIA noted a series of interesting secret visits by Moscow VIPs right after the event. The chief epidemiologist from the Ministry of Health in Moscow arrived shortly after the outbreak began, with several assistants and a large laboratory. Defense Minister Dmitriy Ustinov made an unannounced visit to Sverdlovsk two weeks after the first casualties had appeared. Two days after Ustinov's visit the Soviet health minister, Boris Petrovskiy, also visited the city, again without publicity. About this time the commanding general of the military installation which housed the anthrax institute reportedly committed suicide.

As bodies of victims accumulated, they presented a logistics problem. Although human-to-human contagion of anthrax is considered medically impossible, there were widespread fears. Reportedly the corpses were stored in chloramine. The bodies were not returned to families; empty coffins were buried instead.

As the month of April wore on and the number of deaths mounted, the Sverdlovsk government took action. Officials called public meetings to issue calming assurances that "nothing is happening." Then they published a few general advisories urging people to be careful with meat from private markets. Newspaper articles by Dr. V. Popugaylo and candidate of veterinary sciences N. Lazarev appeared in *Uralskiy Rabochiy* ("Urals Worker") and *Vecherniy Sverdlovsk* ("Evening Sverdlovsk") and in about a dozen factory newsletters. Finally a strangely inconsistent sort of assurance was made that even though "nothing happened, don't panic, it is all localized and under control." At no time did any official statement refer to any actual human cases of anthrax; all the urgent health warnings were general and hypothetical in nature.

Wild animals in the nearby forest were hunted down and killed, along with most dogs in the district. Yet supposedly no cases of anthrax were ever noted among local animals.

By the end of 1979 some highly garbled accounts of the disaster had reached the West. But U.S. government experts did not have much to go on until early February 1980, when the Central Intelligence Agency (CIA) heard from a secondhand witness it deemed "eminently credible." This anonymous Russian evidently was the man who had written an article for the anti-Soviet émigré magazine *Posev*, published in Munich. The article, under the pseudonym "N.N." (the Russian equivalent of "X.X."), had appeared late the previous year and had been quoted in several sensationalist magazines such as West Germany's *Bild*.

At this point the Carter administration finally decided to ask the Soviets formally for an explanation. But the way it was done helped confirm the Soviets in their paranoid reaction to the Western interest in the Sverdlovsk disaster.

There was actually some considerable merit to the Soviet reaction. The American embassy in Moscow had filed its inquiry through diplomatic channels on Monday, March 17, 1980. The very next day Washington officials publicly announced their concern about the incident. Considering the eight-hour time lag from Moscow to Washington, that essentially allowed the Soviets one working day—all of Tuesday in Moscow—to respond. The Soviets smelled a setup. One American embassy official later admitted privately, "We behaved in a way designed to provoke the wild bull."

On Thursday, March 20, Soviet officials issued their "bad meat" explanation and subsequently refused to address any further objections from the U.S. government.

There were more than just U.S. government claims behind the anxiety in the West. One Soviet defector who claimed to have trustworthy sources of information on the incident was Mark Popovsky, who in 1980 was a visiting scholar at the Kennan Institute in Washington, D.C. He was the author of a highly respected analysis of the Soviet scientific establishment, the 1979 book *Manipulated Science*.

Popovsky's evidence is straightforward and unambiguous and supports the DIA hypothesis. In early 1980 he received underground communications from a number of sources in the city of Sverdlovsk, recounting the local versions of the happenings of the previous spring. The disaster reportedly might have been many times worse. "My sources told me the wind blew toward town but then turned around," he told a magazine in late March. Earlier, in 1958, at the same institute there had allegedly occurred a similar incident, in which another wind shift kept fatalities down. "They ask me until what time will God continue to save the city by changing the wind."

According to Popovsky, the Soviet government has been conducting germ warfare research since the 1920s. When he left the USSR early in 1979, he had definite knowledge of two installations, in Kirov and Sverdlovsk, and tentative knowledge of two others, in Kalinin and Novosibirsk. All four facilities were in the immediate vicinity of large cities.

It was from such accounts by Popovsky and other Soviet émigrés, from reconnaissance satellite imagery, from communications intercepts, and from human sources within the USSR that American intelligence analysts assembled their detailed scenario of a germ warfare accident. But however authoritative the scenario may appear, the danger of exaggeration and misinterpretation is always present.

Some accounts received by the DIA told how large areas around Compound 19 were graded and covered with asphalt, but other authoritative reports insisted that satellite photography showed no excessive asphalt-paving activities going on in the aftermath of the explosion. One account reported that satellite photography had shown that one of the buildings in Compound 19 had been virtually abandoned after the date of the explosion. There were no more animals in its outdoor pens, and the snow on its access walks and driveways was not being shoveled through the winter of 1979–1980. This observation was extremely persuasive to a number of American government analysts. Yet another account by an expert with access to the same sources maintained that the abandoned areas were much smaller in area. In any case, abandonment of an area is more typical of radioactive contamination than of bacteriological contamination; with radiation, merely waiting a few months lets the isotopes decay safely, but with dangerous spores, decontamination is needed since the spores, if untreated, could survive and even spread beyond the original area.

In the spring of 1980, when the American government's accusations went public, a number of Western specialists took issue with them.

Dr. Vivian Wyatt, a reader in microbiology at the University of Bradford, published articles in which he dubbed the story implausible: "We may never know what did happen but the story of a germ-warfare disaster does not ring true." This was because the theory required certain actions which he doubted the Russians really would have wanted to take. For one, he doubted that Compound 19 was military in nature: "It isn't likely that the Russians would run the risk of playing around with anthrax near a vital military town." This risk especially had to do with explosive shells: "It is difficult to believe that anyone would keep (or manufacture) such weapons in a research establishment near a large town." Secondly, he was skeptical of the usefulness of the postulated weapon: "It is doubtful if anthrax has been seriously considered as a possible weapon since the late 1950s." Additionally, he was sure that explosions were impossible in the manufacture of anthrax spores: "The growth of anthrax spores either for vaccines or for more sinister purposes would be a routine business, with nothing inflammable or explosive in the area, just a lot of broth at body temperature. To the best of my knowledge there has never been an explosion of any bacterial cultures."

Yet Wyatt's assertions seem particularly unconvincing to me. He was arguing without solid facts but with confidence in his intuition.

Clinical microbiologist Raymond Zilinskas attributed the outbreak to "an infected animal" and concluded: "Most probably, the Sverdlovsk epidemic did not arise as a result of Soviet biological warfare work." The germ warfare theory was rejected on much the same grounds used by Wyatt. "[N]o nation would be so stupid as to locate a biological warfare facility within an approachable distance from a major population center," Zilinskas argued, from faith, not facts. He also expressed confidence in the ease with which any such hypothesized germ accident could have been treated: "Prophylactic medication could have been quickly administered to exposed persons as public health authorities grasped the situation and an epidemic would have been immediately stopped at that point." But in this assessment Zilinskas evidently had greater faith in Soviet public health procedures than did the Soviets themselves, who were busy making excuses for the epidemic they had been unable to forestall. Practicing physicians also have taken issue with Zilinskas's optimistic view, since once victims have been exposed, even high doses of penicillin are not particularly effective, and once septicemia develops, a patient's prognosis is very grave no matter what treatment is offered.

Zilinskas did blame the worldwide spread of suspicions squarely on the USSR: "If the Soviet government allowed open research at accessible facilities and otherwise followed the provisions of the 1972 Convention, these suspicions of illicit

Soviet research and development would probably not have developed."

Dr. Zhores Medvedev is an expatriate Russian living in England, where he is a biochemist with Britain's National Institute for Medical Research in London. He does not consider himself a "defector" since despite his dissident politics, he was willing to return to the USSR, where his twin brother, Roy, still lives, but the Soviet government told him not to come back from a foreign trip. In 1980 he wrote several scathing critiques of the germ warfare theories, in which he pointed out inconsistencies and contradictions among the variations of the story and lambasted the way in which the rumors first were published and circulated.

Medvedev suggested that Compound 19 was manufacturing anthrax vaccine: "The production of the anthrax vaccine entails large-scale cultivation of anthrax bacteria and production of spores." But American analysts had rejected that explanation when they determined that the Soviet standard anthrax vaccine is from an avirulent form of the bacillus, one that could not cause such an epidemic if released. Medvedev did not address this objection.

His article concluded, "The medical authorities in the USSR are certainly responsible for the anthrax outbreak in Sverdlovsk. It was connected either with tainted meat or wool or a laboratory accident. But there are no facts yet to indicate that the production of a bacteriological weapon was the cause of the Sverdlovsk epidemic. . . ."

Among the articles critical of the germ warfare theory, one in particular contained original data, not just reasoned speculations. David Satter, the Moscow correspondent of the *Financial Times* in London, had traveled near the area in mid-1980 and reported on some popular theories about the epidemic. Passengers he met on the Trans-Siberian Railroad told him that the outbreak had been caused by bad meat sold to city dwellers by villagers, that warning leaflets had appeared everywhere, and that many dogs and cats had been destroyed. One man, who claimed his brother had recovered from the illness, said there had been few deaths and no quarantine of the city. On the other hand, a chief doctor of a clinic in the nearby city of Shadrinsk told Satter that he had never been informed of the outbreak at all, a standard practice if the disease had been natural in origin. The paucity of actual hard data on the Sverdlovsk event is accentuated by the obvious unique importance of such gossip as that which Satter picked up accidentally (though the possibility that the testimony was a deliberate plant cannot be entirely discounted).

American biochemist Dr. Matthew Meselson of Harvard, best known for his controversial (and still-disputed) explanation of "yellow rain" in Southeast Asia as a naturally occurring phenomenon involving bee feces, has also rejected the germ warfare scenario. As an independent consultant to the U.S. government, he was allowed to review the classified reports on the incident. "I spent many hours [in 1980 and 1981] looking at very classified material," he later told a science conference in 1986. "I disagree with the conclusions the government reached. That is all I am allowed to say."

One of Meselson's major nonclassified arguments deals with the experience of Donald E. Ellis, a professor of physics and chemistry at Northwestern University. Together with his wife and two small children, Ellis had been in Sverdlovsk the month of the epidemic as part of a scientific exchange program. This fact was unknown to the U.S. government until two years later, when one of Meselson's colleagues discovered it fortuitously. Meselson talked with Ellis, and later, in an interview with Leslie Gelb of the *New York Times*, Ellis reported: "I don't exclude the possibility that something may have occurred . . . but I think either I or my wife would have sensed some effort to protect us from it. We moved freely and were not aware of any restrictions on us." After spending May in Novosibirsk, Ellis and his family returned to Sverdlovsk in June and the following month, on the way to a children's camp, passed very close to Compound 19. There had been no restrictions on such movements.

"One of the few important certainties in this murky business," Meselson argued, "is that the Soviet authorities permitted Professor Ellis and his family to enter, and, most remarkably, to reenter the city. Although not conclusive, this does not readily fit in with the picture of an attempted cover-up of a biological-warfare accident."

These critics of the germ warfare theory—Wyatt, Zilinskas, Medvedev, Meselson, and others—did make several good points in their articles and arguments. One was that the terms *inhalation anthrax* (or *pulmonary anthrax*) and *intestinal anthrax* are misleading if they imply that these forms of the disease are always distinctive in symptoms. Actually, once anthrax germs are inside the body, the disease can progress pretty much the same way. The lymph glands become infected, and this initiates a massive invasion of the bloodstream. The American account required infection through the lungs (via an airborne release), whereas the Soviet account required infection through the digestive tract (from the bad meat); these different origins cannot be as easily differentiated as the American scenario requires.

Throughout 1980 and later the Soviets asserted their innocence and expressed public outrage over the Western accusations. "The Soviet side gave a timely, clear, and exhaustive explanation," insisted TASS resolutely on June 12. It summarized the Soviet explanation this way:

> In the spring of 1979 a natural outbreak of anthrax among domestic animals did take place in the region of Sverdlovsk. As is known, weather conditions were very unfavorable in the districts of the Sverdlovsk region in the autumn and winter of 1978–1979. Some animals were weakened at the end of the winter season. As a result, their susceptibility to infection grew. Cases of skin and intestinal forms of anthrax were reported in people because dressing of animals was sometimes conducted without observing rules established by veterinary inspection. At that time, local newspapers ... published warnings to the population of the city and outskirts. They urged people to observe better rules of personal hygiene while attending to domestic animals, not to buy unmarked meat, wool, undressed hides, etc., from strangers at the markets.

This basic account was to be reworded and repeated again and again.

The Soviet allegations about private-market meat (often mistakenly referred to as "black market" in the West even though the sales were legal) were not implausible. CIA sources established that there had indeed been a large quantity of private meat for sale in Sverdlovsk at the time of the epidemic. Public supplies had been badly depleted by weather and mismanagement.

The Soviets perceived the germ warfare accusations as a

malevolent American plot. Noted Radio Moscow on July 9: "One gets the impression that someone in Washington is feverishly looking for ways of artificially whipping up the psychological war against the Soviet Union after the boycott of the Moscow Olympics failed and the campaign over the events of Afghanistan began petering out." *Literaturnaya Gazeta* was even more explicit, as author M. Mishin explained:

> We will have to recall the story of how the "Urals Sensation" started. It was concocted early this year [in March], when the White House administration and its allies decided to "punish the Soviets for Afghanistan" [the Soviet invasion occurred in December 1979]. . . . First the idea was sent across the ocean and fed to West Germany's *Bild,* to try out such a vile piece of "news" in that gutter rag. . . .

Mishin's attempted "explanation" was pitifully weak and easily refuted. As already noted, some garbled reports of the Sverdlovsk disaster were already circulating in late 1979, well before the Soviet Afghanistan invasion. Furthermore, Mishin's scenario conjured up the image of an American CIA agent reading Sverdlovsk papers about the April 1979 epidemic and deciding to blame it on a germ warfare accident. This, too, was contrary to actual facts: The local papers had repeatedly carried warnings about bad meat; but these were only of a general nature, and they never specified that an actual anthrax epidemic was in progress.

Yet the instinct to blame America (and the CIA in particular) was too useful to forgo. A January 1981 Moscow Domestic Service radio broadcast asserted again: "The story was created in the inner sanctums of departments which are conducting psychological warfare against the Soviet Union."

Soviet press accounts suggested that there had been some mild retribution for the accidental outbreak. Regarding the newly admitted fact that "local organizations carried out poor sanitary control," Mishin's article in mid-1980 stated: "There need be no doubt that they have been called to account for this." And according to another Soviet article, a few individuals were actually convicted of violation of hygiene codes "for the sake of personal gain": V. A. Stafeyev secretly buried a diseased cow, and M. I. Gorina slaughtered three anthrax-infected sheep and sold the meat to her neighbors. No fatalities seem to have resulted from these two cases, since Stafeyev was merely fined and Gorina received a suspended one-year prison term. Whoever was punished for the fatalities was never mentioned.

A Soviet medical magazine did seem to make a vague official admission to a number of victims when it used the phrase *cases of illness.* The article in question appeared in the May 1980 issue of the *Journal of Microbiology, Immunology and Epidemiology;* it probably was in print prior to the American accusations in mid-March, and the official submission date on the paper was the previous August 29. The authors were Ivan Bezdenezhnykh, chief epidemiologist of the Russian (the republic, not the whole country) Ministry of Health, and Vladimir Nakiforov, chief specialist in infectious diseases in the same ministry.

"During March and April [1979]," the Russians wrote, "the slaughter of cattle in individual households increased significantly. The meat was sold privately in the city suburbs. At that time isolated cases of anthrax among humans were recorded, with cutaneous and intestinal forms of the infection occurring." The animals probably had been infected from eating contaminated fodder, the medical experts suggested.

Western observers were thus faced with two inconsistent interpretations of the events of April 1979 in Sverdlovsk. Neither of the theories—the germ warfare accident or the bad meat ingestion—seemed to account for the "facts." Yet the implications for the future of arms control were too crucial to tolerate ambiguity and uncertainty.

To try to make sense of the evidence, Washington set up a special investigative group in mid-1980. There were representatives from the Joint Chiefs of Staff, the National Security Council, the State Department, other federal agencies, plus Dr. Philip Brachman of the Centers for Disease Control in Atlanta, Dr. Joshua Lederberg of Rockefeller University (a Nobel laureate in medicine), and Dr. Paul Doty, a professor of biochemistry at Harvard. Dr. Matthew Meselson of Harvard served as an independent consultant.

The group rejected an initial hypothesis that the outbreak was from a legal vaccine factory. Then it considered the theory of a single explosion spreading virulent spores, which was not substantiated by the fact that the reports spoke reliably of new cases coming in over a six-week period and a single explosion would not have had that long-lasting an effect. The possibility of a lengthy undetected leak from the institute was also considered and rejected.

Next, the group considered the Soviet claim that bad meat was the cause. It rejected this explanation, too. Noted Leslie Gelb: "They [the group members] could find no historical precedent for an outbreak of intestinal anthrax causing so many deaths over a period of several weeks." The high mortality rate argued against this explanation as well, although there are forms of intestinal anthrax with both the symptoms and lethality which at first seemed unique to the pulmonary form.

For example, one nonpulmonary precedent involves an epidemic in Yaroslavl in 1927 in which twenty-seven persons contracted the disease and every one of them died. The cause was established as a batch of diseased smoked sausages.

The scenario eventually produced by the U.S. working group, which was also the preferred explanation of the CIA, had two distinct stages. First was the sudden huge airborne release of virulent spores being used for the development of biological weapons at the military compound. After the initial wave of fatalities, spores infected the local food chain (meat in particular) despite public health measures. Later victims picked up the disease from contact and from eating.

Even then, however, the CIA reportedly estimated that there really was a chance—numerically expressed as "about ten percent"—that the outbreak had occurred for the reasons specified by the Soviets, bad meat, and that all the evidence pointing to a germ warfare accident could be coincidence, misinterpretation, and rumors both distorted and fabricated.

This reconstruction of how American analysts grappled with the Sverdlovsk puzzle is from Leslie Gelb's 1981 article for the *New York Times*. He conducted dozens of interviews with current and former U.S. officials, and with independent experts. His article concluded:

Perhaps there is an embarrassing but acceptable explanation of the event. It is conceivable that the Soviet story about tainted meat is true, but many things have to be explained away for it to be credible. This is where most of the working

group ended up—uncertain but believing the Russians probably violated the treaty. . . . The Soviet mania for secrecy
means that they are never likely to be positive about intrusive
forms of verification. Yet if the Russians are really interested
in arms control, it is in their interest to avoid situations like
the one of doubt and mistrust attending the Sverdlovsk
incident.

There the issue rested for five bitter years of worsening
U.S./USSR diplomacy. The United States fumed about the
perfidy of the Soviets. The USSR glowered at the insults of the
Americans. In Sverdlovsk people became accustomed to the
absence of spouses, siblings, children, or parents, and their
personal tragedies were private ones. On the international
scale, where the Sverdlovsk incident had become a cause
célèbre, real people didn't even count.

Then, in 1986, the information logjam broke. The Soviets
began ever so slowly to release a new story. It portrayed an
embarrassing, clumsy cover-up of a terrible public health
disaster of unprecedented proportions. It was a persuasive
scenario, and it might even be true.

In September 1986 at a treaty review conference in Geneva,
the Soviets presented a Ministry of Public Health official named
Nikolay Antonov to answer specific questions on the 1979
anthrax outbreak. He specified that the outbreak had been
traced to contaminated cattle feed. Cases of the disease appeared over a seven-day period, he stated, allegedly refuting
U.S. allegations of a single aerosol event (in fact, the U.S.
scenario already accepted this long period and accounted for
it). Wide-area decontamination was required, Antonov asserted, because "undisciplined workers" had thrown contaminated meat into open garbage cans, after which stray dogs had
spread the meat throughout many neighborhoods. Antonov's
open discussion completely astounded Western experts at the
conference, although it did not change many minds; it was five
or six years too late for that. Unfortunately, too, its suddenness
did not allow time for newsmen to do sufficient background
research to ask Antonov some really crucial questions.

Some of the other key arguments of the germ warfare
accident hypothesis were also losing credibility. For example,
the DIA's report stressed that military involvement in the

Sverdlovsk cleanup was proof of the military origin of the contamination. But this argument is not persuasive. At the Chernobyl nuclear plant accident in 1986, for example, specialized Soviet army decontamination units had been put in charge immediately despite the civil nature of the catastrophe. This was because they were the only agencies with the appropriate equipment, training, and disciplined organizational structure. By analogy, the appearance of Soviet anti-germ-warfare specialists in a civilian anthrax epidemic that had gotten out of hand would not really have been proof of the epidemic's military origin. Again, the army would have had the best-trained people and equipment for the emergency.

Also in 1986, several Soviet doctors privately delivered to their Western associates what purported to be the authentic medical reports on the anthrax epidemic. The documents could have been an elaborate hoax, of course. But if the reports were authentic, the reason for the earlier secrecy and hypersensitivity on the epidemic became obvious. It had been one of the worst Soviet public health disasters in decades and the absolutely worst human anthrax outbreak of the twentieth century. No wonder the Russians had tried to cover up details of the catastrophe.

The "official" figures released privately were shocking. Seventeen people had contracted the cutaneous form of the disease, and all had been saved by treatment. There had been seventy-nine cases of intestinal anthrax, and sixty-four of them had ended in death. These deaths represented a lethality rate of 83 percent. All but one of the cases were in adults aged over twenty (the single child, a young girl, survived). Two-thirds were males. Two-thirds lived in southern Sverdlovsk; the other third, in the central and northern parts of the city.

The Soviet doctors in 1986 described how contaminated bone marrow used as a cattle feed supplement had not been properly heat-sterilized before being fed to privately owned livestock. This is a plausible explanation with precedents in Europe and America.

One feature of Soviet industrial plants contributed to the rapid and wide spread of the disease. Most plants usually have their own commissaries for workers. The ceramics factory was badly hit because it had bought and distributed some of the tainted meat. There had been a severe winter, and meat was in short supply. Eager customers demonstrably took less care in following safety procedures. Careless disposal of waste scraps of the tainted meat around the plant would have required the decontamination observed by many witnesses.

The doctors confirmed the reports of the slaughter of loose dogs in the city. Furthermore, about thirty sheds and slaughterhouses associated with processing and storing the bad meat were burned. Homes and workplaces were sprayed with disinfectants.

Every antibiotic within reach was reportedly thrown at the patients. Everyone exposed was repeatedly vaccinated, although it takes a few weeks to build up immunity and the effectiveness of the vaccine was generally considered questionable. As for livestock, the normal annual vaccinations were performed ahead of schedule.

The Soviet doctors continued to insist that there had been no military casualties and no military involvement in the treatment. The Ministry of Health had allegedly run the whole show. Since the military had its own commissary system and its own meat supplies, it didn't have to go out to the private market to scrounge for meat, so if the bad meat theory is correct, the lack of military casualties is logical. However, the evidence for military involvement in at least some of the treatment is supposedly very strong. Since such involvement is not proof of military responsibility for the origin of the epidemic, the Soviet doctors' recent denials are inexplicable. If there had been military casualties, it's conceivable that they were treated by the military's own units and the civilian medical teams were never told. If so, the death toll may have been even higher.

If this latest Soviet explanation is true, it confirms widespread Western assumptions that early Soviet accounts were deceptive. The 1980 medical article by Bezdenezhnykh and Nakiforov, which referred only to "isolated cases," had clearly been a deliberate understatement. Further, the leniency of the legal punishments which were reported (fines and suspended sentences) gave the contrived impression that little damage had been done.

Professor Ellis's experiences during his visit in Sverdlovsk were also puzzling, since the recently admitted anthrax epidemic was at its height when he and his family were in the city. Yet the Ellises claim to have noticed nothing unusual as they worked, shopped, and socialized among the roadblocks, fires, warning posters and broadcasts, and so forth. For the new "official" Soviet explanation in 1986, Ellis's testimony of "life as usual" is no longer the corroboration Meselson presents it as. Indeed, it must be dismissed as unconnected with the reality of Sverdlovsk's April 1979 epidemic; the reasons are indeterminable.

For the Soviet explanation to be true, the significance of a number of the CIA's HUMINT reports (human intelligence, or collected word-of-mouth, accounts) must be discounted. For example, the visit by Defense Minister Ustinov, if it occurred at all, must have been a coincidence (not implausible, since the region contained major military installations). Further, the predawn explosion (assumed to have been inside Compound 19) would have to be an unconnected event, which again is not implausible in a heavily industrialized city of more than a million inhabitants.

If the belated Soviet explanation of the 1979 epidemic is essentially accurate (and it probably is), the subsequent downward course of international debate on its nature owes its flavor primarily to endemic Soviet secrecy and distortions concerning potentially embarrassing events. Prompt and candid disclosures could have settled the question immediately and forever. However persuasive the later explanations might be, their very tardiness is bound to leave lingering suspicions.

Victims of the Sverdlovsk anthrax epidemic include more than just the immediate medical casualties and their loved ones. There have been diplomatic casualties as well. The weakening of the arms control process over the issue of verification and accusations of Soviet cheating was not simply a matter of American negativists seizing on any excuse. Western concern over the Sverdlovsk reports could not be attributed merely to "anti-Soviet paranoia." Sincere analysts in the United States were deeply disturbed by this incident and by the Soviet handling of it. Meselson, for all his skepticism, admits as much. "There was evidence to make us concerned," he has stated. The Soviets were the ones with the power—but not evidently the ability—to cut off and assuage this Western anxiety.

2

ACCIDENTS
ON ICE

They agreed that not a word or even a hint of what had happened should be said to their relatives. Possible hold-ups with telegrams were to be explained by poor radio reception.

—Cover-up strategy after catastrophic
fire at Antarctic base, 1982

Soviet behavior patterns of secrecy about technological disasters and defensiveness about asking for foreign help exist in the context of a Russian perception of encircling, hostile "outsiders." To determine how deep-seated are these psychological patterns, we need to examine Soviet behavior in an environment free of hostility, guarded borders, and fears of malevolent foreigners. There is, in fact, just such an environment, although we have to go actually to the ends of the Earth to find it: Antarctica. There teams of scientists work without national boundaries, without weapons, without cultural animosities. They share a common enemy, nature itself, and this has forged a comradeship and cooperative spirit rare elsewhere on the planet. Antarctica is a "blank slate" in terms of history and tradition; under such benign conditions, how do the Russians balance secrecy and disasters?

The Soviet Antarctic station named Vostok was the scene of a major crisis in 1982, and the official handling of that disaster reveals characteristic behavior patterns.

The base's location was different from that of the other Soviet bases, being far inland. The current Vostok station was set up in 1957 by the second Soviet Antarctic expedition, during the International Geophysical Year. It is located on a plateau 11,000 feet above sea level (where the air is half sea level pressure). At 78 degrees south latitude, the station endures continuous darkness from late April to mid-August; in summer, from mid-October through late February, the sun is up continuously. The spot is the coldest on Earth, and the planet's record low temperature (−88.3 degrees Centigrade or −127 degrees Fahrenheit) was recorded there in August 1960. The area is climatically a desert, and the air is very dry; there is very little annual snowfall.

Unquestionably, living conditions there are extreme. One veteran *vostochnik* described it this way in a Soviet book: "Skin chaps, the mucous membranes bleed, and it feels as though a pine cone has got stuck in your throat. You want to drink all the time, and consume incredible quantities of tea and fruit drinks."

The station is supplied by tractor convoys from the Mirniy base on the coast, almost 900 miles and six weeks to the north. For about a month in midsummer (usually January), light aircraft perform the main personnel exchange.

Russian Antarctic operations have been unkindly described as "Mickey Mouse," and visitors to Vostok in particular invariably comment on the crude facilities. One American explorer, with some respect, called the Russian workers "really hard core"; they were roughing it in conditions at least twenty years more primitive than those of other nations' bases. Yet they accomplish real scientific work. Key investigations involve geophysics (the station is located very near the south geomagnetic pole) and ice coring (the glacier beneath the base is 11,500 feet thick).

When disaster struck at Vostok early in 1982, the hardness of the Soviet crew's core was sorely tested. One man died immediately, and twenty other men began a grim struggle for survival. A year later the rest of the world learned about it.

On April 12, as the severe south polar winter was just setting in, a fire broke out in the station's diesel-electric power plant. Both the main pair and the backup pair of diesel generators were destroyed—and with them the source of the station's heat as well as electrical supplies.

The Soviets never said what had caused the fire except to stress that fires can break out easily; that means they should have made better preparations but didn't (serious fires have struck Western camps, too). There were vague references to an electrical short circuit.

The station's winter supply of drinking water had been stored as cut blocks of ice, right next to the power station. But the men threw most of the clean ice onto the flames in a futile fire-fighting effort, so their water supply, too, was lost. The diesel oil supply was also right next to the powerhouse, and as it burned, the flames licked at the tanks. However, the oil (which the men were to need for their emergency stoves) was too cold to catch fire easily.

The station's chief engineer, Aleksey Illarionovich Karpenko, was killed in the fire. Although later accounts portrayed his death as heroic, a between-the-lines reading of what really happened shows it was due to a stupid design of the building. As was called for in procedures, he turned off the generators during the fire. But then the lights went out, and he couldn't find his way to the exit, so he suffocated in the smoke. There were no emergency lights, either automatically activated or otherwise, and Karpenko paid with his life for this oversight.

Other injuries were minor; there were burns, broken ribs, and one man later had to have a badly injured finger amputated.

Station commander Pyotr Georgiyevich Astakhov was faced with potential disaster, even death for the entire team. Evacuation by tractor convoy was impossible as the result of the weather conditions (it was already −96° F). No Soviet aircraft were anywhere near the continent.

As temperatures inside the buildings plunged, the men acted quickly. The first thing to do was protect the station's radio transmitter since if it froze, it would never function again. Much of the food supplies could also be ruined in a deep freeze; they had to be moved into warmer rooms. The radiator water lines in the buildings were immediately drained.

Three old kerosene stoves found outside the main building were brought inside and immediately activated. One was placed in the main hall, where the food was stacked nearby; another was placed in the radio hut, where a small generator from one of the ice drills was brought inside and hooked up to the radio.

Later the same day the base doctor noted in his diary: "In my corner the temperature is already [−22° F], and I can only write with a pencil. The toothpaste has turned to stone. As a test, I used the tube to hammer a nail. . . . The aluminum walls are ringing ominously, like a cable stretched to its limit. They are cracking, too. . . . Those back home are sure to say 'They'll never get out of that,' when they hear about our tragedy. . . ."

After many hours of emergency work, radio contact was reestablished with Molodezhnaya, the main Soviet Antarctic base. Back in Moscow, officials at the Arctic and Antarctic Research Institute began considering various emergency re-supply plans. An airdrop of supplies was suggested, but it was considered very dangerous for any Soviet flight crew since the nearest available airfields were thousands of miles away from the imperiled base.

The Vostok team members soon decided that they could probably survive the winter with the kerosene stoves since there was plenty of food and they could cut more ice for drinking water. They advised Moscow that a risky (and possibly unsuccessful) airdrop wasn't needed. Reportedly they had another request: keep their predicament secret from their families, so as not to worry them.

Their bravado was almost certainly unjustified for several reasons. First, relying on open-flame stoves enhanced the danger of another fire, especially as the weeks passed and everything inside the building became soaked in fuel oil. "When you are handling diesel all the time, you inevitably spill some and get splashed," noted one diarist. "Everything, our clothes, the floor, our beards, the blankets, pieces of equipment, everything is saturated with this smell—it seems as though it isn't blood flowing through our veins, but diesel." In addition, the base's one small generator just couldn't be expected to make it through the winter under the heavy use demanded of it (the men later fortunately found and repaired two large diesel generators from the base dump, which only accentuated how badly they had really needed more generators). Recalled one

survivor: "We were hostages of that power engine. Its sputter-
ing and worn-out knocking [were] treated like the illness of
someone dear."

If anybody considered asking for help from the Americans at
McMurdo Sound or the South Pole station, the idea was
squelched. Soviet officials made no mention of their plight,
either over the radio (Mayak Radio Station continued to
broadcast its regular weather reports every midnight) or
through any of the international scientific channels between the
USSR and everyone else in the world. To the outside world
everything was just fine and cozy at Vostok.

But if another accident were to occur, the men could be dead
within hours, too soon for American rescuers to aid them.
Astakhov, the base commander, had once wintered at an
American base, and he knew American airlift capabilities. But
he risked twenty lives to avoid the humiliation of asking for
help from people who were his personal friends but his
country's enemies. When an American mission commander
later confronted his Soviet counterpart with his lack of request
for aid, the Russian could only silently shrug his shoulders in
evident discomfiture.

Meanwhile, on their own, Astakhov's team members were
"making do" with what they had. They cut up used bottled gas
cylinders and fashioned thirteen fuel oil stoves out of them.
These were placed in three rooms of the surviving building,
and the men spent the next half year huddled around them.

"Beside the stove it was like the tropics," one recalled, "and
beside the wall, like the Antarctic!" Another noted in his diary:
"While you sit, your head is hot, but your feet are in snow boots,
and when you look down you find they have frozen to the floor.
On the floor itself, in the corners, and at the walls there is ice."
The stoves had difficulty burning in the thin plateau air, and
they smoked heavily. Fat flakes of soot floated around the
room, and soot covered the men's faces. "My documents smell
of fuel oil to this day," recalled one of the scientists a year later.
The stoves had to be monitored and manually adjusted around
the clock. Every other day somebody had to climb up on the
roof and clean out the soot from the chimney.

Running the small generator was chancy since it had no spare
parts. The team turned it on for several hours a day, "operating
it as efficiently as possible," in the delicate words of a Russian

reporter. To keep the generator going far beyond its design life, expedition members fashioned spare parts from broken tractors. A supply of paraffin wax was discovered, and the men cast candles to solve the problem of illumination. They later even constructed a small sauna.

On November 23, 1982, a tractor-sled convoy reached Vostok from the Mirniy base after a record 34-day dash (four of the fourteen tractors were lost on the frantic rescue push). The convoy brought a new diesel power plant, building materials, and other supplies. The siege had lasted 225 days. When the survivors got home to Moscow, each was awarded the Order of the Red Banner of Labor; Aleksey Karpenko was buried on a small island near Mirniy, on January 17, 1983, with the epitaph "He came here to stay forever."

Because this was a genuine story of courage, endurance, ingenuity, and hardship, once the story finally broke, the Soviets reported the feat widely. The proper themes were stressed, and the improper ones (questions of bad engineering, why they didn't ask for help, and so on) were ignored.

Reading these published accounts, U.S. Antarctic expedition members who had been in regular touch with the Soviets were astonished. According to Joe Bennett of the National Science Foundation (which coordinates American polar research), the Soviets had spent the whole winter pretending that everything was fine. "There's always an exchange of weather data going on," he explained. "But because of the language barrier, there's not a lot of chitchat. Still, there was no indication of any difficulty, none that anyone detected."

The refusal to ask for assistance offended many of the American South Pole veterans. "There was rather extensive support gear available. At McMurdo we have a warehouse full of equipment to support fieldwork," one veteran pointed out. "There are emergency generators, huts, tents, radios, all sorts of auxiliary equipment."

According to veteran American pilots, one of the American aircraft staged from New Zealand could have reached Vostok within a few days of any call, depending on weather conditions. At the very least, an airdrop could have been made, but under ordinary midwinter Antarctic conditions the Hercules supply plane should also have been able to land to off-load equipment. This is possible because American aircraft operating near the

South Pole have better skis and better engines than the Soviet counterparts. American pilots were also familiar with the route because during the December–January flying season American aircraft used to visit Vostok regularly with personnel and supplies.

One such midwinter rescue mission had even been flown many years previously, when an American base on the high plateau had lost its backup generator (and was thus one failure away from freezing to death). In May 1966 a C-141 had flown into Antarctica, landed to off-load the generator, and then successfully returned to New Zealand, with inbound and outbound refueling stops at McMurdo Sound. In the 1960s four midwinter medevacs had been made, two in June from McMurdo and two others from the Byrd station at the South Pole itself, in April and September (the April medevac had been of Russian exchange scientist Leonid Kuperov, so the Soviets knew the United States could do it). A rescue mission to Vostok in 1982 would have been almost "routine."

Yet in later Soviet reports the possibility of American help was implicitly denied. "Not even the most well-meaning hand of help could reach that deep into the Antarctic," a Soviet account falsely asserted.

American hands have always been willing and able to help the Soviet Antarctic expeditions when asked. There was one case in which the Soviets did call for help and, in doing so, undoubtedly saved the lives of several of their own people. The case may help define the limit beyond which embarrassment is outweighed by humanitarian motives.

On January 2, 1979, an Ilyushin 14 supply aircraft crashed on takeoff from the Molodezhnaya station when its left engine failed. The plane was totally destroyed by fire, three crew members were killed, and nineteen others were seriously injured (mostly trauma). It was the only aircraft the Soviets had on the continent. After two days of consultation with Moscow and balancing considerations of life and death, the Soviet base commander radioed McMurdo Sound, more than 2,000 miles away, for assistance. Several of the injured required special medical attention if they were to survive.

Within six hours a portable medical van was loaded on a ski-equipped C-130 Hercules along with two doctors and several medical corpsmen. The mission was led by William

Morgan, commanding officer of the U.S. Navy's VXE-6 detachment (the Antarctic Development Squadron Six). The plane flew first to the U.S. base right at the South Pole, topped off its fuel tanks, and then flew directly to Molodezhnaya. Captain Morgan located the Soviet base without navigation aids and had to make a poor-visibility approach to get under a low cloud ceiling.

The American plane picked up the four most badly injured Soviets and an escorting Russian doctor. It then headed for Dunedin, New Zealand, where after refueling stops at the South Pole and McMurdo it arrived late on the afternoon of January 5. All five injured men survived.

The reason the Soviets broke with their tradition of not asking for help is still unclear. Perhaps there were high-ranking officials (or sons thereof) among the wounded who would have died if they hadn't been medevacked. Or perhaps the nature of the injuries—and the life-threatening consequences of their inadequate treatment—forced them to seek help. Doubtless the Soviet victims were grateful to be alive. But the incident never seems to have appeared in the Soviet press.

The Soviet behavior pattern of extreme reluctance to admit difficulties seems consistent, as other Antarctic events confirm. On December 30, 1984, an American plane visited Vostok to drop off a visiting French team. Usually such visits are occasions for feasting and serious drinking. But the visitors were struck by the meager spread in the mess hall. Later the American pilot and French team leader were taken aside to a small office, where they were offered half a bottle of vodka. Puzzled, they accepted it for a series of mutual toasts and then went about their business.

After the monthlong visit was over, the French were picked up by the same American flight crew, which then learned the explanation for the earlier uncharacteristically sparse Russian hospitality. The Soviets' tractor supply train from the coast was two months late and hadn't yet arrived when the French were dropped off. The Russians had put out all their remaining food to greet their guests but were too proud to ask for additional supplies to tide them over. Fortunately the food brought along for the French was enough to feed everyone until the tractors did arrive.

In February 1986 the Soviets suffered another Antarctic

accident and again declined to ask for Western aid, which might have saved six lives. An Ilyushin 14 transport was returning to Molodezhnaya after assisting in crew changeovers along the coast. On the 1,200-mile flight from Mirniy, the plane encountered strong head winds under a whiteout condition— no visibility at all. As the wings iced up and the fuel ran low, the pilot attempted to land blind. It was a desperate gamble, and all radio contact was lost.

Clearly hoping the men had survived, the Soviets sent out search planes. But they did not ask American aircraft to join in the search. Alone, it took them five days to find the wreckage, on the Philippi Glacier about 150 miles from Mirniy. Whether the men had died immediately on impact (as was likely) or had survived the landing only to die of exposure while waiting for rescuers to find them was never revealed.

The incident was mentioned in Soviet newspapers the following month. It was the first that American Antarctic operations officials—who would have sent out their own search planes if they had been asked—had ever heard of it.

A number of themes come to mind in the analysis of these incredible stories from the neighborhood of the South Pole. First, the dedication and skills of Soviet Antarctic explorers are manifest and laudable; these are human characteristics any nation would be proud of. Second, the essential Soviet pattern of secrecy is more relaxed there than anywhere else in the world. Once the Soviets even asked for help, and while they generally withheld immediate disclosure of other accidents, some information was eventually released (the existence of any other still-secret major disasters is considered unlikely). However, truly useful information about the accidents, the kind that might enable other national Antarctic teams to learn from the Soviet misadventures and themselves to avoid similar accidents, was never released.

There was some unusual candor in a newspaper article in *Izvestiya* on October 5, 1986, that revealed that the Soviets had lost an entire Antarctic base. The station, Druzhnaya-1, had been temporarily abandoned over the south polar winter but was to host a team of 170 researchers during the USSR's thirty-second regular Antarctic summer exploration season in 1986–1987.

That expedition was to have arrived in December, but now the men allocated to Druzhnaya would have to be accommodated elsewhere because the station had just vanished. It had been located on the Filchner Ice Shelf, two miles from the edge of the glacier, just east of the jutting Antarctic Peninsula which points toward South America. Vast areas of the floating ice suddenly broke loose and moved out to sea, carrying the base with them. It had been the main center of geologic and geophysical studies, specifically in search of oil and gas reserves in the area.

A new twist to the setback appeared in *Pravda* a few days later, just as the first Ilyushin 18D transport took off for the main Soviet Antarctic base. Human negligence, not just nature's hostility, was blamed. It seemed that the Argentines had evacuated a nearby base shortly before the ice shelf disintegrated. The Russians had had plenty of warning, the newspaper complained, so why had they been taken by surprise? Moscow didn't even know the base was missing until another team of explorers, non-Soviet ones at that, had been unable to locate it and had notified the Soviet Antarctic Commission. Since nobody heroic could be found, the search for the guilty had begun.

The base was later found on floating ice, and most of its equipment was retrieved for the new location. Since the scale of the disaster was thus much reduced, the urgency of finding and punishing scapegoats quickly faded.

In an environment where international and ideological tensions seem alien, where cooperation is the enshrined tradition and military confrontation is unknown, the Soviet behavior regarding disasters and secrecy retains a distressingly "typical" character. It seems relaxed only in comparison with usual Soviet behavior patterns everywhere else in the world. Compared with accepted norms in the West, however, it remains—even at its best—an alien, semiparanoid style. The freeze, even at the South Pole, is taking a long, long time to thaw.

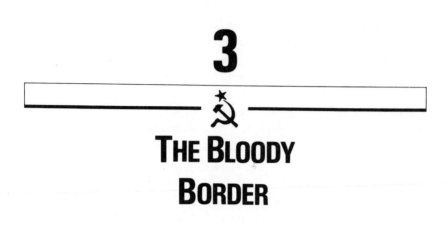

3

THE BLOODY BORDER

The protection of the USSR state border is a very important, inalienable part of the defense of the socialist father-
land. The USSR state border is inviolable. Any attempts to
violate it are resolutely suppressed.

—*Preamble to the*
  "Law of the Border of the USSR"

After five years of official silence Moscow revealed its version of
an aerial tragedy on the USSR's southern border. But as in the
metaphor of nested masks, what the Soviets uncovered was
itself a counterfeit image, and beneath it was not so much
heroic drama but bloody farce.

Soviet Air Force Captain Valentin Kulyapin realized he was
still alive when he felt the blast of cold air on his face. His
parachute had opened properly, and he was descending slowly
toward the ground. His jet interceptor was plunging to the
ground in flames. The intruder plane, its tail badly damaged by
the collision Kulyapin had deliberately instigated, flew into a
mountainside as the Russian pilot watched.

It was July 18, 1981, and the four crewmen of the chartered cargo airliner which had strayed across the Soviet border had just paid for their carelessness with their lives.

On a map the Soviet state border is just a line, like any other nation's political boundary. In real life, however, the Soviet border seems to be unique in the world. It comprises an invisible menace, a life-threatening zone which appears designed to destroy anyone who wittingly or unwittingly crosses it. Other nations have both borders and powerful military forces, but the United States, or Japan, or Sweden, or even China is not known to blow airborne intruders out of the air regularly. Such behavior is not normal by contemporary world standards.

While a simple ideological explanation might attribute such behavior to pure Soviet malevolence, the reasons for the occurrences are sometimes difficult to divine. In large part, however, technological failures and accidents seem to have conspired to reinforce instinctive Soviet paranoia, leading to murderous results.

The doomed aircraft this time, in mid-1981, was a Canadair Limited CL-44 transport, registration number LV-JTN, one of two owned by an obscure Argentine cargo line named Transporte Aéreo Río Platense. Earlier in 1981 the aircraft had ostensibly been chartered through intermediaries to fly cargo from Larnaca (Cyprus) to Teheran (Iran). The airliner, as it turned out, first picked up the cargo in Tel Aviv before flying it to neutral Cyprus and on to war-torn Iran. The cargo consisted of weapons for the war against Iraq.

Aboard the aircraft on the return leg to Cyprus were three Argentine crew members and a British citizen. Héctor Cordero was the pilot; José Burgueno and Hermete Boasso were his crew. Stuart McCafferty was officially listed as "purser," but he was a representative of the brokers handling the arms sale. On July 18 the crew was making its third round trip.

The aircraft departed Teheran and headed northwest toward Turkish airspace. Because of intermittent air-to-air combat along the Iran-Iraq border, the airplane (like most others flying between Iran and points west) flew as far north as possible, skirting the southern Soviet border along the Caucasus Mountains.

There the crewmen made their mistake. Instead of following a heading of about 300 degrees to the Turkish border and then turning left to a heading of 240 degrees direct to Cyprus, the aircraft seems to have been on a course about 5 degrees farther to the right, to the north. That took it over a section of Soviet Azerbaijan which juts southward along the generally southeast-northwest trend of the border. It flew parallel to the border, but on the Soviet side, for ten or twenty minutes.

By Soviet accounts released five years later, the "intruder" disregarded all radio calls (nobody at any Iranian or Turkish control tower seems to have heard such calls) and then ignored signals from escorting Soviet planes. That the Soviet military had botched the contact procedures seems much more likely, considering the level of skill (or lack of it) shown on other, similar occasions.

Kulyapin was one of the Soviet pilots on alert at the time the aircraft was spotted. He was also the deputy squadron political officer, the *zampolit,* a position generally characterized less by flying skill than by ideological zeal. In air-to-ground communication he was "pilot 733." As he approached the target, he heard that jets from other bases were breaking off their intercepts prematurely as the result of low fuel reserves. He was the only pilot to catch up with the intruder.

Kulyapin was keyed up for combat, according to his thoughts as reported in the much later newspaper account. "Who would dare cross the border?" he marveled to himself. He rapidly visualized the terrain over which the intruder was flying and tried to imagine what targets worth spying on could be there.

As he, now alone, approached the target, his controllers radioed that the target was turning toward the border (that is, toward the west). Kulyapin recalled feeling outraged. "What's this?" he wondered. "An evasive maneuver, a trick, or an attempt to slip out unpunished? He won't get away!" As he closed in from behind, he performed an IFF ("Identify—Friend or Foe") radar transponder interrogation, but there was no answer, which meant it was a foreign aircraft.

Kulyapin reported later that once he had caught up with the intruder aircraft, the "enemy" pilot had deliberately ignored him, even though he had performed all standard visual contact procedures. "They flew nose to nose. . . . Kulyapin saw the heads of the foreign pilots turned in his direction," the newspaper account later claimed. "He gave them the conventional signal to make a landing approach on a designated course. In response he got no reaction whatsoever."

As the young Russian pilot was paralleling the intruder off its left wing, it suddenly turned in to him, forcing him to dive and avoid collision. Kulyapin interpreted this as a hostile act designed to force him into a spin. "The intruders, it seemed, were counting on the Soviet pilot panicking and breaking up in the propellers when they made their sharp maneuver," claimed the newspaper account. This left turn also put the intruder on a course out of Soviet territory, toward the Araks River, which was already visible in the distance. Kulyapin was seized by anger. "Who's giving it to whom, huh?" he savagely thought. "Well, we'll see—let's fight."

Most likely the Argentine pilots were oblivious of the intercept and had just made the normal turn toward Cyprus, which was due at about this time. But the Soviet interpretation was entirely different: "The crew of the intruder aircraft arrogantly continued to move toward confrontation. They understood that the Soviet pilot would try to cut them off from the border, which was only a few kilometers away." By fantasizing such lines of thought in the minds of the foreign pilots, the official Soviet account was able to portray them as unambiguous enemies.

"I can't let them push me across the ribbon," Kulyapin realized, thinking of the nearby river border. "733 to base," he called out. "The intruder is not following my orders. He is trying to escape across the border."

Basing its decisions on the excited (if not by now hysterical) accounts by Kulyapin, ground control ordered that the obviously hostile intruder be shot down. Kulyapin's jet (of an unidentified type) evidently had no guns, but it did have missiles. However, Kulyapin concluded that he would be unable to drop back the mile or two needed for a good radar lock-on and missile launch in the few moments before the aircraft crossed the border.

Instead, since he was right up near the airliner, the *zampolit* instinctively decided to emulate the glorious Soviet heroes of the Great Patriotic War (World War II) and ram the enemy plane. He announced his intentions to ground control and was asked to repeat them—but nobody ordered him not to carry out his attack.

Kulyapin looked ahead of him to where the river was growing nearer. On the ground he spotted a moving black spot.

"The intruder aircraft's shadow fell on our territory," went the story. "An evil, nasty shadow."

The ramming plan was not entirely suicidal since the Russian pilot hoped to cripple the four-engine turboprop transport with strategic blows from the top of his own jet. To do this, he flew in close to the right side of the tail and began bumping into the stabilizer. Suddenly his canopy shattered and shards of glass sprayed around the cockpit, bouncing off his helmet and shoulders as he cringed. Nothing heavier hit him, so he pulled back on the control stick and rammed the intruder again.

His own jet began shaking violently as its control system failed. He grabbed the red ejection handles and pulled, noting that the cockpit clock read 1444 Moscow summertime.

Kulyapin never heard the detonation as a tremendous force threw him upward, probably passing within feet of the tail of the airliner. But upon regaining his senses moments later he looked around him. The newspaper described what he saw: "Like an overturned autumn leaf the intruder aircraft was falling in a steep spiral: its right tail fin had been cut clean off." Kulyapin thought: "You never come out horizontal from that flight path." He watched the intruder crash and burn.

Western aviation experts who have examined Kulyapin's account of the encounter are highly skeptical. Pilots who have flown the CL-44 report that air turbulence behind the engines is so violent that it would have been impossible to control a throttled-down jet to hold a position directly behind and below one wing. The consensus is that Kulyapin misjudged a turn and hit the airliner by accident, afterward deciding to make up a story of glorious self-sacrifice.

The cargo plane was quickly reported overdue by the Argentine company, and a check with Turkish air traffic controllers revealed that radar had shown the aircraft disappearing into Soviet airspace. Still, the Soviets were at something of a loss to account for the event, and they took four days to announce that the foreign plane had crashed into a Soviet jet—and then blamed it for the collision. Said TASS: "The crew of the plane did not respond to any inquiries by Soviet ground air traffic control services and to attempts to render help to it, [but] continued the flight over the Soviet territory, performing dangerous maneuverings. Some time later the plane collided with a Soviet plane, was destroyed, and burned." Officially, at least at first, it was a negligent accident. Oddly, TASS never identified the nationality of the aircraft.

At first the Soviets ascribed no hostile intent to the intruder, but soon began the campaign to prove it had really been an "enemy" that deserved to be destroyed. Within two weeks propaganda distortions had begun. Although the plane, for example, had not been flying *into* Soviet airspace when it was destroyed but had been about to cross the border *out* of Soviet airspace, the Soviets conveniently changed its course 180 degrees as proof of aggressive intent. For example, on August 1 a Persian-language broadcast on the so-called National Voice of Iran (a Soviet-run facility which purported to be a native Iranian station) gave this version: "The Soviet Union's aviation authorities ordered the plane to land. However, the said plane, without paying the slightest heed to warnings by Soviet planes, continued its flight into the Soviet Union's airspace. At this point, there remains no alternative for any country, including the Soviet Union, but to prevent further flight of the aggressive plane and to neutralize it."

At the crash site thirty miles southeast of Yerevan (just across the border from the conjunction of Iran and Turkey, in the far northwestern corner of Azerbaijan), Soviet investigators doubtlessly combed the wreckage immediately. The bodies were moved to a morgue in Yerevan. No "spy gear" of any kind could have been found, or the world would have been loudly and self-righteously told about it. The aircraft's flight recorders (if any, and they probably existed) were removed and hidden away (the crew's final conversations would have proved its innocence), and if the Argentines ever asked for the recorders back, they were rebuffed.

But even with such physical evidence the Soviets would still be officially claiming five years later that the plane had been flying without markings. This might initially have been based purely on Kulyapin's testimony that "it was a four-engine military aircraft." Yet Leopoldo Bravo, the Argentine ambassador to Moscow, had been allowed to visit the crash site, and he clearly saw the Argentine flag still distinctly painted on a surviving portion of wing. The Russian pilot should easily have been able to spot it as well.

The charred bodies of the crewmen were returned to Argentine and British authorities. Meanwhile, Moscow's deputy minister of foreign affairs, Zemskov, had assured the Argentine ambassador that the Soviet pilot had also been killed in the tragedy. Otherwise, the Argentine officials undoubtedly would have insisted on interviewing him.

Kulyapin, meanwhile, had actually walked away without a scratch (after learning to his relief that he had come down on the proper side of the border). He was duly decorated with the Order of the Red Banner, was sent to the Lenin Military Political Academy for further ideological training, and by 1986 had been posted as a deputy regimental political officer.

By then the Soviets had built up enough pride in his spirit of self-sacrifice that they were willing to boast publicly about it. The April 6, 1986, issue of *Red Star* published a large portrait of the heroic officer and gave a two-page account of his achievement.

"The heroic deed performed by Kulyapin is practically legendary," the newspaper concluded. "But the pilot doesn't like to talk about it randomly at meetings or dinners, although he shares the experience of having rammed a jet plane with his fellow airmen in detail. They may need to do it in battle to defeat the enemy. And survive!"

This account of Kulyapin's incredibly stupid feat, compounded by the Soviet air traffic control's failure to contact the doomed Argentine plane by radio, is important in that it reveals in detail the thought processes which might be going through the head of a typical Soviet pilot intercepting an "enemy" aircraft on his country's borders. It has happened numerous times before and since, often with similar tragic consequences.

A legendary hero of an earlier intrusion was a pilot named Boris Vegin. Supposedly he had shot down one intruder, perhaps about 1960. In an account published in 1973 he told a Soviet author about frequently watching enemy spy flights over international waters. Once a Soviet interceptor approached such a spy plane only to fall suddenly into the sea. "It was never recovered and the cause of the pilot's disaster remains unexplained," Vegin recounted. "Possibly the spy plane hit him. . . ." The notion of armed spy planes ready to kill innocent Russian pilots would encourage other pilots either to exercise caution or, as in Kulyapin's case, to display zealous combativeness.

Another pilot, identified only as "Captain G. Yeliseyev," had also rammed an "intruder" at some date in the 1970s ("a few years ago" from 1983). He died in the feat and received the USSR's highest posthumous military honors. Since there are no unaccounted-for Western planes near the Soviet border, the plane which Yeliseyev destroyed could well have been Soviet (there are reports of at least two cases in which Soviet planes were in fact mistakenly destroyed by Soviet air defense forces). Interestingly some details parallel Kulyapin's account (the pilot was a *zampolit*, and the intruder was trying to escape across the border), but others are quite different (he rammed the intruder at full throttle and was killed).

The eagerness shown by Kulyapin, Yeliseyev, and Vegin to defend the holy Soviet border, while extreme, was hardly unique, as other concrete examples show. On June 21, 1978, a Soviet jet blew an unarmed Iranian helicopter out of the air when it strayed across the border near Ashkhabad in foggy weather. All eight men aboard the training flight were killed. Claimed the Soviets: "It had ignored warnings to land." By now an observer may deduce a pattern in which such warnings, if ever really given, were totally ineffective because of major technical shortcomings in Soviet radio equipment.

The southern USSR border region's reputation was bad enough after the two aircraft losses in 1978 and 1981, but as the Iran-Iraq War dragged on, the region got even more dangerous. In 1984, for example, Alitalia pilot Benito Niolu told a Rome conference that the Iranian-Soviet border was a region of weak navigation signals where "being buzzed by fighters was commonplace" and "the risk of a mistake [is] great." On his weekly flight between Rome and Teheran he reported being "haunted by thoughts of a repetition of the shooting down by fighters of the Korean jumbo jet after straying into Soviet airspace last year." A spokesman for Alitalia, Italy's state airline, reported that the company didn't consider the route dangerous.

Just how easy it could be for the Soviets to destroy an innocent civil airliner by mistake was demonstrated in 1984 over the western Baltic Sea, near Gotland Island. The Swedish government claimed that on August 9, 1984, a Soviet jet fighter pursued—arguably by mistake—a civilian Airbus 310 jetliner and intruded thirty miles into Swedish airspace, at one point closing to within about a mile of the unaware airliner. Radio intercepts showed that the Sukhoi 15 fighter had armed and locked on its air-to-air missiles. The Soviets, on October 21, officially denied that any such thing had happened and claimed the jet was fifty miles from where the Swedish radars showed it. They provided carefully labeled maps to demonstrate this and even had testimony from another pilot, who swore he was looking at the jet in question on maneuvers over the Baltic when the Swedes claimed it was over their territory. The conclusive proof offered by Soviet spokesman Vadim Zagladin was: "If our jet really got as close, the Swedish aircraft would have been able to photograph it. All aircraft are equipped with photographic equipment, but there is no photograph!" When reminded that the jet was tracked directly behind the airliner, out of sight of any of the windows, Zagladin refused to back down: "Well, this is the situation—no one saw it, no one heard it. And there is no other evidence." The Soviets just were not about to admit the possibility of equipment failure or human error on their part.

Previous experience with trigger-happy Soviet pilots in the Baltic Sea area had been even more frightening. Some encounters involved military aircraft and others involved civil aircraft, and it didn't seem as if the Soviets could tell them apart. On April 8, 1950, a U.S. Navy patrol aircraft had been destroyed by Soviet aircraft only ninety miles southeast of Gotland Island, with the loss of ten American lives. Wreckage of the aircraft, including bullet-ridden landing gear, was recovered and helped establish its location when attacked. On June 13, 1952, a Swedish C-47 Dakota transport was shot down in the same area, with the loss of eight lives. Three days later a Swedish rescue aircraft (a Catalina seaplane) was shot down by two Soviet MiG-15s, but the crew ditched and was rescued. Another U.S. patrol aircraft was attacked over the Baltic Sea on November 7, 1958, but escaped.

In the late 1970s another American reconnaissance mission over international waters in the Baltic was almost attacked by an overeager Soviet pilot. Aboard the modified four-engine RC-135 (Boeing 707), intelligence officers listened to the air-to-ground conversation between the nearby Soviet jet and its ground control. Ground asked the pilot if he could see "the target," and the Russian enthusiastically replied in the affirmative. "It's a B-52!" he claimed, to which the ground replied calmly, "Count the engines" (a B-52 has eight). Aboard the

American plane, listeners heard with vanishing amusement how the Russian pilot counted slowly to eight. "The guys were freaking out listening to this," recalled one official, who recounted the story to journalist Seymour Hersh. Fortunately the Soviet ground control had no doubts about the identity of the "target" and merely instructed the pilot to take a photograph and return to base. His voice was not heard again over the radio frequencies. More confusion (or less sound judgment) at ground control could have led to a more tragic outcome. Arguably that's the way several of the earlier tragedies had occurred.

And that's the way it may have happened on July 1, 1960, when a routine RB-47 patrol over international waters in the Barents Sea (off Russia's northwestern coast) was attacked by Soviet fighters. The Russians were, perhaps understandably, jumpy because of the recent capture of the U-2 pilot Francis Gary Powers when his spy plane had been shot down near Sverdlovsk. They shot down the RB-47, killing four crewmen; two others parachuted safely and were captured by a Soviet patrol boat.

Nikita Khrushchev had his own self-serving version in his memoirs:

> Some U.S. reconnaissance planes were flying over our northern territorial waters, collecting intelligence on our radar installations along the Arctic Circle. We shot one of them down. The American practice in such cases was to announce that their plane had been flying over international waters. But of course, they had no way of proving their claim, and we had concrete proof that the opposite was true. Some of the crew members had been killed, but one or two were captured alive. We returned the corpses to the U.S. immediately, but the survivors we held. Other than that case, the U.S. ceased to violate our airspace. . . .

Oleg Penkovskiy was a high-level Soviet military official at that time as well as an American spy. Shortly after his capture in the early 1960s a document purporting to be his journal was published in the West. His account of the RB-47 incident was entirely different from Khrushchev's and was consistent with the U.S. claim that it had scrupulously avoided Soviet airspace this time.

The U.S. aircraft RB-47 shot down on Khrushchev's order was not flying over Soviet territory; it was flying over neutral waters. Pinpointed by radar, it was shot down by Khrushchev's personal order. When the true facts were reported to Khrushchev, he said: "Well done, boys, keep them from flying even close. . . ." I know for a fact that our military leaders had a note prepared with apologies for the incident, but Khrushchev said: "No, let them know that we are strong."

Almost twenty years later, on April 20, 1978, another tragic shooting incident occurred in the same area when an errant Korean Air Lines 707 strayed over the Kola Peninsula and was attacked, arguably without proper warning, by Soviet jets.

No satisfactory explanation for the course deviation of Flight 902 has ever been produced, the result in no small part of the Soviet refusal to release any of the recovered data, such as flight recorders and the pilots' and navigator's logs (the Soviets even refused to allow the pilots to make photocopies before leaving Moscow for home). Years later the Soviets released a map (almost certainly based on analysis of flight recorder data) which showed that the aircraft had begun a wide right turn soon after reaching Iceland on its Amsterdam to Anchorage over-the-pole route. Such a turn was too gradual to occur manually, and the on-board guidance equipment would have equally been unable to match it deliberately, so a plausible explanation involved a drift in the aircraft's inertial platform or the manual keyboard entry of an incorrect correction factor for Earth's rotation (the apparent path would have been followed if the sign of the correction factor had been reversed).

Soon after entering Soviet airspace, the airliner was met by a Soviet jet. The pilot of Flight 902, Captain Kim Chang Ky, reported that when he caught sight of the Soviet jet—off the right side, not the left as specified by International Civil Aviation Organization (ICAO, pronounced eye-kay-oh) standards—he reduced speed, lowered his landing gear, and flashed his navigation lights on and off, all specified in procedures as signifying willingness to follow the Soviet fighter. His calls on 121.5 were recorded by a Finnish air traffic control tower at Rovaniemi, which also noted the lack of any Soviet calls on the same frequency.

Despite the existence of the Finnish tapes, a Soviet spokesman later still declared: "The Soviet Union did everything possible to land it at an airfield but it would not comply." At that point the Soviet jet fired a missile which blew off part of a wing and showered the fuselage with shrapnel, killing two passengers. *Pravda* later called it a "warning shot."

American intelligence units in Europe had been able to eavesdrop on the Soviet air-to-ground communications as they occurred via some new high-tech eavesdropping facilities, according to a recent book by Seymour Hersh. At first the Russian pilots were convinced by the size of the radar blip that the incoming aircraft was a Boeing 747 and thus obviously a civilian airliner. But then at one point one of the pilots correctly reported that its silhouette was that of a Boeing 707, the same design as the RC-135 intelligence aircraft. The pilot was then ordered to attack and destroy the target.

Remarkably, the pilot argued with his ground control, on the basis of a closer view which showed the Korean Air Lines logo on the aircraft's tail. For several minutes he protested that the airplane was not a military one. Hersh's sources reconstructed the conversation as follows:

> CONTROLLER: Do you see the target?
> PILOT: Roger, it is a civilian airliner.
> CONTROLLER: Destroy the target.
> PILOT: Did you understand me?
> CONTROLLER: Destroy the target.
> PILOT: [Swears], do you understand what I told you?
> GENERAL: [Identifies himself], do you know who I am?
> PILOT: Yes.
> GENERAL: Force down that plane.

The Soviets evidently decided that the markings were false, painted onto a spy plane for just the purpose of confusing their pilots.

One eavesdropping American, recalling the tone of the pilot's voice, later described the conversation as "one of the most dramatic things I'd heard in years. . . . I could see the guy shaking his head and saying, 'We don't shoot down civilians.' " But he followed orders. His first missile did not detonate but his second blew up against the airliner's left wing.

Following the air-to-air attack came the most embarrassing part of the incident, as far as the Soviet air defense forces were

concerned. With air streaming out through holes in his fuselage, the Korean pilot pushed his jet over into a steep dive to get
to a lower altitude with breathable air density. In doing so, he
vanished into a low-lying cloud bank and dropped below Soviet
radar coverage. The pursuing jets overshot him and were
unable to spot him when they circled back. The Soviet radar
screens were masked with ground clutter. The target had
eluded them!

For more than an hour Captain Kim flew at an altitude of
only several thousand feet across the snow-covered peninsula,
seeking a safe landing place. The Soviets had no idea where he
was. He had aborted several approaches to possible sites when
he spotted obstructions at the last moment. Finally, after
nightfall, he found a frozen lake bed, just west of Kem, and let
down smoothly, skidding in to a safe landing.

Meanwhile, both overhead and at ground control points the
Soviets frantically sought out the escaped target. Hours later,
responding to a phone call from a nearby Soviet settlement,
Russian militia officials with a ladder knocked at the side of the
airliner. The target had been found, no thanks to high-tech air
defense equipment.

The incompetent performance of the air defense technology
scandalized the Soviet government. Little concern seems to
have been wasted on the two dead passengers. Instead, the fear
was that American spy planes or even bombers might be able to
utilize similar techniques against Soviet weaknesses to penetrate
defenses. The air defense forces underwent a severe reorgani-
zation, and in the shakeup many leading officials had their
careers terminated.

The result of the 1978 shakeup may have been a military
organization much more eager to shoot to kill at the earliest
opportunity lest their marginal technological capabilities not
allow them a second chance at any future "target." With more
confidence in their ability to find and track intruders, Soviet
military leaders might have been less trigger-happy. But after
1978 all the officers of the air defense forces must have been
grimly determined not to let the next intruder slip away so
easily.

The Soviet failure to cooperate with international investigators in 1978, and Moscow's refusal to turn over the necessary
data, also clearly laid groundwork for later tragedy. Commen-

tators at that time warned about precisely such a danger. "If even deadlier incidents are to be avoided," wrote Anthony Paul in *Reader's Digest,* "the Russians owe it to the world to make the [flight] recorder available, and to publish a full, factual account of what they believe happened." Soviet failure to comply with ICAO standards in investigating the 1978 incident were a direct contributory precursor to the later tragedies.

At the other end of the Soviet Union, along the Pacific coast, American patrol aircraft had also been doing their share toward making Soviet border defense forces jumpy. Regular patrolling for decades, including airspace violations both planned and unplanned, had been punctuated by occasional shooting incidents. As early as October 22, 1949, an RB-29 over the Sea of Japan was attacked (no injuries). On October 7, 1952, an RB-29 was shot down by Soviet fighters six miles north of the Hokkaido coast, killing all eight crewmen. Another RB-29 was destroyed on July 29, 1953, killing another sixteen crewmen. On September 4, 1954, a U.S. Navy (USN) Neptune reconnaissance aircraft was attacked by a Soviet Mig-15, allegedly fifty miles off the coast, and on November 7 of the same year a U.S. Air Force (USAF) B-29 equipped with photoreconnaissance gear with eleven men on board was shot down "near Hokkaido" (ten men survived on parachutes). Subsequent shooting incidents resulted in no additional deaths.

There was one unusual case in which the Soviets did admit they made a mistake. On June 23, 1955, a U.S. Navy aircraft was attacked over international waters near the Bering Strait. Three crewmen were wounded. The Soviets admitted the error and offered to pay half the damage cost. The United States accepted. By today's official Soviet accounts, the last such mistake they made was thirty years ago.

Hersh's 1986 book on the 1983 KAL 007 tragedy provided information on a hitherto secret incident on April 2, 1976, near Sakhalin Island. A fully marked Japanese P-2V Neptune patrol plane inadvertently penetrated a few miles into Soviet airspace and was pounced on by a Soviet Sukhoi 15 jet, whose pilot reported to the ground that he had "visually sighted the target." He was ordered to attack and subsequently fired two air-to-air missiles. Both fortunately missed, and the Japanese aircraft was not damaged.

All these incidents were only preludes to the worst air

tragedy of the Soviet borders, the destruction of Korean Air Lines Flight 007 on September 1, 1983, with the loss of 269 lives. Although the Soviets claimed complete justification, while many Western groups saw it as a deliberate Communist atrocity, careful reconstruction of the incident makes it appear instead to be the worst foul-up of Soviet air defense technology in USSR history. The ultimate guilt is unavoidable: The Soviets shot to kill, all right, but irresponsibly they weren't careful to determine at whom they were shooting. All their expensive equipment and operators never provided data sufficiently convincing to dissuade them from their original instinctive (and wrong) judgment that the blip was an "American aggressor."

The bare facts of the September 1, 1983, KAL 007 disaster have been established, despite attempts by the Soviets and some assorted Western conspiracy enthusiasts to deflect responsibility. As with many airliners before and since, Flight 007 went off course through some unlikely but plausible combination of human errors and equipment problems. Tragically the accidental course deviation put it over Soviet territory.

The Soviets had numerous opportunities to identify the "bogey" as a lost civilian airliner but were unable to fulfill their responsibilities. As the airliner crossed the Kamchatka Peninsula, Soviet interceptors failed to reach it and make visual contact. Later, over Sakhalin Island, the Soviet pilots also nearly missed their intercept. When they finally caught up, there were only minutes remaining before the plane exited Soviet airspace. In the rush the Soviet pilot let off a burst of cannon fire from a position behind and below the "target," where it was physically impossible for the Koreans to see it. No radio calls were heard by anyone in the area on the specified distress frequency of 121.5 megahertz. At one point the Russian pilot was abreast of (and a bit below) the airliner, but despite earlier experience with American RC-135s, he failed to notice—or report—the obvious visual differences (mostly in the running lights). This was especially true since the airliner's lights were flashing brightly, hardly the behavior of a stealthy intruder (to refute this obvious deduction, the Soviets later merely lied about the plane's flying "without lights").

With the border approaching and without ever having performed a proper communications procedure, the Soviets fell into the same routine as they had with the lost Argentine airliner two years earlier. The pilot, call sign "805," followed in the tradition of Kulyapin, Vegin, Yeliseyev, and nameless others. When in doubt, attack to kill. Don't let the "enemy" escape.

And that, horribly, is just what happened. Amazingly there were many people in the West who were surprised. Predictable, too, were the impassioned pronouncements that the Soviets must have known they were killing innocents when another appalling interpretation was that they didn't know—or care—at whom they were shooting, even though they should have been able to determine the aircraft's innocence. Presumption of guilt is easier and safer, at least from the Soviet point of view.

With KAL 007 and the other incidents, a pattern of Soviet claims is apparent. How is a dispassionate observer able to gauge the reliability of Soviet accounts when its side usually has the only surviving witnesses?

Survivors of Flight 902 over the Kola Peninsula in 1978 did provide firsthand accounts that were markedly at variance with the official Soviet descriptions. And another recent border incident gave a similar opportunity to compare and contrast Moscow's accounts with the recollections of non-Soviet witnesses.

In July 1983 the Greenpeace antiwhaling group sent its ship *Rainbow Warrior* to a Soviet whaling station on the Chukchi Peninsula at the far eastern edge of Siberia. Several of the group landed by small motorboat and were distributing literature to Soviet whalers when military units arrived. One American headed back to the ship in the motorboat, carrying the camera with exposed film showing the group's activities.

The official Soviet TASS dispatch on July 21 claimed that the main ship fled at once and "made dangerous maneuvers, deliberately creating a shipwreck situation. . . . The [small] boat . . . capsized as a result of such irresponsible actions. The possible tragic consequences were averted by Soviet frontier guards which raised a helicopter into the air and saved the drowning man."

This official Soviet scenario is a self-serving series of lies from beginning to end. As recounted by Greenpeace participants later, the helicopter itself was chasing the man in the motorboat as he tried to reach the ship. After making several menacing swoops, it lowered a line into his boat, "inviting" him aboard.

Quickly he removed the film from his camera and left it in the boat, then put the boat's tiller hard over as he let himself be hauled up into the helicopter. Others aboard the *Rainbow Warrior* saw the motorboat running in circles and steered toward it; one man was injured when he successfully managed to jump on board, bring the boat under control, and retrieve the film. The *Rainbow Warrior* headed out to sea without interference, leaving several of its crew in Soviet custody.

The photographs retrieved from the boat were widely published around the world. The photographs showed the illegal whaling station the Russians had insisted did not exist. They showed the outdoor boilers for rendering the whale fat. They showed Greenpeacers handing out antiwhaling leaflets to puzzled and resentful Russian workers. The existence of the photographs was documentary proof of the falsity of the Soviet account (none of the Greenpeacers taken into Soviet custody was allowed to keep any exposed film). The captives were treated well and were turned over to Western authorities a few days later.

The number of times the Soviets have resorted to deadly force after botching intercept and communications attempts is appalling. In fact, the last "successful" (that is, nonfatal) intercept of an intruding aircraft seems to have been in 1968, when a chartered Seaboard World Airways DC-8 was diverted to a Soviet field in the Kuril Islands (the pilot still maintains he wasn't in Soviet airspace but prudently went along with the fighters off his wing).

Regarding disasters on their borders, the Soviets showed unusually extreme levels of falsification and fabrication of events, more so than in other kinds of disasters. Presumably the shrill tone of these is to justify the actions of their military forces. Secrecy has always been much more rigid when related to military than to civilian disasters. As for how effective *glasnost* will be in any future military border disasters, only time will tell. So far Western analysts believe that the Soviet military has not responded enthusiastically to *glasnost* or any other Gorbachev reform.

However, since these tragedies there has been one encouraging event. One airliner did cross the Soviet border in an unscheduled manner recently and was not shot down.

In late 1986 a Kuwaiti airliner, en route from Damascus to

Teheran, safely made an emergency landing in Yerevan when a sudden storm shut down all airfields in Iran. The Boeing 727 had turned around and was headed back west but was too short of fuel to reach any airfields in Turkey. The crew desperately radioed to the Soviet air traffic control facility in Armenia.

Once permission had been granted, the airliner crossed the Soviet border near Dzhulfa (less than 100 miles from where the Argentine airliner had been destroyed six years earlier) and made a safe landing at Yerevan. The plane was serviced and fueled and took off the following morning.

Full details never became clear, and several reports described how the airliner had crossed the border while being pursued by unidentified jet fighters. There must have been difficulty in the civil air traffic control officials' contacting military air defense officers on such short notice. But the bottom line was that an airliner abruptly entered Soviet airspace, bet its life on Soviet radio technology, and this time survived.

Whether this was a fluke or a softening of the traditional bloody border policy, the future will reveal. When Mathias Rust flew his borrowed Cessna 172 from Finland to Moscow's Red Square in May 1987, he apparently owed his life to indecision and reluctance to fire on the part of at least two Soviet interceptor pilots who had shadowed him. The most tragic aftermath of Rust's stupid stunt would be a rebirth of Soviet border paranoia and trigger-happiness, ensuring that the next airborne intruders, either innocently lost or gleefully copycatting Rust's exploit, will pay with their lives. In terms of secrecy, the issue may boil down to whether the West notices the shootdown (particularly if there are Western citizens aboard) at all; if not, the Soviets can be counted on to try to keep such bloody border atrocities secret, or failing that, to creatively rearrange reality to fit Soviet preconceptions and propaganda needs.

On the border, that's the lesson of the past and the trend of the future.

4

MILITARY
DISASTERS

You know, we have one formula now: there are no closed topics.

—*Empty boast by journalist Yuriy Schchekochikhin of* Literaturnaya Gazeta, *from the Moscow/San Francisco telebridge on* The Role of the Media in Current Relations, *broadcast on Moscow television May 13, 1987*

Military service anywhere involves dealing with high-energy fuels, machines, and armaments, which through their very nature can conspire with human carelessness to take a toll on human life. What is unique about the Soviet approach to armed forces safety is how eagerly they report Western fighter crashes ("Another Catastrophe!" exclaims a typical headline in *Krasnaya Zvezda* ["Red Star"], the military daily newspaper) while steadfastly maintaining the facade that such events do not happen in the USSR. Military-related disasters are among the most highly classified accidents in the USSR, and in fact, the degree of secretiveness around an event often serves as an indicator of how deeply the military is involved.

*   *   *

As part of a massive foreign aid package, Soviet engineers built a 1.7-mile tunnel through the Salang Pass in Afghanistan in 1956. The tunnel is on a slope; it is also unventilated. In later years cynics often pointed out how the entire highway from the Soviet border to Kabul had been engineered to withstand heavy military traffic, even armored vehicles. The Afghan government had never asked for so sturdy a road, but the Soviet government evidently saw a possible future need for it.

Early in November 1982 the Agence France Presse bureau in Islamabad, Pakistan, filed a sensational report:

> Over one thousand Soviet soldiers and Afghani civilians suffocated in the Salang Pass tunnel last week after a tanker truck full of petrol collided head on with the leading vehicle in a Soviet military convoy, a Western diplomatic source said here today.
>
> Citing reports in Kabul, the source said that vehicles piled up inside the tunnel, the main pass through the Hindu Kush mountains. The death toll was estimated at 1,100 at least. The source said that the Soviets first believed the convoy was being ambushed by Moslem insurgents and blocked both ends of the tunnel. Drivers kept their engines running owing to the cold, and exhaust fumes and the fumes from the damaged tanker led to the huge death toll, with virtually everyone trapped in the tunnel suffocating.
>
> Western diplomats in Kabul estimated that 700 Soviet soldiers died in the accident, believed to have occurred on November 2 or 3, while 200 were affected by fumes. They estimated that from 400 up to as many as 2,000 Afghan civilians could have died in the disaster, with a further 200 affected.
>
> Neither Soviet nor Afghan authorities in Kabul have confirmed the report, but Kabul radio each day reads a list of people who have died, and diplomats noticed a marked increase in the days after the accident is believed to have taken place.

More than a week later, on November 18, 1982, the official Afghanistan news agency, Bakhtar, reported a road accident at the Salang Tunnel, along the main road from the USSR to

Kabul. The account mentioned "loss of life" but denied Western news services' reports that "subversive activities" had been involved. TASS repeated the report, and it appeared in the November 19 issue of *Krasnaya Zvezda*.

In New Delhi a few days later another "Western diplomat" (from a different embassy from the one who had talked to Agence France Presse) gave his own anonymous version of the disaster, which he dated as November 3. Quoting a relative of one of the Afghan victims, he put the death toll at between 500 and 1,000 people, including 80 Soviet soldiers. He was told that two military convoys entered the tunnel at the same time, in violation of the standard practice of allowing only one-way traffic alternately; the lead vehicles collided in flames, and a long traffic backup resulted. Some burning gasoline ran down at least part of the sloping tunnel. This smoke plus the fumes from the idling engines of both convoys quickly poisoned the tunnel air.

The diplomat also passed on unconfirmed reports that many Soviet troops inside the tunnel panicked, mistakenly believing they were being ambushed (the diplomat seriously doubted any hostile action). Reportedly there was gunfire within the tunnel. Troops at both ends blocked both entrances, presumably with armored vehicles since there are evidently no fitting gates. This prevented anyone from escaping. Nearly everyone within the tunnel died.

The event then disappeared almost entirely from the official Soviet media. It had happened, but it hadn't been much. Such was and still is the official Soviet version.

Despite the general belief that the disaster was a tragic accident, several different Afghan resistance groups claimed credit for a deliberate act of sabotage. A man identifying himself only as "Paghmani, formerly Royal Afghan Army, now the Afghan Resistance Movement," wrote an account providing many new allegations:

> I have personal knowledge from the leader of the Afghan resistance of Kohistan, Khwaja Nuruddin, that the lead vehicle in the Soviet convoy was rammed by an Afghan, dressed in Soviet uniform, driving a gasoline truck. . . . This convoy was carrying supplies of poison gas (and what is

worse, nerve gas) for the Soviet garrison in Kabul. . . . Within twenty minutes over 1000 Soviet and pro-Soviet soldiers died. The media have claimed another 300 Afghan civilians died, but this is not true.

The final official Soviet account, more than a year afterward, appeared in passing in the eighth paragraph of a page-three article in the Red Army newspaper on January 14, 1984, which mainly discussed the tunnel in general and the Soviet-Afghan teamwork in guarding it. In an interview an Afghan tunnel guard related how the "sad event" of a year earlier was caused by a truck's engine's unexpectedly stalling, causing the tunnel to be filled with fumes from idling engines. "Many drivers lost consciousness," recalled Senior Lieutenant Abdul Vakeel, "and several people died from suffocation." No collision, no fire, no mass casualties, no Soviets killed at all—but something serious must have gone wrong, because Vakeel went on to say that as a result of this event, the Afghans "requested" help from Soviet traffic control troops, and a Lieutenant Colonel Vasiliy Aleksandrovich Romanov soon arrived to "share" command with the Afghan Army's Colonel Jamaluddin. Reportedly they soon had the tunnel "running like a watch."

Since the "official" Soviet account is even more innocuous than the official Kabul account of a year earlier, and since it describes consequences (the Soviet takeover of tunnel security) all out of proportion to the alleged scale of the stimulus ("several" Afghans dead in a minor accident), it can fairly easily be dismissed as a cover-up. At the same time we can also dismiss the resistance claims of deliberate sabotage, especially Paghmani's, which claimed omniscient knowledge of events to which there allegedly were no surviving witnesses.

We are left with a major convoy disaster and an unknown number of casualties. Only "several" fatalities are implausible; hundreds of deaths seem likely; 1,000 or more fatalities are not out of the question. If there were only a single lane of traffic, many hundreds of large vehicles could have fitted inside the tunnel at any one time, and with drivers and guards alone that puts upwards of 1,000 people between the "north" and "south" portals. Passengers in troop trucks and buses push the total potential victims even higher, by 20 to 50 people per loaded vehicle.

What soldiers of any other army would have done in the face of burning gasoline and exploding ammunition trucks remains an open question. It seems to have been a situation in which mass panic was the outcome. But because it involved Soviet military forces, another outcome was even more likely: almost a total news blackout. Perhaps even the dates of death on gravestones throughout the USSR have been faked to cover up the "nonevent."

On May 13, 1984, possibly the greatest peacetime military disaster in recent Soviet history occurred at Severomorsk, the Arctic Ocean port in the northwestern corner of Russia that is the home base of the USSR's Northern Fleet. A series of explosions destroyed vast quantities of munitions and weapons and killed and injured several hundred servicemen.

The report, first broken by *Jane's Defence Weekly* in London early in July, was "substantially correct" according to high-level NATO sources.

Jane's asserted that the fleet would not be "a viable force for the next six months," adding that "it is conservatively estimated that it will be two years before the facility is fully operational again." The fleet includes an aircraft carrier (officially dubbed an "antisubmarine cruiser" by Soviet spokesmen), 148 cruisers (including Kirov-class nuclear-powered cruisers) and destroyers (featuring the new Sovremenny-class guided missile destroyer), and half of the USSR's nearly 400 submarines (the missile subs reportedly escaped damage). None of the ships was damaged, but their stockpiles of ammunition were gone.

The explosion allegedly destroyed 580 of the fleet's 900 SA-N-1 and SA-N-3 surface-to-air missiles and 320 of its 400 SS-N-3 and SS-N-12 ship-to-ship missiles. Furthermore, the complete stock of about 80 SS-N-22 missiles (capable of carrying nuclear warheads, which are usually stored separately) and many SS-N-19 nuclear-capable antiship missiles were also lost. Some SA-N-6 and SA-N-7 antiaircraft missiles were damaged. Very large quantities of missile spare parts were also allegedly blown up. It "represents the greatest disaster to occur in the Soviet Navy since World War II," alleged the magazine.

The blasts were so powerful that initial appraisals thought a nuclear detonation might have occurred. The explosions were monitored from space, on seismographs, from atmospheric barometric shock waves, and by unspecified "other sources."

Following the initial explosions, fires and secondary explosions reportedly continued for five days. The smoke clouds were so extensive that even low-resolution weather satellites noticed unusual atmospheric effects.

Later analysis of reconnaissance photographs indicated that three separate areas were devastated. These were the tactical missile storage area, the nonnuclear warheads area (including fuel storage and other delicate components), and a naval munitions storage depot about half a mile from the nuclear-capable SLBM (submarine-launched ballistic missile) area, where three of the six bunkers were damaged by blast and by debris. Some of the few undamaged areas included the naval mine storage depot.

The source of the estimate of 200 deaths and an equal number of injuries was not given. Compared with similar Western ammunition and petrochemical explosions, it seems an underestimate.

The cause of the blast was reported to have been "too many munitions . . . stored too close together." Some sort of initial blast touched off "sympathetic detonations around the whole complex." One Western magazine asserted it knew (from anonymous informants) that the trigger for the blast had been a motor vehicle accident involving a truck, carrying missiles off a just returned destroyer, which collided head-on with another ammunition truck. The explosion allegedly "definitely began in or near the ready-use magazine and continued as a chain reaction through bunkers that had their blast doors open."

The same issue of *Jane's* that broke the story also addressed the wider issue of military accidents in general. Reportedly another explosion occurred two days later at the military air base of Bobruysk, eighty miles south of Minsk. That explosion involved a stock of surface-to-air missiles, and ten of eleven munitions arsenals, along with administrative buildings, were destroyed. In all, said the magazine, half a dozen major explosions had struck Soviet military installations since the beginning of 1984. The most recent one was on June 25, at the Soviet military base near Schwerin in East Germany. It later turned out the magazine probably got its original story from the same man who supplied it with classified U.S. spy satellite photographs of a Soviet aircraft carrier under construction; he was caught and later sent to federal prison.

It may be too easy to dismiss such disasters as caused by

carelessness and by disregard for human life. At Severomorsk a string of standard safety practices, from one-way traffic during munitions transport to good blast-door security, seems to have been violated. Yet when high explosives are involved, the Soviet military traditionally behaves very, very cautiously, possibly because of the expense of the explosives, if not the value of the humans nearby.

One first-person account available in the West stresses the Soviet concern for safety at Severomorsk. An ex-Soviet missile test engineer named Mikhail Turetsky, who had worked in the Northern Fleet in the 1950s and early 1960s, somehow was allowed to emigrate in the 1970s. Once in the United States, he wrote a monograph about his experiences. The story has all the earmarks of authentic firsthand experiences by an expert engineer.

Interestingly enough, safety was considered a supremely critical feature of Northern Fleet missile operations. Just how much this was so was illustrated by the severe reactions to an incident in 1961 that Turetsky calls "a major accident" even though no damage or casualties resulted.

Missiles were being supplied to three diesel submarines and one nuclear boat. The dock was partially blocked with snow-banks which had not been properly cleared. Cranes on the dock and the submarine being serviced were transferring missiles and fuel canisters.

Turetsky wrote:

> During the transfer operation, the seventh missile being loaded unexpectedly broke loose from the shore crane at an angle of 45–50 degrees. It then twisted loose from the floating crane, spun about in the air and fell into the snow bank. Even this relatively soft landing fractured the missile; fuel components leaked out into the snow, but fortunately did not ignite. Had the missile spun one more time in the air it would have hit the side of the crane, and the result would have been catastrophic.

The base authorities did not take this incident lightly. Their reaction was severe. An investigation by a special commission appointed by the commander in chief of the Soviet Navy took place in April. The cause of the accident was a manufacturing flaw in the attach points of the crane's grappling equipment:

Welded joints called for in design specifications had been omitted. "Based on this investigation," Turetsky concluded, "the director of the plant which had produced the crane, the head of the plant's quality control department, and the plant's military representative were fired and expelled from the Party. In addition, despite the fact that the Test Base had been absolved of responsibility, the base commander was reprimanded before the Central Committee in Moscow."

Turetsky noted "an interesting follow-up" to this story. Before 1961 the Soviets had provided the Chinese with some missiles and submarines of this same type and with servicing cranes with the same out-of-specification grappling mechanisms. After the 1961 near catastrophe, said Turetsky, "It is almost certain that they were not informed of the accident."

Even if the Soviets showed no concern for Chinese safety, they obviously had great concern for their own. Nevertheless, by not acknowledging their own mistakes, they set up the situation in which somebody else could get hurt in repeating those mistakes. Soviet secrecy may well have cost Chinese lives.

Military jets of all nations crash, some more frequently than others (and not necessarily Soviet jets most frequently). A few recent Soviet incidents that have come to light, however, may illustrate a pattern.

The final incident which convinced MiG pilot Viktor Belenko to defect was a stupid aircraft crash at his base near Vladivostok sometime in early 1976. After three months of senseless road construction work, his unit returned to flying. An aircraft, poorly maintained, flown by a pilot with rusty skills, malfunctioned on takeoff and plowed into a passing civilian bus. Ten people—two men, three women, and five children—were killed. All the bodies were horribly mangled. Belenko blamed bureaucratic bungling for the catastrophe. Of course, official disclosure of the accident was inconceivable.

On August 5, 1976, a long-range Soviet reconnaissance Tu-95 aircraft, returning from Cuba to the USSR, apparently crashed into the ocean southeast of Newfoundland. There were no survivors.

On December 24, 1983, a Soviet bomber reportedly crashed in northeastern East Germany (near the Polish border), killing both crew members. West German tourists were observing a low-flying formation of five bombers when one nosed into the ground and exploded. The accident was never disclosed, presumably since routine military operations were involved.

About 240 Soviet soldiers died in a plane crash near Kabul Airport on October 28, 1984, according to an Agence France Presse report from Islamabad, Pakistan. The troop-carrying jet went down only moments after taking off from Afghanistan bound for the USSR. One explanation was that there had been a collision with another aircraft carrying young Afghans to the Soviet Union; another report was that the plane was downed by Afghan rebels. Since the Soviets never later complained about "attacks on civilian airliners," the hostile action account probably reflected nothing more than wishful thinking. Official Soviet silence implies both embarrassment over the specific accident and traditional military secrecy.

At the same time the Soviet press openly discussed the deaths of two test pilots in a crash in April 1984. Major General Aleksandr Vasilyevich Fedotov and his flight engineer, Valeriy Zaytsev, had taken off late one sunny afternoon in an unspecified type of aircraft, and a malfunction made them decide to head back to the base; they didn't make it. The article stressed the heroic and productive life of Fedotov.

In January 1985 the Presidium of the USSR Supreme Soviet presented awards to six Soviet aircraft crewmen for heroism during a crash that killed all but one. The six had taken off at an unspecified date, from an unspecified airfield, in an unspecified "military airplane," for a long training flight. The plane shook, banked left, and began to fall from the sky. In charge of the aircraft was Colonel Vil Rakhmanovich Tukhvatulin, a thirty-year air force veteran; with copilot Captain Konstantin Konstantinovich Mironov, he struggled with the controls, while ordering the rest of the crew to bail out. According to the official account, "All stayed at their stations, realizing that the plane was over a populated area and must be guided clear." Only at the last moment did one crewman, Captain Aleksandr Ivanovich Yefishin, manage to get out; the others died. The plane crashed in a field, and nobody on the ground was injured. While the official account is a typical "heroic sacrifice" morality lesson, it is oddly inconsistent with standard emergency practices: Only one or at most two crewmen would have been needed to fly the aircraft away from the populated area, while the others would have been ordered out by the commander. More likely, the other men couldn't get out because of command or equipment failure.

These unusual revelations refute the simplistic notion that the Soviets never disclose airplane crashes or even military crashes. But that they usually withhold such information remains true.

"Routine" crashes continue in secret. On February 18, 1985, a Tu-95 Bear was observed to crash into the sea off the naval base of Cam Ranh Bay, Vietnam (at least six crewmen are believed to have perished). On May 16, 1985, a Soviet Air Force helicopter based on Sakhalin Island was observed by a Japanese fishing boat to fall into the sea; there were no survivors. On July 7, 1985, about 6:00 P.M. local time, a Su-15 Flagon was observed to dive suddenly into the Baltic while on a routine reconnaissance mission near Sweden's Gotland Island (the Soviets conducted search and rescue operations for two days, but the Swedes never observed any pilot being picked up by rescue boats). Later that same month (July 21), during massive Soviet naval exercises in the Norwegian Sea, a Yak-36 Forger vertical takeoff and landing fighter failed in midair, and the pilot ejected safely. He was quickly picked up by rescue boats from the Soviet aircraft carrier *Kiev*. The incident was observed and extensively photographed from an F-16 of the 331st Squadron of the Royal Norwegian Air Force.

In the spring of 1986 an Ilyushin 76 cargo plane carrying the USSR's airborne test laser weapon was destroyed by fire while on the ground, according to reports published three months later (which specified "late May or early June" as the date). There were casualties among the crew and systems specialists at the aircraft's base, which probably was the Ramenskoye test center southeast of Moscow.

These few reports can only be considered representative. Sometimes an entire year or more may go by with no reports at all about Soviet military aircraft accidents (a British aviation magazine's survey of flight safety for 1986 listed more than 300 accidents around the world, but none in the USSR). The only military aviation accidents that reach Western attention are either those that occur within sight of Western observers or those that the Soviets choose to glorify for indoctrination purposes. In the latter we have no reason to trust the "facts" as reported by the Soviets; many of the accounts may be partially or even wholly fictitious. In the former there are more subtle reasons to question the extent to which Western military departments honestly and fully report what they know of Soviet military hardware failures. It does not "pay" for Western military organizations to detail the shortcomings of Soviet military forces; just the opposite is much more traditional, especially around budget time.

An example from thirty years ago illustrates such a problem in analysis which probably still continues. In the mid-1950s the Soviets were developing the Mya-4 intercontinental bomber, NATO code name Bison (*Mya* stands for "Myasishchev," the chief designer, a competitor of Tupolev). The Soviets made numerous boasts about its capabilities, and the U.S. Air Force (and, through it, the U.S. Congress) became so thoroughly alarmed by what the bomber's possible potentialities were that hundreds of millions of dollars had to be spent in response.

What had been the real threat of the Bison bomber? There was a reality behind Khrushchev's bluster and the USAF's "worst case" pseudoparanoia. Years later, in his memoirs, Khrushchev made the following appraisal of the system:

> There were other problems [besides insufficient range] with the Mya-4. We weren't sure it could fly through dense antiaircraft fire. Nor did it perform very well in its flight tests. A number of test pilots were killed. As a result, our fliers didn't have much confidence in it. In the end we decided to scrap the whole project because it was costing us too much money and contributing nothing to our security.

With such accidents deliberately covered up, the Soviet policy of secrecy stoked the boilers of the arms race in a pattern which appears to have changed little over the decades. The Bison program, for example, became only a footnote; the Soviets diverted some Bisons to naval reconnaissance roles and got good use out of them. One or two were still flying into the mid-1980s, doing test bed work for the Soviet's space shuttle program. But as intercontinental bombers they were a failure.

It's not just Soviet military aircraft that suffer disasters. Naval forces do as well (a whole chapter is to be devoted to submarines), as the following examples illustrate.

In the late summer of 1974 a Kashin-class destroyer exploded while on a cruise in the Black Sea, according to Turkish fishermen who observed the event and reported: "The ship exploded in flames and sank." The crew probably numbered up to 400, and no survivors were seen. The armament of the warship probably did not include nuclear weapons. Noted the *New York Times*: "The Kashins were the USSR's first warships to rely on gas-turbine propulsion, providing the quick acceleration needed in destroyer tactics. There have been reports in Western Europe that the Russians have had trouble with this engine system and that a Kashin-class ship suffered minor damage from an explosion in the Baltic last year." When asked, a Soviet embassy official in Istanbul replied curtly, "We have no information about this." But Norman Polmar, an expert on Soviet naval affairs, reported the ship was called the *Otvazhniy,* and it suffered an internal fire followed by explosion on August 31; he put the death toll at 200.

In March 1984 a Soviet cruiser observing NATO maneuvers in the North Sea suddenly suffered an explosion or flash fire. The Kresta-class cruiser, which normally carries 460 men, was in the middle of a NATO fleet of 150 ships performing Exercise Teamwork 84, when smoke was observed suddenly to surround the warship. American warships offered assistance, but the Soviet ship radioed back that it was not needed.

Twice in recent years Soviet missiles have accidentally hit the wrong countries, creating significant embarrassment for Moscow.

On December 28, 1984, a Soviet target drone fired during a military exercise in the Barents Sea went off course—or perhaps survived all Soviet attempts to shoot it down within the designated firing zones—and headed for Scandinavia. It zipped across the neck of Norway, which borders on the USSR along the Arctic Ocean, and plunged deep into Finland. It eventually came down near Lake Inari, about 100 miles from the border. Finnish search teams found the craft and brought it to an air force depot for inspection. It was not a modern cruise missile but was a converted winged subsonic weapons carrier from the 1960s, now used for target practice. The Soviets apologized.

On September 11, 1986, the Soviets reportedly hit China with an unarmed submarine-launched missile fired from near

Severomorsk, in far northwestern Russia. The SS-N-8 missile, with a range of 5,700 miles, had been fired from a Delta II submarine, and presumably had been aimed at the regular impact point near the Kamchatka Peninsula. But soon after launch it veered sharply to the right and was not destroyed by the safety officer—if such destruction (via internal destruct charges not usually carried on operational missiles) was even possible. The missile eventually hit the ground just across the Amur River near Khabarovsk, a few miles on the Chinese side and 1,500 miles off course. "Unless they were aiming at China, it was not a very good shot," quipped one unnamed American military official.

U.S. sources released news of the incident, but the Chinese never complained (if they even noticed). In an unusual departure from the routine cover-ups concerning any reports of military malfunctions, a Soviet Foreign Ministry spokesman officially denied that the missile had crossed into China. "One of our missiles was launched during regular maneuvers," admitted Boris Pyadishev, "but it did not go beyond the Soviet border." For their part, the Chinese didn't contradict him.

The Chinese have been no stranger to errant falling Soviet space hardware. Persistent but as yet unverifiable reports assert that in 1968 a Soviet spacecraft intended for manned lunar flight had landed in China's Xinjiang Uygur Province after an unmanned lunar test run. The Chinese retrieved it and eventually put it on display at the Red Army Museum in Beijing. Some Western visitors report seeing it, but Chinese space officials claim to know nothing. Supposedly even the Chinese were amazed at the primitive level of instrumentation inside the spacecraft, which, for example, used spring-mounted accelerometers that had been obsolete for many years in Western equipment.

While Soviet servicemen share many of the same occupational hazards of their colleagues in other armed forces, there is one particular threat to life and limb that seems almost uniquely Soviet: mutiny. Numerous stories circulate about the violent deaths of rebellious servicemen.

Defecting MiG pilot Viktor Belenko has related how his unit near Vladivostok was told in June 1976 that two army draftees from a nearby base had attempted to fight their way to the Sea of Japan and steal a boat. At the beginning of their dash they killed three officers, and before they themselves were hunted down and killed, they killed and wounded a number of additional loyal troops.

According to secondhand accounts from a Soviet émigré who knew the perpetrators, there were two attempts in 1970 to hijack patrol boats from the Soviet Northern Fleet and defect to Norway.

The first attempt in June failed because the two mutineers tried to keep their shipmates under control while heading the patrol boat westward. They were quickly overpowered, arrested, tried, and shot. The second attempt in August was instigated by a Ukrainian draftee who wanted the money he was bound to get from the CIA in exchange for the warship he would bring. The plan involved locking the crew sleeping-compartment door, gassing the crew, then shooting the captain in his cabin. But when the mutineer tried to open the ship's weapons locker, he was unable to force the lock, so he abandoned the plan. In the morning the weapons locker damage was discovered, and the patrol boat immediately headed back to port. There diligent interrogations by security forces quickly smoked out the culprit.

If the navy is unpleasant, the life of a Red Army draftee is just as grim, and the soldiers are kept in line by a number of stories about how resistance is futile. One story heard in 1967 during the military tour of a subsequent émigré was that the previous summer two desperate draftees had stolen automatic weapons and lots of ammunition and had eventually been trapped in the main train station in Kursk, where they were killed in a ferocious firefight.

Probably the greatest mutiny in recent Soviet military history involved the destroyer *Storozhevoy* ("Sentinel"), which made an unsuccessful dash westward across the Baltic for Sweden in 1975.

The ship had just returned to port at Riga after a long series of difficult maneuvers, and most of the 250-man crew were ashore for the November 7 Revolution Day celebrations. The ship's deputy political officer, Captain Valeriy Mikhaylovich Sablin, led a conspiracy which included another officer named Markov and a dozen or so petty officers. They locked the ship's captain in his cabin, tied up some other officers, and then ordered the unsuspecting skeleton crew to head for the open sea.

One sailor managed to jump ship as the *Storozhevoy* headed out of the port at about 3:00 A.M. local time. He swam ashore and hitchhiked into Riga, but it took him two hours to reach naval headquarters and convince anyone that something was wrong. Meanwhile, one officer on board had managed to untie himself and reach the radio, from which he broadcast an emergency message: "Mutiny aboard the *Storozhevoy*; we are headed for open sea."

That message was uncoded, and the Swedish military (at the Defense Radio Listening Institution) apparently overheard it. They kept their interceptions secret but did later admit that Soviet radio traffic "deviated from the norm."

As the *Storozhevoy* headed for Sweden, ignoring radio orders to heave to, Soviet jets opened fire. Unofficial reports from Sweden, however, tell how the crews of some Soviet Air Force planes at first refused orders to open fire. The Swedes recorded "very stormy conversations" with the pilots, who finally obeyed orders to attack and, in Swedish estimates, killed fifty crewmen. One of the Soviet planes never followed orders and refused to take part in the attack.

The Soviet jets actually scored their most damaging hits on a frigate which was pursuing the mutineers. Altogether, American analysts concluded, about a dozen men on both ships are believed to have been killed by the Soviet air-to-surface weaponry. Meanwhile, with only a skeleton crew, the *Storozhevoy* had been unable to return fire.

Six hours out from Riga, and only thirty miles from Gotland Island, the mutineers finally surrendered to a boarding party. In Sweden astonished radio listeners had heard almost the entire sequence of events. The ship, badly damaged, was taken in tow to the naval base at Liepaja for repairs. Sablin and up to eighty-two others (possibly an exaggeration) were reportedly shot.

The root causes of the mutiny were summarized by U.S. Navy Lieutenant Commander Gregory Young, who studied the incident for his master's degree at the Naval Postgraduate School in 1982. "A lot of different things all probably contributed," he wrote. "[There was] a lot of discontent on board, bad living and working conditions, ethnic frictions, alcoholism. And there was also the unusual circumstance of a trusted political officer on board a ship, without much of its crew, and located close to the West." It was obviously an explosive combination. Officially, of course, it never happened.

The *Storezhevoy* mutiny probably made the Soviet Navy a lot more trigger-happy, especially with its own people on suspicious courses. Together with communications foul-ups all too typical of Soviet military operations, this was a recipe for a tragedy when some ship or plane could be incorrectly suspected of mutinying—and consequently, it might be attacked without warning. No such reports have surfaced so far.

Several general observations are possible. The first is that in the USSR, the land of secrets, military-related secrets are, not surprisingly, the deepest kind. Other disasters may "leak," but military accidents rarely do. Only on the rarest of occasions do Soviet officials even deign to deny Western reports of military accidents.

In May 1987 "openness" was thriving in many sections of the Soviet media. But when during a training flight a Soviet jet accidentally dropped a rocket onto the southwestern Polish village of Wilkocin, killing one man and injuring two others, the news came only from private Polish sources. According to the Soviets, it never had happened.

Glasnost has cast no light at all into this corner of Soviet reality, and the Soviet military establishment clearly intends to keep it that way.

5

SUBMARINES

QUESTION: How do you tell a man is from the Northern Fleet?
ANSWER: He glows in the dark.

—*Soviet Navy joke*

The official Soviet explanation was simplicity itself: The missile submarine had sunk because it had quickly filled with water. While analysts chuckled over the tautology, they realized they had witnessed a breakthrough. It was October 7, 1986, and for the first time in half a century of recorded Soviet history, the Soviets had admitted to the loss of one of their submarines at sea.

The United States had lost two nuclear-powered submarines, the *Thresher* off Cape Cod in 1963 with 129 men, and the *Scorpion* in the mid-Atlantic in 1968 with 99 men (the Soviets, describing the *Scorpion* loss, suggest that one of its nuclear torpedoes must have detonated). In the discussion and comparison of such events, the foremost unforgettable fact is that death submerged is about as horrible an end as human engineering has devised. Chemical spills sear skin and lungs, electrical fires devour flesh, ammunition and fuel explosions tear limbs off, high-pressure water jets pierce through bodies, while salt water short-circuits power supplies and electrocutes anyone nearby, collapsing bulkheads crush and maim—and all through the terror-filled final moments, usually in the dark, there is no way "out" since on the outside is death. If death is not instantaneous, it can be hideously lingering as air becomes poisoned (carbon dioxide buildup kills long before breathable oxygen is exhausted). That human element must not be forgotten behind the following catalog of Soviet undersea disasters.

The best available summary of early Russian submarine accident experience is Jan S. Breemer's article in *Navy International* magazine in May 1986. Breemer, who outlined the entire history of the Russian submarine service, pointed out that as early as 1913 Russia owned the world's third-largest submarine fleet, and its safety record was at least as good as (and maybe better than) that of West European fleets. Between the world wars the Soviets had about the same accident rate as the French, British, or German submarine fleet.

Many incidents are known from that period. In late 1927 (Breemer suggests September) there was the loss of *AG-16* (possibly named *Bezbozhnik*, ["Atheist"]) after a collision with a destroyer (only seven survived from a crew of twenty to twenty-five men); on May 22, 1931, the *Rabochiy* ("Worker") was lost in the Gulf of Finland, with thirty-five fatalities; sometime in October 1931 a submarine sank during acceptance trials, but it was later raised; on July 25, 1935, the submarine *B-3* collided with a battleship and sank with sixty-six crewmen (TASS officially announced this disaster); in November 1938 the *M91* sank during a trial run; on July 24, 1939, the submarine *Shch-424* went down off Murmansk after being rammed by a fishing trawler. It is a sad but not unusually costly list.

Breemer noted that information about the period immediately after World War II is very sketchy. However, the introduction of new technologies increased the accident rate (Quebec-class subs in the mid-1950s were nicknamed cigarette lighters in honor of their frequent engine explosions), as did the expansion of operational areas. In the 1950s Soviet submarines began venturing out into the distant oceans, and unfamiliar operating conditions probably exacted their toll.

Additionally, both nuclear power and on-board missiles were being introduced in the 1960s, and a number of accidents must have testified to the "learning curve" of these technologies. Former Soviet submarine missile test engineer Mikhail Turetskiy, in his memoir published in Virginia in 1983, recalls accidents caused by those new factors which occurred while he was on duty at a missile test range at Severomorsk.

One type of sub-launched cruise missile, the P-5 in Soviet nomenclature, was installed aboard large containers attached to a submarine's topside. These containers seriously affected the sub's performance and handling qualities. Finally, according to Turetskiy's account, "An accident put an end to any further testing of the system. A submarine put to sea [sometime in 1960–1962] carrying empty containers and sank on its return voyage. A two-year search for the boat yielded nothing. It is possible that the high position of the containers significantly reduced the stability of the submarine, causing its destruction."

A second incident in 1961 involved newly introduced nuclear-powered submarines on the high seas:

> One of the new nuclear submarines on a return voyage was assigned to practice a salvo-firing of two R-13 missiles [NATO designation SS-N-4] in the Northern Fleet's test range. Near the coast of England an accident in the submarine's nuclear power plant occurred. Crew members and other submarine passengers were seriously contaminated. Parts of the ship, and the missiles themselves, were also contaminated when a cooling pipe broke. The level of radiation was reported to have been five [rem] per hour in the space where the pipe broke.

Soviet rocket engineers suggested that this was a good opportunity to test the effects of radiation on missile components and fuel, and "after a two-month ventilation of the submarine" the missiles were removed, installed on a diesel-powered missile submarine, and successfully launched.

As the 1960s progressed, the Soviets began introducing a series of new submarines. Eventually they had more than twelve shipyards, each producing its specific type of submarine.

NATO designations attempted to keep the different types distinct; Zulu, Golf, Hotel, Yankee, Delta, and other designators were applied to these different models with various types of weaponry and power plants.

As these missile submarines, along with nuclear-powered attack submarines, began patrolling the oceans within missile range of the United States, accidents soared. Some of them were made obvious by sightings of surfaced crippled submarines; in a few other cases data obtained by Western naval intelligence activities were later released (or leaked). Many of the accounts, however, were based on interviews with knowledgeable Soviet citizens who had emigrated and later were interviewed by the CIA's Domestic Intelligence Division (DID); the reliability of such hearsay reports is a major concern, and they must be treated on a case-by-case basis.

An early 1970s incident was related by a Soviet émigré who had served in the navy:

A sailor aboard an unknown class ballistic missile nuclear submarine was exposed to excessive radiation through his own negligence. He was hospitalized and subsequently demobilized from the Navy six months prior to his scheduled discharge. He was continually in and out of hospitals and was hospitalized permanently in 1975. He died in 1976 after spending one year in the hospital. There was no doubt he died from excessive exposure to radiation.

Another émigré reported an incident from "around 1966," on a submarine home-based at Polyarnyy, near Severomorsk. There was radiation leakage in the reactor area. On return to the USSR some crew members were hospitalized for radiation sickness at a specialized center on an island near Murmansk. The interviewee added: "[Many] of those sent to the island did not come back."

The source went on to describe how the sub returned to port: "As the submarine entered port the captain requested permission to proceed directly to the shipyard. Permission was not granted but the captain took the vessel there nonetheless, and as it approached the pier several of the crew members jumped ashore and ran in scattered directions before the submarine was berthed." To repair the sub, a "special brigade" was formed.

Sometime in 1968, according to an émigré, a sub (presumably

nuclear) went down in a bay off the base at Severomorsk. A search was initiated a day or two after it had failed to return, but by the time it was found thirty days later ("on the bottom of the estuary to Kolskiy Zaliv") the ninety-man crew had died. All the food aboard had been eaten, but there hadn't been time for the men to starve; more likely the crew had later suffocated. The submarine was raised, repaired, and recommissioned.

Two years later, on April 11, 1970, in the North Atlantic Ocean 350 miles southwest (and upstream) of England, a November-class attack submarine suffered an internal fire and nuclear propulsion system failure. Crewmen were seen on deck trying to rig a towline to a Soviet merchant ship, but because of worsening sea conditions, the attempts to tow the sub were abandoned. The following morning the submarine was no longer in sight and was presumed lost. The number of crew casualties is not known, but it could have been everyone aboard, as many as eighty-eight.

According to a 1986 statement from Captain Guy Liardet, director of British Naval Public Relations, the Russians still "regularly check it [the sinking site] for any radiation leaks."

At almost the same time in 1970 a second disaster involving substantial loss of life apparently occurred, also off the British coast, according to another émigré. An unidentified nuclear submarine was lost after experiencing a major fire during the Okean-70 maneuvers. Other independent U.S. Department of Defense (DOD) sources corroborate this event.

The full text of the heavily censored CIA interview summary reads:

During the exercise, an unidentified Soviet nuclear submarine (class unknown) was tied up alongside an unidentified submarine tender (class unknown) in the vicinity of the Faeroe Islands. [Passage deleted.] . . . interior of the nuclear submarine caught on fire. The cause of the fire was not disclosed. The fire was fought unsuccessfully, and the submarine captain gave orders for part of the crew to escape to the submarine tender. The political officer, who had not been ordered to leave the submarine, went on board the tender for fear of his life. The captain ordered the executive officer and several crew members, number unknown, to leave the submarine. The executive officer and crew members refused and instead assisted the captain in fighting the fire. The fire could not be controlled and was spreading towards the nuclear reactor. Since there was fear that the nuclear reactor was about to catch on fire, the submarine captain ordered the submarine to be scuttled. The petcocks were opened, and the interior of the submarine was flooded to prevent the fire from reaching the nuclear reactor. The number of petcocks opened and the number of compartments flooded was [*sic*] unknown. The submarine sank "with great loss of life," but the specific number of casualties was not disclosed.

It's conceivable that both these accounts are grossly distorted, independent versions of a single event somewhere off the British coast. In light of what we know about distortion factors in émigré reports, that remains possible.

Two "routine" submarine accidents also are known to have occurred in the following years. During January 1971, in the Mediterranean, a Foxtrot-class attack sub was apparently involved in a collision with a Soviet merchant ship, and a twenty-foot section of its bow was sheared off. Any personnel in the forward area (the torpedo room traditionally doubles as bunk space for several dozen crewmen who continuously rotate into and out of the "hot" bunks) would have been killed. A year later, in February 1972, in the North Atlantic Ocean about 600 miles northeast of Newfoundland, a Hotel II-class SSBN lost all power after a serious propulsion malfunction, possibly involving several deaths. The sub was taken in tow for return to the USSR.

In December 1972, in the Atlantic Ocean a few hundred miles off the North American coast, an unidentified Soviet nuclear submarine experienced radiation leakage in a nuclear-armed torpedo storage compartment in a forward section. Consequently the compartment was sealed off with some crewmen inside. One account by an émigré was that the sub had to be towed home at a speed of two to three knots. This source (who also had described the 1968 Severomorsk submarine disaster) recounted what happened to the men in the isolated compartment. Evidently they could not be reached because of contamination of their surroundings and themselves, although it is appalling that the Soviets couldn't get them out quickly and put them through a decontamination procedure. "The crew

members . . . initially consumed dry rations that were permanently stored in the compartment, and later they received food
through a small opening from the weather deck." At Severomorsk they were evacuated from the compartment and hospitalized. Several crewmen had died shortly after the accident
(from radiation, burns, poisoning?—we don't know), and others
died later. "The majority of submarine crew members suffered
some form of radiation sickness," the source reported.

On August 28, 1976, in the Mediteranean, an Echo-class
submarine was involved in a surface collision with the USS *Voge*.
Photographs released by the U.S. Navy show the submarine (its
conning tower and periscope visible just over the surface)
heading straight for the side of the frigate. Another view shows
the sub's conning tower akilter following the impact. The navy
claimed the sub had followed the American ship on a parallel
course for an hour before turning in to it. Some hull damage
was noted on the submarine, but crew injuries probably were
minor.

According to another Russian émigré, about October 1976,
in the Atlantic Ocean, an unidentified nuclear submarine
(possibly a missile sub) suffered a fire in its missile launch
compartment. Casualties were reported to be three dead; the
sub returned to the USSR under its own power. Another
émigré reported that sometime the following year, 1977, in the
Indian Ocean, an unidentified nuclear submarine suffered an
internal fire, possibly caused by an outdated reactor. There was
an unknown number of deaths; the sub was towed home to
Vladivostok.

The CIA's account of the interview gave an intriguing view of
just how this report leaked out. According to the informant, it
had to do with the general Soviet housing shortage:

> Housing accommodations for wives and dependents at Soviet
> naval installations were extremely inadequate. Because of
> this, many students at the various naval academies and
> installations in Leningrad established residence in Leningrad
> upon graduation and maintained them throughout their
> naval careers. Because of [this], in 1977, when a fire of
> undetermined origin occurred on a Soviet submarine in the
> Indian Ocean, a select number of people in Leningrad were
> aware of the event while the fire was still under way. Several

.crew members were killed in the fire, and their wives and dependents in Leningrad were informed that the accident had taken place at that time. The submarine was forced to surface in an attempt to extinguish the fire which lasted for several days. Eventually, the fire was put out, and the submarine was towed by a Soviet trawler to a port near Vladivostok. Nothing on this accident appeared in the Soviet press at that time even though the event was well publicized in the world press.

A submarine in tow through the Sea of Japan is newsworthy, and Japanese television and print reporters regularly charter aircraft to fly over the embarrassed Russians and photograph the crippled boat. There are no press accounts of this happening anytime in 1977.

However, there was such an incident on October 13, 1978. According to a Reuters dispatch from Tokyo, "A 3,200-ton Soviet submarine, armed with anti-shipping missiles, was reported under tow by a destroyer in the Sea of Japan tonight with a typhoon bearing down from the Pacific. The Japanese Defense Agency said a navy reconnaissance aircraft spotted the Juliet class submarine." This could be the publicity the Soviet source referred to. The error in the year of the incident (if indeed it is an error) would not be particularly unusual or troublesome.

The source reported that pre-1960s nuclear subs used liquid sodium as a heat transfer fluid, but because of its aggressive flammability, it was subsequently replaced by water. "It is possible that the submarine which caught fire in the Indian Ocean could have been one of the older types whose reactor had not been changed from liquid sodium to water."

At about the same time ("late 1970s), aboard a prototype Alfa-class submarine in the Barents Sea, there reportedly was a catastrophic reactor meltdown. The reactor used liquid sodium for a heat transfer agent. News of this accident allegedly comes from U.S. naval intelligence sources, but the accident is not on official U.S. lists.

In 1977, in the Atlantic Ocean off North America, an unidentified nuclear submarine experienced radiation leakage so dangerous that twelve crewmen were immediately evacuated to the USSR. They were put on a Soviet fishing trawler, shipped to Canada (probably Gander, Newfoundland, which is serviced by Aeroflot), then returned via their national commercial air transport to Leningrad. The source is the same émigré who reported the Indian Ocean event of 1977.

On August 19, 1978, in the Atlantic Ocean 140 miles northwest of Scotland, an Echo II-class missile sub suffered a breakdown in the nuclear power plant and was taken in tow; casualties (if any) are unknown. More details were available from a series of articles in the *Times* of London:

> The 5,600-ton submarine broke surface on Saturday night after sending out calls for assistance to other units of the Soviet fleet, the Navy said. She was taken in tow by a tug boat, which is stationed off the Shetlands for such emergencies. . . . Escorting them were a Kresta II class guided-missile cruiser, a Kashin class guided-missile destroyer, a minesweeper, an oiler, and a survey ship. The Russians made no request for assistance, the Navy said.

According to a dispatch the following day, the Soviet Northern Fleet first began stationing a tug in that area after a Hotel II-class missile submarine broke down several hundred miles off Newfoundland.

Some advice offered by Breemer in his mid-1986 survey is worth repeating here: "Caution is also warranted in assuming that an engine casualty is the reason each time a Soviet submarine is seen in tow. The Soviets have had a long-standing practice of 'piggy-backing' their submarines to and from operating areas."

On August 21, 1980, about 6:00 A.M. Tokyo time, in the Pacific Ocean 290 miles east of Okinawa, an Echo-class nuclear submarine suffered an internal fire and was taken in tow. At least nine crewmen were killed and three were injured.

The submarine suffered a power breakdown so complete that it had to send a team (including the captain) aboard the nearby British freighter *Gari* to use its radio to call for help. "We saw a white signal flash," the British captain later told a Tokyo television station. "There was smoke flowing. Three officers boarded our ship and radioed a message to the Soviet embassy in Tokyo." The British reported seeing several bodies on the deck and other crewmen receiving artificial respiration.

When a Japanese patrol boat reached the sub, it was told no

aid was desired. A helicopter crew observed about 50 crewmen on the sub's deck (some under a makeshift tent and others wearing hooded white garments), and by sunset the Soviet freighter *Meridian* had picked up about 55 of the sub's 100 crewmen.

Seeking the fastest route back to Vladivostok, the Soviets requested permission to pass through Japanese territorial waters. Japan refused unless it received assurances that there was no reactor leak and no nuclear weapons on board. The Soviets assured the Japanese government that this was the case (no radiation leak was ever detected by monitors) and were allowed to proceed. But the odds of the submarine's actually having no nuclear weapons are remote; plausibly the Soviets just lied about it and correctly figured there was no way to get caught.

Long afterward Soviet embassy sources in Tokyo disclosed that the nine crewmen had been suffocated by the ship's fire-fighting system. Such a system would discharge fire-suppressant gases into the sub, possibly on the presumption that all crewmen had already been evacuated. The fire must have been so serious that the suppressant was triggered even though there were men still alive in the same compartment; one of them could have triggered it himself.

The same sort of accident tragically happened again in that general area only a few years later. On September 20, 1984, in the Sea of Japan, a Golf II-class missile sub suffered a fire, possibly the result of an electrical overload. Casualties (if any) are unknown. For two days the sub (supported by a Natya I-class minesweeper, which supplied water) made strenuous fire-fighting efforts, repeatedly surfacing (at which point white smoke was observed billowing from its conning tower) and diving. Finally the 3,000-ton sub headed for Vladivostok under its own power.

Two years later, in Janaury 1986, the Japanese were again watching a Soviet submarine in distress, this time in the East China Sea. An Echo II-class SSBN was first spotted (by Japanese maritime authorities) in tow by an Ingul-class salvage vessel. The nature of the accident and the extent of casualties (if any) are unknown. The 6,200-ton sub and some crewmen in its conning tower were extensively photographed by newsmen in hired aircraft as it passed Japan's Kyushu Island.

*   *   *

A good case study in the difficulty in evaluating émigré reports deals with accounts of a September 1981 Baltic Sea accident, in which an unidentified nuclear submarine suffered a "series of sudden physical shocks" which made the boat "no longer navigable." It was taken in tow to Kaliningrad (formerly Königsberg). An unknown number of crewmen were hospitalized for radiation exposure.

A second account of this event also exists, but it is impossible to determine if it is an independent corroboration or a same-source retelling. This brief, heavily censored U.S. intelligence report released in mid-1984 said:

> Sep 1981, Soviet submarine operating in the Baltic. . . . On an unspecified date, the submarine underwent a series of strong and sudden physical shocks. An emergency was declared and [words deleted] crew members were sealed into the compartment in which they were standing duty. The submarine was no longer navigable following the [deleted] and was taken under tow. It was towed for a total of 36 hours but was actually moved only during darkness. . . . [Lines deleted.] The sub was towed to the harbor of [about sixteen letters deleted; *Kaliningrad* has eleven]. The sailors who had been sealed in the compartment were then flown to [four- or five-letter name deleted—Kiev? Riga?] and hospitalized. . . . [Six lines deleted.] The Soviet Military Medical Personnel in charge told [deleted] had to be insulated [isolated?] because they might spread an epidemic. . . . [Deleted] observed that in a period of 10–14 days [deleted] hair had completely fallen out and he had suffered an extreme loss of weight. Based on [deleted] medical background, [deleted] was suffering from severe nuclear radiation poisoning. The same symptoms were observed in the others in the isolation ward. [Deleted] opinion, all of the victims were terminally ill. . . . [Five lines deleted.] Most of the sailors were reported to be of Latvian and Estonian extraction. [Deleted] there is a hospital in Riga which was well known for its research in epidemiology and suspects that this is the hospital in which the sailors are located since it [deleted]uld be equipped with highly secure isolation [deleted].

The difficulty in reading such an account with its blizzard of deletions is bad enough. Add the uncertainty regarding the ex-Soviet source's ideological intentions, technical background, proximity to firsthand accounts, and powers of memory, and the idea of reconstructing an accurate account of the alleged incident must be considered chancy at best. Somewhere in the USSR are surviving witnesses and official reports; the odds of ever finding either are minuscule.

Real submarine disasters continued into the early 1980s. In June 1983, in the North Pacific off the Kamchatka Peninsula, a Charlie I-class nuclear submarine sank. But it was salvaged two months later. Casualties were probably substantial (if not total) among the ninety crewmen. The attention of American military intelligence agencies was reportedly drawn to the area by the vigorous rescue and recovery operations, which culminated early in August with the raising of the submarine.

In September 1983, in the North Pacific Ocean, an unidentified nuclear submarine was reportedly involved in an unspecified accident. This may be an émigré's garble of the June 1983 sinking, or it may be an independent event.

Soviet submarine troubles very often reveal military secrets, and it often has not been the fault of the Soviets. Twice within six months in 1983 and 1984, submarines were damaged during "close encounters" with American warships.

The first incident occurred on October 31, 1983, in the Atlantic Ocean off South Carolina. A new Victor III-class submarine got its propeller entangled in a towed-array cable from the USS *McCloy*.

Although the Soviets may have recovered the American ASW (antisubmarine warfare) device, code-named SQR-15, the incident was termed "an intelligence bonanza" by U.S. naval experts ("the intelligence community is extremely delighted," one source told the *Washington Post*. It was the first time that one of the Victor boats, one of the Soviets' frontline attack submarines, had been seen on the surface for any length of time. The 341-foot-long 6,000-ton vessel went into production in 1979 and is currently being produced at a rate of three per year. It is the first Soviet sub with its own towed-array sensors. For armament, it carries six torpedoes and has nuclear-tipped SSN-15 antisubmarine missiles with a range of thirty-five miles. Reportedly it can reach speeds of thirty knots underwater.

While waiting four days for assistance, the sub bobbed helplessly in the six- to eight-foot ocean swells. U.S. Navy officials related how it must have been very uncomfortable inside for the ninety-man crew. "You can bet they're barfing their borsht right now," noted Lieutenant Commander Mark Neuhart. "It would be very uncomfortable because subs are not designed for traveling on the surface."

Retired Admiral Mark Hill, a former assistant chief of naval operations, observed: "I think it's a terrible embarrassment, and that's really the story. . . . I think it reflects the fact that they put far less emphasis on the safety of their individuals and far more on having a presence off our coasts and around the world." Although Hill's newspaper interview alluded to earlier Soviet submarine accidents, his evaluation in this case may have been unfair since it was probably the snagged American cable, not bad Soviet technology, that had brought the submarine to grief. Although the Victor III-class attack subs reportedly have two nuclear power plants, each has only a single propeller shaft.

Despite the propeller problem, the submarine was able to proceed south very slowly. Finally it had to be towed to Cuba by the *Aldan*, a Purga-class tug.

The second U.S./USSR naval run-in occurred on March 21, 1984, in the Sea of Japan. A 3,600-ton Victor I-class boat collided with the U.S. aircraft carrier *Kitty Hawk*, leaving the Soviet sub dead in the water. Casualties (if any) are unknown.

Vice Admiral Robert F. Schoultz, deputy chief of naval operations for air warfare, detailed the incident to a congressional subcommittee the day after it happened. He explained that the sub had been following a group of supply vessels toward which the carrier was heading. It was dark (10:10 P.M. local time, precisely), and, he said, ". . . the *Kitty Hawk* closed in on her from behind and she did not see it." (Since the carrier was approaching from almost directly behind—in a fanlike zone called "baffles"—the sub could not hear its propellers. The sub was known to be in the area but allegedly was not being tracked in the time before the collision.) The submarine captain "made an error and got in the way, in my view," Admiral Schoultz concluded.

During the same hearings Rear Admiral Dan Cooper, budget officer of the navy, said that "if I were on that submarine, coming to periscope depth, I would clear my baffle so I could hear anything in that area that might have been masked. . . . It sounds like it was not very good submarining practice that the submarine skipper was following. . . ."

The submarine broached immediately after the collision, and the carrier turned a searchlight on it. The American crew did not see a great deal of damage, but there must have been underwater damage because the sub soon came to a halt. As the American ships sailed on, the Soviet sub was soon lost in the darkness.

Both Victor-class accidents introduced a new theme into the dangers of Soviet submarine operations. The victims were among the newest, not the oldest, class of deployed boats. Seamanship, not equipment breakdowns, was probably the central cause.

All such collisions couldn't be blamed on American malevolence. On September 21, 1984, in the Strait of Gibraltar, a Victor I-class sub was involved in a surface collision with a Soviet merchant vessel, damaging its forward hull section. Casualties were unlikely. Emergency repairs were made in Hammamet, Tunisia. Officially it never happened.

In October 1986, in the Atlantic Ocean 550 miles northeast of Bermuda, the most publicized Soviet submarine disaster in human memory occurred (this is the incident which opened this chapter). A twenty-year-old 9,400-ton Yankee I-class missile sub with about 120 crewmen suffered an explosion in its missile launch compartment. Officially there were 3 Soviet seamen dead.

This was the first case on record since before World War II in which official Soviet sources had ever admitted to an accident aboard Soviet nuclear submarines. This is the full text of the TASS announcement, which first moved over the English-language TASS wire at about 1500 GMT on October 4:

A fire broke out in a compartment of a Soviet nuclear-powered submarine with ballistic missiles on board, which was in an area some 1,000 kilometers north-east of the Bermuda Islands, on the morning of October 4, 1986. The submarine's crew and other Soviet ships, which sailed up to help, are dealing with the consequences of the fire. There are casualties aboard the submarine. Three persons died. After analyzing the situation, an expert commission in Moscow reached the conclusion that there is no danger of any authorized action of weapons, a nuclear explosion or a radioactive contamination of the environment.

Western observers were not the only ones caught by surprise by the suddenness and candor of the official dispatch. When the Soviet embassy in Washington, D.C., was called for further details, it said it knew nothing at all; when the TASS dispatch was read to a Soviet official, he blurted out in disbelief, "We told you guys that?"

Photographs released by the U.S. Navy showed one of the submarine's missile tube hatches blown away ("The hatch was peeled back like a sardine can," a navy spokesman declared), as well as another hole in the side of the sub. The explosion which caused this damage occurred underwater, so its tremendous force can be appreciated, and its consequences in other quarters of the ship must have been enormous.

In fact, the submarine was in serious trouble right after the initial explosion, according to one naval source: "They didn't immediately rise to the surface. We think they got up as soon as they could, but that wasn't real fast. They're definitely not moving now." The first sign of trouble had been the sound of klaxons picked up by external microphones on an American attack submarine trailing the Russian "boomer." Noted another Pentagon offical: "I can't go into details, but let's just say they made one hell of a lot of noise under water with their fire alarm" and with the subsequent explosion. "The force of the explosion," noted Secretary of Defense Caspar Weinberger, "was very, very great."

The USS *Powhatan,* an auxiliary rescue ship, was ordered into the area, but the Soviets declined a U.S. offer of assistance. Several Soviet merchant ships soon reached the stricken sub, and they took off most of its crew. The day after the accident eight Soviet sailors were seen circling the submarine in a small boat, obviously assessing external hull damage and probably seeking signs of continuing leaks.

Two days later, during the night of October 5–6, shadowing Western patrol craft suddenly noticed a flurry of activity. The submarine had been observed to be floating lower and lower in the water. Green and red flares sliced through the predawn sky, and the towline to a Soviet merchant ship was cut. The *Powhatan* again offered assistance, and the Soviets again radioed it to "remain clear." The last of the crew took to lifeboats, and the sub sank within half an hour.

The last man off was the captain, and according to intercepted radio messages, he was none too eager to be rescued. After leaving the sub on a small raft only minutes before it sank, he refused assistance from a boat from a nearby Soviet freighter. "We don't know what his problem was," a U.S. official told the *Washington Post*. "Maybe it was pride or fear, or maybe he wanted to paddle all the way to Virginia." Soviet naval officials radioed stern orders that the captain go aboard the Soviet ship, and he finally did.

A second (and last) dispatch was issued by TASS at about 1700 GMT, October 6. Like the first, it was sparse and to the point:

> From October 3 to 6, 1986, the crew of the Soviet submarine in which an accident happened, and the crews of the Soviet ships which approached the scene, were engaged in an effort to keep her afloat. Despite the efforts, the submarine has not been rescued. At 11:03 AM [Moscow time, 3:03 A.M. Bermuda time] on October 6, it sank to a great depth. The crew has been evacuated to the Soviet ships which appeared on the scene. There have been no other losses among the crew, apart from those which were reported on October 4. An effort is continuing to find out the circumstances which resulted in the loss of the submarine, but the immediate cause is the speedy flooding of water from the outside. The reactor has been shut down. According to the conclusion of specialists, the possibility of a nuclear explosion and radioactive contamination of the environment is excluded.

Such a catalog of underwater catastrophe can be justified only if it provides some insight into Soviet submarine capabilities, including comparative reliability and safety, along with an explanation of why in 1986 the long-standing complete secrecy policy was set aside.

To do the first task, however, requires knowledge of the total time spent at sea by Soviet submarines, and this is hard to estimate. Mere numbers of subs cannot be directly compared since American missile subs spend so much more of their time actually at sea than do the Soviets. Nevertheless, in Jan Breemer's words, "The weight of evidence leaves no doubt that the American submarine fleet has been much less accident prone than its Soviet opponent."

Understanding how the secrecy policy has been modified is even more difficult. Submarine disasters have traditionally fallen under the "military affairs" policy of total secrecy for reasons of national security. For routine submarine malfunctions, the Gorbachev regime evidently expects the world to understand that nothing has changed. But when the stricken submarine carries nuclear missiles aimed at U.S. targets, and when photographs of the boat's gaping holes are published around the world, traditional silence would have been impossible without repudiating *glasnost* before the entire planet. Western expectations thus propelled Moscow along a course of disclosure which it never would have been likely to choose from internal motivations.

Such moral pressure was more powerful than that of water at great depths, which has crushed more Soviet submarines than we probably know about. The pressure of expectations of *glasnost* broke the hull of Soviet maritime defense security, at least this once. But as mathematicians can demonstrate, it takes more than one point to define a line, to describe a trend. The next Soviet submarine disaster and Moscow's reaction to it will define how far underwater the sunlight of *glasnost* extends. To judge from past experience, there won't be long to wait.

6

DISASTERS
AFLOAT

Disaster teaches you a lot—that is true. But these times
demand different methods of learning.

—*Geydar Aliyev, Soviet maritime accident
investigation commission chairman, 1986*

As the Soviet freighter *Mekhanik Tarasov* listed forty-five degrees off the Newfoundland coast, a Danish trawler approached
and radioed an offer of aid. It was February 16, 1982, and the
Soviet ship had been bound from Quebec to Europe with a load
of newsprint when it endured a battering by a heavy storm. The
oil rig *Ocean Ranger* had just gone down in the same area with
great loss of life.

The Russian captain waved off the would-be rescuers, pre-
ferring that his forty crewmen wait for the arrival of a nearby
Soviet ship rather than accept help from foreigners. This
second Soviet ship, the *Ivan Dvorskiy*, eventually showed up
three hours after the *Mekhanik Tarasov* had sunk. The *Ivan*

Dvorskiy was in time only to help the Danes pull some of the last bodies from the water. Seven survivors and eighteen bodies were eventually picked up.

Once again, ordinary Soviet people had paid a bitter price for the official Soviet policy of refusing assistance from "enemies."

One of the most famous "official" Soviet maritime disasters is the loss of the icebreaker *Chelyuskin* in February 1934 and the daring rescue of its crew. The ship was crushed by ice fields in the Chukotsk Sea (at the far eastern tip of Siberia), and 104 people on the ship had to abandon the sinking vessel and seek refuge on the ice field. Under severe conditions, half a dozen Soviet pilots made repeated flights to the site and over a period of days picked up all the survivors. This drama was covered live by radio. The pilots became the first in the USSR to be honored with the supreme award of the country, the title of Hero of the Soviet Union. And the Soviets did it all themselves; a plan to save time by flying pilots to Alaska and buying rescue planes there was rejected as politically unacceptable. If the stranded *Chelyuskin* survivors couldn't be rescued by Russians, they were not going to be rescued at all.

Aleksandr Solzhenitsyn documented another kind of maritime emergency along the same coast. In the spring of 1938 the steamer *Dzhurma* was transporting 3,000 or 4,000 slave laborers from Vladivostok to the Kolyma goldfields, which required passing very close to Japanese-held Sakhalin Island. Some of the prisoners got loose and looted a storeroom, setting it afire. As smoke poured from the hold of the ship, a Japanese naval vessel pulled alongside and offered assistance in fighting the fire. The captain refused the offer and ordered the hatches sealed, suffocating the fire and the thousands of political prisoners as well. Once the Japanese ship was out of sight, the bodies of the dead were thrown overboard.

"Decades have passed since then," the fuming Solzhenitsyn wrote in a footnote to this episode, "but how many times Soviet citizens have met with misfortune on the world's oceans, yet because of that same secretiveness disguised as national pride they have refused help! Let the sharks devour us, so long as we don't have to accept your helping hand!"

Even in recent years Soviet seafarers have lost their lives while seemingly well within range of Western rescuers. On December 31, 1966, a fishing fleet refrigerator ship sank thirty-five miles north of the Aleutian Island of Unimak, with the loss of fifty lives. On February 28, 1967, the fish-processing ship *Tukan* sank in the North Sea fifteen miles off Denmark, drowning fifty-seven of the seventy-nine men aboard. On March 23, 1969, a fishing trawler off the North Carolina coast was rammed by the tanker *Esso Honduras,* and about twenty-five Soviets drowned. Doubtlessly there have been dozens of other such ocean accidents which escaped the attention of Western ships, probably because the endangered Soviet vessels never issued general distress calls.

Space technology of the 1980s is already changing all that. In the near future even Soviet sea disasters will be immediately known to rescue organizations around the world. Lives will be saved in the process, at the not inconsiderable cost of potential Soviet embarrassment over the loss of secrecy about their accidents afloat.

Since 1983 a series of Soviet and American satellites have carried small piggyback radio relays designed to listen in on international distress frequencies and forward any calls to centralized coordination offices. The Western term *SARSAT* stands for search-and-rescue satellite; the Soviet term *KOSPAS* is a Russian-language abbreviation with the same meaning. The Soviets have taken justifiable pride in their role in this rescue system called SARSAT-KOSPAS.

In the first three years of operation the SARSAT-KOSPAS net saved more than 600 lives by detecting emergency signals nobody else could hear, alerting rescuers in time to get to the crash or sinking site. Noted a Novosti news agency report: "Among the survivors most (some 300) are from the U.S. and Canada, and 20–30 people each from Spain, France, Norway and some other countries." But there was something very, very odd about the published list of "saves": There wasn't a single Russian name on it.

The Soviets, in other words, never admitted to having any plane crash or ship sink that potentially required help from any of the satellites in the network. Supposedly their participation in the international project was purely altruistic; they expected to gain no benefit for themselves and allegedly had not done so.

The initial system used simple radio repeaters (transponders) which operated on the existing emergency beacon system on

121.5 megahertz (MHz). Any overheard distress signal was relayed down from the satellite as soon as it was received. But for a rescue control center to hear the relayed emergency signals, the satellite had to be in direct line of sight of both the distressed sender and the rescue control center site.

In Western Europe there are two rescue control centers, one at Toulouse, France, and the other at Tromsö, Norway. Both are within line of sight of satellites flying over Soviet territory, although the French site covers only the far western edge of the USSR. The French have never recorded any Soviet distress beacons, but the Norwegian site has. "The Norwegian Mission Control Center [NMCC] has detected distress signals within USSR boundaries," a Norwegian official disclosed in November 1986. The Norwegians immediately forward all such calls to their Soviet counterparts. "[But] the NMCC does not get any feedback if the Kospas/Sarsat locations on 121.5 MHz relates to a real distress or a false alarm when the source is within the USSR area of responsibility." The French reported that the Soviets do not return that favor: "The Soviet Mission Control Center does NOT presently forward to the French Mission Control Center the 121.5 MHz beacon locations that the Moscow and Arkhangelsk ground stations might have performed in areas where the French authorities are responsible for distress alerting."

The American station on Kodiak Island in the Aleutians also from time to time hears distress beacons from within Soviet territory. That information is passed on to Soviet operators at their Siberian rescue center at Nakhodka, and is generally acknowledged and identified as either a test or a false alarm. The Soviets have never admitted that any of these U.S.-relayed reports was a genuine emergency.

Both American and French SARSAT officials have provided an identical (and reasonable) explanation for the lack of news about Soviet rescues on the 121.5 MHz space relay system: It may be possible that there indeed have been very few (if any) authentic Soviet distress calls on that frequency. Anything picked up could indeed have all been tests and mistakes.

Although the USSR is believed to have about 50,000 radio beacon packs set to 121.5 MHz for aviation use, these are carry-on units which must be manually activated by crash survivors. The widespread installation of shock-activated 121.5

MHz beacons in tens of thousands of Western aircraft had no equivalent in the USSR, and initially the Soviets were uninterested in that frequency. Instead, they had all along planned to develop a more sophisticated system with special-purpose beacons operating on 406 MHz. They agreed to install 121.5 MHz transponders on their prototype system at the request of Western rescue agencies, but they saw little utility of such transponders for themselves.

Once the Soviet standard 406 MHz system becomes widespread, it will be much more capable—and revealing—than the current 121.5 MHz system. The beacons will transmit specific data on the nature of the emergency, on vehicle type, ownership, other information, and on precise location. In addition, the satellite transponders will perform "store-dump" operations in which all signals picked up all around the world are recorded and later relayed to Earth. This will mean that all Soviet aviation and maritime disasters will be quickly known to rescue centers, both Soviet and Western.

Such advanced hardware is to be launched in the late 1980s aboard new Soviet and Western satellites. Results will be very different from those of the initial system, especially regarding revelations of Soviet commercial sea and air traffic disasters— unless perhaps the Soviets demand international agreements to restrict release of such data under some "privacy" consideration!

The original network had consisted of five satellites; three were launched by the USSR (on June 30, 1982, March 24, 1983, and June 21, 1984) and two by the United States (National Oceanic and Atmospheric Administration weather satellites launched on March 28, 1983, and December 9, 1984). Although the Soviets explicitly designated their satellites as KOSPAS vehicles and meant people to believe that function had been the entire mission of the satellites, in reality the specific transponder equipment hardly constituted more than a small fraction of the payload, which served other purposes: The vehicles were military navigation satellites to guide Soviet missile submarines, a fact the Soviets were understandably unwilling to admit.

A startlingly negative inside view of the KOSPAS spaceborne rescue system in actual operation appeared in a Soviet newspaper in August 1987. The author complained bluntly that the system "still falls far short of being adapted to our country's needs." After years of boasting, the candor was refreshing—and shocking.

It seems that an An-2 aircraft had recently crashed on the Taymyr Peninsula, on the Arctic Ocean. Passengers and crew were uninjured and were able to manually activate their emergency beacon. They were not far from an airfield and a rescue team soon reached them. But there were disquieting aspects of the story.

"Equipment installed in stations for receiving signals from space has not been perfected," complained the article, "and does not allow coordinates of disaster victims to be calculated quickly and precisely. Rescue teams usually obtain this information from tracking stations of other countries. Moreover, malfunctions occur regularly in our stations' apparatus. Recent exercises employing 'KOSPAS' have demonstrated this graphically." Implicit in the litany of complaints was the scandal that the crashed An-2's survivors owed their lives not to Soviet experts but to operators in either Norway or Alaska.

The astonishing aspect of this unsurprising admission that there really are Soviet victims requiring aid from KOSPAS is that such life-saving aid usually must come from Western rescue centers, which are unaware of the critical nature of their work. They do routinely relay beacon coordinates to their Soviet equivalents, but—as earlier testimony has documented—the Soviets for their part have never returned so much as a thank-you for the lives that are being secretly saved.

The explanation for the refusal of Soviet officials to admit to domestic KOSPAS rescues may thus now be clear. Most of those rescues are because of data received from foreign rescue centers—and any published list of specific cases could be compared to messages to Moscow on file in the foreign centers. It would be humiliating for the Soviets to expose their dependence on foreign assistance to make the KOSPAS system work. Far better to remain silent.

But meanwhile if the foreign centers, unaware of the life-or-death criticality, don't always expedite the transmission of beacon data, Soviet lives could well be lost because of delays in rescue operations. Yet for officials, this may be a small price to pay to maintain the facade of national pride in a rescue system they boast of having pioneered.

*　　*　　*

Some Soviet maritime disasters widely published in the West may go unreported in the USSR for the simple reason that they actually never happened. This seems to be the case with the reported loss of the steamer *Eshghabad* with 270 passengers and crew, in a storm on the Caspian Sea, on May 14, 1957. The Teheran correspondent for the Associated Press originated this report. He quoted Iranian newspapers in the port of Pahlavi (formerly and now again called Anzali), which in turn relied on word-of-mouth accounts from local Soviet shipping officials who had allegedly received the report by confidential cable from the port of Baku, inside the USSR. Three days later another Teheran correspondent filed a brief report that the Iranian naval department insisted it had "no evidence" to substantiate the original press reports—but that account was not published as widely as the initial story.

No further corroboration of the claim ever came out, although the original AP story soon was incorporated into general Western reference books such as the *1958 World Almanac and Book of Facts* and similar compendiums. Later, Western press summaries accompanying subsequent major maritime accidents listed the *Eshghabad* as one of the worst such sea disasters in history.

But there are a lot of suspicious features about the account. The name "Eshghabad" is not a proper transliteration of any Cyrillic spelling and it is strange for a Soviet ship to carry a Moslem name. The name may actually be somehow connected to the small village of Eshaqabad, southwest of Mashhad. Meanwhile, there is no *Eshghabad* (or any similar name) listed in the 1957 edition of *Lloyd's Register of Shipping,* which contains descriptions of all British and foreign merchant ships over 100 tons. *Lloyd's List,* published by the renowned British maritime insurance combine, ordinarily records shipping disasters both major and minor, but has no such report for 1957.

So it is overwhelmingly likely that the "famous Soviet sea disaster" never happened. Soviet press officials, meanwhile, never complained about the Western reports, possibly because they themselves knew they couldn't be sure it never happened!

In the past, real Soviet ship accidents were kept almost invisible. A few oceangoing and river disasters had become known in recent years, but suddenly in 1986 and 1987 an unprecedented openness was apparent. To appreciate the difference, a comparison with the past is necessary.

In 1977 a new-model Soviet cargo ship made a near-record-breaking crossing of the Atlantic: It completed a trip from Hamburg to New York in fifty-one days, "one of the slowest trans-Atlantic passages since the advent of steampower on that ocean," according to the "Port Notes" column in the *New York Times.* An advanced reverse-pitch propeller malfunctioned halfway across, and the ship completed its crossing in tow by a Soviet oceangoing salvage tug (probably the one normally stationed off Newfoundland to pick up broken-down nuclear submarines). Repairs were made at the Bethlehem Steel Corporation repair facility in Bayonne, New Jersey. The Soviet news media never commented on the embarrassment.

Other accidents were not nearly as benign or comical. On August 1, 1977, a major Soviet ship disaster occurred, this time on the Volga River near Gorkiy. Soviet newspapers reported that several people were killed. Later unofficial reports put the death toll at twenty-eight and described how the explosion of the river tanker carrying chemicals had badly polluted the Volga.

On June 5, 1983, the cruise ship *Aleksandr Suvorov* hit a railway bridge over the Volga near Ulyanovsk. A freight train on the bridge was reportedly tumbled onto the boat. At first at least 400 people were feared dead; this was later scaled down to between 170 and 250. A navigation error had sent the ship under the wrong span, and the top decks (where the passengers were watching a movie) had been scraped off. There was unusually swift publication of an official communiqué which mentioned "loss of life" and the establishment of a high-level state commission of investigation (headed by Politburo member Geydar Aliyev).

On February 26, 1981, the Soviet freighter *Komsomolets Nakhodki* was lost in a storm in the Tsugaru Strait off Japan, on its way from Muroran (north of Hakodate) to the USSR. A distress call was received from the ship, but before Japanese rescue patrol boats could reach the scene, the ship went down with all thirty-eight hands. There never was any official Soviet announcement.

On February 16, 1986, the passenger ship *Mikhail Lermontov* ran aground on rocks on the north coast of New Zealand and sank with the loss of 1 crewman. The 737 crew members and mostly elderly passengers were rescued. The Soviet captain, Vladimir Vorobyev, was dismissed and transferred to "work ashore," and Sergey Stepanishchev, the navigator, was given a suspended four-year prison sentence and a $29,000 fine.

Bare details of the New Zealand sinking were published in the Soviet press, presumably because it happened in sight of Western eyes and was bound to be reported over foreign radio broadcasts. But where secrecy was possible, it was evidently the strategy of choice for Soviet news officials.

In comparison with covering up their own maritime disasters while scrupulously reporting all such Western accidents, the Soviet press has consistently exaggerated the scale of Western misery. Once it even fabricated a sea disaster.

In September 1984 five American seamen were held for a week after their ship, the *Frieda K.*, accidentally intruded into Soviet waters near Little Diomede Island, between Alaska and Siberia. The Soviets convinced themselves it was an innocent mistake and escorted the men in their ship back to international waters.

But the official news agency had another version for domestic consumption. According to TASS, the *Frieda K.* had sunk in a storm! The five Americans were then rescued from certain death in the frigid waters by heroic Soviet naval units, which treated them to Russian hospitality before turning them over to an American ship in the area. The sinking and heroic rescue were totally fictitious, but they fed the Soviet mythos of the hospitality and humanity of their border guards, a year after the Korean airliner had been shot down in the same area.

The greatest Soviet maritime disaster in decades, and one of the most publicized Soviet disasters of all time, occurred on August 31, 1986, in the Black Sea.

About 10:30 P.M. on Sunday, the thirty-first, the vacation liner *Admiral Nakhimov* left port at Novorossiysk, bound for Sochi. Aboard were a ship's crew of 346 and 888 passengers, who included some families of crewmen, 1,234 people altogether. Inbound for Novorossiysk was the bulk carrier *Pyotr Vasyov* with a load of oats and barley. It was a warm, clear night with unlimited visibility.

The *Nakhimov*'s captain, Vadim Georgiyevich Markov, had held the rank of long-voyage captain since 1959 (his age was not given but he must have been in his late fifties); Captain Viktor Ivanovich Tkachenko of the *Vasyov* had held his rank for six years.

The pilot of the *Nakhimov* saw the freighter coming on from about his one o'clock, from ahead right. He was disturbed to note that the "angle-off" was not changing, indication of an impending collision. When called by radio, the freighter responded, "Don't worry, we will pass clear of each other. We will take care of everything."

Yet the *Vasyov* did not change course. Second Mate Chudnovskiy, on duty in the *Nakhimov*, called Captain Markov to the bridge. They watched incredulously as the freighter drew near. Markov never gave any alarm, although it would have taken only the pushing of a button, and he never took evasive action. At the last moment the *Vasyov* reversed engines in a futile attempt to stop.

The freighter struck the old passenger vessel on its starboard side, at its absolutely most vulnerable point, the bulkhead between the engine room and the boiler room. A huge hole (about 1,000 square feet) was torn in the side, and water rushed into both sections at a rate later estimated at 100,000 gallons per second. The ship rolled over on the impact point and within fifteen minutes sank to the bottom in 150 feet of water, just two miles off the lighthouse at Cape Doob.

The accident commission later concluded that "no contemporary ship could have stood up to such a blow," rejecting concerns that the old ship just caved in because of its decrepitude. "The design, however, was far from perfect. The Admiral Nakhimov had only one compartment and was easy to sink."

"Even in a nightmare one could not imagine that such a huge steamship could sink in only seven minutes," a Russian newsman wrote later for the official weekly *Moscow News*. "What a ruthless absurdity. There wasn't one—not even the slightest— excuse for the tragedy." That kind of statement was highly unusual for the Soviet media.

There was no time to launch any lifeboats, but numerous rafts were deployed for people to hang on to. Water temperature was sixty-eight to seventy degrees Fahrenheit, no problem for the people floating in it. Fuel oil was floating on the water, too, and it coated most of those people.

Survivors reported that the ship was struck with no warning and that the emergency lights came on only for a few moments before failing. In the darkness hundreds were unable to find their way to the open. Those who did slipped overboard, often unwillingly.

The Soviet media were filled with the kind of sensational first-person disaster account commonplace in the West. For example, Mikhail Lebedev is a research associate at the Moscow Institute of Natural Science and Engineering, and he recalled what happened aboard the *Nakhimov* this way:

> On the instant of the collision my mind could not accept the trouble. When the lights went out in the bar where we were sitting, I didn't feel fear. My first desire was to find the barman and pay. But suddenly he shouted: "Everyone to the deck!" Up on deck, I saw the ship beginning to list. There was no time to look for a life vest. Already in the water, I let go of the ship and with difficulty swam away from it. People were all around. Suddenly everything fused into a single spot. I realized that I had lost my eyeglasses. Coastal lights loomed dimly ahead. Some ship stood nearby like a dark huge bulk. Help had come just in time: some sections of the inflated raft had burst. Aboard our rescue vessel the seamen took off their clothes in an attempt to warm us up the best they could.

A fleet of rescue ships set out quickly, and most survivors were picked out of the water within a few hours. As the night wore on, the good weather changed, and strong winds began whipping up the waves, making it more difficult to locate and retrieve survivors. By the following morning the wind was whipping along at fifty miles per hour. No more survivors were found.

Vladimir Soldatov, chairman of the Novorossiysk City Executive Committee, later mused to Russian reporters about how his city's people had risen to the disaster:

> That night the city did not sleep. Immediately after the tragic news came, all doctors voluntarily showed up at the hospital. Blood was immediately brought in for transfusions and medicines were prepared for those who had suffered from the cold. In less than an hour, all the hotels were made ready to receive people. Telegrams were transmitted immediately

if coded "disaster." The workers of cafés and restaurants brought hot meals to the hotel rooms. Even while the rescued were being wrapped in blankets (many had no time to dress) shop directors and their assistants came rushing in. They learned people's suit, dress, and footwear sizes. Even new spectacles were brought for those who had lost theirs. And in the morning a huge crowd assembled in the City Executive Committee. The inhabitants of the city donated money, requested that the rescued be sent to their apartments, and offered warm clothing. And they got angry when their requests were turned down or if they were told that nothing was necessary, that there was plenty of everything.

The first official Soviet disclosure on the disaster was released at 4:00 P.M. the following day. It even beat out Western news services, which had been chasing down rumors all day. The real revolution in Soviet disaster news policy had caught them flat-footed.

At the accident scene on Tsemesskaya Bay, rescue operations turned into recovery operations, as Soviet newsmen watched and reported. Through a powerful hydroacoustic apparatus, rescuers called for anyone trapped in an air pocket: "If you hear me, give two strikes with a metal object against the side." Rescuers listened and heard nothing. A spokesman later elaborated: "Divers were the first to go down to check whether an air pocket had formed somewhere. They found no air pocket."

By Tuesday the first of a series of regular press conferences was held in Moscow by Soviet officials. It was revealed that by that time, 836 people (including 5 children) had been rescued, and 29 of them remained hospitalized; 79 bodies had been recovered from the sea; 319 people were missing. The final death toll was almost 400. Meanwhile in the port of Novorossiysk, daily evening press conferences were organized in a hall at the Seamen's Palace of Culture.

Survivors were given medical and material help, and travel arrangements were made to get them home as soon as possible. The vacationers had come mostly from the Ukraine, Belorussiya, and the Baltic, with scattered representatives from Moscow and from Central Asia. Party organizations back home were alerted to prepare receptions. A traditional Western media response to disasters is for local newspeople to interview hometown survivors for a regional perspective on the disaster, but this is a strategy which hasn't yet caught on in the USSR. Mercifully the survivors were allowed to get home without bright videocamera lights being shoved into their faces.

Some early rumors which had reached Western news agencies were quickly exposed as exaggerations. Agence France Presse carried the account of "an unofficial source" who claimed the passenger ship had sunk so fast because it had been "literally cut in two" (it hadn't been). The Soviets later complained (in *Moscow News*) that Western news accounts blamed the fast sinking on the age of the ship (I have been unable to locate any such account); in general, however, they were satisfied with Western media treatment. Their astonishing policy of unprecedented openness doubtlessly contributed to this result.

The Soviet public was presented with hitherto unfamiliar details about the experiences of professional rescuers. They learned that this was the biggest ship that the Black Sea Fleet's search and rescue unit had ever had to deal with. "I have dealt with different accidents on the high seas and oceans for twenty years," noted Captain First Class Artur Rogozhin in a newspaper interview. "I have seen many things—but nothing like this, both in scope and complexity." Of course, the Soviet public had rarely, if ever, seen news of any of the earlier accidents, with which Rogozhin and his colleagues had contended.

Press reaction was quick to blame the crews. *Pravda* wrote that the crash was evidently caused by "violation by captains of both ships of rules of safe navigation," and both were arrested shortly thereafter. Other newspapers laid the blame on "slovenliness and carelessness." *Izvestiya* criticized the "obvious negligence" and attacked the liner company for being unable to provide a passenger list.

National newspapers unleashed investigative reporters on the affair and published what they dug up. For example, Moscow's *Komsomolskaya Pravda* sent special correspondents V. Gorlov and V. Yunisov to Odessa, the headquarters of the Black Sea Line, to nose around. They obtained a list of near misses at sea, "caused by crews' poor discipline and irresponsible attitude to duty." Among the scandals associated with the *Admiral Nakhimov*: drinking binges among the crew; outmoded lifeboats, which would have taken thirty minutes to lower to the sea; a captain who had been transferred from international shipping lines for committing various offenses; no emergency drill for passengers; no warning to the passengers. The *Vasyov*'s crew was also severely criticized for such stupidities as not shutting down engines immediately, and thus running over many floating survivors. The correspondents also made vague allegations about "the behavior of one particular senior officer in charge of passengers who neglected fellow crewmen and passengers to save himself." A report in *Sovietskaya Rossiya* described conclusions reached at a session of the Russian Republic's Council of Ministers: "This year alone hundreds of cases of fleet commanders being at work in a state of intoxication have been established, and more than 200 of them have been disqualified. Connivance at, and underestimation of, the situation have resulted in the accident rate remaining high. . . . Accident investigations are quite often of a poor standard and do not reveal the causes and attendant conditions." These kinds of shocking indictments reverberated throughout the Soviet news media.

Politburo member Geydar Aliyev was again called upon to head a maritime disaster investigating commission. Only three years earlier a special commission of the Merchant Marine Ministry had launched an investigation into Black Sea Line operations after a series of collisions (none of which had been announced at the time). "The incidents happen mostly through the fault of their crews," the commission reportedly concluded. Clearly the corrective procedures instigated in 1983 were inadequate.

Aliyev talked to a *Literaturnaya Gazeta* correspondent ten days after the disaster, and his anguish and anger surfaced. "Every day we are meeting with parents, children, husbands, and wives of people who died, and we look into their eyes. That is a terrible test. But we can meet those eyes." Although Aliyev asserted that none of his associates was directly to blame, he did allow that by tolerating sloppiness in the past, they might have encouraged conditions which made the accident possible.

By November the commission's report had been completed and forwarded to the Politburo for consideration of actions, including criminal prosecution. The process was publicized at every step. In the meantime, the government had instructed the USSR's Maritime Fleet Ministry Collegium to take radical measures to improve shipping safety as well as the discipline and organization in the work of maritime transport. It was noted that leaders of the Ministry of the Maritime Fleet had been tolerating "major shortcomings in work with cadres and in ensuring navigation safety and preventing accidents at sea," while the Central Council for Tourism and Excursions had been caught committing "gross violations of established procedures for sales of tourist travel vouchers and the organization of sea cruises." A major shakeup in top-level personnel had already occurred.

The trial of the two captains ended in March 1987. Both were sentenced to fifteen-year prison terms and large fines. In addition, a special ruling criticized the Ministry of the Maritime Fleet for laxity in personnel standards, and the court suggested a legal inquiry be made into "shortcomings in the activity of the Emergency Rescue Service, whose boats arrived late in the area of the catastrophe." The latter recommendation must have come as a surprise to Soviet readers; all previous press accounts had criticized the liner's crew and management but had expressed unreserved praise for all the rescuers. Evidently some "shortcomings" took longer to be publicized than others.

Shortly after the sinking, at one of the regular press conferences in Moscow, a correspondent from the *Los Angeles Times* had a particular question: "Your desire to provide full information at a press conference of this kind has been very widely and positively viewed. What could you say on this?"

Albert I. Vlasov, first deputy chief of the propaganda department of the Central Committee of the Communist party of the Soviet Union (CPSU), replied: "In my view we are giving you full information, such as we know it. It is not just on matters of this kind, but also on others. We are for openness and frankness, and we are openly and frankly talking to you." Astonishingly his statement was considered credible, and with justification.

Vlasov's promise was tested and fulfilled almost immediately. On November 11, 1986, there was an emergency on a Soviet passenger liner in the Sea of Japan. A TASS report from Vladivostok promptly described a fire aboard the liner *Turkmenia* which broke out shortly after midnight on November 10. Captain V. G. Kim ordered all passengers (consisting of 300 holidaying schoolchildren and their escorts) into lifeboats, and they were picked up by rescue ships within two hours. Meanwhile, the blaze had spread to the ship's superstructure and was not put out until the morning of the following day. Two crewmen were killed fighting the fire. TASS announced their deaths without comment.

If "Ping-Pong diplomacy" in the 1960s helped open the American road to better international relations with Beijing, a similar result with regard to Moscow may result from "McDonald's diplomacy" of 1987. A few considerate American gestures during yet another Soviet maritime disaster sent soothing diplomatic signals at a time of U.S./USSR tensions.

On March 14, 1987, the Soviet freighter *Komsomolets Kirgizii* sent out an urgent distress call. It was being severely battered by a storm a few hundred miles off the New Jersey coast, and its Cuba-bound load of Canadian flour had shifted dangerously in the hold after the ship's engines had failed. Waves were crashing over the vessel's pilothouse, and the ship was listing badly. The captain decided the ship was doomed and appealed for rescue.

Three U.S. Coast Guard helicopters were dispatched from Cape Cod and were able to take on board the entire crew of thirty-six plus a child of one of the crew members. The storm continued into the night, and by the following morning all that was left afloat was an oil slick and some flour sacks.

The Russians had been flown to a Coast Guard station near Atlantic City, then driven to a U.S. customshouse in Philadelphia, where they were joined by a Soviet embassy official. By midnight they had been checked into a suburban Philadelphia motel. Their arrival triggered considerable excitement as the motel staff reopened the restaurant kitchen and quickly served cheeseburgers, eggs, chopped steak, chef's salads, ice cream, and beer.

The following day the Russians were driven to the Soviet embassy compound in Washington, and they spent Monday shopping and experiencing local cuisine (such as at the "Golden Arches"). Before departing on a scheduled Aeroflot flight on Tuesday, they met briefly with President Reagan at the White House.

The Soviet press reported the ship's loss and the rescue of the crew. An official government note expressed "thanks for the expeditious and effective help rendered as well as for the care and the friendly treatment accorded to the Soviet seamen." The

Soviets had admitted difficulties, had asked for help—and had evidently not been embarrassed to accept it.

The marked difference in news reporting on the *Admiral Nakhimov, Turkmenia,* and the *Komsomolets Kirgizii* from that reflecting previous policy on earlier Soviet sea disasters is simply stunning. Western newspeople covering the *Nakhimov* story were faced with a surfeit of candid, cooperative Soviet officials and underwent "culture shock"—was this really still the Soviet Union? And the depth of the new and genuinely more open policy was even more graphically demonstrated by the unleashing of Soviet newsmen on at least some of the sordid aspects of the story and by the official willingness to publish such material. Something fundamental really had changed in these particular subjects, and it turned out that it hadn't even required intervention from above (in the form of all-seeing rescue satellites). Soviet maritime secrecy/openness policies had metamorphosed one step ahead of the technological revolution that was about to make such secrecy impossible anyway.

There are still some Soviet bureaucratic issues to be resolved. In June 1987 TASS carried a short, happy news item about how the U.S. Coast Guard had saved the life of a Soviet citizen off the coast of Alaska. The dry-cargo freighter *Grigoriy Aleksandrov* had radioed for assistance when crew member Valentina Prudnikova, twenty-nine, required emergency surgery. Some Americans at Attu rowed out to the freighter in an inflatable boat and brought the woman back to the island's small airstrip, where a Coast Guard plane was waiting. She arrived at an Anchorage hospital in time to save her life.

All in all it was a heartwarming story. The Soviets had asked for help (a few years ago they probably would have tried to operate on her on the freighter, and the woman would probably have died). They had not been embarrassed to accept American help or express gratitude for it.

The official Soviet news agency encountered one problem in researching the story. Nobody at the Soviet Shipping Ministry could obtain any information about the incident. TASS was forced to resort to paraphrasing a United Press International wire story from Anchorage. For future stories, Soviet newspeople still have to develop their own information channels within the Moscow bureaucracy. Even under *glasnost,* this is likely to be a monumentally challenging task.

7

ON LAND...

There are some know-it-alls who keep count of all disasters—Chernobyl and the Admiral Nakhimov, the loss of the atomic submarine, the coal mine explosion—and see them as proof that if anything has changed in our country it is for the worse. No, it is not that there are more disasters, but that there is more honest and frank information about them and, had there been such openness before, there could be less negligence and fewer disasters today.

—Academician Vitaliy Goldanskiy,
  New Times, *Moscow, May 1987*

Nothing could illustrate more graphically the official nonexistence of disasters than a street scene in Moscow on September 3, 1976. As flames raced through a six-story block of apartments less than twenty-five yards from the Soviet Foreign Ministry, rush-hour crowds hurried by, seemingly oblivious of the blaze, their eyes straight ahead. Flames shot from the tops of buildings, firemen in heavy coats scaled icy ladders—but no Muscovites tarried to gawk at the dramatic scene. To look at the fire would have been to acknowledge its reality and the falsity of official denials, many may have thought, consciously or unconsciously.

A few muttered in passing to the handful of Western

journalists observing the scene. "It's a nightmare," one said, referring to the blaze or the crowd's unwillingness to look at it. Another acted more true to Russian form: When a foreigner raised a camera to photograph the scene, he was accosted by an elderly woman who shouted, "Why would you want to take a picture of that?" Why indeed? Merely because it was reality, a consideration of minor weight in determining the content of official Soviet news dispatches.

While fires doubtlessly occur throughout Moscow as well as in the whole USSR, the ones mainly noted by Western reporters are in hotels frequented by foreigners who can serve as witnesses. But these may provide typical Soviet patterns of behavior.

On February 25, 1977, at least twenty (some said forty-five) people were killed, and twelve seriously injured, at a late-evening fire at the Hotel Rossiya. The fire on the upper floors of the 6,000-bed hotel started "by a technical fault" of equipment in an elevator shaft (an elevator motor). Among the dead were five foreigners: one West German, two East Germans, and two Bulgarians.

Edmund Stevens of the *Times* of London filed a dispatch which criticized Soviet emergency procedures:

> Firefighting equipment was unaccountably slow in reaching the scene. The water flow from the few hydrants available did not have the volume or force to reach the upper floors. No foam or chemicals were used in fighting the flames, and there were no jumping nets that might have saved the lives of some of those who leapt from windows. . . . The most serious indictment may be against the hotel planners and builders. Most of the partitions between the hotel rooms consist of the sides of wooden wardrobes, ideal fuel for fires. Although the building was only ten years old, there was nothing resembling an automatic sprinkler system.

During the fire Western reporters tried to film and photograph the ongoing disaster. But they were stopped by police who confiscated their film.

Lynn Jones of ABC was one of several who filed written protests with the Soviet Foreign Ministry. According to Jones, he was prevented by police from filming even the following morning, when the hotel manager insisted the event was of "little interest." A West German cameraman got some film before policemen chased him off with a warning: "You are only looking for sensation, you should not laugh at our misfortune!" Several other resident correspondents and tourists reported being detained by police when they tried to take photographs.

This Soviet attitude is typical and has been encountered over many years. The photographs would have been a "sensation" primarily because Soviet practices made them so rare; photographs of fires in the West frequently appear in the media, and they are considered routine news coverage, not sensational at all. As for "laughing at Soviet misfortune," such a paranoid misimpression of the role of Western newspeople in Moscow appears to be deliberately fanned by the government to engender hostility and defensiveness.

The event itself was downplayed but not totally ignored by the Soviet press. A message of condolence from the Central Committee of the Communist Party and the Soviet government was finally published on the front page of *Pravda*.

Two days later a flash fire broke out at the Merchant Marine Ministry, and Marks Prospekt was sealed off temporarily. Officially the fire never happened.

Almost a decade later, during the early-morning hours of September 28, 1986, a serious fire swept the ancient Zagorsk Monastery, in the building of the Moscow Ecclesiastical Academy and Seminary. "There are casualties," TASS announced briefly the following day. "An investigation into the causes of the fire is under way." Although no further news was ever released to the Soviet public, for foreigners the English-language *Moscow News* later disclosed that five young students had died in the fire in their dormitory. However, the priceless relics were saved. The emergency drew more fire brigades than any other fire in living memory.

TASS continued its new habit of disclosing such disasters (at least the ones that foreigners were going to see anyway) when another Hotel Rossiya fire killed a woman on January 29, 1987. The official Soviet press released the simple facts the following day. Other fatal fires must also have been occurring throughout the capital, but officials counted on their not coming to the attention of foreign journalists, so they were never announced.

*   *   *

For ordinary citizens in Moscow, the most dangerous form of transportation, after automobile accidents, is the metro, the subway. Arguably it may be among the most dangerous subway systems in the world. But the Soviets are immensely proud of its architectural grandeur and react defensively to any criticism (there is the old story of how a Westerner admired the decor but asked why they had to wait an hour for a train, to which his Soviet host snapped, "But what about the Negroes in the South?").

On June 10, 1981, eyewitnesses told Western correspondents that at least seven people died in a fire that broke out in a subway station. It rated only five lines on page eight of the *Times* of London on June 12 since only the sketchiest information was available and there were no human-interest details so popular in Western accident reports. No official Soviet confirmation ever appeared.

Nine months later, on February 17, 1982, many people (between 15 and 30, said first reports, later settling on 32) were killed and more than 100 injured when an escalator collapsed into a shaft during evening rush hour at the newly opened Aviamotornaya subway station in northern Moscow. There was widespread public concern over the metro disaster. It's easy to imagine Western news coverage of such a catastrophe: detailed chronologies of the suffering, probing questions to the designers of the equipment, investigations of similar accidents and near accidents, testimony from whistle-blowers on ignored early-warning signs, and so forth. There was no official Soviet comment.

The next year, on March 30, 1983, several passengers were killed when two subway trains collided in the Belorussky station on the Circle Line. A senior official of the Moscow metro told foreign reporters there had been no accident and that the closing of the station had been due to a breakdown of rolling stock.

Doubtlessly other fatal Moscow subway accidents have occurred without any word being given to Western correspondents (and there are subways in other Soviet cities, too, with no reports of accidents ever reaching the West). Subways are a feature of "Soviet reality," in which people take particular pride, and the image is not to be tarnished with the reality of suffering and death.

*   *   *

Even when disasters do not reflect badly on Soviet technology, there may be political implications which also deny them official reality. Terrorist bombings, for example, are officially almost nonexistent within the USSR.

On the evening of Saturday, January 8, 1977, a powerful bomb was set off in the last car of a crowded subway train entering the Kursk station. It had been left by a "swarthy man" who had leaped out of the car as it was leaving the previous station. Seven persons were killed, and thirty-seven others were injured seriously. The bomb had been deliberately set by terrorists.

There were unconfirmed rumors about two other bombs also going off, one in a garbage can on 25th of October Street and the other in the vestibule of a building near Lubyanka Square. Casualties were reported in both these explosions as well.

TASS released an official announcement only of the subway blast. Some high-level Soviet sources blamed "dissidents," while in contrast Andrey Sakharov said he could not "dismiss the feeling" that the KGB had staged the incident to justify a crackdown on political dissidents. He was soon told that such "deliberately false and slanderous concoctions [that] smear the Soviet state and social system" could make him liable to prosecution under Article 70 of the Soviet Constitution, forbidding anti-Soviet agitation.

Late that year three Armenians from the Caucasus were arrested and charged with the bombing; shortly thereafter they all were shot. The case was closed, and the disaster disappeared from official consciousness.

Other bombings never even achieved such status of official recognition.

On Saturday, September 1, 1973, inside Lenin's mausoleum in Red Square, an elderly man was blown up by a bomb he had concealed beneath his clothes. Two women in line next to him were also killed. He was thought to have been intending to blow up Lenin's embalmed body only a few yards away. Officially little damage was done to the interior and the mausoleum was open to the public one day ahead of schedule on Monday (it's usually closed on Mondays), presumably to quiet rumors; one such rumor was that the damaged "Lenin" had been quickly replaced by "another wax and straw simulacrum, the sixteenth so far"! The incident had been witnessed by a large number of tourists (from upper floors of the Hotel Rossiya, many could see masses of mixed white and black smoke rising from the building, even though soldiers had quickly cordoned off all of Red Square), and by nightfall the city was abuzz with miraculous stories of the entire building's being demolished but Lenin's body's being preserved unscathed (or immediately replaced). Another rumor, possibly official in origin, alleged the bomber had recently been released from a mental institution. His identity and motives have never been established, but his anti-Lenin passions could have been based on personal suffering in the gulag or in an insane asylum for political dissidents. Any notes he left behind in his home were seized by the KGB; even his identity was not learned by the Western press.

On June 11, 1977, a bomb went off in a taxi parked outside the Sovietskaya Hotel. Almost a month later, on July 6, TASS announced the arrest of a man who admitted committing the crime "out of base motives." This explanation was no explanation at all, but it satisfied Soviet propaganda requirements that all enemies of "public order," as defined by the Communist party of the Soviet Union, are either insane or evil people. The real meaning of "base motives" was never made clear. A jealous husband, an extortion scheme, an attempted hijacking, or similar actions satisfy Western understanding of the phrase, but the Soviets could as easily have meant politically inspired anti-Soviet violence.

On February 16, 1981, a bomb went off near the KGB headquarters, killing a soldier. In discussions with Western contacts, some Soviet sources identified the dead man as "an engineer" and hinted that a personal vendetta was behind the act. Soviet officials, asked about the rumors of the explosion, did not deny the event but denounced its being reported as "a provocation." There was no news release. Terrorism is something which officially exists almost exclusively in the sick, dying societies of foreign countries.

One of the scariest automobile rides I've ever experienced was during my stay in the USSR one summer. Cars and buses rushed down the highways all night long without their headlights on (the midsummer "white nights" provided some small twilight illumination). At other times of the year weather conditions are terrible. Roads are often in poor shape and are badly repaired (and repair work is poorly marked with cautionary warnings). Add the high level of drunkenness among both drivers and pedestrians, and the prescription for traffic slaughter is complete.

Robert Kaiser commented on this in his book on Russia:

> Though no complete statistics are published, the Russians apparently have a staggering number of traffic accidents. Partial figures for individual republics have slipped into print, and they suggest that on a per-vehicle basis the accident and casualty rates may be five to ten times what they are in the United States, for example. Many of the victims are pedestrians, who still are not used to sharing the streets with fast-moving cars.

Yet little news gets out. Sometimes years go by without any accounts of Soviet traffic accidents' appearing in the Western press. The *Times* of London, however, published a series of short pieces in the summer of 1977. Perhaps their correspondent found a unique and temporary human source in some Soviet ministry or the Moscow first-aid service who gave him restricted information on what was legally a state secret: traffic accident data.

The series was sketchy in the extreme. On June 9 eight people were killed and eighteen were injured when a truck ran out of control and crashed into a crowd at a bus stop in central Moscow. On July 9 about fifteen soldiers were killed and several other people injured when an army truck collided with a bus outside Moscow. In early August an entire dance troupe of the Georgian Chorale (about eight people) died in a road crash in the Caucasus. On August 25 eight women were killed in Armenia when a billboard was knocked over onto them by a car; thirty children were left motherless. That was all the West ever found out about Soviet traffic fatalities for the whole year.

The London paper's unusual window into Soviet traffic deaths closed as quickly as it had opened, and no further reports appeared in the *Times* for six whole years (a Swiss insurance company claims to know of a bus catastrophe which killed twenty-one people on March 3, 1980). This merely illustrated the fluke nature of these kinds of news stories getting out at all. Then, on March 2, 1987, TASS suffered a fluke of its own: The news agency reported that eight people had been killed, and nine injured, in the Caucasus Mountains when a truck carrying cement went out of control in foggy, icy weather and hit a bus. If the accident was hardly unusual, the official Soviet acknowledgment certainly was.

In mid-1987 the Soviets went "all the way" on traffic deaths: They released a national total for the previous year. With perhaps a tenth as many private cars as Americans own, the Soviets had suffered almost the same number of deaths. For 1986, 39,000 Soviets had been killed, and a quarter of a million injured (the article in *Izvestiya* bluntly stated that the Soviet fatality rate was "several times higher" than the American or West European rates). Nearly a quarter of the deaths resulted from inadequate emergency medical care, the article complained. Many of the accidents were directly due to either bad road design or alcoholism. It was an unprecedented, scandalizing article, and it was clearly meant to shock the general Soviet public.

Accidents are caused not just by vehicles and drivers, as the article pointed out, but also by failures in roads and bridges. A few earlier examples had slipped out through official secrecy. On August 18, 1977, near Gorkiy, a crowded footbridge over a main railway line collapsed, dropping people thirty feet to the track below and killing at least ten of them; no official mention appeared. On September 20, 1986, a bridge collapsed during tests at the Kegumskaya hydroelectric station in Lithuania, dumping vehicles and pedestrians into the water. Ten people were killed, and fourteen injured, and this time the disaster was mentioned in a local newspaper. Dozens of other such incidents must have occurred in the same time period; only official Soviet statisticians, and the families of the victims, remember them now.

Railways and railway disasters have been a feature of civilization for a century and a half. Recent American experiences with Amtrak disasters should be sufficient motivation not to point the finger at Soviet disasters in any attempt to replicate the Soviet distraction gambit—one side's reveling in the other side's misfortunes.

In any event the Soviets have undoubtedly had their share of such tragedies. Turetsky's memoir mentioned a 1960 passenger train collision with a missile rail convoy that killed hundreds. In April 1975, for example, there was a brief report from the *Times* of London's correspondent in Moscow: "Scores and even hundreds of people are feared to have died when a crowded commuter train in Lithuania ran into a military goods train loaded with petrol." There were no further reports and no official news release, ever. To judge from past experience in evaluating disaster rumors, if the event occurred (as is probable), the death toll was probably considerably below that given in the rumor. At the same time there were doubtlessly many other fatal wrecks of which the West is not even aware. It's conceivable that even in Moscow nobody has a complete tally of such disasters.

Over the following decade only two accounts reached the attention of the West. Sometime in 1977 a blaze started in a dining car on the Moscow–Leningrad express. The fire was caused by the carelessness of a drunken waiter, who died along with three apprentice firemen (short Soviet newspaper reports in November mentioned the tragedy briefly). On June 24, 1981, seventy people were killed when an express and a local train collided near Gagra in the Caucasus, but only word-of-mouth travelers' reports reached Moscow (there was no official announcement).

Railway accidents undoubtedly continued to occur—in secret. Then, suddenly, another "routine" accident became the vehicle for a revolution in news coverage.

On November 12, 1986, TASS reported a collision of two passenger trains at the small station of Koristovka, near Kirovograd in the Ukraine, at 3:02 A.M. on November 6. The accident "involved human casualties," but no specifics were provided; traffic was reportedly restored within three hours of the collision. Both trains, the Kiev–Donetsk and the Krivoy Rog–Kiev, were behind schedule when they simultaneously arrived at Koristovka. "The Central Committee of the Communist Party of the Ukraine and the Council of Ministers of the republic have expressed condolences to the victims of the accident, the bereaved families. They have been granted material aid." In addition, the obligatory notice of the founding of a government commission of inquiry was given, although preliminary investigations reportedly had already revealed a pattern of "indiscipline and criminal negligence."

Three weeks later the commission's findings were also published: "Investigation showed that the accident took place as a
result of criminal negligence and the crossing of a stop signal by
a locomotive team from the Taras Shevchenko depot. Engineer
A. Galushchenko, through whose fault the accident took place,
was permitted to convey passengers on insufficient grounds,
after a long break from driving trains." He had decided to take
a nap, and his drowsy assistant missed a stoplight. Three
officials at the depot were reprimanded and fired, and two
others merely received stern reprimands. Galushchenko got
fifteen years; the assistant got twelve.

The speed and openness of the published findings were
remarkable. This clearly wasn't due to any feature of the
accident itself, except perhaps its location in the Ukraine
(where the Gorbachev regime was still being resisted by old-
guard bureaucrats). Policy in Moscow had seen to it that this
accident, and perhaps future ones as well, would be more
honestly reported.

The trend was continued at least sporadically into 1987. In
January the newspaper *Sovietskaya Rossiya* reported on an
accident in Sonkovo, 140 miles north of Moscow. Untended
freight cars rolled down a slope and ran into a passenger train,
igniting a fire that killed two people and injured twenty-three
others. Soviet newspaper readers were being given a new diet
of news topics, and in-country accidents were now, at last, on
the menu.

The transformation in news style was complete by the time
the next rail catastrophe occurred on August 7, 1987. Reporting the disaster at Kamenskaya had no political or practical
motives—the accident just happened, and *mirabile dictu* that was
sufficient rationale to report it and even show on-the-scene
reportage on the nightly news program *Vremya*.

A freight train with failed brakes had been gaining on a
Rostov–Moscow passenger train. Controllers had several minutes' warning and tried to find a siding or alternate track for the
passenger train. Failing that, they ordered the train to proceed
at maximum speed, to stay ahead of the runaway. But while
passing through a station, a conductor—assuming the engineer
had forgotten to stop—pulled the emergency cord. The runaway rammed into the passenger train, demolishing the rear
two cars and badly damaging a third.

"Tens of people lost their lives," officials said, and the toll could have been as high as eighty. Nobody seemed to have been at fault, but there were no suggestions that officials should have ordered the rear trains evacuated in the five to ten minutes during which the emergency was known. One tradition remains unchanged: Warning the public only worries them.

Disaster news could also be used by the Gorbachev regime in its struggle with entrenched bureaucracies in Moscow itself. Observe the following contrast of reporting policies.

On December 2, 1984, a gas explosion devastated a nine-story apartment building in Tbilisi, killing at least 100 people. Official reaction: none on record.

Two years later, on January 8, 1987, a gas explosion devastated a five-story apartment building in Kondopoga, on Lake Onega northeast of Leningrad, killing three and injuring nineteen. Official reaction: fully reported on page six of *Pravda* on January 13.

The story by A. Minayev named names and seemed to pull no punches. The correspondent found that for years the city officials had been requesting that Gosplan (the national economic planning agency) increase heating for residential sections of the city. The heating was supposed to come from excess thermal capacity of the local pulp and paper mills; but there hadn't been any such excess for a long time, and people were regularly using electrical heaters and cookstove gas for apartment heating. This was already a violation of existing safety regulations.

Then in early January, when especially fierce − 40° F cold enveloped northern Europe, gas supplies to one apartment block were cut off by freezing gas condensate in the main line. Two gas company workers, Yu. Kiselev and V. Mikhaylova, purged the line with nitrogen but, because of the "searing cold," "skimped on a number of operations"; the result of their "grossly violating the safety regulations" was a gas leak which rapidly filled the basement of the building.

Minayev's article carried a confused and misleading account from eyewitnesses. They saw that the building "seemed to be wreathed in mist. Was it steam or smoke? Then it began to tumble down noiselessly. And a moment later it was shaken by a powerful blast." Evidently Soviet journalists are so inexperienced at reporting disasters that nobody correctly interpreted a distant eyewitness's report by taking the speed of sound into consideration; somebody a mile away would have seen the effects of the explosion five seconds before the sound reached him, even though the blast had obviously preceded the dust cloud and collapse.

Of the seventy apartments in the building of the Sunskiy poultry factory residential area, thirty-two were totally destroyed; 112 people were left homeless. The blast knocked out windows for blocks around. Yet emergency repairs were effected quickly in the face of the severe cold, according to *Pravda.*

The newspaper also focused on the "good news" angle. "I spoke with many people, including victims," Minayev wrote. "You are struck with their powers of endurance and calm. People were convinced that everything would be done for them within the shortest possible time. And that was indeed the case. No one was left in trouble." Whether the homeless would get new apartments soon remains an open question, along with whether or not *Pravda* would report on it.

Why the candor about the blast, compared with official silence only two years earlier? It may have been simply Soviet newspeople flexing unexercised journalistic muscles now that some restraints are perceived to have been lifted. But it also could be useful for internal political reasons; potentially the release of the story was connected with the fact that the centralized Gosplan bureaucracy is apparently engaged in a power struggle with the Gorbachev administration, and this tragedy was reported to make it subtly but unavoidably the fault of unresponsive Gosplan bureaucrats.

The Russian newspeople kept flexing their *glasnost* muscles, whatever the motivation. Twelve days later, on January 20, 1987, a gas explosion killed three people in Moscow itself. TASS promptly reported it and announced: "A commission has been set up to supervise work to remove the consequences of the explosion and investigate its causes." No ulterior motives can be divined behind the release of this news item; the newspaper seems merely to have had the extraordinary desire to tell truthfully and completely what happened.

In the past some Soviet industrial disasters have been bad enough or instructive enough to be reported or have been useful in power struggles to remove entrenched bureaucrats. For example, on March 11, 1972, a serious accident at a radio engineering plant in Minsk killed an estimated 100 workers. The plant produced 7 percent of the USSR's radios and television sets.

According to an official investigation, "errors in the design of the cabinet-making department's ventilation system, as well as negligence of safety engineering regulations in operating it" led to the disaster. Factory director L. Zakharenko was dismissed for a "criminally careless" attitude toward safety. In addition, Valery Kalmykov, minister of the radio industry, and two deputy ministers were officially reprimanded.

The safety lessons don't seem to have stuck. Another electronics factory reportedly exploded on January 8, 1982, killing fifty workers. Reports reaching the West did not even include the location of the disaster, and there was no official Soviet word.

Early in 1983 the Communist party's Central Committee took unusual action in revealing that an explosion had claimed "many lives" at a synthetic rubber factory in Sterlitamak, in the southern Ural Mountains. Diplomats speculated the death toll must have been "catastrophic" to generate an official announcement.

If the industry has any military connections, furthermore, the traditional military security requirements absolutely prevail. On March 4, 1982, at about 7:30 P.M., an explosion rocked a factory in Davidkovo (a western section of Moscow) that produced spacecraft hardware, and one eyewitness claimed there were many casualties (several hundred people worked at the plant round the clock). Flames reached the tops of nearby sixteen-story buildings. "One would have thought one was in a bombing raid," the eyewitness recalled; others reported a series of explosions "like shelling." Some of the witnesses were Westerners, and they counted forty fire trucks and several dozen ambulances rushing to the site. "Dozens" were reportedly killed, and about 100 injured, but official Soviet sources said nothing. Meanwhile, firemen sifted the ashes for three days, searching for the remains of additional victims or for top secret hardware and documents.

Later rumors said the explosion had occurred in a prototype assembly workshop where highly flammable magnesium was stocked.

There was a very oblique reference to the disaster in the single word of an official release. A brief obituary subsequently appeared for an "Engineer Colonel Ivan Butin," who worked "in the construction sector." Wrote the army newspaper *Krasnaya Zvezda*: "Soviet Defense Ministry announces with sadness the brutal passing . . ." Observers assumed he had been in charge at the factory when it blew up.

Early in 1985 reports circulated about a munitions plant disaster in Siberia. According to Russian contacts of Western reporters in Moscow, hundreds of people had been killed in mid-December during an explosion near Leninsk-Kuznetskiy, not far from Novosibirsk. The facility was described as a deep underground "ammunition research and production center" in a disused mine. The entire region was reportedly being sealed off by the KGB, and many party and government officials went to the area immediately after the accident. No further reports were ever received, probably because of the military affiliation of the facility.

A year later, in early January 1986, the disaster was replayed, this time in the western Siberian town of Biysk. A missile factory reportedly blew up, but no information about casualties was available.

Only a few months later, however, another industrial accident was reported entirely differently. According to a report in *Pravda* in mid-1986, a hitherto undisclosed fire and explosion the previous winter had occurred at a coal-fired power plant at Ekibastuz in Central Asia, causing energy problems throughout the region. The report blamed an untrained worker trying to change an oil filter without turning off the fuel supply; the plant had reportedly been plagued by inefficient management and inexperienced personnel. Two of the plant's eight 500-megawatt units were knocked out for several months.

To avoid having to close down several factories for lack of power, the Krasnoyarsk hydroelectric power station on the Yenisey River was ordered to make up the power shortfall. Engineers warned of the downstream flooding consequences of increasing the water flow through their generators, but they were ordered "from above" to proceed. As a result, river levels rose, and winter ice cracked and flowed, destroying some bridges and shore equipment and tearing loose a year's harvest of lumber stored along the river.

The chronicle of disaster and the laying of blame on a wider scale than just individuals were unprecedented. There was no further news of punishments, but the publication seems to have served political ends in an industrial internal power struggle. As a peripheral fallout, however, the Soviet public became better informed.

It was concern over the high accident rate at his coal mine in Donetsk that in the early 1970s led sixteen-year mine veteran Vladimir Klebanov into the dissident movement. An "unrealistically high plan" had led to overwork and fatigue among mine workers and consequently to more than a dozen deaths and many hundreds of injuries annually in Klebanov's mine alone. The authorities kept the casualties as secret as possible and refused to investigate the causes, and for complaining, Klebanov was judged "insane" and sent to a psychiatric prison. Complained former shift foreman Klebanov: "Our unions don't defend our rights."

But nobody responsible for mine safety paid him any attention. Accidents at Soviet coal mines continued, without either Klebanov's or the general public's attention. For example, in the early 1980s a methane explosion in a coal mine near Karaganda wiped out an entire day shift, about 100 men, but it wasn't officially "real." Then, in late 1986, one was treated very differently.

In late December 1986 another major Soviet disaster was reported promptly. Leaking methane in the Yasinovskaya-Glubokaya coal mine sixty-five miles east of Donetsk in the southern Ukraine set off an explosion at 11:15 A.M. on December 24. The underground blast killed a large number of people, according to official reports that hinted at heavy casualties and severe damage (later accounts listed seven dead). The fire took four or five hours to put out.

Soviet television carried videotape of cleanup teams at work at the mine. Chairman of a special "state commission" on the accident was Aleksandr Lyashko, who was asked about whether all the casualties had received aid. They all had, he said. "No family has been left without attention. The commission will also receive each family specially in order to establish the set pension and other benefits." Presumably the quickness and courage of rescue workers, and the thoroughness of relief organizations, constituted sufficient "good news" to allow public revelation of the event.

The "bad news" followed: Violations of safety standards and sloppy work practices had caused the deaths. A damaged flexible cable to a rock-loading machine kept popping a circuit breaker. With power off, the fans keeping methane from building up stopped working. Several times the workers jury-rigged the cable and turned their machinery back on. But the last time came after methane had accumulated to the danger level, and a spark from the bad cable ignited an explosion.

Whenever the fans went off, the miners should have been evacuated from the area, in accordance with safety regulations. The damaged cable should have been replaced, and a new cable had been available. The specialist in air monitoring, a woman named Blokhina, told investigators she had informed mine controller A. Krutchevskiy about the fan stoppages and the need for temporary evacuations; he denied ever hearing about it.

Izvestiya correspondent N. Lisovenko added a personal conclusion to his special report, which was published only two weeks after the tragedy. "Safety procedures are still breached very much and very often," he wrote. "In actual fact, a comprehensive inspection carried out while the government commission was working revealed numerous breaches of safety rules. Additional breaches were revealed even at the Yasinovskaya-Glubokaya mine, which suffered so cruelly."

Lisovenko's radical conclusions could well apply to all types of Soviet disasters, and perhaps they were meant to do so:

> No, it is not the mines as such that are dangerous, as it may appear to uninformed people. What is dangerous in mines, just as anywhere else, are sloppy workmen; what is dangerous is the hope that "things may work out" that has taken root in many of us, the carelessness that has become almost a norm of life for many people, the lack of conscientiousness and the lack of precision in observing rules which have been proved sometimes by the grimmest of workers' experiences. And all this can create calamities against which any equipment is powerless—clear though it is that equipment must also be improved.

The article in the official Soviet government newspaper ended, in a lesson which used the mine disaster only as an excuse, with: "The technical consequences of the accident have already been determined, studied, and largely eliminated. But have we learned all the moral lessons of this calamity? And have we firmly assimilated them?"

Some new lessons, at least, were assimilated. In mid-May 1987, when disaster struck at the Chaykino mine near Donetsk ("loss of life" was officially reported), the reporters were again there and were again reporting the scene. The explosion this time turned out to have been caused by a sudden surge of the explosive methane into an old ventilation shaft that housed a mechanical drive shaft which tended to give off sparks.

The absence of truthful reporting about Soviet accidents led to more accidents than would have occurred if people had been more aware of the genuine dangers inherent in modern society. Secrecy cost Soviet lives, these recent commentators were asserting.

Whatever the motivations behind the new policies, the Soviet public is having its consciousness raised on a weekly basis by new, lurid (by Soviet standards) revelations of human disasters throughout their country. Additionally, for the first time in their careers many Soviet journalists have "tasted blood" in genuine investigative exposés. Gorbachev has loosed a new force at the grass-roots level; it remains to be seen how accurately (if at all) it can be aimed once its momentum gathers strength and how easily it can be shut down if new policies appear.

8

DISASTERS
IN THE AIR

There are still many blank spots in our 70-year history,
there are many as yet undescribed events, events and
situations that have not as yet been analyzed well or in
sufficient depth. Our history is not as yet sufficiently
populated with its real protagonists, with people.

—*Sergey Kolesnikov, deputy editor in chief,*
  Kommunist, *"Questions of Theory" TV panel,*
  Moscow television, May 28, 1987

Veteran Moscow correspondent Hedrick Smith's marvelous
book *The Russians* contains a particularly pathetic story about
the human side of disasters in the USSR. In 1971 a young
woman had boarded a plane in Karaganda to fly to Moscow in
order to take her entrance exams for Moscow State University.
She was expected to return after a week, but when she was
three days late returning home, her parents grew worried. Her
father flew to Moscow to look for her and found no sign that
she had ever arrived; the university told him she had never
taken the exams, and friends she had planned to stay with had
not seen her. Finally, at a police station an officer delicately
suggested he might inquire at the airport police station. There

he was told—after being sternly instructed to keep the information confidential—that she was dead, killed with all the other passengers on her flight from Karaganda. He was stunned by the news, of course, as well as by the notion of an undisclosed aviation catastrophe. Meanwhile, since such crashes are officially nonexistent, Aeroflot makes little effort to obtain passenger lists or addresses of next of kin for use in such impossible situations as crashes. This results in numerous cases of such anguish, in which loved ones actually vanish from the earth, their bodies being cremated and buried somewhere at the airport's convenience, their friends and relatives remaining ignorant of their fates. Smith's source was a Russian scientist who must have made the rounds of the Moscow foreign press corps: Robert Kaiser had the same story in his book on the Russians.

The opposite fate once befell another Russian family in Soviet Central Asia when they were promptly informed that they had lost a member in a fiery aviation disaster. Hours later the man showed up at the front door, sparking consternation as well as relief. It turned out that he had been thrown off the plane at an intermediate stop for excessive drunkenness and had been held overnight at the airport lockup. For once, alcoholism had saved a Russian life!

Author Kaiser also related an illuminating interview with Irina Kirilova, editor of *Pravda*'s Information Department. Airplane accidents were not of interest to her newspaper, she explained, since "the reader must know something new and good. . . . If there is some connection with heroism, courage, or overwhelming a great risk, then we write about it." As for planes that crash, "What's the point of writing about every one? It happens that accidents occur for technical reasons—that doesn't interest us very much." The role of "news" as a "morality play" is distinctly Soviet.

The lack of official media interest in Soviet airplane accidents does not extend to those that happen in the West. Such disasters in Europe and the United States are of great interest to *Pravda,* which indefatigably reports them. This is fully consistent with the propagandistic purpose of the Soviet media: Make Soviet citizens thankful they live in the USSR, not somewhere else.

If the Soviets ignore their own air accidents, they seem to care little about their victims either. Unconsciously perhaps they resent the reminder of officially denied fallibility exhibited by grieving survivors. The standard practice has been to pay a 300-ruble (about a month's salary) indemnity to a family, to provide the urn with the victim's ashes (presumably of the victim, since identification procedures are likely much less rigorous than in the West), and to deliver a stern warning not to disclose the victim's cause of death.

Since Aeroflot is the world's largest airline, it naturally can be expected to have the greatest number of accidents. In addition, Soviet flying conditions are among the worst in the world, with bitter cold and long darkness much of the year. The Soviet Union is the biggest country in the world, with great distances between airports. An accident rate higher than average would be entirely understandable under such adverse conditions.

Any Western effort to catalog such accidents must serve two purposes: first, to "set the record straight" on official Soviet claims (and official silences) and, second, to search for patterns in the frequency and type of accidents and in the way they were reported (or not reported) by Soviet officials. Both purposes can be satisfied by beginning the chronology in the late 1960s, when such information was becoming more readily available to foreigners.

Accidents were doubtlessly occurring, but the information was hidden away unless there was non-Soviet next of kin to notify. If there were foreigners among the dead, news of the accident was bound to get out (even if the Soviet press never printed anything). A good example occurred on February 17, 1966, when a Tu-114 airliner, inaugurating service to Brazzaville, Congo, crashed on takeoff from Moscow. Aboard were a high-level Soviet trade delegation and an African delegation. The Soviet Civil Aviation Ministry reported eight dead; unofficial sources put the death toll at forty-eight. Since foreigners were aboard, the Soviet government was compelled to make a brief public statement.

Where there were no foreigners, there was no news. On August 26, 1969, an Il-18 airliner (conflicting rumors put the city of origin as Norilsk or Sochi) made a wheels-up crash landing at Moscow's Vnukovo Airport, killing 16 out of 102 passengers. A year later, on July 18, 1970, an An-22 airliner vanished over the North Atlantic en route from Iceland to Halifax, with 8 crew members and 15 passengers (Western aviation authorities knew of the disappearance because of mandatory flight plan filing procedures). On December 13 of the same year, an Il-18 airliner crashed on takeoff from Leningrad's Smolniy Airport, killing all 90 people on board. Less than a week later, on December 19, 1970, an An-22 cargo airliner caught fire and crashed on landing at Panagarh, India, killing the 17 aboard (the Indian press reported it). The following August 11 it was rumored that a Tu-104 airliner with 97 aboard had recently crashed and exploded at Irkutsk, leaving no survivors (different accounts had the accident occurring either on takeoff or on landing). A month later, on September 14, a Hungarian MALEV Tu-134 airliner crashed on its approach to Kiev, killing 8 crew members and 41 passengers. On October 13, 20 people were killed when another Tu-104 crashed somewhere in the USSR. On May 18, 1972, an An-10 airliner crashed on approach to Kharkov, killing 6 crew members and 102 passengers. All these accidents and probably others—which occurred at about the time of the disappearance of the college-bound young woman from Karaganda—went unmentioned in the Soviet press.

A key feature in airline safety is the individual skill and combined teamwork of Soviet aircrews, and this is extremely difficult for foreigners to determine. Soviet published accounts could hardly be expected to admit more than an occasional human frailty among Aeroflot personnel.

Yet there was one type of occasion in which Soviet flying skills were directly observable by U.S. pilots. When Kremlin VIPs flew to the United States, their aircraft also carried American escort pilots. One of them prepared a summary report in 1971, when President Nixon was considering flying on Soviet-made aircraft during his upcoming China trip. The American pilot strongly advised against it if the Chinese flew like Soviets (it turned out they didn't).

"Below-standard procedures utilized by Soviet VIP crews are continually being observed," the report began. Soviet pilots were observed using commercial road maps and hand-drawn charts, not proper aeronautical charts. They wandered from approach paths, often too low. Poor fuel management resulted in emergency landings. "Approach procedures were completely disregarded," one account related, describing how different crewmen switched directional beacons and argued with each other when ground control told them they were miles off course. Preparing for a return flight to Moscow, a Soviet crew was unable to start one engine and discussed taking off from New York on only three engines (they admitted having done so on other international flights); at that point the U.S. escort pilot announced he would leave the aircraft before going along with such a dangerous procedure. All these incidents were observed among what must have been regarded as the best, safest Soviet aircrews, and they certainly must raise some concern over general flight safety standards.

Also widespread among Soviet flight crews is a cavalier attitude toward fuel reserves. Carrying a safety margin (such as enough to divert to an alternate airfield in bad weather) reduces payload, and since Soviet aircraft are notorious gas guzzlers, they reportedly fly routinely with only enough fuel to reach their scheduled next stop. Soviet pilots privately mock any of their colleagues and ground officials who actually insist on loading fuel margins called for in published regulations. The result is bound to be many unnecessary desperate landing attempts at airfields where dangerous weather conditions have suddenly developed.

Even under these conditions Soviet aircraft accidents seemed to be occurring at random and not unreasonably often. But in late 1972 a terrible fifteen-month period of air slaughter began.

Near the beginning of October an Il-18 airliner crashed on takeoff from Sochi, killing about 100 people on board. Ten days later an Aeroflot Il-62 airliner crashed in a heavy rain in a muddy swamp near Moscow, three miles short of Sheremetyevo Airport: all 176 persons aboard died. The passengers included 38 Chileans, 5 Algerians, 1 Frenchman, and 1 Briton. It remains to the present day the worst Soviet civil aviation accident in history, but it warranted only forty-two words on *Pravda*'s back page, about one for each of the 39 foreigners on board. Unofficial reports said that the plane's instrument landing system was inoperative and that the plane made three unsuccessful approaches before crashing on the fourth approach. A month later, on November 28, a Japanese DC-8 crashed minutes after takeoff from Sheremtyevo Airport, Moscow, killing 61 of 76 aboard. Eyewitnesses report it "burst into flames after leaving the ground."

On February 19, 1973, a Tu-154 airliner en route from Moscow to Prague crashed 200 feet short of the main runway, killing 66 of the 100 people aboard. The captain survived; his report described how the "stabilizer [tail plane] locked as we came in to land." A few weeks later, on March 3, a Balkan-Bulgarian Il-18 airliner crashed at Moscow's Sheremtyevo Airport, killing 7 crew members and 18 passengers. The accident was later attributed to tail plane icing.

A bizarre and mysterious aviation catastrophe occurred on May 7, 1973, when a Tu-104 airliner on the way from Moscow to Chita exploded in midair 100 miles from its destination, killing all 100 people aboard. One rumor was that the explosion was the result of a skyjacking attempt by a man who had demanded to be flown to China. This is supported by émigré reports that passengers who had left the flight at intermediate points such as Novosibirsk and Irkutsk were questioned by police. Another account is that the plane was shot down by Soviet fighters as it crossed the border outbound. Alternately, it could have made a simple navigation error, missed any attempts at radio contact, and then been destroyed by Soviet air defense forces.

On June 30, 1973, a Tu-134 airliner with eighty-four people on board overran a runway in Amman, Jordan, killing one crewman and one passenger. Seven other people on the ground were killed during the unsuccessful takeoff.

The end of 1973 saw an acceleration of the already high accident rate. On October 13, twenty-eight people were said to have been killed in the crash landing of an Aeroflot Tu-104 airliner, although unofficial sources did not even know the location. Later, on December 8 or 9, an unidentified jetliner crashed in bad weather, just short of the runway at Domodedovo Airport, Moscow, killing thirteen of seventy-two aboard. A week later a Lithuanian newspaper reported on an air crash between Vilnius and Moscow which killed all on board, including three prominent Lithuanian pediatricians and one West German citizen. Other sources identified the aircraft as a Tu-124 airliner, and the crash site as about 100 miles out of Moscow.

By late 1973 Aeroflot was reeling from this horrifying series of accidents. Moscow sources told Western journalists that within little more than a year there had been at least seventeen Soviet airlines crashes (including two Tu-104 crashes and four Tu-154 crashes within four months), very few of which the world ever learned about. These commercial aviation disasters killed more than 600 people. The above chronicle has been able to define significant details of only eight major crashes which cumulatively killed more than 500 people.

Safety understandably became a Russian preoccupation. The monthly magazine of the Ministry of Civil Aviation devoted its lead article to "Increasing Flight Safety." The article made accusations that there were certain shortcomings in Aeroflot's operations, including inadequate crew training and lax equipment checkouts. On December 12, 1973, Deputy Prime Minister Nikolay Baibakov went out of his way to assure the Supreme Soviet that the airline was "taking further measures on providing flight reliability."

Meanwhile, according to a dispatch from the *Washington Post*'s correspondent in Moscow, even without official news reports the Soviet public's concern over the crashes became so pronounced that official statistics reflected a dropoff in passengers. Many Russians were becoming afraid to fly Aeroflot.

One fanciful rumor attributed some of the crashes to problems with icing. The problem was allegedly isolated as ground personnel drinking the alcoholic windshield deicer and then topping off the ground storage tanks with alcoholic urine. Enough water was in the replacement fluid to freeze over the windshields.

Whatever the cause (or causes) of the accidents, no results of official investigations were ever announced in Moscow. But something worked, or the luck changed, because suddenly in early 1974 the Soviet aviation accident rate seemed to return to normal.

The only known Soviet civil aviation disaster in 1974 occurred on April 27, when 118 people died aboard an Ilyushin 18 turboprop leaving Leningrad for Krasnodar. An engine caught fire on takeoff, and the plane hit the ground about two miles from the end of the runway. Travelers, including Westerners, reported seeing cars stopped along a nearby road and people running to the crash site. They also saw "a stream of ambulances" rushing from the city to the airport. There never was any official disclosure.

Two small fatal accidents are known to have occurred in 1975. On January 16 an Aeroflot An-2 cargo plane en route to Sam Neua, Laos, crashed into a mountain, killing four crewmen and eight passengers. Then, on July 25, a Yak-40 airliner crashed at Batumi, killing twenty-eight people. There were no announcements.

Sometimes Soviet aviation accidents take bizarre forms. On September 3, 1975, a navigator aboard an Ilyushin jet from New York to London was shot in the head, reportedly "a suicide." Most of the 102 passengers were American tourists headed for the USSR. Two hours out of London the plane's pilot reported "an incident." When the plane landed, Soviet embassy staffers from London were there to greet it. Scotland Yard made inquiries and issued a statement that the police "are satisfied there is no evidence of a criminal act and that the wound was self-inflicted."

After several years of relatively safe air travel, the accident rate suddenly skyrocketed. On January 3, 1976, a Tu-124 airliner at Vnukovo Airport, Moscow, exploded on takeoff en route to Brest, killing all 83 passengers and 4 crew. Two months later, on March 5, an Il-18 airliner crashed at Yerevan on a flight from Moscow, killing an estimated 100 to 120 people on the airliner and 7 more people on the ground (Western reporters learned from contacts that a list of the dead was available at Yerevan Airport for persons inquiring after relatives). On June 1 a Tu-154 airliner crashed in Africa, killing all 46 on board. The flight from Luanda, Angola, to Moscow went down in dense fog shortly before it was to land at its intermediate stop of Malabo in Equatorial Guinea. The passengers included a Hungarian, 3 Russians, and 32 Angolans, 20 of whom were wounded soldiers going to the USSR for treatment, and most of the rest students; even then the Soviets left all public statements to Angolan airline officials. On September 6, 1976, at Sochi on the Black Sea, about 80 or 90 people were killed in a midair collision between two aircraft on approach to the same runway. Then, on November 28, 1976, a Tu-104 airliner on flight from Moscow to Leningrad crashed about five minutes after takeoff, killing all 72 aboard (one was a Czech citizen; the rest were Russians). Authorities gave condolences to relatives. This was the fifth Aeroflot secret crash of the year.

*   *   *

Statistics released to the International Civil Aviation Organization by countries around the world showed interesting patterns throughout the 1970s. ICAO is affiliated with the United Nations and headquartered in Montreal, Canada. As an international body it accepts the data provided by members, although the way it treats those data often shows how much credibility it gives such reports.

The USSR had been providing ICAO with scheduled airliner safety records throughout the 1970s, and ICAO published them—but only in a special supplement. One set of figures showed "World Flight Safety (without USSR data)" and a second set showed "World Flight Safety (with USSR data)" ICAO left it up to the reader to choose which set to believe.

Extracting the Soviet-supplied information from the two sets of statistics is a simple arithmetic operation, and it shows why ICAO evidently gave so little credence to Moscow's official figures. The Soviets claimed their fatality rate (per passenger mile) was only about half as high as the rest of the world's rate for the same reporting periods. This was absolutely implausible, just considering the flying weather alone. For example, in 1973, when even Russians grew fearful of flying aboard Aeroflot, the official Moscow statistics claimed the USSR had only three scheduled flight crashes with ninety-eight fatalities, for an overall fatality rate only 56 percent as high as the averaged rest of the world's. The Soviet statistics were patently phony.

But 1976 was different, for some reason. Five major accidents were known to have occurred, and the official Soviet report acknowledged them all. There were 385 official fatalities, very close to unofficial estimates. Moreover, the accident rate reflected this more honest reporting: It was, even officially, nearly three times the lower than normal rate experienced by the rest of the world, and it was several times as great as the official Soviet figures of previous years.

It's difficult to understand what prompted officials to report more honestly. But the more accurate reports continued into 1977 with an official Soviet rate still almost twice the rest of the world's rate. At that point all such Soviet reporting to ICAO ceased entirely.

Three bad aviation disasters are known to have occurred in 1977, and the possibility that releasing such negative data to ICAO would have embarrassed Soviet officials could account for the decision later that year to stop reporting any such data.

On January 13, 1977, 96 people died in the loss of a Tu-104 airliner as it exploded at an altitude of 3,200 feet during its final approach to Alma Ata in Soviet Central Asia (reports reached Western correspondents in Moscow from foreigners living in Alma Ata; no official statement was ever made). On February 15, an Il-18 airliner (which can carry up to 110 passengers and usually flies full) crashed while flying from Tashkent to Mineraliye Vody in the Caucasus (Aeroflot sources told a Reuters correspondent about the crash, but no official statements were ever made). Then, on May 27, an Il-62 airliner crashed near Havana en route from Moscow, killing 68 (there were 2 survivors, an East German and a Russian). Many of the passengers were Cuban students returning from Moscow, along with West German, Swedish, and British citizens. The plane hit palm trees short of the airport's main runway in poor weather.

The May 27 crash was the fourth major Il-62 air disaster in the past five years. There is a story told in the Western airlines industry about international repercussions of these (and later) Il-62 crashes. It seems the Chinese had bought a number of such airliners for their domestic fleet and had even obtained a license to manufacture them in China. Several years later the program was suspended and all Il-62s in China were grounded. The reason was the occurrence of several catastrophic in-flight structural failures, each resulting in the total loss of the aircraft and all its occupants. The Russians accepted no responsibility and provided records showing safe Il-62 statistics. They blamed the crashes on shoddy Chinese manufacturing, even though the faulty airliners turned out to have been the ones originally bought directly from the USSR. Chinese aeronautical engineers had supposedly spotted serious design flaws in the Il-62's structure when they were setting up the manufacturing program. They had warned against use of the Il-62 on the ground that midair breakup was a distinct danger. When the Chinese verified this through tragic losses (probably duplicating previous Soviet air disasters which had not been revealed, in order to make a foreign sale), they scrapped their Soviet airliners and opened talks with Boeing. They now build their own 707s under license.

*   *   *

No Soviet civil air crashes are known to have occurred in 1978. In fact, almost two years passed without any reports of aviation disasters. It was a safety record Aeroflot justifiably deserved to be proud of, but it couldn't afford to boast because people would wonder about the earlier level of accidents the comparison was being made with.

Then, on March 17, 1979, bad Russian climate struck again. A Tu-104 airliner crashed in freezing rain after takeoff from Moscow for Odessa. Aboard were 90 people; some reports say all were killed, while others list only 25 dead. On August 11, 1979, human error and bad luck struck. Two Tu-134s crashed at 25,000 feet over the Ukraine, one on an eastbound Tashkent to Minsk route, the other flying westward from Chelyabinsk to Kishinyov; 173 people were killed. Neither disaster was announced, but in the latter case news quickly spread by word of mouth because of the presence on one of the aircraft of the popular Pakhtarov soccer team.

A similar, "average" number of accidents occurred in 1980. On June 5, 110 people were rumored to have been killed in an Il-18 crash. A week later, on June 12, an Aeroflot Yak-40 hit high ground in Tadzhikstan, killing all on board (an unknown number). On July 7 a Tu-154 airliner crashed at Alma Ata, shortly after takeoff for Simferopol in the Crimea, killing all 163 aboard. This last crash was thus the second worst Soviet aviation disaster in history. Unofficial rumors about it filtered out over the next ten days; it had been briefly reported in the local paper *Kazakhstanskaya Pravda*, without details on casualties.

The Soviet aviation accidents which have become known to Western reporters have taken a terrible toll on life and property. As for those that remain unknown, there must, of course, be a great many. On the basis of obviously doctored statistics released to the ICAO and rates known at well-observed sites such as Moscow, it is reasonable to assume that there may be as many as an equal number of "secret aviation disasters" as of "known disasters." No accidents are documented from such far eastern cities as Vladivostok and Khabarovsk; there are few, if any, foreigners there to see them, and the regions remain heavily militarized, enhancing "ordinary" secretiveness.

If a tree falls in a forest and there is nobody there to hear it, philosophers still argue over whether or not it made a sound.

When a Soviet airliner goes down in distant Siberia and word never reaches the West, the victims are just as dead.

Sometimes the Soviets have been moved to announce domestic air disasters if sufficiently important Soviet citizens were on board. The best recent example of that occurred on February 7, 1981, when a Tu-134 airliner crashed on takeoff from Leningrad and killed up to 70 people (all on board). Twenty-three Soviet admirals and generals, including Admiral Emil Spiridonov (commander of the Pacific Fleet), Vice Admiral Vladimir Sabaneyev (head of the Pacific Fleet's political department), and Lieutenant General Georgiy Pavlov (head of the navy's air forces) were among the dead, along with "warrant officers, ensigns, sailors, and civilian employees." The military contingent had been in Leningrad for a political meeting to elect delegates to the twenty-sixth Congress of the Communist party. Their combined obituary said they all died in an air crash "while carrying out their official duties," although details of the crash itself were not revealed. A similar circumstance occurred a year later, on January 23, 1982, when 150 people (including 2 high-ranking army officers) were killed in an airline crash at Krasnoyarsk. The deaths of the military officials were mourned, while details of the crash itself (including any official estimate of total casualties) were omitted.

Foreigners, too, continued to earn official recognition for any air crashes which killed them. On July 6, 1982, an Aeroflot Il-62 airliner, en route from Moscow's Sheremetyevo Airport to Sierra Leone in West Africa, crashed soon after takeoff (the cause is believed to have been uncontained engine failure). All ninety people aboard were killed. Many of the dead were African citizens. TASS broadcast news of the crash and expressed condolences to the next of kin. An official at the Botkin Hospital, reached by telephone by a Reuters correspondent, said nobody could have survived the crash. "The catastrophe was so serious, so horrible, that we did not need to give medical attention to anyone."

As usual, the deaths of ordinary Soviet citizens were not deemed newsworthy. On September 30, 1982, an Aeroflot Il-62 airliner landing in Luxembourg skidded from the runway following an asymmetric brake malfunction (the pilot reported asymmetric reverse thrust also), killing 7 of the 67 passengers. A year later, on August 30, 1983, a Tu-134 airliner was lost at

Alma Ata, and all on board (probably 100 people or more) were killed. Yet another year later, on August 5, 1984, an Aeroflot An-12 cargo plane and its crew of 3 were lost on a flight either to or from India. The plane had crashed near Nawabshah, Pakistan.

Secrecy was hard to maintain for a major air disaster later that year. On October 15, 1984, a Tu-154 airliner was destroyed on landing at Omsk when it crashed into a fuel truck on the runway. All on board the airliner were killed. The Moscow correspondent for Radio France International, Jean-Pierre Quittard, filed this report, which went out over Paris International Service on October 19: "According to several witnesses, Soviets as well as Westerners who were at Omsk that day, . . . the aircraft had just landed and was still traveling rather fast, and therefore was unable to avoid the fuel truck, which was literally blocking the main runway. Despite the efforts of rescue workers, all the passengers are thought to have burned to death." Another rumor, attributed to an Aeroflot employee in Moscow, was that the plane had actually been taking off for a night flight to Krasnodar in southern Russia when it hit the truck. The Tu-154 has a crew of 10 to 12 and a maximum capacity of 167 passengers; since domestic flights on that route are almost always booked to capacity, the total death toll could have exceeded the figure of 176, which was the Soviet record high up to that point. When a UPI reporter called the Omsk airport, he was told by an official that all questions must be referred to a special commission set up to investigate "an incident." The Russian would not even define the nature of the "incident." Later callers attempting to make long-distance phone connections from Moscow were told that the lines were "closed." Moscow never released any official information about the "incident," nor were there condolences expressed publicly. This major disaster is particularly notable in the scope of official silence; it seems to have been the last major civil air catastrophe which the government seriously attempted to cover up.

Throughout 1985 a new policy was seen to be gradually emerging. Accidents were being announced as they occurred, but only in local publications. Still, it was a major advance, as four examples demonstrate (there aren't any rumored civil crashes in 1985 which were *not* reported).

On February 1, 1985, the government of Belorussiya released this communiqué:

> On February 1 of this year, a Tu-134 passenger airplane which was making a flight over the route Minsk–Leningrad crashed in the vicinity of the airport of the city of Minsk. There were casualties. The causes of the catastrophe are being investigated by a special commission. The government of the republic expresses profound condolences to the victims and to the families and friends of those who were killed.

Unofficial reports put the death toll at about eighty.

Three months later, on May 3, an Aeroflot Tu-134 collided with a military aircraft, both on approach to Lvov, with an unofficial death toll of near eighty. The route was Tallinn, in Estonia, to Lvov to Kishinyov in Moldavia, at the far southwestern edge of the USSR. Because of the airliner's point of origin, the official announcement appeared only in local Estonian newspapers. "The passengers and crew perished," said the stark account. "The U.S.S.R. Ministry of Civil Aviation expresses deep condolences to the relatives and friends of the deceased. . . . The reasons for the crash are being investigated by a special commission." Independently the Soviet military newspaper announced that a group of high-ranking officers in the same region had "tragically perished" in the line of duty the same day.

Two months later, on July 10, a statement was released by the Uzbek Communist party's Central Committee: "There was an aviation disaster involving a passenger plane on a Karshi [near Samarkand]–Ufa [in the Urals]–Leningrad flight. The passengers and crew perished. The causes are being investigated by a special commission. The Uzbek Communist Party Central Committee, the Supreme Soviet Presidium, and the Council of Ministers of the Uzbek Soviet Socialist Republic express their deep sympathy to the relatives and friends of the victims." The news release was strikingly similar in wording and overall content to the earlier announcements from Belorussiya and Estonia: It was obviously following a new formula for information release which had been promulgated on a nationwide basis.

On October 13 an Aeroflot Yak-40 crashed at the Black Sea resort town of Poti, killing about a dozen passengers. Local news agencies admitted the crash and relayed "official condolences" to the families of victims.

In October 1986 the weekly Moscow newspaper *Nedelya* reported that a Tu-134A passenger jet loaded with vacationers from Vorkuta in the northern Urals had crashed near Syktyvkar in a heavy rainstorm en route to Moscow (the crash occurred on the sixteenth). There were eighty-two people on board; two crewmen were killed, and several were injured. The story was reported as a straight news item, with no moralizing or scapegoating. It had happened, and the newspaper decided to tell the public about it; however, no other Soviet newspaper seems to have mentioned it.

On December 12, 1986, an Aeroflot Tu-134 on route from Minsk to East Berlin's Schönefeld Airport crashed in a forest in suburban East Berlin, killing sixty-nine people. Soviet news coverage was brief, quoting the East German news agency: "On board the aircraft were 73 passengers and 9 crew members. Rescue teams have managed to free 17 people from the burning wreckage. The precise number of victims has not yet been established." TASS declined to quote from the East German news reports, which mentioned the possibility of pilot error. But ten months later, the Soviet press carried the official conclusion: The Russian crew had been confused (due to their poor grasp of English instructions from the control tower) and had approached the wrong runway. The disaster had been their fault and the Soviet press reported it.

A remarkable interview in *Pravda* in June 1987 gave a novel view of Soviet aviation accidents from the perspective of a Russian investigator. Pilot Vladimir Gerasimov, a twenty-six-year veteran of Aeroflot, had spent more than half his career investigating accidents and devising techniques to prevent them.

Gerasimov discussed his work in finding the cause of Tu-134 and Tu-154 aircraft's swerving unexpectedly off runways just after landing, and mentioned a big accident which had occurred in Bratsk, deep in Siberia, on July 13, 1981; although nobody was killed, the airliner was totally destroyed—and Western correspondents in Moscow had never heard a peep about it. Gerasimov examined this and several hundred related cases and developed a theory that gas streams from the reverse thrusting after touchdown were reducing the effectiveness of the aircraft's control surfaces used for left-right steering. Although he found numerous aviation engineers eager to follow up his theory, the research proposal "was not covered by the plan," so there was no official funding. He and his associates worked on holidays and at night and corroborated the theory; this led directly to corrective engineering, an end to uncontrolled swerves, and the reinstatement of 300 pilots who had been blamed for wrecking big Aeroflot airliners by running off runways. "But there is also an element of shame and vexation here, if I am honest," admitted Gerasimov, because of the fact that the engineers who helped him had received no recognition or reward from their aviation institutes (that was because the successful solution of this problem had not been planned and thus earned no credit from the Aviation Ministry).

In another accident an airliner landed at night on a runway filled with airport vehicles. The air traffic controller was asleep. He was severely punished, but Gerasimov demanded that investigators look beyond the single event to seek out a pattern. The man had dozed off after many hours had gone by without any aircraft arriving; he lived in a single-room apartment with a wife and two children, and he was taking college courses part-time. A year and a half after the tragedy another traffic controller was discovered asleep at the same console. Gerasimov's call for a "human factors" approach had been ignored in preference for traditional Soviet "strict punishment" of individual transgressors.

Accidents still happen, Gerasimov complained to the newspaper. Airplanes still collide in midair: "They happen more often than they could or should." The veteran investigator presented his explanation. "The main difficulties are posed by social and moral rather than technical problems," he announced. "Guilt and responsibility are invisible but inevitable shadows behind every accident. The attempt to escape these shadows sometimes raises a real storm." Candid, shocking discussions of forbidden topics such as aircraft accidents raise real storms of their own, and Gerasimov, dedicated, unafraid investigator of real causes, is clearly going to be in the center of these storms of controversy.

There were mixed signals in the disclosure policy followed in the next Soviet air disaster. It occurred on October 20, 1986, when an Aeroflot Tu-134A crashed on landing at Kurumoch Airport, near Kuibyshev on the Volga River. There were a large number of fatalities, but no hint of the aviation catastrophe reached Western correspondents (this supports the supposition that a vast number of crashes are probably occurring at remote provincial airfields without ever being noticed by the West).

The accident was eventually disclosed officially after the pilot had been sentenced to a fifteen-year prison term. He had been practicing a "blind landing" needed to satisfy his proficiency rating, but had violated regulations in this situation. The airliner hit the ground too hard, broke up, and caught fire. The official report released nine months later also faulted the airport's emergency services as being ill equipped, untrained, and much too late in arriving at the crash scene. The delay in reporting was attributed to the case being *sub judice,* and when it finally came out, the depth of detail was remarkable.

Notwithstanding such public calls for honest, thorough accident investigations, the Soviet regime soon demonstrated utter disregard for these desired principles of full disclosure. When political and diplomatic reasons called for it, the official Soviet aircraft accident investigation process was readily prostituted.

On October 19, 1986, a Tu-134 flown by a Soviet crew crashed while attempting to land in Maputo, Mozambique. Aboard the flight from Lusaka, Zambia, was President Samora Machel of Mozambique. The plane had been flying south toward Maputo when, after it had begun its descent, it suddenly turned to the right and a few minutes later hit the ground. Machel and thirty-six others were killed. The crash site was in South Africa, about a mile from the confluence of the South African, Swaziland, and Mozambique borders and less than fifty miles from its goal.

Within days (on October 24), Moscow's Radio Peace and Progress had begun using the tragedy for a venomous anti-American campaign:

It is perfectly apparent that [the catastrophe] could not have occurred due to any ordinary disruption. President Samora Machel and those accompanying him were flying with a plane that certainly was thoroughly checked. The safety of these planes cannot in any way be compared to that of the so-called concern shown to passengers who fly aboard various modifications of Boeing and "DC" planes. It is common knowledge that on diverse occasions, due to serious defects, the planes of these firms have been taken off from flights for long periods of time. It is also well known how often accidents had occurred on the planes of these manufacturers in flights from Paris to Istanbul, Nairobi, or New Delhi, bringing death to hundreds of passengers who had trusted Western airlines.

On November 12 Ivan Vasin, deputy minister for civil aviation of the USSR, issued through TASS a statement in which he could suggest only three possibilities for the crash: a shelling of the plane from the ground; an explosion on board the airliner; or deliberate radio interference. He elaborated that the plane could have been diverted thirty-five degrees to the right as the result of powerful interference generated by radiotechnical devices run by the "South African racists."

One surviving Soviet crew member was flight engineer Vladimir Novoselov, who suffered leg fractures. He told a Leningrad TASS correspondent: "In our crew there were airmen of the highest qualifications, and I am prepared to vouch for the faultless actions of the pilots and also for the good technical working order of the presidential aircraft."

But the cause of the crash turns out in have been almost certainly a combination of flight crew misjudgments (based on fatigue) and tragic misunderstandings with the Maputo traffic control (neither side was adept in English). Understandably the Soviet and Mozambique governments have excellent reasons to dispute such a conclusion.

Under international aviation agreements the "state of incident" (South Africa) has full responsibility for the investigation, assisted as desired by the "state of manufacture" (the USSR) and the "state of registration" (Mozambique). Despite the political chasm among them, all three nations did set up a cooperative investigation team to decode the airliner's cockpit voice recorder and flight data recorder. Subsequently the Moscow and Maputo teams pulled out when they didn't like the direction in which the evidence was pointing, and the South Africans tried to enlist other nations and international groups in their investigation, to ensure impartiality—or at least its appearance. Nobody else in the world wanted to get involved, but eventually a special commission, which included both the former head British aviation accident investigator and the former head of Eastern Airlines, ex-astronaut Frank Borman, was established.

The Soviet crew members had begun their return flight to Maputo with insufficient fuel to reach their weather alternate, Sofala (Beira), Mozambique. They had neglected to file a proper flight plan and hadn't even accurately counted their passengers. During the southbound flight they had listened to music, exchanged stories, debated how to share some beers and Cokes they'd been given, and failed to perform basic cross-checks of navigation performance. When a directional indicator called for a partial right turn, they had assumed they had drifted to the left of the desired course and performed the turn, not using other available navigation aids to verify their position (one of the pilots probably had momentarily mistuned the radio to a nearby station). They had continued to descend through the clouds, without seeing the runway lights (this was a violation of instructions they had been given) and, to explain the absence of airport lights, mistakenly assumed there had been a massive power failure in Maputo. As their confusion grew, they had taken no precautions, and when the ground proximity alarm went off, they had ignored it and continued to descend. Moments later they had hit the top of a hill.

"Totally unprofessional," a French aviation expert testified about the crew performance; "pandemonium" was how Frank Borman styled the cockpit procedures, ". . . the sloppiest I've ever seen." The official Soviet reaction to this interpretation was extreme. "Reactionary anti-Soviet circles, using these events in provocative purposes, try to whip up another wave of anti-Soviet hysteria," complained USSR Deputy Aviation Minister Vasin.

The Soviets insist that their crew members performed flawlessly and that a phony radio beacon lured them off course to their deaths. That's a nitwit excuse, since without gross malperformance by the crew the plane would still have been safe even with such a beacon. But by concentrating on phony "causes" (i.e., an assassination attempt) for propaganda purposes, the Soviets risk not fixing the true cause (poor discipline and communications). This attitude leaves open the potential for repeat aviation catastrophes. In such a situation, the Soviets thus appear congenitally incapable of learning from even their own mistakes.

Themes of political intrigue and foreign attack had been inappropriate the previous March, when a Soviet-flown An-26 Curl transport crashed at Pemba Airport, killing seven Mozambique government officials, along with Maria Chipande, the defense minister's wife. At that time the Soviets did not report the crash. Neither did they complain about the malice of the South Africans or of any "plot." More likely, little propaganda value was seen at that time in exploiting a "minor" tragedy, an ordinary plane crash. In Mozambique, meanwhile, reportedly the new leaders today use Western aircraft and flight crews. They, at least, may have learned the right lessons.

The motivations and practices of Soviet air disaster secrecy have obviously undergone a tremendous evolution in recent years. Evidently government officials concluded that passengers on Aeroflot, both foreign and domestic, were the ones who stood to lose the most from cover-ups and subsequent ignorance of accidents. Additionally, other national airlines that fly into the Soviet Union's airspace are at some risk using Soviet facilities. Midair collisions are a failure of ground control; accidents caused by inadequate deicing fluid are a failure of ground servicing. The gradual easing of secrecy on accidents which do happen may alleviate many concerns about lax Soviet attitudes toward flight safety.

The trend in reporting aviation disasters is thus clearly positive in direction. But it cannot be forgotten that each point on the chart which defines such a trend actually represents the terrible deaths of many airliner passengers and crew members. If by some miracle the Soviets, having decided to report all airliner accidents, go for months or years without reporting any, the plausible (and pleasant) conclusion would have to be that no such accidents have occurred. That is a consummation devoutly to be wished, especially by all those in the West who have flown aboard passenger jets and contemplated, however briefly, the prospect of becoming traffic safety statistics themselves.

9

SUPERPROJECTS

"Soviet technology is the best in the world," boasted a Muscovite to his wife in a joke current in Moscow in the mid-1970s. "Now we have satellites to relay television all the way from Vladivostok and a supersonic plane that can take passengers cross-country in only a matter of hours. Do you realize what this means to our lives?" His practical wife immediately knew how they would benefit: "Indeed, yes, that's wonderful. When we see on television there are eggs for sale in Vladivostok, I can take that plane out there to buy a few!"

The *Maxim Gorkiy,* or ANT-20 (designed by A. N. Tupolev), registration code L760, was the largest passenger plane in the world in the mid-1930s: It could carry up to fifty people. It had eight 900-horsepower engines, weighed forty-six tons, had a 206-foot wingspan, and was equipped with a radio station, a printing press, a photography laboratory, film projectors, loudspeakers, and illuminated signs (it was intended to be a flying propaganda studio).

Khrushchev in his memoirs recalled the tragic events of Sunday, May 18, 1935:

The Maxim Gorkiy went up for a demonstration flight. It was escorted by a fighter [an I-5] painted red so that the people watching on the ground could compare the size of the two planes. The pilot of the fighter was a famous air ace—I forget his name [it was N. Blagin]. He started showing off his skill by executing all kinds of dives, loops, and tricks. In the midst of these dare-devil aerobatics, he miscalculated and hit the Maxim Gorkiy. Both planes crashed and everyone was killed [there was a crew of eleven plus thirty-six passengers]. . . . If I'm not mistaken, the passengers were award-winning workers. I think so because I was a member of the committee that arranged for the funerals of the famous people who perished in accidents. Stalin was furious about the crash, and his wrath was directed at us, the Moscow city officials. He decided to punish Bulganin and me by making us carry the urns with the ashes of the crash victims from the crematorium to the Hall of Columns. I didn't mind at all. I considered it a special honor to participate in this funeral and to pay my last respects to these courageous people who had died so tragically.

Tupolev, who was already in political trouble for suspected ideological unreliability, fell deeper into disgrace. He soon wound up in a special prison laboratory for the untrustworthy but technologically useful. Tupolev was, to put it mildly, out of official favor, and so was his superproject. Despite the apparent utility of such an aircraft, the Soviets never built another one.

Half a century later another giant airplane, designed to show off Soviet glory, soared through the air—and then dropped out of the sky and out of Soviet consciousness. It was the Tu-144, designed by Andrey Tupolev's son, Aleksey.

A small-scale model of the plane was first shown at the Paris air show in 1965. By 1968 a full-scale flying prototype was being completed. Moscow Radio announced it would become operational "in the nearest future." On New Year's Eve of 1969 the prototype Tu-144 (equipped with ejection seats, later removed) took off on a brief subsonic test flight, beating the Anglo-French Concorde into the air by two months. The pilot was Eduard Yelyan, and the copilot was Mikhail Kozlov.

The Tu-144 flew supersonic in 1969, and by 1971 the Congressional Research Service at the Library of Congress in Washington assessed it as "clearly an aircraft which is competitive with the Concorde." The Soviets thought so, too, and hoped to sell twenty of them to world airlines after building ten for regular domestic use by Aeroflot.

When the Russian plane's configuration had first become known in the West, it was quickly dubbed the "Concordeski" because of striking visual similarities to the competing Anglo-French supersonic airliner, the Concorde. The Tu-144's long, swanlike fuselage and delta wings did give it a superficially similar appearance to its commercial rival.

But upon closer consideration it became clear to aviation observers that the Soviet aircraft was a unique plane, not a copy. It was slightly larger and faster than the Anglo-French plane and was meant to carry more passengers. Its four engines were grouped together in one block under the mid-body, unlike the Concorde's widely spaced pairs; these engine nacelles were twice as long as the Concorde's. While the Concorde forward fuselage had a circular cross section, the Tu-144's was markedly flattened on the bottom, and the surface blended smoothly into the wings (the Concorde's wings were joined to the fuselage along the aircraft's lower body, but the bottom surfaces were not flush). The Tu-144's wings were shaped in a double delta silhouette (much like the NASA space shuttle), while the Concorde's wings had a swooping ogival curved profile with a complex twist at the ends.

The engines were distinctly different, too, and this was to be the key to the Soviet plane's ultimate failure. The Tu-144's turbofan engines, built by the Kuznetsov design team, were unable to run at temperatures as high as those of the Concorde's turbojet Olympus engines. To compensate for the resulting loss of cruise power, the Tu-144 had to run its engines on afterburner for its whole flight, not just at takeoff and landing. This led to crippling fuel consumption rates—30 to 40 percent higher than Concorde's. (The Soviets eventually recognized the seriousness of this problem and at one point in early 1977 even tried to purchase advanced electronic engine control equipment from Lucas Aerospace Ltd. in England. Because the same equipment was also used on the new Tornado jet fighter, the British government scotched the deal.)

One of the leading British officials in the Concorde program, Sir George Edwards, had first seen the Soviet design in 1967, when the prototype was nearly finished. He later recalled thinking that there were many things that were transparently not right about it.

He said so to "young Tupolev," the fifty-year-old designer. "You'll have to change a lot of things," he told him. "You've got the intakes and the engines in the wrong place, for one." Tupolev reportedly replied, "Well, I know that, but we just can't get the control system to work with the engine-out [engine failure] case." As Edwards recalled, that problem was also stumping the Concorde team, but they later mastered it.

Edwards also told Tupolev: "You've got too unsophisticated a design of wing, with no camber [curved cross section] or twist. . . ." And he added that although bypass engines were going to help with airport noise (which he wouldn't have thought in Russia was a very sensitive issue), he presciently told his Russian counterpart that he was going to lose a lot of efficiency when it came to cruise performance.

"They never were good at powered controls," Edwards also noted. "The Ilyushin 62, which was very similar to the VC-10, had manual controls, for the simple reason that they didn't know how to design powered ones." His reference to the Ilyushin 62 was ironic because it was generally considered too similar to the British Aircraft Corporation's VC-10 (by Vickers-Armstrong) to be merely coincidental. Each used side-mounted pairs of aft engines and an elevated tail. The Il-62, Russia's first long-range four-jet aircraft, initially flew in January 1963, six months after the VC-10. Ultimately 200 were built.

According to Greville Wynne (who had been the spy Penkovsky's contact officer), British counterintelligence had identified a "mole" within the VC-10 aircraft bureau in England who was funneling detailed technical data to the Soviets. Rather than arrest him, the officials contrived an elaborate plot to feed high-tech disinformation to Moscow. The spy was transferred to the Concorde project and for several years, up until 1969, when the Tu-144 began actual flight testing, he was fed specially doctored test data and design specifications. The spy obligingly forwarded them to Moscow via his contact, an East German trade official who had become a double agent for the British.

What the Russians did with their counterfeit data is not known. They certainly had their own studies and flight tests to provide firsthand results. Still, the Soviet practice of aping

Western designs and trusting Western technology over home-grown alternatives is deep-seated. The damage done to the Tu-144 project by the British disinformation may have been considerable.

In any case, the Soviet aeronautical engineers were obviously thinking along the lines of Edwards's criticisms. At the biannual international air show in Paris in 1973 a Tu-144 was displayed. It was the second production version, and its design had been substantially modified. "Moving the engines from underneath the body halfway out on the wing was no light achievement," Edwards told a writer for *Jane's* some years later, "and that had to be a big compromise because the undercarriage was already where the engines were to be. They had also changed the wing, which had camber and twist incorporated. . . ."

Another feature of the redesigned plane which appeared at Paris in 1973 was its canards, the small extra wings in the front of the fuselage. These retractable winglets allowed the plane to reduce its takeoff and landing speeds, so it could land on shorter runways than could the Concorde.

On June 3, the last day of the air show, the two different Mach 2 airliners flew head to head before a crowd of 200,000 aviation fans. First the Anglo-French Concorde made a magnificent flyby and circuit of the field, performing more like a fighter jet than a passenger airliner. The crowd was impressed. Then it was the Tu-144's turn.

Pilot Mikhail Kozlov did his best to outperform the Concorde, completing a series of maneuvers with a low flyby along Runway 060. As he came along the runway in front of the main reviewing stand, many aviation experts and journalists grew apprehensive over the airplane's low airspeed. They saw the plane's afterburners kick in, painting shock diamonds behind the four engines. As the plane reached the end of the runway, it pulled up into a climb which rapidly became dangerously steep. "Shoot him, shoot him!" one bureau chief cried to his cameraman. "He's not going to make it!"

Kozlov's nearly vertical climb had had its intended effect: The crowd oohed in amazement. The admiration then suddenly turned to horror. As clearly shown later in photographs, the left canard broke clean off from the stresses, which went far beyond the design limits of a commercial airliner. It smashed into the wing root behind it, and a small orange flare blossomed as the ruptured fuel tank exploded. The plane nosed over and dived straight into the ground "like an arrowhead," one horrified newsman recalled years later. Six people aboard the aircraft and seven on the ground were killed.

Accident investigation was hampered by the lack of flight recorders. One recorder broke open and its photographic film was ruined; another was never found. The Soviets hinted it had been stolen, perhaps by a souvenir hunter or one of the hundreds of technical intelligence specialists who flock to such air shows. But getting such a bulky box out of the sealed-off neighborhood would have been a major problem, even for anyone who found it first; it was equally possible that it had never even been installed by the Soviets.

The accident was reportedly the occasion of a major inter-service battle between the two Soviet intelligence agencies, the well-known KGB and the lesser-known GRU (military intelligence). As it turned out, the KGB agents at Le Bourget missed the disaster and got no film; the GRU, long suffering as the KGB's lower-status partner in espionage, had managed to obtain a complete high-quality record of the entire aerial breakup of the Tu-144. But before turning the film over, the GRU apparently dickered long and hard over operational concessions from the KGB on a number of long-standing points of dispute.

The news was broken to Soviet citizens in a brief report buried on the back page of *Pravda*. No heroic funeral or interment awaited Kozlov and his crew. Meanwhile, Tupolev's team eventually concluded that pilot error was the immediate cause of the disaster, although nobody wanted to determine who had pressured Kozlov to attempt to upstage the more capable Concorde.

Two years passed. With some changes the jet was soon readied for operational service. At the end of 1975 Tu-144s began what the Soviet Ministry of Civil Aviation touted as the world's first commercial supersonic services, on a twice-weekly basis. Flying out of Domodedovo Airport near Moscow, the aircraft supplied Alma Ata, capital of Kazakhstan, in Central Asia, with high-priority oil field equipment, mail, and agricultural foodstuffs. The plane covered 1,900 miles in just under two hours.

The first passenger service was slated to begin in June 1976,

U.S. Defense Intelligence Agency map shows presumed distribution of wind-blown anthrax spores from alleged germ weapons' accident in Sverdlovsk in 1979. Soviets wrapped the genuine anthrax outbreak in deep secrecy (and downplayed actual losses), so that worst-case scenarios became plausible and couldn't be disproved.

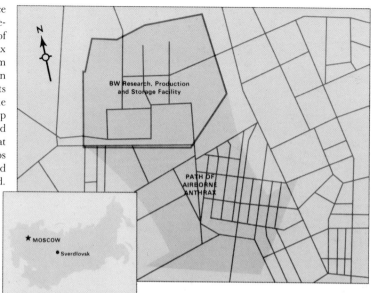

N

BW Research, Production and Storage Facility

PATH OF AIRBORNE ANTHRAX

★ MOSCOW

● Sverdlovsk

Vostok, a Soviet science base in Antarctica, suffered a major fire disaster in 1981, but the two dozen survivors refused to ask for available American emergency assistance. The catastrophe was kept secret until months after Soviet rescuers had arrived.

Soviet air defense forces have been on a hair trigger to attack unidentified intruders. In 1981, Major Valentin Kulyapin (*above left*) fanatically rammed a lost cargo airliner near the Iranian border, killing all four crewmen, and in 1983 another pilot, identified as Major Vasiliy Kuzmin (*above right*), obediently fired missiles into an unknown target (the Korean Airlines Flight 007) over the Sea of Japan, killing 269 people. Propaganda cartoons fictitiously portrayed intruders as carrying spy gear.

Комментирует художник

ГОСУДАРСТВЕННАЯ ГРАНИЦА СССР

МЕЖДУНАРОДНАЯ ВОЗДУШНАЯ ТРАССА

— Держитесь подальше, господа!   Рис. Бор. Ефимов

In October 1986 near Bermuda, a Soviet nuclear-powered submarine carrying nuclear-armed missiles suffered a severe internal explosion. U.S. patrol planes photographed the dying sub, a hole visible above its missile compartment. This is the first undersea disaster admitted to by Moscow though dozens of similar incidents have occurred.

Salang Tunnel in Afghanistan was the site of a major military transportation catastrophe in 1982 when more than a thousand Russians and Afghans might have been killed from fire and asphyxiation.

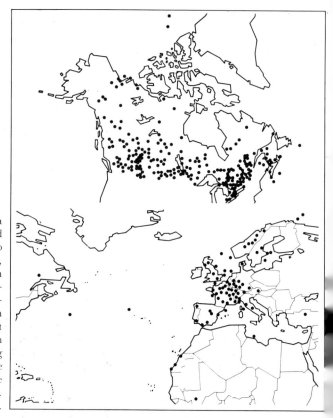

This summary chart of air/sea rescues, involving both U.S. and Soviet space satellites, shows no problems within Soviet territory, even though rescue centers in Norway, France, and the Aleutians frequently overhear emergency beacons sounding within the USSR. In early 1987 a Soviet sea captain broke with tradition when his grain ship was sinking off the coast of New Jersey. He radioed for help, and the entire crew was rescued by the U.S. Coast Guard.

When Valentin Bondarenko, a Soviet cosmonaut trainee, burned to death in a space cabin test in 1961, Moscow kept the disaster secret for a quarter century (unwarned, three American astronauts perished in a shockingly similar accident in 1967).

Despite some recent releases of historical information, many former cosmonauts remain "missing in action," their official anonymity enforced by photographic forgeries that seek to expunge them (and their presumably tragic fates) from history. This missing cosmonaut from the 1969–1971 period was in several pictures released carelessly but has been removed from some later versions, for reasons unclear. His name and fate remain unknown.

The most famous of the "missing cosmonauts" was first noticed in a few Soviet space photographs from the 1960s (he is second from the left in the back row in this group shot released in 1971). Subsequent official editions of the same photograph erased him. The original clumsy retouching was itself touched up to include fake background such as a stairway or bushes. Widespread Western publication of these forgeries embarrassed Moscow into allowing disclosure of the man's name and fate. Grigoriy Nelyubov was expelled from the space program in 1961 (due to an unpardonable act of arrogance), and thereafter he sank into alcoholism and died.

Forged versions of these group portraits taken at the Sochi resort just after Gagarin's successful mission in 1961 tried to excise a total of five failed cosmonaut candidates. They appear in the original frontal group shot, but an oblique group shot taken almost simultaneously has been retouched to remove them all.

NEW YORK POST

METRO SPORTS FINAL

Friday May 2 1986

35 cents

TV Ratings: P. 118

Late word from inside Russia:

MASS GRAVE = FOR 15,000 N-VICTIMS

Relatives give the grim details | **RED ADMITS: THE CRISIS RAGES ON** | *Top U.S. doc summoned by Soviets*

INSIDE: SIX PAGES OF LATEST STORIES and PHOTOS

Post-Chernobyl rumors in 1986 spoke of vastly exaggerated casualties and damage (the headline is from the *New York Post*, May 2, 1986), and the Soviets responded by blaming such distortions on deliberate Western lies. The cartoon shows panic emanating from a radio labeled MADE IN USA. But such rumors (and many others like them about other Soviet disasters) sprang up naturally within the Soviet population without the slightest need for any Western instigation or encouragement.

РАДИОактивные злопыхатели.

Рисунок Д. Циновского.

but as that year progressed, the cargo flights to Alma Ata were reduced to once a week, then stopped altogether. The Tu-144 dropped out of official existence. No new projections for passenger service were issued, and all that Aeroflot officials would say was: "The supersonic passenger plane Tu-144 is being assimilated into Aeroflot." Repeatedly spokesmen passed up opportunities to boast about the new plane. Aviation Day passed on August 15, 1976, with no mention of it at all, and in October, when Aeroflot celebrated twenty years of Soviet civil jetliners, little or no mention appeared anywhere in the press. Between May and November the newspaper *Grazhdanskaya Aviatsiya* ("Civil Aviation") carried only one brief mention of the plane, and on December 1, 1976, in a report on Soviet passenger planes expected to be in service by 1980, the Tu-144 was absent.

Another full year passed before the first passengers boarded a Tu-144 bound for Alma Ata. Each had paid eighty-five rubles for a one-way ticket (a third over the regular fare). On November 1, 1977, the first of what were promised to be weekly runs to Kazakhstan took off. Although the plane was configured with 133 seats, the first trip had only 80 seats filled. The second flight was delayed a day because of a national holiday, and the November 15 and 22 flights were canceled altogether because of weather (passengers, many already seated on the Tu-144 for hours, were offered seats on an Il-86 jetliner). The following week snow at the Moscow end frustrated the flight. Part of the difficulties was associated with the fact that there were no full-service facilities at Alma Ata for the Tu-144, so that the plane could not leave Moscow without some confidence it could return.

Passengers complained of poor air-conditioning and high noise levels, particularly in the rear (where people had to converse with written notes). These were only passenger comfort features, however, which have never rated high in Soviet design philosophy anyway. More serious operational problems involved vibration and excessive fuel consumption.

The weekly service limped along into the new year. The flights were irregular, often being delayed for a day or more, sometimes being canceled altogether. On June 6, 1978, the last paying passengers rode the Tu-144 on its return from Alma Ata to Moscow. It was the airliner's hundred and second and final passenger flight. Four aircraft, tail numbers 77105 through 77108, had supported the operation, but by the end of September they had disappeared from Domodedovo Airport and never returned. Another Tu-144 disaster at the end of May had helped Aeroflot reach its decision. No passengers were involved. It had been a pure test flight which crashed at the Ramenskoye flight test center forty miles southeast of Moscow, killing two persons and seriously injuring three. A specially modified version, the Tu-144-D, also had made test runs from Moscow to Khabarovsk on the USSR's Pacific coast, a distance of 3,914 miles, beginning in June 1978. New problems cropped up there, too.

"I don't think they have ever really overcome their basic problems of drag and excessive fuel consumption," one senior aerospace engineer told the *Times* of London at the time. Evidently things were so serious that the Soviets decided to seek Western help. This highly unusual step testified to the level of desperation of the Tupolev Bureau. In late 1978 Soviet representatives approached Concorde officials with an unprecedentedly explicit description of their problems. They requested help improving the design of the variable-geometry engine inlets. They disclosed metal fatigue problems at the tip of the aircraft's vertical stabilizer. They asked for information on a series of items (listed by *Aviation Week*):

> [A]nti-icing devices for the leading edge of the air intakes, fuel-system pipes and devices to improve the life of such pipes, mud flaps, emergency power supply, drain valves for fuel tanks, passenger cabin interior appointments, fireproof paint, navigation-piloting equipment, speed stability control unit, fire-fighting system, including warning devices and lightning protection, acoustic loading of airframe and controls, and improvements in residual strength of fuselage (with damage) and life of the undercarriage units.

This shopping list revealed technological weaknesses throughout the project.

Soviet candor included a thorough listing of malfunctions encountered on the commercial passenger flights. About 600 malfunctions were detected in the whole year; 226 were on the passenger service flights. The most serious was an engine oil leak around the O ring seal of the central support (all engines on all planes were subsequently adjusted). Other specific problems surfaced on: December 27, 1977, when reduced cabin pressure forced the crew to make the entire flight subsonically at 36,000 feet; January 29, 1978, when a faulty switch indicated falsely that the landing gear had not retracted; March 14, 1978, when excessive temperature in an engine exhaust duct forced the aircraft to return to the airport.

There was nothing unusual or particularly shameful about these problems, which seem typical of any new aircraft. But while the Soviet officials were being so forthright with their Anglo-French counterparts, not a word of the problems—or of the Russian approach to the Concorde team—ever appeared in their press. Their openness was clearly a unique result of a particular need in a program not under control of the Soviet military; nevertheless, it was an impressive break with Soviet tradition.

Several years of redesigning and testing (and of media silence) followed. By early 1981 a spokesman for the Ministry of Aircraft Production was able to announce that the tests "are coming to an end" and the aircraft would be back in service soon. It never was. During this period Western pilots heard rumors that two more aircraft had been lost on long cross-country flights and their wreckage never even found, much less recovered.

In mid-1984 Nikolay Poluyanchik, director of Aeroflot's international division, confirmed to Western journalists that the plane would never fly again. He blamed it on operating costs: "We are not prepared to use an aircraft which is inefficient." Concorde had barely escaped cancellation for the same reason, despite its significantly higher fuel efficiency (and ticket price).

Up to eight aircraft remained. Three test prototypes flew in the early 1970s; two of the later production versions were known to have crashed, and perhaps others as well. Their current disposition is unknown. In view of the Soviet policy of wiping the program from the national memory, none of the remaining Tu-144s is likely to wind up in a public museum.

Concorde design official Sir George Edwards, in what could have been the Soviet plane's obituary, observed:

I would have said that the reason the Tu-144 had petered out was that they [the Soviets] had reluctantly come to the conclusion, having been hacking across Russia with mail and freight, that it really wasn't a going concern for carrying passengers across the Atlantic. The aeroplane just wasn't refined enough. These things stand or fall by half per cents. You don't have to be dramatically adrift. I don't think there was the refinement in the design to enable them to do it.

Clearly the Soviets had overestimated their technological capabilities (as had many Western analysts). When the problems mounted to an unbearable level, they must have decided just to scrap the whole system. The design simply could not be "Band-Aided" into a workable aircraft.

Years have passed without the plane's being mentioned in the Soviet media. After the 1970s, full of boasts, the 1980s saw the Tu-144 become the "plane that never was." Yet if one approaches Aeroflot officials, they grudgingly may produce a press release presenting a standard set of excuses about "Why supersonic aircraft (specifically Tu-144) do not operate on regular air routes." The document contains some delightful twists and turns of fact and logic, and is a classic in excuse making.

First, the official Soviet excuse was "environmental protection," which consisted entirely of "deleterious effects on people's health due to the sound shock wave passing" (no ozone depletion problems in Soviet skies, apparently). Although the Soviets acknowledge that the Concorde continues to operate, it does so over "deserted ocean areas," and in the USSR "there are practically no such airways." Actually, the 1977–1978 commercial routes of the Soviet plane took it across the deserts of Central Asia and the taiga of Siberia, where the population density is probably even less than that of the heavily trafficked North Atlantic beneath the Concorde.

Secondly, the Tu-144 was accused (accurately) of being wasteful of fuel; its fuel consumption was ten times that of subsonic aircraft. Not mentioned was the central, fatal flaw of the Tu-144: that it was *so* inefficient that its unrefueled range was too short to cross the Atlantic and thus to compete for the most profitable runs. "The operation of supersonic aircraft is still unprofitable," the Aeroflot statement concluded. But for priority passengers and cargo, ticket surcharges could have alleviated this problem, and the Soviets run many other big projects without regard for cost, purely for the prestige.

In short, the Soviets tried to make the airplane's technological failure into a positive endorsement of their concerns over human health, waste, and cost. But while it lasted, the program taught the Soviets—and the West—a great deal about both the limits of their advanced aeronautical technology and the limits of their secrecy.

The biggest telescope in the world is in the Soviet Union. The Soviets take pride in having the biggest anything, but they are especially proud of the telescope.

The Big Alt-Azimuth Telescope (BTA) is located forty kilometers (twenty-four miles) south of Zelenchukskaya, at a complex called the Special Astrophysical Observatory (SAO). Visitors fly to Mineralniye Vody ("Mineral Waters") in the northwestern Caucasus, then take a three-and-a-half-hour drive to the site. The observatory is one and a half miles above sea level.

The BTA is an impressive instrument. The main mirror is six meters (twenty feet) in diameter, the largest in the world. Building a mirror that size was a monumental challenge. The original mirror, cast of Pyrex glass in Leningrad in the 1960s, cracked badly. A second one cracked, too, but was made usable by having its bad sections covered to prevent degradation of the total image. By 1986 a second replacement mirror was under construction. Thick glass (the mirror alone weighs forty-two metric tons) takes a long time to reach a uniform temperature; until it does, the temperature differences cause the mirror to flex slightly, defocusing the image. In the "miniclimate" of the telescope dome, it can take hours to adjust to changing thermal conditions.

The 800-ton telescope is mounted on a revolutionary computer-controlled framework which rotates horizontally and pitches vertically. This requires control in two axes rather than one (the traditional, lighter telescope is built with its rotation axis pointed toward the North Star, and it merely rotates around that axis to counter Earth's spin). The Soviet BTA had to have a two-axis framework because of its great weight. It seems to work well, except it cannot point straight up.

Observations can be made of stars of twenty-fourth-magnitude brightness, the dimmest objects that can be seen by any telescope on Earth. In essence, the telescope can see everything within the natural, physical limit placed on all Earth-based stargazing by the atmosphere's airglow. More important, spectral bands can be distinguished for extremely dim objects, down to the sixteenth magnitude. These are remarkable levels of sensitivity. The instrument's major advantages are in observations of distant galaxies, which are both dim and extended (not pinpoint) sources. There, every photon counts, and the immense light-gathering capacity of the large mirror is advantageous. The large mirror also has high spatial resolution, which allows it to create separate images of objects that are close to one another. Many foreign guest observers have expressed immense satisfaction with results obtained on the BTA ("A most effective instrument," one spectroscopic observer commented after several days of observations in 1980).

Yet astronomers have noted that while the instrument can and does make useful observations, the kinds of major advances to justify its immense price just don't seem to be there. "I'm not aware of any major breakthroughs coming from the telescope, no major findings," noted Stephen Maran of NASA's Goddard Space Center. "Their published papers indicate rather routine discoveries."

An analysis by noted physicist Freeman Dyson of the Institute for Advanced Study in Princeton, New Jersey, remarked on the "stupidities" of the Soviet superproject that may have crippled Soviet astronomy for a generation, while feeding nationalistic pride. "[In 1978] I went to the Caucasus Mountains to visit the new Soviet observatory at Zelenchukskaya," Dyson wrote. "The observatory had been under construction for twenty years and was just beginning to go into operation. The six-meter telescope was finished and was sitting quietly in its gigantic dome, but unfortunately the slit of the dome was blocked by masses of ice and could not be opened." Dyson noted a vast visitor's gallery overlooking the telescope and a unique feature, "a white wall for visiting dignitaries to sign their names on. The wall is huge, about a hundred feet long, and every square inch of the wall was tightly packed with names. The visitor's gallery and the wall must have been given some real priority, so that they were in full swing for many years before the telescope was ready."

Dyson also noted that the location seemed to be inappropriate: "I was on the mountain for three nights and did not see the sky. At Zelenchukskaya the weather is consistently bad for the greater part of each year. The site is far too close to the high Caucasus peaks, which are regularly stirring up storms and clouds." Another American astronomer noted: "The telescope is better than it's given credit for—the mountain is bad."

The weather patterns of the Caucasus Mountains are such that the wind comes out of the steppes, causing stormy and cloudy weather along the northernmost range. The southern ranges experience clearer weather but lie in the non-Slavic republics of Armenia, Georgia, and Azerbaijan. Reportedly government officials had rejected all the earlier site suggestions for political reasons and insisted that the world's biggest telescope be located in European Russia.

The climatological shortcomings were explained by another Western visitor, who made some pertinent observations. Noted Dr. Anthony Fairall of the University of Capetown Observatory:

> The observatory is surrounded by magnificent alpine scenery, including much forest. Since there has to be a climate to support [the forest], such could hardly be ideal for astronomy. . . . The presence of moisture in the air also greatly affects what astronomers call "seeing," the degree of blurring from the atmosphere which can badly curtail the performance of telescopes. I believe that this may account for the telescope not being as productive as it could have been.

One of Dyson's Soviet colleagues told him in confidence that "the Zelenchukskaya project had set back the progress of optical astronomy in the Soviet Union by twenty years." For two decades the project soaked up the majority of funds allocated to telescope building. With the same level of funding the government could have built and equipped "four or five first-rate modern observatories of modest size at optically excellent sites in central Asia, and a whole generation of astronomers might have been saved from frustration." But in that case, Dyson noted cynically, "the political officials in Moscow would not have had the satisfaction of building the biggest telescope in the world, and there would have been no hundred-foot wall for the visitors to write their names on."

While popular Western media accounts describing the instrument as "hopelessly flawed" are exaggerated, it would be plausible to say that with massive cost overruns and political site selection the installation fell far short of the capabilities promised for it a quarter century ago, when the project was approved. Soviet astronomy does not appear to have particularly benefited from the project, but in commissioning the construction of another "biggest in the world" for Russia, Moscow officials likely had given very little consideration to such motivations anyway.

Probably the most expensive and little-known Soviet superproject flop was the man-to-the-moon program of the 1960s. During the race the Soviets were explicit about expecting to be first. Following the U.S. Apollo successes, and thus having failed in their attempt to send Russian cosmonauts to the moon ahead of American astronauts, the Soviets did the next best thing: They initiated a propaganda campaign that the USSR had "really never intended" to send men to the moon. Supposedly the American success was a "nonvictory" in a "nonrace."

Nevertheless, the evidence that the Soviets were lying and had actually fully intended to be first to the moon is convincing. They had expended budget sums equivalent to the cost of the Apollo program, tens of billions of dollars. In terms of available resources—money, high-quality engineers, physical plants, Western currency to buy computers—the sacrifice was greater because they had fewer such resources to begin with. And they got back essentially nothing since the project was canceled. Rather than come in in second place and admit there really had been a race, the Soviet government chose not to go at all.

"I'm only sorry," Khrushchev recalled in his memoirs, "that we didn't manage to send a man to the moon in Korolev's lifetime" (the Soviet space chief died prematurely in 1966 at the age of fifty-nine). Korolev had been working on that very man-to-the-moon project; his successors were unequal to the engineering and management challenges.

In 1967 and 1968 the Soviets flew some Zond probes out around the moon and back. These were modified versions of the manned Soyuz spacecraft, intended eventually for manned lunar flight; published Soviet statements at the time made this clear. Pictures showed the spacecraft being tested with a launch escape tower, a piece of hardware reserved for manned vehicles. The spacecraft transmitted dummy biomedical telemetry and followed a gentle reentry trajectory optimized for crew survival.

To their own news media, Soviet cosmonauts boasted of getting to the moon ahead of the Americans. In face-to-face chats they discussed with American colleagues expectations of their own personal lunar voyages.

From 1969 to 1971 the Soviets made a number of flight tests of moon-related hardware, usually under cover names but distinguishable by their distinctive flight profiles. Western analysts concluded that one particular flight—Kosmos 434 in 1971—had been a test of the lunar module needed to land men on the moon's surface (the Russians translated the term as *lunnaya kabina,* or "lunar cabin," when they reported on Apollo missions). But officially Kosmos 434 had been only a scientific probe to explore outer space. Years later the satellite plunged into the atmosphere and burned up near Australia. The Australian government was concerned because a Soviet nuclear reactor had only recently fallen on Canada. So Canberra dispatched an official inquiry to Moscow. A spokesman for the Soviet Foreign Ministry (after checking with spaceflight officials) assured the Australians there was nothing to worry about. The satellite had no nuclear reactor on board; it was just an old "prototype lunar cabin." Somebody had forgotten the old cover story and had evidently told the truth by accident.

Mars, the Red Planet, has proved to be one prize in the sky that has remained stubbornly beyond the grasp of Soviet exploration. For nearly a decade and a half the Soviets experienced practically uninterrupted disasters with their space probes toward Mars. The experience was so discouraging that the program was abolished in the mid-1970s and not revived until recently. The planned July 1988 launchings of the international Fobos missions, to what the Soviets had originally vainly hoped was to be the "Red Planet," will inaugurate the third major phase in Soviet attempts to explore that planet; the first two phases were dismal failures.

In 1960 the USSR's first shots at Mars ended in catastrophe when one rocket exploded during checkout, killing dozens of technicians (see next chapter). Mars had been the target, but the rocket had hit—and hurt—much closer to home.

Earth on the inner track lapped slower outer Mars once more, and in late 1962 the interplanetary launch window opened again (as it does about every twenty-six months). On October 24 the first new Soviet Mars probe blasted off in deep secrecy (to be announced only if successful). The probe and its injection stage went into a temporary low parking orbit. But half an hour later the stage exploded into dozens of fragments.

This cloud of objects then zoomed up over the horizon and appeared without warning on American attack-warning radars in Alaska. The Cuban missile crisis was at its height, and for a few moments the unannounced and unpredicted Soviet space failure looked like the long-feared massive Soviet ICBM attack. Tracking computers quickly determined that the fragments were not aimed at the United States, and the debris soon fell back into the atmosphere and burned up harmlessly. The Soviets have never to this day acknowledged their failed Mars shot which might have set off World War III.

A week later, on November 1, the rocket fired perfectly, and Moscow immediately announced the successful launch of Mars 1. Although the launch was hailed as the world's first space probe sent toward Mars, the 2,000-pound vehicle's radio broke down five months out, three months short of Mars, and no data were obtained about the target planet.

On November 4, meanwhile, a third rocket headed for Mars, but like the first, it disintegrated while still in its parking orbit. Moscow never acknowledged its brief existence.

Again, the planets circled the Sun and resumed their convenient mutual alignments when Earth–Mars shots are feasible. At the end of November 1964 the Soviets made more launchings. These, too, failed to reach their target planet. At this point the Soviet Union's first Mars program fizzled out and was canceled. Nine known launchings had been made, and perhaps more, and scores of people had died. Russian engineers had proved unable to design either a reliable booster or a sufficiently long-lived payload for the demanding outbound voyage, so all interplanetary efforts were henceforth concentrated on nearer Venus, while a new generation of Mars hardware—both booster and payload—was prepared.

In the late 1960s the Soviets advanced to a second generation of Mars probes. These were to be carried atop their new Proton booster, which had three times the thrust and, if anything, even more troubles than the first booster system. At least one launching, at the end of March 1969, reportedly blew up early in flight (perhaps a second one did so as well). At least one other attempt during that period never got off the launchpad. No successes were achieved until the launching of Mars 2 on May 19, 1971, and Mars 3 on May 28 (an attempt on May 10 got stuck in parking orbit—again!—but this time Moscow covered up by labeling the satellite "Cosmos 419," allegedly another routine scientific satellite for the exploration of space).

The Mars 2 and Mars 3 probes each weighed about five tons, five times as big as the first-generation vehicles of the early 1960s. Each consisted of a landing capsule and a carrier spacecraft with a rocket engine to brake from a flyby trajectory into an orbit around Mars. The capsule was designed to be dropped off on the approach leg, prior to the braking rocket burn.

On November 27, 1971, the first probe arrived at Mars. It ejected its capsule as scheduled, but the landing failed. For three days Soviet space engineers made futile efforts to establish contact, then gave up. Moscow nevertheless announced a great success, the "first landing on Mars," which carried metal pennants engraved with the coat of arms of the USSR. No mention was made of the unfortunate detail that the probe did not survive the descent (in fact, it may have burned up in the atmosphere).

On December 2, 1971, the second probe arrived, and this time the lander touched down alive and began sending signals. But after twenty seconds the signals ceased. Soviet engineers tried in vain for five days to recontact the lander before any announcement of the arrival was made in Moscow: another "great success for Soviet science."

Some observers, perhaps influenced by traditional excuse making in Moscow, suggested that the fierce planetwide dust storms then enveloping Mars had been responsible for the failure of the two landers. But in 1976 Viking data were to show that surface conditions would not have been too severe, even at the height of the storm. Professional Sovietologists had long been bored with the recurrent Soviet complaint that bad weather was once again responsible for yet another disastrous agricultural harvest, but this was the first known time that the Soviets had publicly complained about bad weather on *another planet* interfering with Soviet productivity.

The next window to Mars was open in midsummer 1973, and it was the last one before the USA's scheduled Viking probes of 1976. These American robot Mars explorers were to involve highly sophisticated orbital and surface science programs. So the Soviet engineers were evidently under great political pressure to carry out a successful landing mission, however primitive, to upstage their American competition.

But in 1973 it was not possible to make a simple repeat of the 1971 launchings. This was because the Earth–Mars trajectory was a little steeper this window, and this required a higher final velocity at Earth departure. This velocity could not be achieved by the rocket carrying the full five-ton payload; the engineers could promise only three and a half tons at most, considering the required extra speed.

The solution to this problem demonstrated the ingenuity of Soviet engineers and the urgency attached to the politically inspired beat-the-Vikings effort. Each 1971-class five-ton vehicle was split into two parts (to be launched separately): The lander was attached to an orbiter type of vehicle with empty propellant tanks (so it would not be able to go into Mars orbit), and the intended orbiter had full tanks but no lander capsule attached (the orbiter was needed to provide a radio relay link back to Earth).

Two pairs of spacecraft thus needed to be launched. The two orbiters went first (Mars 4, launched on July 21, and Mars 5, on July 25), followed by the two landers (Mars 6 on August 5, and Mars 7 on August 9).

Mars 4 reached the Red Planet on February 10, 1974; but its retrorocket did not fire (the Soviets never explained why in their brief announcement), and it flew past the planet into oblivion. Mars 5 came next, and it successfully braked into a 1,100- by 20,000-mile orbit (with a period of twenty-five hours, just over one Martian day in length) on February 12; the probe began an observation program while waiting to act as a radio relay for the lander vehicles which were following a few weeks behind it.

Of the landers, Mars 7 pulled ahead of Mars 6 on the outbound trajectory and arrived at Mars on March 9. The carrier vehicle was targeted to pass Mars at a range of 1,000 miles, dropping off the lander on the way past; but the probe was already a dead, tumbling derelict, and the landing attempt was abandoned. Mars 6 arrived three days later and did enter the atmosphere, where it transmitted grossly misinterpreted readings on the atmospheric composition (excessively high argon readings were not refuted until Viking landed two years later) and then went dead just at the scheduled touchdown time.

The expensive and complex Soviet "double double" Mars gamble of 1973 had been Moscow's last chance to beat the Americans to a successful Mars landing and score another spectacular "space first." A new flight attempt coincident with Viking in 1975 was apparently out of the question for political reasons; even a success would compare poorly with the sophisticated Viking probes. So for the second time in less than a decade an entire Soviet Mars probe program was scrapped as a dismal failure, and efforts were redirected and concentrated toward Venus, an easier, closer target. The cost of the Mars probe program would be somewhere in the neighborhood of $3 billion.

It took another fifteen years before the Soviet space program got up enough nerve to launch another probe toward Mars.

The Russians have a clear-cut national lust for "biggest, highest, farthest" projects, totally admirable in their goal, if not in their achievement. Their failures indicate that they sometimes go into superprojects overestimating their capabilities and their luck and probably underestimating the difficulties. Their advanced strategic planning for such activities is not nearly as thorough as it should be and is overshadowed by the whims of their political leaders.

And since imagery was often the prime motivating force for undertaking such superprojects, cover-ups of the subsequent failures are mandatory. Fortunately for foreign observers trying to penetrate such false fronts, these cover-ups have generally been ad hoc and poorly contrived. They have failed, for the most part, just as dismally as the projects they were intended to conceal.

10

DEAD
COSMONAUTS

> The family of Senior Lieutenant Bondarenko is to be provided with everything necessary, as befits the family of a cosmonaut.
>
> —*Special Order, signed by Soviet Defense Minister R. D. Malinovskiy, April 16, 1961, classified Top Secret. NOTE: Prior to 1986 no Soviet book or magazine had ever mentioned the existence of a cosmonaut named Valentin Bondarenko.*

In 1982, a year after the publication of my first book, *Red Star in Orbit.* I received a wonderful picture from a colleague who had just visited Moscow. The photo showed cosmonaut Aleksey Leonov, hero of the Soviet Union, holding a copy of my book—and scowling.

Leonov was frowning at a picture of what I called the "Sochi Six," the Russian equivalent of our "original seven" Mercury astronauts. They were the top of the first class of twenty space pioneers, the best and the boldest of their nation, the ones destined to ride the first manned missions. The picture was taken at the Black Sea resort called Sochi in May 1961, a few weeks after Yuriy Gagarin's history-making flight. Just beneath that picture in my book was a copy of the same photograph—with the figure of one of the heroic six cosmonauts erased. One of the original top cosmonauts had been "unpersoned," and the two versions of the same 1961 photograph proved it.

Soviet space officials—including Leonov—had taken a great deal of trouble to cover up some episode in their space history involving the man whose face had been erased. Now Leonov had good reason to scowl. The deception was revealed, and a ghost had risen from the dead, from official Soviet oblivion.

For decades nobody outside the cosmonaut program knew about Grigoriy Nelyubov. He had been an egotistical young jet pilot. Despite such a character flaw, his academic and flying skills were so impressive that he had been the favorite candidate of several top officials for the honor and glory of humankind's first flight into space. Failing that, he was considered certain to receive one of the next spaceflight assignments following Yuriy Gagarin's pioneering mission in 1961.

But late that year Nelyubov and two other cosmonaut trainees were returning from a weekend pass when they got into some sort of altercation with an army patrol at a train station. Blows may have been exchanged when they were unable to bluff their way through a checkpoint for which they didn't have proper credentials. The three, who may also have been drunk, were subdued and placed under guard in the station duty officer's office.

It was quickly established that they were indeed cosmonauts, as they claimed, and the military security officials were willing to forget the whole thing. One officer, however, insisted that the cosmonauts apologize to the patrol members (suggesting that the cosmonauts had come out ahead in the brawl before being overwhelmed). Nelyubov's two colleagues readily agreed.

Nelyubov, however, refused to apologize. He was, after all, soon to become his nation's third or fourth man in orbit, and he demanded respect and subservience from his captors.

Lacking this simple gesture of reconciliation, the duty officer filed his report. It quickly reached the cosmonaut corps commander, an old air force veteran named Nikolay Kamanin, who became incensed at his men's all-too-public irresponsibility. In response, Kamanin expelled the three from the cosmonaut corps. Their space careers were aborted; they went back to flying jets in Siberia.

The other cosmonauts were as aghast at the severity of the punishment as they were outraged at Nelyubov's conceited intransigence. He wouldn't be missed, but the other two men (second-string space trainees named Ivan Anikeyev and Valentin Filatyev) had been very popular. "They burned down in concert" was the Russian figure of speech for Nelyubov's taking his well-liked buddies down in flames with him.

Nelyubov was transferred to an interceptor squadron based near Vladivostok, where he bragged to everyone that he had once been a cosmonaut. He was embittered that few believed him. Then he watched his colleagues one by one go into orbit, to fame and glory: first, the rest of his equals among the Sochi Six (Nikolayev, Popovich, Bykovsky in 1962 and 1963); next, some of the second team, whom he had already outranked (Komarov in 1964 and Leonov the following year); then, also in 1964, men he didn't even know (Feoktistov and Yegorov), who had not even been cosmonauts when he was expelled.

Sinking deeper into depression and alcoholism, he experienced "a crisis of soul," as a Russian journalist tactfully put it. In the predawn hours of February 18, 1966, while drunk, he stepped in front of a train near the Ippolitovka station, northwest of Vladivostok, and was killed. Whether it was intentional or accidental, nobody could tell.

None of this was known when I wrote *Red Star in Orbit* and published his photograph. For fifteen years, since I first saw his photo, I had sought this man's identity and his fate. The tragic story was finally revealed in April 1986 as a short part of a series of newspaper articles on the twenty-fifth anniversary of Yuriy Gagarin's flight into space.

That incredibly revealing series in *Izvestiya* was written by Russia's leading space journalist, Yaroslav Golovanov. He had probably researched it years before but had been unable to publish the truth until the policy of *glasnost* and relentless pressure from Western researchers (myself among them) had made the revelations possible.

The candor of 1986 contrasted sharply with the misrepresentations in interviews a decade earlier, when cosmonauts had rebuffed Western inquiries into the fates of the missing spacemen. Cosmonaut Aleksey Leonov (later to come face to face with the Sochi Six forgeries in my book) had earlier been shown the picture of the "missing cosmonaut" (Nelyubov, it turned out) by a Dutch journalist and had given a phony explanation: "In 1962 or 1963—I don't remember exactly—during a [run] in the centrifuge he developed excessive spasm of the stomach. He then disappeared from our ranks." As for my pictures of the young blond pilot who turned out to be Ivan Anikeyev, Nelyubov's partner in disgrace, Leonov had given this description of his fate: "He was removed from the team because of his general physical condition. That was, I think, in 1963." It is virtually impossible to believe that Leonov had so completely forgotten the scandalous expulsion of the arrogant Nelyubov and innocent Anikeyev; rather, he made up an innocuous cover story with the expectation that the facts would never come out to embarrass him.

The Russians had always presented their march to space as a smooth road to glory, the outgrowth of sound planning and monolithic support. The Soviets' traditional practice of boasting, covering up, lying, and retouching aspects of their own history made most Western observers doubt this rosy image. Contradictory information came out in bits and pieces, sometimes suggesting a picture worse than it was. Golovanov's articles in 1986, five years after my *Red Star in Orbit* came out, were the first tentative attempt to set part of the record of the past straight. And there was such a lot to set straight by then.

Even before the first announced Soviet spaceman blasted off in 1961, rumors reached the West about the existence of secret graves of anonymous dead cosmonauts, killed on unannounced missions. Moscow vigorously denied them all, to no effect. Lists of dozens of dead cosmonauts circulated in the Western press for many years. The Soviets denounced the originators of such material as "enemies."

Then, in 1986, Golovanov revealed in *Izvestiya* that indeed there had been a cosmonaut fatality back then after all, and it had been kept secret. His article even included the dead cosmonaut's name, Valentin Bondarenko, and the date of his death, March 23, 1961.

"Valentin was the youngest of the first batch of cosmonauts (he was 24 years old)," Golovanov wrote. A small, grainy formal portrait accompanied the article. It showed a very young man attempting to look stern and important. The photograph had been taken only a few days before his death.

Bondarenko had been undergoing routine training in a pressure chamber, which was part of a ten-day isolation exercise. At the very end of the exercise he made a trivial but fatal mistake. "After medical tests," explained Golovanov's article, "Bondarenko removed the sensors attached to him, cleaned the spots where they had been attached with cotton wool soaked in alcohol, and without looking threw away the cotton wool—which landed on the ring of an electric hot plate. In the oxygen-charged atmosphere the flames immediately filled the small space of the chamber."

Under such a condition of high oxygen concentration, normally nonflammable substances can burn vigorously. The cosmonaut's training suit caught fire. Unaccustomed to the vigor of high-oxygen fires, Bondarenko would only have spread the flames further by attempting to smother them.

When the doctor on duty noticed the conflagration through a porthole, he rushed to the hatch, which he could not open because the internal pressure kept it sealed. Releasing the pressure through bleed valves took at least several minutes. And for all that time Bondarenko was engulfed in flames.

"When Valentin was dragged out of the pressure chamber," continued Golovanov's account, "he was still conscious and kept repeating, 'It was my fault, no one else is to blame. . . .' " He died eight hours later from the shock of the burns.

He was buried in Kharkov, in the Ukraine, where he had grown up and where his parents still lived. He left a young widow, Anya, and a five-year-old son, Aleksandr ("Sasha"). Anya remained at the cosmonaut center in an undisclosed job. When he grew up, young Aleksandr became an air force officer.

Golovanov's candid story, in which he disclosed Bondarenko's death, may have astonished his countrymen, and it briefly made headlines in the Western press; but it was hardly news to informed "space sleuths" in the West. They had been hot on the trail of exactly this incident, and Soviet news censors knew it. The cause and effect of Western digging into a Soviet catastrophe, followed by Soviet large-scale (but still not full-scale) release of an "official account," are quite clear-cut. The broad outlines of the "Bondarenko tragedy" had already slipped past the Soviet cover-up.

In 1982 a recently emigrated Russian Jew named S. Tiktin discussed Soviet space secrets in a Russian-language monthly magazine published by anti-Soviet émigrés in West Germany. He mentioned in passing a relevant incident. "Soon after the flight of Gagarin [in 1961] the rumor spread about the loss of cosmonaut Boyko (or Boychenko) from a fire in a pressure chamber," he wrote.

In 1984 St. Martin's Press published a book, entitled *Russian Doctor,* by the Russian émigré surgeon Dr. Vladimir Golyakhovsky. He described the death of a cosmonaut trainee in a pressure chamber fire. Half an entire chapter was devoted to the incident—and with authority—since, incredibly, Golyakhovsky (a specialized surgeon-traumatologist) had apparently been the emergency room doctor at the prestigious Botkin Hospital when the dying cosmonaut was brought in.

As Golyakhovsky remembered it, a severely burned man identified only as "Sergeyev, a 24-year-old Air Force Lieutenant," was brought in by stretcher. "I couldn't help shuddering," Golyakhovsky recalled. "The whole of him was burnt. The body was totally denuded of skin, the head of hair; there were no eyes in the face. . . . It was a total burn of the severest degree. But the patient was alive. . . ."

Golyakhovsky saw the man's mouth moving and bent down to listen. "Too much pain—do something, please—to kill the pain" were the tortured words he could make out.

"Sergeyev" was scorched everywhere but the soles of his feet, where his flight boots had offered some protection from the flames. With great difficulty the doctors inserted intravenous lines into his feet (they couldn't find blood vessels anywhere else) and administered painkillers and medication. "Unfortunately, Sergeyev was doomed," Golyakhovsky remembered realizing immediately. "And yet, all of us were eager to do something, anything, to alleviate his terrible suffering." The man lingered for sixteen hours before dying.

Afterward Golyakhovsky reported talking with a small young officer who had waited by the phone in the lobby while the burned man lay dying. The doctor requested and received an account of the original accident. Details included "an altitude chamber . . . heavily laden with oxygen" and "a small electric stove [with] . . . a rag burst[ing] into flame." Golyakhovsky was also told that it had taken half an hour to get the pressure chamber open, with "Sergeyev" on fire until the flames consumed almost all the oxygen inside the room.

Sometime later Golyakhovsky saw a photograph of this

deathwatch officer in the newspapers. He had been Yuriy
Gagarin, who became the first man in space.

Despite minor distortions, the Tiktin and Golyakhovsky
material turned out to provide fundamental, direct, and invaluable leads into a major catastrophe in the early Russian space
program. It was left to the Soviets only to fill in the details about
the real death of Valentin Bondarenko, and they did in April
1986.

Golovanov's article also provided some new confirmation of
many other things we knew or suspected. It had already been
known that of the twenty men chosen for space training in
March 1960, a prime group of six finalists had later been
selected for the first mission. But Golovanov filled in unknown
details. One of the original six, a man named Anatoliy Kar-
tashov, had already been grounded after experiencing skin
bleeding during a centrifuge run. A second "sixer," Valentin
Varlamov, was dropped after injuring his neck in a stupid
diving mishap (he died several years later of an unrelated
medical problem). Their replacements became some of the first
men in space; a quarter century later even Golovanov's *glasnost*
still couldn't publish their photographs.

Another of the twenty cosmonaut trainees (the one named
Mars Rafikov) had left later for personal reasons (because he
was the only non-Slavic cosmonaut ever selected, his motivation
is subject to speculation). The last casualty, Dmitriy Zaikin, was
grounded in 1968 for medical reasons (ulcers) after serving on
a backup crew.

None of these details had been known at the time, in the early
1960s. Instead, in the absence of Soviet candor, Western
observers filled in their ignorance with guesses and rumors,
mostly wrong and almost always far worse than the truth.

My own first major Soviet space history research project was
undertaken in 1972 and 1973, and it dealt specifically with the
dead cosmonaut stories. What they lacked in quality they made
up in quantity, and the sheer volume of the legends stampeded
many specialists into concluding that at least perhaps a few of
them were authentic.

By 1973 I had compiled an imposing list of rumors about
missing cosmonauts:

Cosmonaut Ledovsky was killed in 1957 on a suborbital space
hop from the Kapustin Yar rocket base on the Volga River.

Cosmonaut Shiborin died the following year the same way. Cosmonaut Mitkov lost his life on a third attempt in 1959.

An unnamed cosmonaut was trapped in space in May 1960, when his orbiting space capsule headed in the wrong direction.

In late September 1960, while Khrushchev pounded his shoe at the United Nations, another cosmonaut (sometimes identified as Pyotr Dolgov) was killed when his rocket blew up on the launchpad.

On February 4, 1961, a mystery Soviet satellite was heard to be transmitting heartbeats, which soon stopped (some reports even described it as a two-man capsule, and several "missing cosmonauts" were listed as Belokonev, Kachur, and Grachev).

Early in April 1961 Russian pilot Vladimir Ilyushin circled the earth three times but was badly injured on his return.

In mid-May 1961 weak calls for help were picked up in Europe, evidently from an orbiting spacecraft with two cosmonauts aboard.

On October 14, 1961, a multiman Soviet spacecraft was knocked off course by a solar flare and vanished into deep space.

Radio trackers in Italy detected a fatal space mission in November 1962, and some believe that a cosmonaut named Belokonev died at that time.

An attempt to launch a second woman into space ended tragically on November 19, 1963.

One or more cosmonauts were killed during an unsuccessful space mission in April 1964, according to radio intercepts by Italian shortwave listeners.

Following the Apollo 1 fire in 1967 which killed three American astronauts, U.S. intelligence sources reportedly described five fatal Soviet spaceflights and six fatal ground accidents.

What is an observer to conclude from this barrage of stories? "Where's there's smoke, there's fire" is a trite proverb, but all the same, the consensus seemed to be that not all the stories could be spurious; some, perhaps two or three, must have been based on actual events.

But my 1972 study was entirely negative. After considering their sources and their details in the hindsight of subsequent space activities. I concluded that all such stories dealing with alleged flight fatalities were baseless.

Simultaneously, however, I uncovered persuasive evidence

that a large number of early cosmonaut trainees had in fact vanished. One could only speculate on the circumstances under which these men left the cosmonaut program, and it was probably a good guess (to be confirmed more than a dozen years later) that some of them were indeed dead. But unlike the 1960s contemporary myths of dead cosmonauts, these men had just not died on space missions.

This new evidence was primarily pictorial in nature. In 1972 and 1973 I had reviewed frame by frame a number of early 1960s Soviet newsreel releases on the cosmonaut program and found at least half a dozen unidentified faces among the obvious trainees. It was unlikely these men were still around, waiting their turns, since the last man from that original class had flown in space in 1969. Some of these faces also appeared in group photographs newly released in 1971 and 1972 in honor of the tenth anniversary of Gagarin's flight (for example, the original of the Sochi Six photograph was in a book by a Russian space journalist, released by a New York publisher).

In 1973 I was astonished to discover different versions of some of these group photographs. Certain faces were air-brushed out of photographs in books published inside the USSR although these "nonpersons" still remained in the same pictures used in Soviet books published for non-Soviet readers.

The most notorious photo-doctored set was the one showing the so-called Sochi Six, including the doomed Grigoriy Nelyubov second from left in the back row. This pair of photos was what Leonov was to scowl at in *Red Star in Orbit*. And several years later British researcher Rex Hall found two different versions of yet another group picture from that same day; that shot had included all sixteen active cosmonauts in one version, but only eleven in the other. Nelyubov was one of the deleted ones, along with his partners in eviction, Ivan Anikeyev and Valentin Filatyev, plus two other future failed cosmonauts, Mars Rafikov and Dmitriy Zaikin, and a parachute instructor named Nikitin, who later was killed on a jump. The original picture ("Sochi-sixteen"), which Hall found in an obscure Soviet space book, was later used to illustrate Golovanov's *Izvestiya* article, with the inaccurate boast "Published for the first time."

These "missing cosmonaut" faces were originally unidentified, so for convenient reference I labeled them with the code names XI, X2, up to X9. Photographs of many of these men had been published with my articles as early as 1973. The one figure I had designated X2 appeared to be special. He was the one erased from the Sochi Six group photograph. In photos and in text he was apparently closely associated with Gagarin's flight. At the same time, however, occasional veiled references to "Grigoriy" in historical accounts and memoirs suggested he was not a very nice person. He turned out, of course, to be Nelyubov.

In 1986, when Bondarenko's photograph appeared in *Izvestiya*, I went back and checked my X series photographs of the unaccounted-for early cosmonaut trainees. One of them, whom I had labeled "X7," almost certainly was the doomed pilot Bondarenko.

In apparent response to the widespread Western publication of the "before" and "after" cosmonaut photographs in the mid-1970s, the Soviets subsequently grudgingly produced an "explanation" for these "extra" cosmonaut names and faces. A 1977 book of Georgiy Shonin, a pioneer cosmonaut, first disclosed the existence of eight "dropouts" in the first cosmonaut class. It revealed the first names only of the eight dropouts from the 1960 class (nine years later Golovanov released their last names as well). Shonin's book (and several other later books by cosmonauts) gave sketchy accounts of their departures from the cosmonaut programs, which purportedly involved medical, academic, and disciplinary problems, clearly indicating that all eight had left the program alive. Shonin even provided a two-page character sketch of the "young Valentin" (Bondarenko, we later learned) without any hint of tragedy. These partial explanations and attempted deceptions were clearly in response to continuing Western press interest in the mystery of missing Soviet spacemen.

By the time I wrote *Red Star in Orbit* in 1980, the completeness of the Shonin story was under strong suspicion. I was skeptical that all eight were still alive or that we would ever know their true fates. On the first point, I was right; on the second, I turned out to be wrong, and happy about it.

Meanwhile, Soviet press officials, obviously responding to the side-by-side publication of the Sochi Six before and after forgeries in my books and articles, initiated artwork to repair what I had mockingly criticized as the clumsiness of the original forgery. In the original retouched version (published in Moscow in 1972), the missing cosmonaut had been removed and a shadowy, crude background painted in his place. In the two new versions of the photograph (published in 1982), inconsistent backgrounds were added. In one, a careful graphic artist had filled in the gap with a reconstruction of a missing staircase (visible in other photographs made at that same session but blocked by the missing man's body); in the other, a less conscientious but more creative artist had conjured up an intricate rosebush to fill in the space of the missing man! Placed side by side, the two new Sochi Six forgeries looked even more ridiculous than the original forgery.

For years I had been one of the lone voices in the West denouncing most of the lost cosmonaut stories as fiction. Imagine my astonishment in April 1986 when one of Golovanov's *Izvestiya* articles (the one entitled "Slander") accused a certain "Dzheymz Oberg of Khyuston" of being a leading instigator of the "secret dead cosmonaut" rumors! Supposedly I was the one who had originated the malicious slanders about the deaths of pseudocosmonauts Dolgov, Grachev, Zavadovsky, and Ledovsky. "I have never heard these names before," Golovanov dramatically asserted after allegedly trying to understand the source of "my" rumors. "Then I suddenly remembered: What am I racking my brains for, the whole thing is simply a fabrication!"

An official English-language "synopsis" of the Golovanov series, released by Moscow's Novosti news agency, went even further. "James Oberg maintained that four Soviet cosmonauts perished in space between 1957 and 1961. He gave their names as Dolgov, Grachev, Zavadovsky and Ledovsky," the agency alleged. "We should ask James Oberg of Houston to clarify who Grachev, Zavadovsky, and Ledovsky are, because he was the one who came up with those names." But I hadn't. Other writers had originated the names, and I had debunked them.

Golovanov also explained who they were only a few weeks later, in May 1986, in another of his articles in *Izvestiya:* In 1959 they had been testers of high-altitude aviation crew equipment who had been interviewed in Moscow papers and subsequently misidentified as "cosmonauts" by Western journalists.

In one of his April 1986 articles Golovanov scolded all those he accused of slandering the Soviet space program: "Fie, gentlemen. Shame on you!" I didn't feel particularly ashamed. He was the one who was misrepresenting my conclusions while plagiarizing my published research. When I learned that the newspaper was going to publish the series of articles in booklet form, I fired off a barrage of letters complaining of the errors and requesting corrections.

Golovanov's answer came not by return mail (I never got an apology or an explanation) but, in typical Soviet fashion, in a revision of history. The booklet was in due course published, and it purported to be based on the original newspaper articles—but it wasn't entirely. The section on my work was completely rewritten in full accord with my complaints; now I was a good guy, denouncing the "dead cosmonaut" rumors while (in Golovanov's own words) "preserving [my] reputation as a solid and objective journalist."

That's about as close to an apology as I ever expect to get, and I accepted it with the grace and humor Golovanov intended. He had made a clever pun on my name—*preserving* in Russian is *oberegaya*—and had gone out of his way to set the record straight (I now presume the original newspaper attack was based on a bad translation of my articles, not an ad hominem smear).

A disturbing aspect about the Soviets' reaction to revelations of their secrets was the insistence that any Western attempt to explore these secret mishaps had to have been inspired by malice, not by an understandable interest in the truth. Even during the period of *glasnost* the ancient and strident Russian paranoia toward foreign curiosity about their failures is very evident.

An ironic example of this attitude is provided by the story of Dennis Ogden, a British correspondent in Moscow in 1961. Just before Gagarin's flight, Ogden came up with the story that a pilot named Vladimir Ilyushin had been launched into space a week before Gagarin but had returned badly injured and had been hidden away. Golovanov wrote in *Izvestiya*:

I initially felt a certain irony and disgust [about the Ilyushin story]. This is a well thought out anti-Soviet propaganda campaign, whose authors have been striving for many years now to dupe millions of people and belittle our country's scientific and technical achievements. . . . It is quite natural and only to be expected that our enemies should desire to undermine the significance of [Gagarin's flight], to find some flaws in it, and to compromise it in some way. . . . Reports of this kind were designed for utterly ignorant and obtuse readers. I repeat: this is a campaign.

With Gagarin accorded near sainthood in the Soviet Union, the invocation of his name and the portrayal of Golovanov's targets as enemies of Gagarin were likely to be extremely effective in arousing hatred among his readers against his targets.

The ironic aspect of Golovanov's railing against "enemies" and using the Ilyushin story as a soapbox was that the story didn't originate with the USSR's enemies at all. It came from its friends. The author was Dennis Ogden, Moscow correspondent of the *Daily World,* the official British Communist party newspaper.

Ogden was in Moscow in 1961 and may have gotten a highly garbled version of Bondarenko's death, which, as we now know, really did occur twenty days before Gagarin's flight. Or he could have combined the fact that the pilot Ilyushin lived in his building and had suffered injuries (in an auto accident, it turns out) with the rumors about cosmonauts' injuries circulating around Moscow at the time. He played a good hunch that turned out to be wrong—but not out of malice for the workers' paradise, which, in fact, he adored.

Meanwhile, new reports about additional dead cosmonauts, still secret, keep coming in. Golovanov's 1986 article essentially denied there were any others after Bondarenko, but that is hardly credible. After all, it had been chief cosmonaut Vladimir Shatalov, on a visit to Houston for Apollo-Soyuz mission planning in 1973, who told his American counterparts that "six or eight" trainees had died (so many that he, as head of training, could not remember the exact number!). One of the women members of the 1973 Soviet delegation to NASA told her American contacts that she was the widow of cosmonaut trainee Anatoliy Tokov, a former test pilot, who died in 1967 while in training for a spaceflight.

In the mid-1960s there were credible reports of one parachute jump fatality and at least one automobile accident fatality (the same source fairly accurately claimed that several trainees had been expelled for participating in a drunken party— probably a reference to the Nelyubov scandal). So there apparently are many more names and many more young men whose sacrifices have not earned their memories the honor they deserve.

When author Michael Cassutt, researching a book on cosmonauts, submitted a Freedom of Information Act request on "cosmonaut training fatalities between 1960 and 1975" to the CIA, he received a curiously suggestive reply. His request for release of such documents was denied, but to aid him in his expected appeal, the CIA told him the dates of nine documents which fitted the description in his request. There had been one report on April 6, 1965 (soon after the Voskhod 2 space walk), three at the time of the Soyuz 1 tragedy in April 1967 and two others later that same year, and three more in the 1973–1975 period (possibly dealing with revelations during Apollo-Soyuz meetings). The existence of such documents certainly suggests the additional existence of reports of training fatalities, but further speculation is useless until the full reports are declassified.

When Golovanov listed dead American astronauts, those killed in training, airplane crashes, and space-related accidents, he perhaps significantly left out one name. Astronaut Edward Givens had been killed in an off-duty auto accident in 1967, and Golovanov did not list him as a "dead astronaut." Perhaps he felt that car crashes don't count as "training accidents." That might be a subtle hint that he did know of similar Soviet accidents and thus modified his standards so as not to have to include them on a list of "cosmonaut fatalities" if they were off duty when killed.

So the Soviets may have suffered several such off-duty cosmonaut fatalities but felt they didn't count. I have found more doctored pictures which show other faces retouched out and photographs of other faces not seen in any later official histories. Since these mysterious figures have been treated the same way as Nelyubov and Bondarenko, they may have shared similar tragic fates. The search goes on.

The Bondarenko tragedy in 1961 bears disturbing similarities to the catastrophe at Cape Kennedy in January 1967, when three Apollo astronauts also died in an oxygen-rich fire. Without knowledge of the Soviet disaster, NASA engineers grew careless in their own use of pure-oxygen atmospheres. On Apollo 1 (as in the Soviet cabin) there was material that turned out to be highly flammable under oxygen-rich conditions; on Apollo 1 (as in the Soviet cabin) there was no quick-release hatch; on Apollo 1 (as on the Soviet cabin), there was no effective fire-fighting equipment.

Could knowledge of the Bondarenko fire have prevented the Apollo 1 fire and saved the lives of Virgil ("Gus") Grissom, Edward White, and Roger Chaffee? The mere knowledge that a Soviet oxygen-rich fire had killed a cosmonaut might have been enough to forestall an American repetition of the disaster.

Khrushchev was Soviet premier at the time of the Bondarenko tragedy, and ten years later, during his enforced retirement, he remarked in his oral memoirs that in general such accident data should be shared. Discussing the Soyuz 11 tragedy, which had just occurred, he said:

> I believe the cause of the accident should be announced for two reasons: first, so that people who still have no idea what happened may be consoled; second, so that scientists might be able to take the necessary precautions to prevent the same thing from ever happening again. On top of that, I believe the United States should be informed of what went wrong. After all, Americans, too, are engaged in the exploration of space.

Yet when he had the chance, in 1961, Khrushchev did nothing to carry through this policy. Perhaps he regretted it.

His successors, including Gorbachev, continued this policy of nondisclosure, to the detriment of all space travelers. When in 1965 a space-walking cosmonaut on Voskhod 2 nearly died as the result of his difficulties in holding on and moving around outside the spacecraft, the Soviets did not warn their American colleagues at all. Instead, in numerous public statements, they raved about how easy and effortless the whole activity had been (only after nearly a decade did the cosmonauts admit to Western journalists that they had faked their initial reports). Consequently NASA planners and astronauts underestimated the troubles they could face in similar activities, and in mid-1966 an American astronaut was nearly lost in space when he unexpectedly encountered the same difficulties. Even as late as

1985, when cosmonaut Vasyutin faced a life-threatening infection in orbit, the Soviets refused to share the diagnosis of their problem with American space doctors. For the sake of the safety of future space farers, a bit more "cosmic glasnost" is required.

The Soviets, of course, have suffered their share of public space tragedies. The events were well known in generalities, but specific details were hard to come by.

In April 1967 cosmonaut Vladimir Komarov was killed when the parachute of his Soyuz 1 spacecraft failed during the return to Earth. Although the Soviet press deified Komarov's sacrifice, the full story behind the disaster was never reported. It involved intense Kremlin pressure for overambitious plans to reclaim the lost Soviet lead in the "space race."

Years later Victor Yevsikov, a Russian engineer who had helped develop the Soyuz heat shield, emigrated to America. Once here, he wrote a memoir of that period. He recalled:

> Some launches were made almost exclusively for propaganda purposes. An example, timed to celebrate international solidarity, was the ill-fated flight of Vladimir Komarov in Soyuz 1. . . . The management of the Design Bureau knew that the vehicle had not been completely debugged; more time was needed to make it operational. But the Communist Party ordered the launch despite the fact that four preliminary launches had revealed faults in the coordination, thermal control, and parachute systems. . . . None of the tests were successful. During the first test flight the heat shield burned during descent. This was due to a defect in the stopper in the frontal shield, where the module had been mounted on the lathe for machining. The module was thoroughly damaged. The three other failures had different causes. Malfunctions in those test flights were due to a breakdown in the temperature control system, malfunctioning of the automatic controls of the attitude control jets, and burning of the parachute shroud lines [by the pyrotechnic ejection system]. In those cases, the head shield served well.

Understandably these failures were never disclosed to the Soviet public. Neither was the Kremlin responsibility for the decision to launch Komarov's doomed mission prematurely. "It was rumored that Vasily Mishin, the deputy chief designer who headed the enterprise after Korolev's death in 1966, had objected to the launch," Yevsikov wrote, referring to the politics-inspired decision. "The flight had taken place despite Mishin's refusal to sign the flight endorsement papers for the Soyuz re-entry vehicle, which he had considered unready." It was a lesson in political pressure that NASA might have profited by as it prepared to launch *Challenger* on January 28, 1986.

Komarov's death has attracted its share of rumors, and the most gruesome is that his death screams were recorded by American monitoring stations. According to this account, he knew while still in orbit that he was doomed and took part in a series of tear-jerking conversations with his wife, with Premier Aleksey Kosygin, and with his associates in the space program. As he began his death dive back to Earth, he reported rising temperatures, then began screaming.

It is difficult to reconcile these accounts with what is reliably known about the Soyuz 1 space disaster. According to Yevsikov, major problems struck the spaceship almost immediately; at one point, an angry Komarov raged, "Devil-machine, nothing I lay my hands on works!" While he did have trouble orienting his craft for reentry, he eventually succeeded. And his descent crossed far northwestern regions of Soviet territory not normally covered by American space-tracking facilities likely to overhear him. A fouled parachute, which was the official Soviet explanation, would probably not have been noticeable to the pilot; alternately, disintegrating on reentry would have occurred during the normal "blackout" period when all radio communications are normally cut off. The "death screams" rumor just doesn't seem credible. Yet in April 1987, with *glasnost* in full swing, the anniversary-crazy Soviets ignored the twentieth anniversary of Komarov's death. Full official candor about the Soyuz 1 tragedy remains out of reach.

In March 1968 Yuriy Gagarin's death shocked the Soviet Union and the world. He had been on a routine jet training flight, with Vladimir Seryogin, his flight instructor. But the official Soviet news media never explained the crash, and dozens of private theories sprang up to account for it. In some, Gagarin was drunk, or hot-rodding, or actually attempting to shoot a moose from the opened cockpit. In others, the Kremlin had done away with him to avoid embarrassment over his womanizing or because he was a "Khrushchev creature." Officially Gagarin has become a "patron saint of space travel"; the details of his death appeared irrelevant to official histories. Only in early 1987 were the accident investigation files opened to Soviet journalists; while debunking rumors about drunkenness, the records were not kind to Gagarin's sainthood when the published reports attributed the crash to "pilot error."

In January 1970 cosmonaut Pavel Belyayev became the first spaceman to die of natural causes. He had reportedly been the lead pilot for a Soviet manned moon shot that was eventually canceled. The official cause of death was peritonitis following surgery for a bleeding ulcer. No explanation was ever offered for how such a simple operation could have gone so wrong for such a hero.

On June 30, 1971, the three cosmonauts of the Soyuz 11 crew perished on return to Earth. The USSR was plunged into national mourning, and eventually the fact of their deaths was turned to proof of the leading role of the Soviet Union on the space frontier (only stay-at-homes avoid the risk of dying). During the Apollo-Soyuz project Soviet engineers told their American colleagues about the air leak which caused three deaths, but such basic factual information has never been published in the Soviet media. It is enough for Soviet citizens to know they died gloriously. It is not necessary that ordinary Russians know how they died or to understand why General Nikolay Kamanin, the head of the Soviet cosmonaut program (who had fired Nelyubov a decade earlier), was himself summarily sacked soon after the tragedy.

On April 5, 1975, two cosmonauts were dumped onto the Altai Mountains in the world's first manned space launch abort. Pilot Vasily Lazarev and flight engineer Oleg Makarov survived a harrowing 20 G descent and then a bouncing ride down a mountainside before their spacecraft came to a safe stop. They came as close to dying as anyone can and later talk about it. Privately Soviet engineers told American colleagues that explosive separation bolts between the second and third stages had been miswired. For many years the Soviet public was left in the dark about these details.

All these events were known to the Soviet public and to the world, at least in broad outline. My own book *Red Star in Orbit* addressed these disasters, and others, in great detail. By coincidence or not, within a short time, a remarkable new series of Soviet newspaper articles began appearing, filling out details of events I had described.

The first article was published in *Krasnaya Zvezda* on January 29, 1983. An editorial preface informed readers that this was to be the first in a series to appear under the rubric "Orbits of Courage." The theme was to be the "difficult roads of space," and it would be handled by the unprecedented disclosure of many new details of Soviet space emergencies. There were just four installments over a three-month period; but it triggered similar articles in other newspapers in a chain reaction that went on for almost a year. All the articles were extraordinarily candid. The facts filled out were these:

In the first article cosmonaut Vasily Lazarev recounted the events of his aborted space shot on April 5, 1975, when his Soyuz 18-1 booster malfunctioned and his capsule bounced down a Siberian mountainside near the Chinese border. There had never before been a detailed written description in the Soviet press.

In the second article flight director Viktor Blagov gave a detailed account of the suspenseful Soyuz 33 mission in the spring of 1979, when a two-man spaceship was nearly stranded in orbit. The spaceship's main engine exploded, and specialists feared that it had damaged the emergency engine as well. Russian cosmonaut Nikolay Rukavishnikov was the first nonpilot to command a Soviet space mission, and he had a poorly trained Bulgarian guest named Georgiy Ivanov along as a copilot, for diplomatic purposes. Ivanov's most valuable suggestion, as it turned out, was that they break out the cognac they were carrying as part of the cargo to the space station they now could never reach. "I had a very little," Rukavishnikov recalled, "and Georgiy took a good drink."

In the third installment, which appeared in two parts on successive days to mark Cosmonaut Day (April 12), three-time space veteran Vladimir Shatalov, chief of the cosmonauts, reflected on how training helps cosmonauts prepare for emergencies. He recounted the landing control problems on Voskhod 2 in 1965 and the emergency unexpected splashdown of the two-man Soyuz 23 on a salt lake in Central Asia in 1976. He also disclosed the hitherto unknown fact that he himself had been waiting inside Soyuz 4 in 1969 when the launch was scrubbed and rescheduled. This happens fairly often in the American program, and the Soviet press always makes fun of such delays; but it never had admitted to having had any experience like it until this article.

The fourth installment was by cosmonaut Vladimir Titov, who described in detail the failure of his Soyuz T-8 to dock with the Salyut 7 space station. He and two crewmates had been launched only a few days after the publication of the preceding article. Upon their return a flood of letters from readers suggested that the cosmonauts be invited to tell their whole story in the same forum, and they subsequently did. The spaceship's radar boom had jammed, and without it they could not measure their position and speed relative to their target. "What we encountered in the actual flight was nothing like any of the unplanned situations known to us," Titov admitted in the article. An alternate procedure was developed overnight ("Now we were moving onto a completely untrodden path," Titov recalled thinking), but when tried, it did not work. "Velocity still seems quite high," the cosmonaut thought. "This is dangerous. Perhaps we will collide. I burn the engine to take the vehicle downwards. We are flying past the station. And so we failed to dock." Titov summarized in the uncharacteristically forthright report: "This experience in orbit was a difficult one." His account was published less than four months after his actual mission, with no prompting from the West. The Soviet space candor was at its apex.

Early in 1984 a lengthy article in *Literaturnaya Gazeta* provided even more graphic details of the emergency nighttime splashdown of two cosmonauts eight years earlier. During their hours on the icy lake the men were in grave danger of suffocation, drowning, or freezing, as extremely difficult weather conditions kept rescue helicopters from reaching them. All this drama and courage were barely hinted at back in 1976, when the splashdown had actually occurred.

The candor exemplified by the "Orbits of Courage" series abruptly ceased when Yuri Andropov died. This may or may not have been a coincidence. Under the brief rule of Konstantin Chernenko, there were no articles of this type. Dramatic failures occurred from 1983 to 1985, but the Soviets blandly reported that all was going well. The 1986 *Izvestiya* series by Golovanov, published under Gorbachev, rates as high as

"Orbits of Courage" in candor, though like its predecessor, most of its significant revelations were prompted by earlier fragmentary disclosures in the West.

Paradoxically the hero-worshiping Soviets denied at least one genuine space age hero—Valentin Bondarenko—his proper tribute and recognition because of their irrational, insistent secrecy. His tragic death in 1961 in the line of duty was not revealed for a quarter of a century. In the meantime, the Apollo 15 astronauts had left a plaque on the moon in 1971 in honor of fallen space heroes, both American and Russian. Bondarenko's name is not on it, and it should have been. How many other names should also have been there remains to be determined.

11

EXPLODING
ROCKETS

As the incident was later reported to me, the fuel somehow ignited and the engine prematurely fired. The rocket reared up and fell, throwing acid and flames all over the place. . . . Dozens of soldiers, specialists, and technical personnel [died]. Nedelin was sitting nearby watching the test when the missile malfunctioned, and he was killed.

—*Nikita Khrushchev's memoirs*
(not published in the USSR)

"I wish I could show you the satellite photographs," the retired American general told me across his desk in Washington, D.C. "The scorched area was just tremendous."

We were talking about what I had once dubbed the "Nedelin catastrophe." In terms of human lives lost, it was probably the greatest disaster of the space age, and it had been obscured in official Soviet (and American) secrecy since it happened on about October 24, 1960. It had taken me twenty years to piece together the information carefully, and disclose my preliminary conclusion in a full chapter of *Red Star in Orbit*. Unlike their recent tendency to come clean begrudgingly on some issues (such as dead cosmonauts) when they were prompted by the

West, nothing but nothing has caused the Russians to tell the story of their worst-ever space-related disaster.

The space age was barely three years old when the Nedelin disaster occurred. During that now all but forgotten era there was intense Kremlin pressure on Soviet space engineers to produce a series of "space spectaculars" (before an aroused America forged ahead, as it eventually did by the mid-1960s). First there had been the *Sputnik* on October 4, 1957, followed a month later by the "muttnik" satellite with a dog on board. In 1959 the Soviets launched a series of probes which first flew past the moon, then hit it, then swung around behind to photograph the hidden back side. In 1960, again well ahead of American efforts, the Soviets began orbital test flights of a recoverable spacecraft designed to carry a human pilot into space and back.

On October 10, 1960, they attempted another spectacular first, a probe toward another planet—Mars. Intended to send back data on Mars's environment, the unmanned spacecraft instead fell back into the atmosphere and burned up when its booster rocket's upper stage malfunctioned. A second launching four days later repeated the same problems and the same results.

There were three chances at success because three spacecraft and boosters had been built. The third booster and spacecraft were prepared with special care after the first two failed. Naturally there was intense pressure on Field Marshal Mitrofan Nedelin, commander in chief of the Strategic Rocket Forces, which launched Russia's space rockets, to produce the desired space spectacular before the launch window closed in a couple of days, causing the entire program to be delayed until the ever-shifting planets realigned themselves properly again, in two years.

When the launching command was given for the third shot on the evening of October 24, something different went wrong: The main rocket engines did not even ignite. All of the rocket's explosive charges were armed, and its fuel tanks were fully pressurized, and the signal to start the engines had been sent— but nothing happened. It just stood there on the launchpad, bathed in searchlights and fuming white clouds of supercold liquid oxygen.

Caution demanded that the rocket be carefully disarmed, its

fuel drained and its electrical systems deactivated. But to return it to launch-ready status would take many weeks, since corrosive chemicals had already been introduced into numerous pipes, and the batteries were already discharging. There just wasn't that much time left.

Under these circumstances, Mitrofan Nedelin made a fatal error and committed a gross violation of elementary rocket safety standards. From the launch bunker, where he had prepared to watch the expected success, he ordered a team of engineers to inspect the booster rocket immediately, as it unexplainably stood there on the pad. Since he was an experienced combat commander, he would not send men into peril he himself avoided, so he walked out to the base of the rocket while the inspection was being made. His staff stood dutifully nearby, and someone brought a chair for him.

The worst happened. The rocket exploded while being inspected, and scores of men, Nedelin included, were killed. A million pounds of kerosene and liquid oxygen flared up in a pyre which must have been visible for hundreds of miles.

An official obituary of Mitrofan Nedelin appeared in the Soviet press on October 26, 1960, saying that he had "died tragically in the line of duty" in a plane crash. There was no mention of a disaster or other casualties. The other victims were probably buried quietly with very localized mourning. Nothing else was ever officially released in the USSR, nothing to the present day.

Within weeks rumors of the disaster reached the West. An Italian newspaper reported on December 8 that there had been "a catastrophic explosion" at an unidentified missile site. Many observers mistakenly connected these rumors with others about an expected manned space shot.

The first mention of the disaster by a Russian source was made five years later. In 1965 the *Penkovskiy Papers*, the heavily edited (and possibly posthumously expanded) memoirs of the spy executed in 1962, gave this account: "When the countdown was completed, the missile failed to leave the launching pad. After fifteen to twenty minutes had passed, Nedelin came out of the shelter, followed by the others. Suddenly there was an explosion. . . . Over three hundred people were killed." In his account Penkovskiy mixed in a rumor that the rocket was nuclear-powered; it was not. He must have also exaggerated the number of people involved, just as others did after Chernobyl in the absence of hard news about the disaster. The ground crews would not have been that large. Nonetheless, Penkovskiy's account reflects rumors circulated within the Soviet government.

Khrushchev's posthumous memoirs, smuggled to the West on tape and subsequently published in 1970 and 1974 (and generally considered authentic on the basis of voiceprint analysis of the tape recordings), had this anecdote in the 1974 volume: "Just before the accident happened, the [chief designer] happened to step into a specially insulated smoking room to have a cigarette, and thus he miraculously survived. Dozens of soldiers, specialists, and technical personnel were less lucky."

In 1976, in an article in a British magazine, Russian exile Zhores Medvedev (widely considered a reliable commentator) gave his own description of what he called "an irreparable catastrophe": "When the [lift-off] was ordered, the ignition did not take place. . . . Nedelin irresponsibly decided to investigate the fault immediately. . . . Suddenly, the ignition started to work. The rocket fell because it was blocked by ladders. All the men and women in the area were killed."

Then the publication of my book *Red Star in Orbit,* with its full chapter on Nedelin, led directly to the unveiling of the most concrete and plausible explanation for the catastrophe. In 1982 Russian émigré N. Tiktin, now living in Israel, prepared a commentary on the book and submitted it to the Munich-based anti-Soviet magazine *Posev.*

According to Tiktin, the October 1960 catastrophe happened this way. After the launch command had not worked, safing (stand-down) commands were sent to the vehicle, but for some reason the new interplanetary stage did not receive its own command, and its internal timer kept clicking toward its planned ignition moment, about one full Earth orbit (ninety minutes) ahead.

Meanwhile, in the launch bunker, enough time had passed that Nedelin felt confident in going outside, up to the still-fuming booster. "They sent one engineer urgently for some piece of equipment," Tiktin wrote. "He jumped into a jeep and headed off," presumably to the assembly building for special tools and for additional personnel. They soon arrived in several buses and set to work.

In the simpleminded electromechanical brain of the fourth stage, the flight was proceeding normally. On the basis of the movement of its internal clock, it assumed that the four strap-on boosters had exhausted their fuel and fallen away after two minutes and that the main core stage had carried on for another several minutes before shutting off. A smaller third stage then was to carry the payload into a low parking orbit, about 100 miles high, before separating. During the brief coasting period a small control unit was to trim out any speed dispersions and aim the seven-ton fourth stage at a proper point in space. At a preset moment, when the rocket was precisely lined up for its path toward Mars, its own small rocket engine would ignite for several minutes, hurling the 2,000-pound payload forever free of Earth's gravitational grip.

(In a private letter to me, Zhores Medvedev had disclosed that he also had learned that the explosion was associated with a failure in the upper stage of the booster. This tiny detail from 1977 did not fall into place until years later, when Tiktin's material appeared.)

But when the expected moment came to break free of Earth's gravity, the fourth stage was really still sitting attached to the rest of the booster rocket, only 120 feet above the launchpad. Nevertheless, the canned instruction program commenced with a burst of flame.

Less than a foot directly below the fourth stage's nozzle was the top of the third stage's kerosene tank. It could have taken only seconds for the blowtorch flame to pierce the thin metal wall and detonate the twenty tons of kerosene.

People around the rocket might have had time to look up or even cover their heads as they shouted pungent Russian curses such as *Blyadskiy rot!* The explosion of the third stage would not necessarily have been fatal to those nearby, but it was not the end of the fireworks either.

In the five cylinders of the parallel-staged core and strap-on units were upwards of a million pounds of kerosene and liquid oxygen. The fiery blast from the small upper stages would have ignited all the lower stages simultaneously, and a fountain of flame would have cascaded down over the launchpad area.

Tiktin described the result as a "sea of raging fire" that swept for hundreds of yards "with a monstrous roar." But it was not a powerful concussion, in the sense of an explosion; it did little physical damage to hardware, and as Khrushchev recalled, one man inside a fireproof shack survived right on the launchpad. Only a 100 or 200 yards away several bus drivers were sitting (or sleeping) in their vehicles when they were showered with burning kerosene. Although terrified and somewhat burned as they fled, they were uninjured by the detonation. Apparently the buses' windshields were not even broken.

The launchpad itself was scattered with the smoking fragments of the rocket and the charred corpses of dozens of engineers and military officers. Belowground in the launch bunker those remaining at their posts would have been unharmed physically.

Why take the risk? Tiktin tried to explain it:

> Why did Marshal Nedelin so grossly violate the principles of safety? Soviet developments in rocket technology had gone through all the stages as had the German and American. Previous explosions of rockets on launch, even if they were secret, happened nevertheless. Could it again? Is it possible that among his staff of specialists (and not fawning courtiers, that was at other times) there wasn't a single one who understood just how dangerous was a rocket full of fuel— and a defective one at that? Surely it was known. But stronger pressure came from decades of the psychological complex of Soviet rule: the authorities know what to do; they are higher, things are clearer to them.

So the staff members went along, whatever their private feelings. And they died.

The debris was swept clean, and the scaffolding and piping were replaced. Damage to the concrete was patched up. By December a new booster had been mounted on the pad and was launched successfully on an earth satellite mission.

Tiktin's revelation has the flavor of a first- or secondhand account, rich in accurate detail, unpolluted by extraneous themes or exaggerated numbers. He has the refreshing habit of not speculating when he doesn't know something for a fact.

It is interesting to note that although the Soviets elsewhere made vigorous denials of various space catastrophe rumors, they have never made a single denial of the Nedelin explosion theory. At the same time, for more than a quarter of a century, there has been no confirmation.

It is proper to speculate on whether full disclosure of the

factors which led to the Nedelin catastrophe could have aided American space officials in avoiding our own disasters. There is one intriguing feature common to the Soviet 1960 tragedy and NASA's loss of the *Challenger* space shuttle in 1986.

As with the Soviet Mars probes in 1960, the pressure of planetary windows opening and closing was a key factor in the careless decision to launch *Challenger*. All three available orbiters—*Columbia, Challenger,* and *Atlantis*—were tightly committed to rigid launch windows: *Columbia* carried a number of experiments devoted to the study of Halley's comet, while *Challenger* and *Atlantis* were scheduled to deploy probes toward Jupiter (the fourth orbiter, *Discovery,* was already assigned to Vandenberg Air Force Base in preparation for a military launch). Because of earlier launch delays, the prelaunch processing for all these flights was behind schedule and was falling further behind day by day as the *Challenger* flight was put off for various minor reasons. So it seemed essential that *Challenger* be launched and get back so that it could be prepared for its reflight. The NASA launch schedule could not slip at all without forfeiting the planetary opportunities for more than a year in the two Jupiter missions and for seventy-six years in the case of Halley's comet.

So both the United States and the Soviet Union suffered terrible space catastrophes as a result of their not sufficiently comprehending the inexorable schedule demands of planetary missions and the fatal consequences of haste.

The Soviets have shown mixed degrees of frankness about some of their less spectacular space failures. Some spokesmen maintain the strict policy of stonewalling efforts at revealing information while others have produced bursts of unprecedented openness.

The textbook Soviet version of those early years of the space age remains unchanged: There were no Soviet space failures, and the latest encyclopedia is still bare of any troubling information. Cosmonaut Gherman Titov, who spent twenty-four hours in space in August 1961 and was subsequently grounded for medical reasons, explicitly denied even a single launch failure in a nostalgic propaganda piece published in 1985. It was history as pure perfection.

"In the USA there began a feverish race for leadership,"

Titov wrote. "From October 1957 to September 1959, when the first Soviet apparatus landed on the Moon, 35 space launchings were undertaken in the world. Nineteen of them ended in failure and all nineteen were American. Soviet launchings were five of the 35, and all were successful."

Titov was not speaking the truth. Western records show that there were at least five Soviet space launch failures in the same period, with more in the following months. The Soviet failure rate was comparable with that of the Americans, but the Russians have been much more successful at lying about it.

In private, Titov's boss, Nikita Khrushchev, was more candid in his memoirs:

Finally Korolev's rocket—which was called "semyorka" ["old number seven"]—was ready for testing. The first one exploded, as I recall. In fact, I think we had several unpleasant incidents. They either blew up on the pad or during liftoff. Fortunately, there were no human victims, but these accidents wasted a lot of money. However, such mistakes and sacrifices are inevitable when technological progress is at issue. After a while the "semyorka" was successfully launched.

Maybe nobody told Titov; he was only supposed to ride on a *semyorka,* not know anything about it and its dangers.

Newly declassified documents from the Lyndon B. Johnson Presidential Library, obtained and published by spaceflight historian Curtis Peebles, have detailed what intelligence sources knew of other Soviet space failures in that period. The first Soviet ICBM launch on May 15, 1957, ended in failure, as did all the next several. The first success occurred on August 3, and preparations then began to launch the *Sputnik* artificial satellite (on October 4). The third *Sputnik* in 1958 was preceded by a launch failure, and the first announced moon shot (in January 1959) followed three unpublished failures. Two more successes in 1959 were announced; three more failures in the same period were not, and have not been.

The document showed that in 1963 the Soviets resumed unmanned lunar probes, but their ambitions far outstripped their technology. As the CIA summary worded it, "They have attempted five lunar probes in the past 17 months, with only one partial success." That was in mid-1964. By early 1966, after another half a dozen failures, they finally succeeded in crash-landing a working television camera on the moon. The success is enshrined, justifiably, in the history books; the failures are not even in the footnotes.

Peebles also drew attention to some previously unknown incidents in the history of the Kosmos satellite program, which was a cover name for both small scientific satellites and large spy satellites. The first announced Kosmos was launched in the spring of 1962, but we now know that this success was preceded by two launch failures the previous autumn. The first Soviet spy satellite was launched at the end of 1961, but the booster failed; the first successful mission occurred the following spring. Both programs quickly achieved a success rate of 80 to 90 percent, but sporadic failures continued throughout the reporting period.

These revelations were merely confirmations of long-suspected estimates. It was hardly surprising that Soviet rockets failed about as often as American ones and that they were least reliable in the earliest launchings. Still, it was satisfying to have official American reports on the public records, since for too long both the Soviet government (in its pose of perfection) and the U.S. government (in its protection of intelligence methods) were engaged in a bizarre conspiracy of enemies to keep the world in ignorance of Soviet space failures. The Soviet motivation may be obvious, but that of the American intelligence services is not. Some sources and techniques may need protection, but it's also possible that confirming too many Soviet space and missile failures would reduce the image of the "threat" so useful to the Defense Department at budget hearings. Neither side wanted to publicize the truth.

As for revelations of Soviet space failures, more were to follow. The uncharacteristically candid Gagarin anniversary articles in *Izvestiya* in April 1986 revealed two completely secret launch failures in 1960 involving unmanned Vostok capsules, one on July 22 and the other on December 22. So we now have Soviet confirmation, the exact dates and the precise nature of the failures Peebles assiduously uncovered in declassified American documents. The July malfunction apparently merely involved the failure of a booster to lift off when commanded (although a midair explosion could have been what the author was delicately hinting at). The December failure involved a premature shutdown of several of the first stage's twenty engines, with the spacecraft automatically performing an abort sequence which saw the dog-carrying capsule jettisoned from the booster and safely recovered 1,000 miles downrange from the launch site. The unannounced December launch failure had followed an announced failure earlier that month, when a capsule burned up on return into the atmosphere.

The later launch failure had actually been mentioned once in the West, in Leonid Vladimirov's unfairly maligned *The Russian Space Bluff*, published in 1971. Reviewers considered this book inconsistent with their high opinions of Soviet space technology—that is, they thought the book just plain unbelievable. Hindsight continues to accumulate corroboration of more and more of Vladimirov's then-controversial assertions.

Soviet stonewalling still surrounds what is easily the second most spectacular and costly catastrophe in the space age, again involving the explosion of a giant Soviet rocket. The Soviets set a record here, the biggest rocket in history ever to blow up on the launchpad, but they have understandably declined to file with Guinness.

This happened on about July 4, 1969, only weeks before Apollo 11 landed the first men on the moon. On a launchpad at Tyuratam in Central Asia, a giant booster equal in power to America's Saturn V moon rocket was nearing its first flight test. The Soviets had been counting on further delays in the Apollo program, preparing their own teams of cosmonauts to circle the moon and then land on it—with any luck, ahead of American astronauts.

It never happened. The first booster, called "TT-5" by the U.S. military intelligence analysts (to designate the fifth new type of missile seen from Tyuratam), exploded on the pad. It might have been a launch attempt; it might (worse) have been a fueling exercise mishap, with support personnel nearby. Some rumors suggest fatalities, and others deny any.

The explosion at what the CIA called the "J complex" was tremendous (reportedly the pad has never been rebuilt to this day), and its shock waves were allegedly picked up on barographs in Stockholm 2,000 miles away. Weather satellite photographs supposedly showed the cloud; spy satellite photographs soon also showed the hole in the ground.

Not only has no Soviet-source information ever come out

about this event, but nothing has ever been released about the two subsequent in-flight failures (in June 1971 and November 1972) which led to the cancellation of the entire program. Face-to-face inquiries of Soviets are rewarded with blank stares or sincere-sounding denials. This truly was the "spaceship that never was."

Perhaps now that the new-design Soviet space superbooster, the Energiya, has successfully been launched, some hints about earlier setbacks may come out (many of the same rocket engineers were doubtlessly involved). But maybe not, since the motivation for not ever revealing these failures is understandable. The Soviets would have to admit that they had lost the moon race, even with the head start the whole world knew they had. They prefer to preserve the fiction that they never tried to send Russians to the moon.

Some catastrophic rocket explosions have eventually been publicized, after years of Western nagging and teasing.

When a manned Soyuz booster caught fire and exploded on the launchpad at about 11:36 p.m., Moscow time, September 26, 1983, the two-man crew was saved by the firing of their capsule's escape tower, which whisked them into the air seconds ahead of the explosion. Although the Soviets did not announce the event (choosing instead to crow over a near accident on a U.S. space shuttle mission a few weeks earlier), the American intelligence community detected it and leaked word to Washington journalists.

In the weeks that followed the explosion, Russian space officials in Moscow were confronted with a phalanx of curious Western reporters, and they responded uncharacteristically—with some truth. This was still during the period prior to Andropov's death when Soviet papers were running "Orbits of Courage" (see previous chapter) and other unprecedented disclosures. Later, at a postflight press conference with the team that had been in orbit at the time of the explosion (the new crew was to have relieved them on duty aboard the Salyut 7 space station), those cosmonauts also answered directly all questions from Western journalists, including details of the launchpad accident.

The events of that near-fatal night were highly dramatic. As the countdown was nearing zero, a fire broke out at the base of the booster. Perhaps it was electrical in origin; perhaps it was a fuel line leak. It may even initially have been in support equipment which had no connection with the rocket itself. Cosmonauts Vladimir Titov, thirty-five, and Gennadiy Strekalov, forty-three, were strapped into their seats with their hands folded in their laps, since the launch sequence was entirely automatic.

When the automatic fire-fighting equipment on the pad failed to put out the flames, the launch director had no choice but to order the capsule jettisoned. At any moment, as the flames ruptured the rocket's main kerosene tank, the entire booster was going to go up in a fireball replay of the Nedelin disaster of twenty-three years earlier.

The next seconds were ones of shock, panic, and desperation. The firing of the capsule's escape tower was supposed to be commanded by dual radio links once the rocket had lifted off and by a wire cable while it was still on the pad. When the abort command button was pushed, however, nothing happened; the flames had already cut the signal wire. The launch director then ordered that the radio command be issued, but the abort radio command console was not supposed to be armed until lift-off. There were frantic dashes up and down corridors at the launch control center, while horrified flight controllers at mission control in Moscow could only watch helplessly. As the seconds passed, the fire grew in intensity until on television monitors the entire spacecraft was enveloped in flames.

Somehow the proper signal was sent, and the capsule blasted free at an acceleration ten times the force of gravity. Within three seconds the capsule hit Mach 1 straight up. Far below, the booster exploded. The two cosmonauts were bounced in their seats as the capsule's emergency parachute popped open (they were too near the ground for the main chute to deploy properly); they slammed into the steppe two miles from the launchpad. They were battered and bruised but alive and within ten minutes were gratefully accepting a rescue worker's hip flask filled with vodka.

From their landing point, the cosmonauts could clearly see the flames roaring up from the launchpad. According to leading space engineer (and former cosmonaut) Dr. Konstantin Feoktistov, the booster wreckage burned for twenty hours.

Nothing ever appeared in TASS, or on the *Vremya* television news show, or on Radio Moscow.

The abort left the orbiting cosmonaut pair, Vladimir Lya-khov and Aleksandr Aleksandrov, in a real quandary. Their space station was in need of repair (they had suffered a nearly catastrophic fuel leak a few weeks earlier), and their return capsule was exceeding its design lifetime in orbit. As they struggled to carry out repairs originally assigned to their now-grounded relief crew, the Western press speculated that they were in danger of being stranded in orbit.

The Soviets denied it, of course, and the cosmonauts even-tually did land safely. Before then, however, NASA made a quick private study to see if the space shuttle *Columbia,* then being prepared for the first Spacelab mission, could reach the Salyut and rescue the cosmonauts. NASA engineers decided that they could carry out such a mission within thirty days of an official go-ahead. But they were not ever asked to do so. "There is no leakage . . ." insisted Soviet space scientist Yevgeniy Ta-bakeyev in mid-October. "The cosmonauts are alive and living normally."

In contrast with the official cover-up, cosmonauts were willing to admit the truth. On December 12, at his postflight press conference, Lyakhov was asked about the explosion. His words, captured on private tape recorders but absent from the official transcript, were entirely honest. "This is true," he confirmed. "The launching was planned for September 26. It is true there was an accident, but the crew was catapulted out and landed safely. We were told about this immediately, and as a result, our flight lasted longer than expected and our program of work was expanded." The next day all that the Soviet press reported was that after their prepared speeches "the cosmo-nauts then answered questions from newsmen." The bland Soviet papers did not report a single question or answer of that incredibly truthful press conference.

More than three years later, after commiserating over the *Challenger* disaster, the Soviets eventually got around to admit-ting that they, too, had blown up a manned spaceship, although fortunately nobody had been killed. In the spring of 1987 the news came out in quick succession from several different publications; perhaps some official had opened the floodgates on this long-suppressed story, but more likely it was another Soviet media push to define their new limits, with each publi-cation emboldened by the successes of earlier ones.

First on the streets was the weekly *Moscow News,* which

slipped the story deep inside a big article on spaceflight safety. A month later the crusading new editor of *Ogonyok*, Vitaly Korotych, told the National Press Club in Washington: "We had a big fight, but we finally published it." The accident had been very serious, he went on, admitting that "we were six seconds away from a Soviet *Challenger*." The following month two major newspapers (including the official Defense Ministry publication *Krasnaya Zvezda*) carried the story in even greater detail.

Little was new as far as Western experts were concerned, but for Soviet citizens it must have been a shocking revelation. Nobody seems to have asked why the explosion had been kept secret for so long.

The cosmonauts' first-person accounts added to the dramatic nature of the incident. "I didn't like the way the craft behaved," recalled Vladimir Titov, the pilot, describing the moments leading up to the explosion. "I sensed a ripple of unusual vibrations." At T minus twenty-five seconds, the cosmonauts noticed an unusual reddish yellow flame outside and black smoke rising past their small porthole. Nobody told them anything.

When the escape tower fired without warning, snatching their capsule to safety, the men quickly figured out that something was seriously wrong. There wasn't any time for fear. Had he felt relief at discovering he was still alive? No, Titov described experiencing an entirely different emotion as he descended by parachute from the world's shortest spaceflight: "Of course, we felt bitter at the efforts wasted in the preparation for the mission."

The new official Soviet candor on the accident was carefully circumscribed. It evidently was now allowable to talk of how the men felt. It was still forbidden to reveal what had caused the explosion in the first place. Also off-limits would be any speculation on whether full and prompt Soviet disclosure of the near tragedy might have reminded overconfident American space officials about just how dangerous spaceflight really is. NASA clearly forgot that teaching in early 1986; the Soviets (in particular two of their cosmonauts) had been given a cheap lesson on precisely that theme two years earlier but had chosen not to share it until it was too late for seven American astronauts.

*   *   *

After the secret dramas of 1983 the Salyut 7 space station entered a sort of "Twilight Zone" of space operations, in which even more than usual there were two parallel (and nonintersecting) dimensions of space activity, the real and the official. Over the next year and a half it twice suffered extremely serious breakdowns, first in its propulsion system and then in its power system. Both times courageous and ingenious teams of ground controllers and cosmonauts managed to repair the damage. However, all during these dramatic and suspenseful repair operations, Soviet spokesmen continued to claim that all was normal during "routine" space activities. Afterward the same officials boasted (justifiably) about outstandingly heroic work carried out in the face of incredible difficulties. Of course, it was news to the Soviet public that anything had ever gone wrong to start with.

First, in 1984 cosmonauts made an astounding six space walks to locate, diagnose, and fix a breakdown in the station's fuel plumbing. Yet officially the men were only performing "preventive maintenance and servicing," and the word *repair* did not appear in the press releases until the truly heroic job was completed.

Then, in early 1985, when another crew was in the final stages of training for return to the Salyut, all radio contact was lost with the temporarily unmanned space station. The Soviets assumed the worst and wrote the station off, and on March 1 TASS announced that "the planned program of work aboard the Salyut 7 orbital station has been fulfilled in its entirety." That notice of Salyut's death turned out to be premature. In the weeks after the official announcement space planners developed a strategy to send a fix-it crew into orbit and repair the station. In June they actually succeeded in doing so, and after (only after!) completing the repair were they allowed to boast about it publicly. Cosmonaut teams worked aboard the Salyut well into 1986, more than a full year after TASS had declared that all planned work had been completed.

Moscow's secrecy about rockets, exploding or otherwise, has accidentally caused the Soviet government considerable embarrassment as authorized statements fall into the yawning gulf between what is and what is said. Several striking examples from the pages of unofficial Soviet space history can provide elucidation and entertainment.

A series of nighttime launchings from the top secret Plesetsk Cosmodrome (several hundred miles north of Moscow) were witnessed in the sky by millions of ordinary Russians, and a major domestic UFO panic was ignited by a particularly heavy launch rate between 1977 and 1981. The government, eager to maintain the secrecy of the rocket base, was more than willing to encourage ordinary citizens to think the lights were from outer space—just not from a secret Soviet military rocket base. But by mid-1983 the Western press had been making so much fun over the official Kremlin discomfiture about "rockets that shouldn't have been there" that *Pravda* actually carried an article admitting to the existence of the hitherto nonexistent space center. The newspaper article even confessed that spurious UFO reports had often been caused by Plesetsk launchings.

In 1967 the greatest "UFO wave" in Russian history was set off by a specific but secret series of Soviet space weapons tests. Dummy thermonuclear warheads were placed into orbit from launchpads in Central Asia, circled the Earth once, and then plunged back into the atmosphere over the southwestern USSR just after dusk. Millions of startled and even frightened eyewitnesses were spread across vast areas of the Ukraine, the Caucasus Mountains, and the lower Volga Valley, and they described sensational overflights of "crescent-shaped UFOs" (actually the Mach 25 shock waves of the reentering warheads). An official commission from the Soviet Academy of Sciences, led by noted astronomers Lev Gindilis and Nikolay Kardeshev, concluded that the apparitions represented a genuinely anomalous phenomenon, certainly not anything to do with secret Soviet testing of illegal space bombardment weapons. That silly cover story has withstood the tests of time and, so far, even of *glasnost*.

On June 21, 1985, a secret Soviet rocket failure and subsequent Soviet government interagency confusion placed Moscow in technical violation of a major international space treaty. A new launch vehicle (called the "SL-16" by the American CIA) was carrying a test payload into orbit when the engines shut down prematurely. As the rocket fell back toward the atmosphere, several small pieces of the upper stage were routinely jettisoned and pushed into orbit by their extra forward speed. The pieces were so small—about the size of garbage-can lids— that Soviet space-tracking radars apparently missed them. The sharper-eyed American radars did not. When the time came for the monthly Soviet launch summary report to the United Nations, in accordance with the Convention on Registration of Outer Space Objects, the June 21 launching was not mentioned since as far as the responsible Soviet agency knew, it had failed (or never ever existed). That omission placed Moscow in clear-cut violation of the UN treaty's requirement that all rocket launchings putting anything into orbit had to be reported. Fortunately for the Soviets nobody at the U.S. State Department noticed the omission either, so the Americans never complained. The small junk Sputniks had quickly fallen out of orbit and burned up in the atmosphere, and the Soviets had by dumb luck avoided a major public relations debacle in being caught unambiguously in violation of international space law.

Such examples, both large and small, underscore the way that supersecrecy can trip up a government trying to conceal space activities and space failures. Rockets and satellites are highly visible to radars and eyeballs. Activities are bound to be observed, so the USSR's next best trick to maintain secrecy is probably to help those observations get misinterpreted as something misleading and harmless—such as flying saucers.

For centuries countryside shoppers have known better than to buy a "pig in a poke"; all merchandise for sale must be available for inspection by prospective purchasers. That time-tested maxim has recently been applied in its most traditional form to Soviet space and rocket technology, and the astounding result has been Moscow's official unveiling of space secrets about past and present failures.

The merchandise consisted of Proton booster rockets. The Soviet government, through a new commercial ministry called "Glavkosmos," has set out to sell orbital launch services to Western customers in the wake of the *Challenger*, Titan, and Ariane failures. Moscow offered to commercialize for "space transportation" its medium-scale Proton booster for Western communications or weather satellites, both for propagandistic pleasure and for cold, hard Western cash.

One major sticking point with potential Western customers

was full disclosure of the Proton's reliability. Without complete launch statistics (failures as well as successes), potential customers declared themselves unable to estimate the likely risks and the level of required insurance. Glavkosmos officials eager to do business with foreign customers accepted the demands for unprecedented candor. Some obscure and behind-the-scenes conflict with the space news censors ended in victory for Glavkosmos.

In August 1986 Dmitriy Poletayev, deputy director of Glavkosmos, was interviewed by a Soviet journalist on the commercial prospects for Proton launch services. "Reliability of carrier rockets is a matter of special urgency today," Poletayev remarked. "As regards the 'Proton,' its reliability factors are higher than all other types of rockets. . . . Out of a total of 97 launches since 1970, only seven were unsuccessful." The very existence of these seven big rocket failures had never been mentioned before.

A month later the agency's chairman went even further. At the annual International Astronautical Federation (IAF) congress in Innsbruck, Austria, Aleksandr Dunayev brought more detailed information packages for distribution to potential customers. According to Dunayev's data, the seven failures involved two scientific probes (on February 6, 1970, and again on October 16, 1975) and five heavy communications satellites being sent toward the standard twenty-four-hour geosynchronous orbit high over the equator. Three of those five failures had occurred over a five-month period in 1978 (which also saw three successful Proton launchings): On May 27 there had been a first-stage failure; on August 17 there had been a second-stage failure; on October 17 there had been another second-stage failure. Two more Proton rocket launch failures occurred in the second half of 1982: On July 23 another communications payload was lost during a first-stage failure, and on December 24 yet another communications satellite was lost as the result of a Proton second-stage failure. These official disclosures were absolutely unprecedented.

Almost all these unsuccessful Soviet spaceflights had been unknown to the Western public, although presumably the high-security military intelligence agencies had observed and noted them. Classified military documents on these subjects did occasionally "leak"; the Washington, D.C., newsletter *Soviet*

Aerospace on October 23, 1978, carried a report that a geosynchronous Proton launch failure had been detected by Western intelligence agencies the "previous week." This turned out to be accurate, for eight years later, as noted, Dunayev admitted to the failure of October 17, 1978. Separately, in testimony before Congress in 1983, U.S. intelligence officials disclosed that there had been three Soviet launch failures the previous year. Dunayev's 1986 list gave two Proton failures for that year (the third must have been an as yet undisclosed routine launch of a smaller rocket).

While the Soviet disclosures were astonishing, Western space scorekeepers did note a few omissions. Nothing was released about the first five years of the Proton's operations (1965–1969), when only five of about fifteen shots succeeded. And one Proton failure from the supposedly fully revealed 1970–1986 period somehow got overlooked; it was the May 1971 Mars shot which got stuck in parking orbit (see Chapter 9) and was officially mislabeled ("dislabeled"?) as the "Kosmos 419 scientific satellite." Additionally, about twenty other Proton boosters had been launched since 1970, carrying payloads destined only for low Earth orbit (they did not carry a so-called D-stage for extra kick to higher altitudes), and at least three of them were already known to have failed (a test flight in August 1970; a Salyut space station in July 1972; and a mysterious space plane test in August 1977). But these were just minor details which only accentuated the unusually open authorized revelations of other deep Soviet space secrets about what had only recently been a completely taboo topic, space and rocket failures.

It hadn't just been the big rocket's batting average which had been top secret. For twenty years the Proton rocket's very appearance had been a Soviet state secret, and no photographs or drawings had ever been released. But beginning with the USSR's launchings of the robot Vega probes toward Halley's comet in December 1984 atop Proton rockets, videotapes became available. Then, in early 1986, a large-format picture book on Soviet space activities, published in Moscow, contained more than a dozen high-quality views of Proton launch vehicles from almost all angles. The one exception was the engine compartment at the base of the rocket, which contained the powerful rocket motors; it was not portrayed anywhere.

Belgian space journalist Theo Pirard confronted Glavkosmos's Dunayev with this oversight, during an interview at the IAF congress at Innsbruck. "Why are you not disclosing in Proton pictures the engines of the first stage?" he asked. Dunayev gave a flippant and irrelevant reply. "Is it so necessary to see these engines?" he countered. "They are working perfectly. Is it only to satisfy curiosity? The Proton vehicle is like a woman: its lower part could remain the most mysterious one. . . ." But then he promised to show such pictures to "serious customers," and later reportedly did so.

Dunayev was apparently feeling confident about his product, as any good salesperson should. In mid-December 1986 he issued another sales pitch to potential customers, bragging (correctly) that "No single failure has occurred in the last 35 Proton launches." Dunayev's intemperate boast seemed too big a temptation for the fates to overlook, so the outcome was predictable: On January 30, 1987, the very next Proton launching, which could have been Dunayev's thirty-sixth straight success, wasn't. Carrying a routine communications satellite, the rocket failed ignominiously in a low parking orbit and burned up the next day. Even worse, another Proton launching the following April also failed when it deposited its three navigation satellites into a hopelessly lopsided orbit.

A Glavkosmos delegation visited the United States shortly thereafter. The Soviets had tied their sales strategy to candor, and this now was the test. The January failure, they explained, had been caused by miswiring which prematurely instructed the payload to cut loose from the still-firing booster; the April failure had involved a new-model upper stage, specially modified for a unique type of target orbit (commercially available Proton rockets would still use the standard tried-and-true version). With their recent experiences of other types of full disclosure from the Soviets' spaceship salespeople, the Americans who hosted the Glavkosmos delegation discovered that they found the Soviet explanations plausible and credible.

If a generalization is possible on this theme, it seems to be that exploding rockets are mighty difficult to cover up successfully for long and that the Soviets, in the recent past, appear to have realized this. Just how much more deeply they now will dig into their less glorious early chapters of space history remains to be seen. Perhaps, for hard Western currency, Glavkosmos might even be prevailed upon to sell archival Soviet documentary film of the vast scorched areas which once marked the funeral pyre of Mitrofan Nedelin and the others who died with him at the launchpad that tragic October evening so long ago. But perhaps, for now at least, that is still expecting just a bit too much.

12

REACTORS FROM THE SKY

Those who circulate absurd rumors about the Kosmos-954 and who are trying to cash in on them undermine the basic principles of international cooperation in the exploration and use of outer space and are doing serious harm to the cause of strengthening mutual trust and understanding between peoples.

—*Leonid Sedov, USSR Academy of Sciences, 1978*

At the dawn of the space age, as Sputniks and Explorers and Vanguards orbited the Earth, some humorists had joked that the saw about "what goes up" no longer deserved its mandatory ending of "must come down."

For many cases, this turned out to be true. There are satellites in high orbits that will take millions of years to fall back to Earth, and there are probes which have forever escaped Earth's own gravity and even that of the Sun itself.

But for several glaring counterexamples in recent years, the proverb has reasserted itself with a vengeance. Smaller satellites fell frequently but flared harmlessly in the atmosphere as they disintegrated. In 1979 the giant plummeting hulk of the derelict American Skylab space station delivered the lesson as it landed in fragments large and small on Australia. Of even more concern, falling Soviet RORSATs (the term, invented by U.S. military intelligence analysts, stands for "Radar Ocean Reconnaissance Satellites," or all-weather naval space spies powered by nuclear reactors) ignited worldwide anxiety during unpredictable but unavoidable death plunges.

The fall of Skylab became a world media event, as planet-wide anxiety followed its final weeks, days, and hours. But when the significantly more dangerous Soviet satellites fell, Moscow remained silent for as long as it could and then issued only bland and baseless assertions that there was nothing to worry about. But the realities of space operations make it a safe bet that such a radioactive satellite fall will happen yet again, and if Moscow's lack of warning and cooperation is repeated, the dangers may be even higher.

Since 1967 about four dozen Soviet satellites of the RORSAT class have been launched into orbit. As a first approximation, such vehicles can be identified by their distinctive orbital path and subsequent maneuver sequences. Reliance on these characteristics is necessary since Moscow consistently and inaccurately labels them "routine Kosmos payloads" for "scientific exploration of outer space" and has always insisted that the satellites were devoted to purely peaceful purposes.

The only two satellites which were ever explicitly admitted to carry reactors, and then only after the fact, were Kosmos 954 (the one that crashed onto Canada in January 1978) and Kosmos 1402 (which dropped pieces onto the South Atlantic and Indian oceans in early 1983). But all the other nuclear-powered ROR-SATs share the distinctive orbital flight paths of the ill-fated Kosmos 954 and 1402. Their initial orbit is only about 150 miles high, inclined to the equator at sixty-five degrees. Backtracking the flight path shows their launch site to have been Tyuratam, east of the Aral Sea in Soviet Central Asia.

Normally, after several days or weeks, each satellite suddenly separates into sections, with some pieces burning up quickly and another piece (the one with the reactor on board) rocketing 500 miles higher into space, where it goes dead and begins a slow derelict tumble in an almost permanent graveyard orbit. This has happened nearly all the time whenever such a satellite has been launched.

The explanation for these puzzling maneuvers lies in the nature of the mission. The satellites are using active radar pulses to seek and track naval forces on the world's oceans. Each transmits a radio pulse, then listens for the returning echoes and picks targets out of the patterns. Since both outgoing and returning pulses dissipate at the famous inverse squared law (twice as far means only a quarter as powerful), the combined efficiency of such a passive search radar system follows an inverse fourth power law: At twice the range the signal would be only one *sixteenth* as strong. Since effective range is so limited, the satellite must fly as low as possible, and the satellite almost has to graze the upper atmosphere. A powerful electrical source is needed. Large wings of solar cells would vastly increase the satellite's air drag and hasten its already precipitous decay rate, so the Soviets chose to use a small nuclear reactor called the "Topaz." It puts out up to 100 kilowatts of heat, which is converted into about 10 to 20 kilowatts of electricity. But the reactor, fueled with 100 pounds of uranium dioxide pellets (more than 90 percent of which consists of the U-235 isotope), also produces highly radioactive isotopes (the "daughter products" in the reaction). These isotopes, if dropped back into the atmosphere, could endanger anyone coming in contact with the debris.

These dangerous isotopes are the motivation for the boost at the end of the mission. The reactor portion is parked in an orbit sufficiently high that it will not fall back to Earth for many, many centuries. By that time the "daughter products" will have cooked down to much lower levels of radioactivity; well before then some sort of orbital tow truck service may have been able to recover them safely anyway.

The two spectacular failures in this flight plan (at least the two we found out about) were due to problems with this last, "parking" phase. Kosmos 954 was launched on September 18, 1977, but after about ten weeks the satellite suddenly and unexpectedly "died" for no apparent reason. Soviet ground controllers repeatedly radioed commands to fire the final boost rocket motor; but this sequence never occurred, and the whole satellite fell back into the atmosphere within a few weeks. Kosmos 1402 was launched on August 30, 1982, and it performed properly up until the final boost phase, which was commanded to occur on December 26. The satellite separated into the appropriate sections; but the reactor section's rocket motor never fired, and the unit rapidly slipped back into the atmosphere.

Both occasions were similar in that the Soviets remained mum about their problems until American officials made discreet diplomatic inquiries. In 1978 the Carter administration made a high-level decision not to go public with its knowledge of the impending fall, allegedly out of altruistic concern over worldwide public panic. More probably State Department officials realized that the Soviets might use public disclosure as a pretense to refuse any cooperation at all (such as privately passing on crucial data on the satellite design), whereas they might show their appreciation for American cooperation in the cover-up by dribbling out technical details useful in any possible recovery or cleanup operation. But they didn't; their disclosures consisted almost entirely of data which Western experts already knew or had guessed. Long after the satellites had broken down in space, Soviet spokesmen (including top scientists from the prestigious Academy of Sciences in Moscow) were still faithfully assuring the world that "all is normal" in orbit— and it wasn't.

Leonid Sedov, a leading space scientist with the Soviet Academy of Sciences, insisted the Kosmos 954 satellite had been launched "in accordance with our program for the exploration and use of outer space," not even hinting the "use" was as a military spy vehicle. The fall to Earth wasn't even the USSR's fault, Sedov claimed. "It may be assumed that the satellite collided in flight with some other object [on January 6]."

The official Soviet sequence of events, as chronicled by Sedov and others, was grossly deceptive. The satellite, launched on September 18, had completed its low orbit mission by the end of October. But instead of being boosted to a safe higher orbit, the satellite began slipping closer to the atmosphere. It was still under ground control, so it remained "horizon stable" in a low-drag orientation. At that rate, reentry was not expected until April. But on January 6 the satellite went out of control, probably because of some internal breakdown or exhaustion of consumable supplies (Sedov's collision excuse is preposterous; the satellite was already doomed two months before), and as it tumbled occasionally sideways along its orbit, its air drag soared and its decay rate increased by five or ten times. Instead of a mid-April reentry, three months away, American analysts in mid-January saw that the satellite was coming in within ten days! On January 12 White House National Security Adviser Zbigniew Brzezinski contacted Soviet Ambassador Anatoly Dobrynin. Only at that point, months after they had known that the reentry was unavoidable, did the Soviets acknowledge the problem.

Even in the last days of the satellite's fall, predictions of its final target were uncertain. In the hours prior to its actual impact, Kosmos 954 had crossed Mexico, central North America, Iceland, Scotland, central Europe, Greece, Egypt, West Africa, the Indian and Pacific oceans, California and central Canada, the North Atlantic, Spain, Algeria, the length of central Africa to Johannesburg, then the Indian and Pacific oceans again (including right over Hawaii) before it finally plunged into northern Canada. Had the satellite survived for another few hours its path would have taken it over the North Atlantic, West Africa, the Indian Ocean, eastern Australia, the Pacific, across northern Canada again, and so forth. It could as easily have come down anywhere along that line.

Fortunately the RORSAT hit a lightly populated region with white snow cover, making the detection of debris relatively easy. But even in such a sparsely inhabited area people were accidentally exposed. Two adventurers on a cross-country trek spotted a large tangled piece of plumbing from the satellite lying on a frozen creek, walked over, and picked it up. Luckily it was later determined that this particular piece was not radioactive.

Shortly after the crash Sedov discussed the whole affair on Radio Moscow and sincerely assured his Soviet listeners that "the termination of the existence of the Kosmos 954 over the northern part of Canada did not create any danger for the population of the area." That was patently untrue. The worst pieces, which could deliver fatal doses within hours if anyone had picked them up, had not even been located at that point. Sedov inaccurately asserted that the reactor "was designed in such a way as to ensure its destruction and burning up on entry in the dense layers of the atmosphere." This, too, was untrue, but the Soviet press never informed its public that the Canadians were recovering many substantial pieces on the ground.

Over the subsequent several months a joint U.S. and Canadian exercise named Operation Morning Light combed the entire search area, between Yellowknife and Baker Lake. Using highly sensitive airborne radiation detectors, the searchers located debris down to fingernail size and smaller. Everything was picked up. The teams recovered basketfuls of debris, some the size of pepper flakes but some many feet in length. Most pieces were dangerously radioactive because of contamination from the reactor core's isotopes (the virulently radioactive daughter products, not the much more gently decaying U-235, were the culprits) and could have posed genuine health hazards if they had fallen over a more populated area.

The search would have been greatly facilitated if the searchers had known what to look for and what sort of radioactive isotope might be out there waiting for them. The Canadians officially asked Moscow for specific details. What were the full nature and amount of the fuel, and the type of reactor, and its construction? What was the chemical and alloy composition of the components of the reactor? What kind of shielding had been employed? Most particularly, what particular items and indications would the Soviets have looked for if the satellite had landed in the USSR (that is, what had they already prepared to look for, in their own undisclosed contingency recovery plans)? There were many questions, but even only a few answers would have been helpful.

The Soviet responses were useless for the search. They essentially said "nothing." The Soviets did allow that there had been 100 pounds of U-235 on board but blandly assured the Canadians that "there is no danger of an explosion" (the last thing anybody was afraid of). Moscow expressed regret that its offer to send technical teams had allegedly been refused (the Canadians didn't know what this remark referred to) and also expressed annoyance that the Canadians had taken so long to notify them officially that the satellite had hit Canada (as if the Soviet embassy in Ottawa didn't get newspapers). They waived all rights to the return of the pieces and allowed Canada to "continue to dispose of them at its own discretion."

Months later the Soviets did respond to Canadian lists of recovered debris with assurances that all had been found and the searchers could stop looking. On May 31 they belatedly stated, "The beryllium reflector included six moving elements that already have been found by you, and several tens of rods of cylindrical form, most of which were discovered." It was a waste of time to keep looking for the rest, they said. "The probability of all those rods in the reflector reaching the surface [intact] after the reactor's core disintegrated is excluded." But these assurances no longer carried any credibility.

The Canadian historian of the recovery operations, C. A. ("Dick") Morrison, had this succinct description of the value of Soviet inputs to the problem: "The lack of specific technical information, both before and after impact, was a serious problem. In this regard the Soviets were being, and would continue to be, singularly uncooperative." The official Canadian damage claim later used much the same wording: The "clear and immediate apprehension of damage" was not ameliorated by the Soviet failure "to provide timely and complete answers to the Canadian questions. . . ." Yet Sedov had told the Soviet public on February 4 that "the Canadian government was informed about the satellite, its power unit, as well as measures that might have to be taken in case the remnants of the satellite were discovered." Sedov was departing from the truth; to put it most charitably, he was grossly exaggerating the value of meager information which Moscow did release.

With his misunderstanding (or misrepresentation) of events, Sedov expressed outrage at some Western reactions to the fall. He denounced "absurd accusations" that the satellite was a flying bomb or carried a laser gun (nobody to my knowledge had ever seriously suggested these). He scrupulously (and arguably not by accident) avoided addressing the most common Western accusation: that the satellite was a naval spy platform.

Article II of the 1972 United Nations treaty entitled "Convention on International Liability for Damage Caused by Space Objects" states that "a launching State shall be absolutely liable to pay compensation for damage caused by its space object on the surface of the earth." The Canadian government filed a claim for $6,041,174.70 with the Soviet ambassador in Ottawa. Negotiations were held throughout 1980, and on November 22 the Soviets agreed to pay fifty cents on the dollar, Canadian.

The 1978 failure had cost the Soviets much more than just the damage claims. They surely spent at least ten times as much in redesigning, rebuilding, and requalifying the ROR-

SAT hardware. But the military mission to locate Western naval fleets was important enough that they spent the necessary time and money, and two years later, without any fanfare or even discreet diplomatic warnings, they quietly resumed launching RORSATs.

While there was some minimal press coverage of the resumption based on analyses by Western experts on Soviet space activities (the Soviets refused to comment), nobody in the West took much notice, and nobody complained (who wanted to question Soviet intentions and be branded an enemy of world peace by Sedov?).

Although Western experts didn't know it at the time, the Soviets had implemented an additional safety feature in their reactor disposal procedure. In the gap of more than two years between the Kosmos 954 debacle and the resumption of the RORSAT program, with Kosmos 1176 on April 29, 1980, two modifications were made in the standard flight program: The low-orbit active mission duration was almost doubled, to more than four months, and the high-orbit parking phase included the reactor section's jettisoning a small package after reaching its final high orbit. The increased lifetime was evidently due to use of a more advanced model of the reactor and to larger supplies of rocket fuel to counteract the mile-a-day orbital decay induced by atmospheric drag. The jettisoning turned out to be the ejection of the reactor core itself from its surrounding structure, an additional safety feature which proved to be crucially important.

After two years of routine operations (consisting of eight launchings), disaster struck again. Kosmos 1402 was launched on August 30, 1982, and it completed its operational mission on December 28. But the boost to high orbit failed. The news came out from private sources, since the governments involved apparently again had intended to keep it secret to "avoid panic." Noted the highly critical *New York Times:* "One failure is bad luck, two is bad management. . . . The Soviet Union is playing Russian roulette with the world. That the odds are long is no excuse for exposing others to some danger. The rain may fall on the just and the unjust alike, but no one should have to expect being showered with radioactive space junk from a bungled military spy mission."

The news of an impending RORSAT crash again swept the

world, even as far as Moscow. At a press conference on other space activities, held on January 6, 1983, academician Vladimir Kotelnikov (director of numerous international cooperative space projects) was asked about the rumors. "Programmed operations are being conducted with the satellite," he assured his audience (a week after it had gone dead). "At present there are no dangers at all regarding the destiny of this satellite." Again, the official Soviet assurances were patently phony.

However, the new safety features implemented after the Kosmos 954 incident had already been activated aboard the doomed Kosmos 1402. The isotope package was automatically jettisoned from the reactor (probably by a "dead man timer," which would not even need ground command). Hence the isotopes were not going to be protected by the satellite's structure during the fiery atmospheric reentry. They could be expected to pulverize completely, and the most radioactive material would thus be safely dispersed in the upper atmosphere at concentrations well within safety levels. The large reactor structure's debris, which could be expected to survive passage through the atmosphere, would also therefore not be badly contaminated.

After the Kosmos 1402 troubles had become public, Soviet spokesmen (after belatedly admitting the satellite was indeed falling back to Earth out of control) bravely asserted that this new improved design was "perfectly safe." But cynics would not let them forget that five years earlier a similar coterie of reassuring officials had been piously proclaiming, even after the Canadians had begun gingerly to retrieve the "hot" remains of Kosmos 954, that the "brilliant design" of that satellite had "absolutely ruled out any possibility of ground contamination." If the new design really was so perfectly safe, the cynics asked, why did the primary Soviet flight plan even bother to boost the reactor into the high graveyard orbit? That maneuver required many times as much fuel as would be needed for a controlled reentry over the USSR itself. Surely such confidence in the safety of the backup system should lead to a decision to use it all the time, since it was so much more fuel-efficient.

In counterattack on this new group of Western complaints, the Soviet press began a campaign of ridicule for precautions being taken. Such Western concern, reported the Soviet news media, had more ominous implications. "In the West they launched a noisy propaganda campaign around the 'fall of the Soviet satellite,' " TASS said. "It is not difficult to guess who needed that provocative hullabaloo and why. The militarists from Washington and NATO use it as a smoke screen to cover up their own aggressive preparations."

A leading Soviet space scientist provided some unusually candid insights on January 16 (shortly before the satellite plunged back into the atmosphere). In a long interview in *Pravda* Dr. Oleg Belotserkovskiy, rector of the Moscow Physico-Technical Institute, hinted broadly and for the first time that Kosmos 1402 wasn't doing precisely what had been planned for it from the beginning. "There can be factors preventing the transfer to a high orbit from occurring," he admitted, "and therefore additional measures are envisaged in order to guarantee safety from radiation." The one chosen for this case (the Soviets never admitted having launched dozens of similar reactors) was dispersal in the atmosphere. "The withdrawal of the fuel core with its radioactive fission products from the reactor ensures guaranteed conditions for it to burn up in the dense strata of the atmosphere and for the materials to be dispersed into finely divided particles."

That apparently was exactly what happened. The main body of Kosmos 1402 burned up over the Indian Ocean on January 23, 1983, after passing across Central America, the Appalachian Mountains, Iceland, Scandinavia, Estonia, the Ukraine, the Caucasus, and Iran; the smaller core itself flamed out over the South Atlantic a few weeks later. In both cases searching American aircraft found no trace of radioactivity above background levels.

The Soviets must have been satisfied with the safety of their modified RORSAT hardware. Only a year and a half later, on June 29, 1984, they launched Kosmos 1579, allegedly just another "scientific research satellite." It was a new RORSAT, and it was followed by others in the subsequent years. Until one falls out of the sky again, it's likely public concern won't be aroused.

There are different ways the world could find out, and an official Soviet announcement is not a leading candidate. Perhaps the reactor jettison safety system will work again, and a Kosmos 1402 replay will result. Or perhaps next time the satellite will go dead before this ejection can occur, and a

Kosmos 954 replay, with the dangerous isotopes shielded through reentry by the satellite's structure, will occur. Or perhaps there will be some new variation of "the reactor in the sky is falling."

Meanwhile, the actual safety of the "reactor graveyard," the high orbits where the dead RORSATs are parked, has been questioned recently by space experts. They have pointed out that the growing belt of space junk circling Earth is thickest just at the altitude chosen by the Soviets to dump their reactors. Also, expended rocket stages from various Soviet programs crisscross that region of space, raising the distinct probability that one or more of the reactor vessels could be ruptured by a collision. The debris could even be knocked closer to Earth. In any case, the smaller fragments, once formed, would tend to decay much more quickly than expected and could be hitting the atmosphere within decades instead of centuries. So far none of the reactors being tracked shows any sign of giving off pieces, but the statistics of space junk say it is only a matter of time.

The Soviets have already been the apparent victim of one orbital "hit and run." In 1982 one of their navigation satellites suddenly disintegrated. Exploding satellites are not at all rare, but their destruction usually results when leftover on-board fuel mixes, boils, or otherwise goes unstable. This satellite had no such fuel, and the dispersal pattern of the fragments was more characteristic of impact with a piece of space junk than of internal explosion. The Soviet government never acknowledged the disintegration (it was probably a piece of an old Soviet satellite or rocket that had hit the new spacecraft) but reportedly professed even more interest in international efforts to control space pollution by junk and debris. Meanwhile, Western space experts were reassured that their statistical projections of space collisions had been verified.

A late-1986 report by Soviet-spacecraft expert Nicholas Johnson of the Teledyne-Brown Corporation office in Colorado Springs, Colorado, expressed anxiety that the existing expended reactors could suffer the same fate as the navigation satellite. "The threat posed by these [reactors] extends not only to contamination during eventual reentry into Earth's atmosphere, but also to other Earth orbiting satellites, including manned spacecraft," Johnson wrote. "Current space storage practices, particularly by the Soviet Union, are insufficient to ensure the protection of the Earth's biosphere from unnecessary radioactive elements in both the near term and the far term."

Officially the Soviets refuse to acknowledge their responsibility for the dozens of radioactive hulks in orbit. All inquiries have been rebuffed. The only two nuclear reactors ever launched aboard Soviet spacecraft, according to the official view, were aboard Kosmos 954 and Kosmos 1402. The orbiting reactor graveyard, in Moscow's eyes, does not exist, and therefore, there can be no danger from it, nor any Soviet responsibility for it.

The Soviet safety record on RORSATs is probably much worse than even the two reentry events and the careless orbital storage of dead reactors suggest. On several other occasions trouble seems to have developed with such satellites. On a few occasions additional radioactive contamination probably occurred.

The earliest test flights were the most troubled, as is hardly surprising in any space program. On the first six flights, between 1967 and 1973, only one payload exceeded ten days in its operational orbit before being boosted and parked. A few were hurriedly retired after only a day or two in space, suggesting immediate massive control failures. On April 25, 1973, a launch attempt failed when the booster rocket fell back into the atmosphere west of Hawaii; another launching attempt reportedly failed in January 1969, when the rocket blew up on the launchpad.

The accident near Hawaii reportedly resulted in significant radioactive contamination of the atmosphere, as detected by dust-collecting American research aircraft. The mix of isotopes revealed a startling and dangerous Soviet practice: The nuclear reactor was apparently turned on—that is, it was made to "go critical"—on the launchpad, prior to blast-off. Standard safety practices endorsed by the United Nations now call for all reactors to be launched "cool"—that is, not generating the highly dangerous "daughter isotopes"—and subsequently commanded on by remote control only after they have reached a safe, stable orbit. The Soviets did not start out following this UN-approved procedure, possibly because the Topaz design requires a very precise alignment of control hardware to avoid an unstable meltdown, and such a ticklish operation could not be remote-controlled. There is no evidence if they have subsequently adopted it.

Soviet publicity behavior with the RORSAT accidents shows variations on typical themes. The Soviets never volunteered information about accidents without strong Western prodding, and even then they responded only occasionally and with minimal information. No acknowledgment of the true purposes of the RORSATs, or technological explanations of the likely causes of their failures, was ever made. The charade about the RORSATs' being "peaceful scientific satellites" was steadfastly maintained. To their own people, the Soviet officials posed as cooperating fully with Western nations yet routinely withheld data which could have been useful to Western monitoring and cleanup activities. The continued existence in space of dozens of other still-radioactive Soviet space reactors was ignored.

Anyone questioning any aspect of the Soviet line was attacked with paranoid vigor as an enemy of international understanding and goodwill. To object to the Soviet endangerment of the whole world was, in Moscow's view, to play into the hands of "aggressive NATO circles."

Even the Kosmos 954 and Kosmos 1402 accidents are in the process of being wished out of existence by Soviet space historians. The latest edition of the massive *Encyclopedia of Cosmonautics* mentions the fall of Skylab but not of the radioactive Soviet counterparts. Discussing the dangers of falling satellites, one Soviet scientist in 1986 wrote, "We all remember Skylab!" Another, denouncing American "Star Wars" plans to put nuclear reactors in space, wrote: "The dangers in such a move are obvious—look at Skylab, for example." People in the West, fortunately, remember a lot more about falling satellites than just Skylab, and they don't have to be enemies of international understanding at all—just the opposite.

13

THE URALS DISASTER

We crossed a strange, uninhabited and unfarmed area.
Highway signs along the way warned drivers not to stop for
the next 20 to 30 kilometers. The land was empty. There
were no villages, no towns, no people, no cultivated land.
Only the chimneys of destroyed houses remained.

—*Soviet émigré's account of a 1961 automobile
excursion in the Ural Mountains*

By 9:00 A.M. on May 1, 1960, Francis Gary Powers was in
Russian custody on a collective farm outside Sverdlovsk, deep
in the heart of the Soviet Union. His U-2 spy plane had been
shot down by a new-model SA-2 antiaircraft missile.

The who-how-where-when of the U-2 incident has been well
established. But major questions remain. First, what target of
major importance had brought the American pilot and his
cameras so deep into Russia? Secondly, what kind of facility was
so important to the Russians that they guarded it with their very
newest missiles even though it was more than 1,000 miles inside
their borders? Above all, had Soviet secrecy—especially about

technological disasters—attracted American interest to this particular region of Russia?

It was in the same region that the infamous Urals nuclear disaster had apparently occurred two years before in early 1958. The nature of that disaster is still obscure. Something happened, but exactly what remains uncertain. The Soviets tried to keep it secret, buried as deep as its victims, but their official cover-ups only forced many of the stories to fester underground before bursting forth in wildly mutated forms.

The occurrence of the disaster, whatever it was, became widely known to Soviet scientists soon after it happened. A few talked to non-Soviets, and within a year of the incident some sketchy reports had appeared in the Western press. The first, which went unnoticed for many years, was in an obscure German-language newspaper in Argentina on July 29, 1958. An independent report in *Die Presse* of Vienna on March 18, 1959, received a short-lived flurry of attention from other European papers. According to *Die Presse,* an anonymous East European (possibly East German) physicist received the description from a Russian physician from the Soviet Academy of Medicine, who himself had been sent to Sverdlovsk in the autumn of 1958 to work at an infirmary for those injured in the accident. This report corroborated the Argentine account, even though the two articles were not compared for twenty years.

Both articles reported that a nuclear accident had occurred in the Ural Mountains in February 1958. Both accounts said the disaster was not a single catastrophic episode, but the gradual breakdown of a filtering system on smokestacks at an "atomic test station." Consequently, dust from many large reactors contaminated an area of several thousand square miles to the northwest of the point of origin. Within a few weeks many cases of severe radiation burns had been recorded (the Argentine account said 1,118; the Vienna newspaper report said about 100). Twelve villages and a number of collective farms had been evacuated.

The Vienna account located the disaster in the Sverdlovsk-Chelyabinsk area (this includes the small city of Kyshtym, which turned out to be the actual site). The Argentine report said, "Werchnnuralski," evidently a distorted, Germanized version of "Verkhneuralsk," a small city about 100 miles southwest of

Sverdlovsk (and only about 150 miles from Kyshtym). The accident resulted in the whole area's being placed off-limits to all foreign travelers.

Other brief, nebulous reports of some disaster soon surfaced, with different postulated causes. A 1962 U.S. survey of nuclear industry safety was merely able to note: "Unconfirmed report of a major reactor incident."

The United States actually had a group of government personnel on the ground in Sverdlovsk in July 1959, a little more than a year after the accident. Their primary mission was diplomatic; it was part of a goodwill tour led by Vice President Richard Nixon and by Milton Eisenhower, the president's brother. The city had been chosen by the Soviets, but Washington evidently decided to take advantage of the opportunity to learn more about a region known to be the center of nuclear weapons work.

Nixon had been briefed on intelligence targets by the U-2 photoanalysis team. The "ground truth" of facilities spotted by U-2 overflights would be extremely valuable. Additionally, some members of the American party were armed with dosimeters and were looking for radiation. Hyman Rickover, the founder of the U.S. nuclear navy, was also along, and it was he who coordinated the radiation measurements as the party visited different locations in the city.

In a recent book on the U-2 affair, author Michael Beschloss revealed (and then evidently overlooked the significance of) a short report he had received during his research. Rickover, he was told, had interpreted the radiation readings to indicate "some sort of atomic explosion" near Sverdlovsk. This tantalizing tidbit suggests that some U.S. officials suspected the existence of the Urals disaster within a year of its occurrence.

Even without the heightened interest in the region which such reports would engender, Sverdlovsk would have been a major intelligence target solely because of its concentration of military industries. More U-2 flights followed, including one on April 9, 1960, and the ill-fated Powers flight on May 1. On that mission the U-2 apparently passed over Chelyabinsk, Kyshtym, and the southwestern section of Sverdlovsk before being destroyed.

As years passed, the CIA collected from Russians more verbal descriptions of this area and its nuclear industries. These reports became available mostly in the 1960s and 1970s from the wave of Soviet émigrés. One account from declassified CIA files is given at the lead-in to this chapter (it was released in the late 1970s). The witness also said, "I asked the driver to stop because I wanted to drink water. The driver refused. 'One doesn't stop here. You drive quickly and cross the area without any stops,' he said." This Russian source was subsequently identified as Dr. Lev Tumerman, a Soviet biophysicist now living in Israel. He had been attending a clandestine meeting of anti-Lysenko biologists in Chelyabinsk, and a biologist colleague offered to drive him the 140 miles back to Sverdlovsk to catch his plane, along a rarely used shortcut. Other Soviet émigrés independently corroborated this description of empty, forbidden lands. "We were not allowed to open the windows of the bus," one noted.

Behind the Urals nuclear disaster lies a mysterious Soviet bureaucracy with the innocuous title of Ministry of Medium Machine Building. It has a street address in Moscow, but its main facilities, at which it manufactures nuclear weapons and missiles, are spread throughout the USSR.

The Soviet nuclear research program had its origins in the 1930s, but it received major acceleration in 1943, when Stalin demanded his scientists build an atomic bomb such as the one he knew the Americans were working on in secret (Joseph Stalin evidently knew about the Manhattan Project before Harry Truman did). The Soviets launched a massive espionage campaign against the American A-bomb project. It was so successful that when in the spring of 1947 they built their first nuclear reactor in Moscow, its characteristics and dimensions were virtually identical to those of the "H305," the fourth American reactor built at Hanford, Washington. Meanwhile, while World War II was still raging, the Soviets also began a vast purchasing program from American suppliers, to support their nuclear weapons program. This included heavy water and many tons of uranium. According to historian Peter Kelly, "The U.S. government helped directly because the trade officials involved were not aware of the Manhattan Project and were unaware of the implications of the orders."

Under the oversight of Lavrentiy Beria, chief of the secret police, the Soviet A-bomb project was administered by an organization called the "First Chief Directorate." Beria's hand set in motion patterns which continue to this day. They include absolute priorities of production over human safety, the wide-scale use of forced labor (including the use of doomed inmates from "death camps" for particularly dangerous jobs), and utter secrecy enforced by the existence of sealed-off societies called "atomgrads," entirely devoted to the nuclear weapons efforts.

The heart of the Soviet program was located at a series of supersecret atomgrads built in the Ural Mountains near Chelyabinsk and Sverdlovsk. These were the plutonium factories for processing raw materials and spent fuel as well as the assembly facilities for the actual nuclear weapons.

The dawn of the nuclear era around the world is replete with stories of victims of radiation's still-unknown deleterious effects. But the Soviet toll seems to have been substantially elevated by an appallingly callous disregard for human safety from the very outset. Carelessness that could lead to loss of precious equipment and material was not to be tolerated, but if the casualties involved merely people or the natural environment, few precautionary measures seem to have been taken.

Professor Mikhail Antonovich Klochko, who sought political asylum in Canada in August 1961 at the age of fifty-nine, had been the head of one of the Academy of Sciences' nuclear chemistry laboratories in Moscow. Once in the West, he wrote long, detailed accounts of his personal experiences in the Soviet nuclear weapons program. "Stalin set the Soviet atomic scientists the task of making the bomb in the shortest time, at any cost," he wrote. "To achieve that goal, the authorities spared neither material expenses nor human lives."

The atomgrads in the Urals appear to have been particularly dangerous in the 1950s. "The appearance of these people was sickly, tired," recalled a native of Chelyabinsk who frequently met atomgrad workers. "It could be assumed that they worked in heavy conditions, and ate poorly. But they insisted that they worked normally and ate well." After a trip to one of these nuclear centers, an unnamed colleague had confided to Klochko: "You cannot imagine the colossal death rate among the scientists and technical personnel there. Each time I visit the plant I find that the cemetery has doubled in size."

In the Urals one of the USSR's most important nuclear weapons centers was the atomgrad called "Kyshtym 40." The original town was along the banks of the Techa, a river whose waters ran successively into the Iset, the Tobol, the Irtysh, the Ob, and then the Arctic Ocean. Construction of the atomgrad had begun in 1945 on the site of an old munitions works as the first Soviet plutonium production plant. Kyshtym 40 had its own reactors and its own reprocessing plant. It also was the first and for a long time the only large-scale Soviet nuclear waste storage facility. By 1947 there was already a sizable "secret city" with thousands of inhabitants.

Ample water supplies were needed for cooling the equipment and for chemical reprocessing, and the chosen area had many lakes. Forested regions had been selected, some observers suggested, to conceal the extent of ground facilities from American photoreconnaissance aircraft. Until the mid-1950s, when the Kremlin decided to disperse its nuclear weapons industry, Kyshtym may have been the site of the only two plutonium production plants in the USSR.

Whatever the ongoing level of radiation contamination, as described by Klochko, many reports still referred to a single catastrophic event which seems to have occurred in early 1958. The Soviets tried to keep it secret, and for twenty years they by and large succeeded.

The Urals radiation disaster finally reached the consciousness of the West beginning in 1976, when exiled Soviet biochemist Zhores Medvedev described it briefly during the course of an article about political interference in science. Noticing the subsequent sensational press treatment of his revelation, he expressed amazement that the story was unknown in the West because everybody in Russia supposedly knew about it. He wrote:

A tragic catastrophe occurred in 1958. The catastrophe itself could have been foreseen. For many years nuclear reactor wastes had been buried in a deserted area not more than a few dozen miles from a Urals town. The waste was not buried very deep. Nuclear scientists had often warned about the dangers involved in this primitive method of waste disposal, but nobody took their views seriously. Suddenly, there was an enormous explosion like a violent volcano. The nuclear reactions had led to overheating in the underground burial grounds. The explosion poured radioactive dust and materials high up into the sky. . . .

It was difficult to gauge the extent of the disaster immediately, and no evacuation plan was put into operation right away. Many villages and towns were only ordered to evacuate when the symptoms of radiation sickness were already quite apparent. Tens of thousands of people were affected, hundreds dying. . . .

The irridiated population was distributed over many clinics. But no one really knew how to treat the different stages of radiation sickness, how to measure the radiation dose received by the patient, how to predict what the effects would be. . . . Many towns and villages, where the radioactive level was moderate or high, but not lethal, were not evacuated. . . .

Many Western commentators evaluated Medvedev's report in the context of the ongoing debate about nuclear power. Pronuclear experts generally denounced the story as "impossible" and "preposterous." Antinuclear groups saw it as a powerful argument in support of their position. In Washington Ralph Nader's Critical Mass group immediately petitioned the CIA for relevant material, under the Freedom of Information Act, for use in its antinuclear campaigns. It received about a dozen heavily censored documents (mostly raw reports of interviews). A dozen other documents were acknowledged to exist but were still classified; these could have included U-2 analyses plus Rickover's 1959 on-site report.

Some stories were particularly grisly, hence perhaps "useful" to antinuclear groups such as Critical Mass. In one account there had been a hospital full of victims, and a witness described them: "We could see the skin on their face, hands, and other exposed parts of the body to be sloughing off. . . . It was a horrible sight." (Such skin effects were also seen among Marshall Island victims of fallout from an American H-bomb test.) Another report quoted an anonymous informant as saying, "Hundreds of persons perished and the area became and will remain radioactive for many years." Nader accused the government of keeping the material secret in order not to frighten people about American nuclear activities.

Yet the dozen-odd documents did not paint a clear or even reasonably consistent picture of any single plausible event. No primary eyewitnesses were found; the people were reporting what they had heard from indirect sources. For instance, the first report indicated merely that "in the winter of 1957, an unspecified accident occurred at the Kasli atomic plant [a small town near Kyshtym 40]." The second document in the officially numbered stack made several observations about the interviewee, including that "in the spring of 1958 . . . he heard . . . that large areas north of Chelyabinsk were contaminated by radioactive waste from a nuclear plant . . ." and also that "in March, 1958, an explosion wrecked part of the nuclear plant at Kyshtym." The fourth document reported that "the occurrence of an accidental atomic explosion in the Chelyabinsk Region during the spring of 1958 was widely known throughout the USSR. Rumors are that many people were killed; however, the generally accepted version is that only several score (individuals) died." The fifth document indicated "on an unknown date prior to June 1959, an accident occurred in the Chelyabinsk Region which caused radioactive contamination of the soil." The sixth document stated, "In early May, 1961, a terrific explosion occurred somewhere in the Chelyabinsk Region. . . . The explosion was so terrific that the ground and buildings shook." The seventh document mentioned "a mysterious explosion in the Chelyabinsk Region in April 1960 [with] possible radioactive fallout causing destruction of trees and vegetation, and many people burned as a result of the explosion. The hospital [at Chelyabinsk] was completely filled with victims of the explosion." The eighth document said that about 1956 "there was a nuclear explosion near Chelyabinsk . . . [at] a production site for nuclear devices." The ninth document reported that in the 1957–1958 period there occurred a "Soviet detonation of a twenty megaton device in an above-ground test." The tenth document said that the "1958 Kyshtym disaster" was a "nuclear accident involving plutonium waste from military nuclear reactors." The eleventh document stated, "In the spring of 1958 hundreds of persons were exposed to radiation and injured as a result of an explosion at the Kyshtym plant. . . ." Several other released documents were just the retyped texts of non-Soviet newspaper clippings.

One of the most detailed and authoritative accounts of the Urals disaster comes from a former inhabitant of nearby Chelyabinsk named Ya. Menaker. He recalled how ordinary people in the region frequently entered the forbidden atom-grad zones, sometimes just to hunt, to harvest mushrooms and hay, or to collect firewood, but sometimes to try to purchase unavailable foods and merchandise in the special zone stores.

Menaker's account of the aftermath of the disaster itself is vivid and detailed, betokening a personal involvement. One autumn "high radiation was discovered" over a vast region stretching about 100 miles eastward from Kyshtym. Control points were set up by specially clothed MVD (the forerunner of the KGB) troops, and all population movement was forbidden. Special supplies of food and water were distributed, but the population remained in place for more than a month while transport was assembled. Finally, everyone was given a new set of clothes (evidently leftover czarist army uniforms from some long-forgotten warehouse) and allowed to take only money and documents with them. MVD troops shot all the farm animals, burned the villages, and bulldozed the rubble into large mounds. "Several hundred villages and settlements were erased," Menaker recounted.

One of the refugee camps was set up near Chelyabinsk, in the small village of Petrovskiy. "These people settled in lean-tos, and it was like the small hamlet grew into a big village," Menaker reported. "But still faster there grew the small hamlet's cemetery, accepting the refugees who died from the radiation. Enlarging to huge dimensions, the cemetery and word-of-mouth stories were the only source of information on the quantity of those dead from radiation."

The Techa River was bounded on both sides by thick barbed-wire fences. Where important bridges crossed the river, some villages were left untouched. Menaker reported that he was often on those roads and bridges and sometimes looked down onto the radioactive waters. "Big pike swarmed there," he recalled, but most other species of fish—in particular, whitefish and roach—had vanished. Birches grew unchanged, but pine trees died. Muskrats thrived in the forbidden zone, and only a few years passed before the natives were cutting through the fences to catch muskrats (for their pelts) and pike (which were sold in village markets).

These hearsay accounts were moving and tantalizing, but they provided little hard data on which Western experts in the late 1970s could base a reconstruction of the original disaster.

Another important avenue of research was about to open, and the new evidence was contained in Soviet government documents.

While traveling in the United States in early 1978, sometime after his original article had appeared, Zhores Medvedev visited the American nuclear center at Oak Ridge, Tennessee, where he discussed what he knew about what was becoming known as the "Kyshtym disaster." A team of skeptical Oak Ridge scientists agreed to survey Soviet scientific literature, looking for clues. They soon made some remarkable findings, and in mid-1979 they released their results. By references to many published Soviet reports which discussed the ecological effects of nuclear contamination in some unspecified region, the Oak Ridge scientists could reconstruct a major radioactive contamination of several large lakes somewhere in the Urals in the late 1950s.

Medvedev used these findings and other evidence for his own 1979 book *Nuclear Disaster in the Urals*. He elaborated on the nature and effects of the disaster, which he'd first described in passing in his magazine article. Careless handling of nuclear waste and callous disregard for human health were central themes in his scenario.

Medvedev's account was seriously questioned in late 1979 by four leading scientists at Los Alamos, New Mexico, site of the top American nuclear weapons laboratory. They proposed, instead, that the radiation was merely fallout from some distant nuclear tests. They argued against Medvedev's speculative reconstruction of the mechanisms of the explosion, and they deemed "unlikely" the careless Soviet practices which had been suggested as explanations for the disaster. They suggested that the CIA's interviews with ex-Soviet citizens were grossly exaggerated or entirely fantasy. Lastly, they found it "hard to believe that an area of this magnitude could become contaminated and the event not discussed by more than one individual [Medvedev] for more than 20 years." That is, they somewhat arrogantly asserted that had the event actually happened, they would surely have known about it long before.

Meanwhile, the "pro-Medvedev" team of Oak Ridge nuclear scientists, led by Dr. John Trabalka, continued its research into the articles published in the Soviet scientific literature. In late

1979 these scientists released a major report which in all essentials confirmed Medvedev's scenario.

The Oak Ridgers surveyed more than 100 Soviet scientific papers about environmental contamination. These dealt with thirteen lakes and some land areas which were studied over a fifteen-year period. Oddly, the sites of the ecological research were not identified by the Soviet authors (although with controlled experiments, they usually are). However, the flora, fauna, climate, and topography were consistent with the Urals. Furthermore, the documented radiation levels were much higher than normal studies and were so high they were "producing either genetic effects or demonstrable toxicity." Additionally, these studies involved much larger areas, both land and water, than were typically involved in deliberate environmental contamination studies.

One of the papers explicitly referred to a single aerosol event, and many of the others obviously implied it. One even described the effects on a forest of strontium 90 fallout.

The Oak Ridge team referred to the disaster area by the nearby town of Kasli, not Kyshtym. Kasli, twelve miles northeast of Kyshtym, was nearly in the middle of the region's complex of nuclear weapons facilities. The U.S. scientists reported:

> We have concluded that a major airborne release occurred . . . in the winter of 1957 to 1958. . . . The available evidence indicates that the most likely cause of the airborne contamination was the chemical explosion of high-level radioactive wastes associated with a Soviet military plutonium production site . . . where long-lived, high-level fission wastes had been improperly buried for many years.

An independent study at Britain's Atomic Weapons Research Establishment in 1983 and 1984 came to conclusions similar to those of the group at Oak Ridge: A nuclear waste explosion had caused an atmospheric release. However, the British developed a slightly different waste processing scenario, which nevertheless led to a similar chemical explosion. "The data hang together," noted lead analyst F. Morgan, "though none of the fits is exact."

The Oak Ridge group studied Soviet maps of the Kyshtym area published in the years before and the years after the event and found they showed the deletion of the names of more than thirty villages in two zones. In one thin swath of missing towns which ran more than forty miles northeast from Kyshtym, every village was gone by the late 1950s, and in a second broader but shorter swath which ran southeast from Kyshtym, along the Techa River, some village names remained. The northeastern swath corresponds to the wind direction in winter; the southeastern swath probably was connected with contamination of the lakes and rivers, which flow in that direction. These vanished towns, with thousands of inhabitants and with good Russian names such as Petrovka, Boyevka, Yugo-Koneva, Russkaya Karabolka, Belokataiski, Kuptovykh, Techa-Brod, Metlino, and Asanova, were known to have been prosperous settlements. The total population of the evacuated areas had exceeded an estimated 10,000.

These "missing villages" have been widely publicized in the Western media as victims of the Urals nuclear disaster. But the cause-and-effect relationship turns out to be considerably more complex than that. The southeastern corridor appears now to predate the 1958 accident. The northeastern corridor and its vanished villages may have a plausible nonradioactive explanation, despite the coincidence of the wind direction.

Looking at charts published by the U.S. Defense Mapping Agency and presumably based on satellite reconnaissance photography, one sees a vast array of smokestacks and industrial parks in the Kyshtym area. About ten miles east of Kyshtym, on the southern shore of Lake Kyzyltash, is an industrial area several miles wide, crisscrossed by rail lines, major roads, and power lines; this is the supposed site of the plutonium production plant, including reactors, radiochemical separation facilities, and waste storage areas. About twenty miles north (and just north of Lake Silach) is another industrial area with railway, road, pipeline, and power line connections; this may be the actual nuclear weapons production facility.

In addition to these features, there is a major complex of parallel high-tension power lines moving off to the northeast. This double row of power lines precisely follows the northeastern corridor discovered by Trabalka and his associates at Oak Ridge.

This congruence can hardly be coincidental; the villages are probably gone because the power lines are there. Perhaps the peasants were evacuated in accordance with strict Soviet medical restrictions on habitations near high-power lines. Equally plausibly, the peasants could have been moved out on KGB orders to protect the lines from potential sabotage by local residents outraged by the radioactive rape of their lands. Another explanation is that the land might have been temporarily evacuated because of fallout but then been permanently taken over by the weapons industry as the most convenient place to locate the power lines. Least likely is the suggestion that the villages are still there but have "disappeared" only because they have been absorbed into the supersecret atomgrad complex; the roads on the maps would not support such "invisible" towns.

Menaker's account gave a different (and larger) description of the affected area, which included both the depopulated corridors discovered at Oak Ridge. He had drawn a map with a boundary running from Kasli to Tyubuk to Bagaryak in the north, to Brodokalmak in the east, thence to Miasskoye, Argayash, and Kyshtym along the south.

Could radiation levels from the 1958 accident have been bad enough to drive out local inhabitants? On the basis of their studies of the Soviet scientific reports, the Oak Ridge scientists were unable to reconcile what they had deduced about the levels of local radioactive contamination with the reports of numerous serious civilian casualties. The accident which they had reconstructed would have been nowhere severe enough to cause massive immediate loss of human life. If, however, as Medvedev, Menaker, and even the two 1958 reports alleged, the local population was left in the contaminated regions for weeks or months, cumulative dosages could have led to serious health damage and even death for many victims.

Without additional evidence about the sequence of events in the northeastern corridor and the extent and duration of evacuations, a more precise reconstruction appears impossible. The simple scenario of a fallout plume followed (after some delay) by evacuation may be correct, but the role of other factors such as the power lines confuses the issue.

The other evacuation corridor, to the southeast along the Techa River watershed, has been explained without recourse to sudden nuclear catastrophes. Researchers at Los Alamos argued against the contamination's being caused by a single catastrophic event. Instead, while admitting that a small-scale event might have occurred in the winter of 1957–1958, they established that massive radioactive pollution of the region had already occurred years earlier than 1958. They showed that the nuclear facility's cooling lake (upstream of the Techa River) had probably become dangerously radioactive by 1953 and that evacuations of river village inhabitants began at about that time in response to episodes of radioactive water containment failures. "Soviet carelessness coupled with general disregard for the citizenry and the environment are [sic] the prime causative factors, not a nuclear waste accident," they argued.

A particularly important source was uncovered by Dr. Frank Parker of Vanderbilt University, during a 1981–1982 study he conducted on the medical consequences of the disaster. He found a Russian construction engineer who had actually worked at Kyshtym for ten years but had then been allowed to emigrate (his job had evidently been so secret that the emigration screening process failed to discover it). He had been one of the chief construction managers, and he was aware of numerous routine mishaps over the earlier years ("There was a fine hospital in the town where patients could be treated for radiation injuries," he recalled). In particular, on several occasions the dirt dikes around cooling ponds would give way and radioactive water would flow into the Techa River. Things got so bad that evacuations were ordered, and he himself had been in charge of moving 2,000 people out of one area (he estimated a total of more than 10,000 people were moved from the river area alone, prior to the 1958 accident). This is consistent with the missing villages from the southeastern corridor discovered by the Oak Ridge team.

Further indications that the local watershed had become dangerously contaminated came from analysis of the maps. Some lakes in the area appear to have been bypassed by a series of canals, which take upstream water past the now-isolated lakes into the downstream Techa River basin. These bypassed lakes and several new reservoirs, alone among the major bodies of water in the region, did not appear in published fish-stocking records for the district, indicating they were "dead." The disappearance of villages from the banks of such bodies of water is hardly surprising. This also corroborates Menaker's first-person account of a quarantined river lined with barbed wire.

*   *   *

The Soviet scientific papers even provided evidence of the nature of the nuclear accident. In analyzing the isotope ratios consistently reported in the Soviet ecology reports, the Oak Ridge team discovered one remarkable feature: "The radioactive 'fingerprint' provided by the field studies seems to indicate an accident involving radiochemical separation operations or waste storage operations associated with the production of weapons-grade plutonium, or both. . . . These isotopic ratios are what one would expect in reprocessed fission wastes (after a decay time of approximately 1 to 2 years). . . ." The researchers noted a curious depletion of the isotope cesium 137 (in some areas, but not in all) and cited one Soviet paper which indicated that the Soviets were separating that isotope from the original broth for agricultural and industrial purposes. If they used the aluminum alum process first exploited in the United States (and they referred to it in the paper), that process would have left the broth rich in ammonium nitrate, which has well-known explosive qualities. If a coolant system in a waste storage tank failed, the overheated broth could reach a flash point and spontaneously blow sky-high, rupturing nearby tanks and spilling their liquid wastes into the watershed.

The Soviet engineer from Kyshtym who was Parker's source disagrees with the cause of *the* 1958 blast. The nuclear fuel reprocessing plant he described having built was a pipe-for-pipe copy of the Purex reprocessing plant in Richland, Washington (the Soviets even used the same jargon for special-purpose equipment; evidently a very successful Soviet spy had stolen the complete blueprints in the early 1950s). The engineer heard later from friends that six months after he had left Kyshtym, there had been a major explosion in his building involving nuclear material ("I was told that the accident took place early in 1958," he told Parker). There was widespread radioactive contamination, but he was unaware of any waste handling or storage accidents.

It is possible to conclude that this 1958 nuclear accident almost certainly happened. This judgment is based on testimony of people such as Menaker and the Soviet engineer from Kyshtym, from other secondhand reports, and on the evidence of the Soviet scientific papers which had collectively eluded the censor's attention (there have been no more such papers published since 1979, when Medvedev and the Oak Ridge team first drew public attention to their significance). This accident occurred in an existing context of widespread environmental contamination by the nuclear weapons industry in the Kyshtym area.

The human toll is much more difficult to gauge. However high the casualty rate near the blast site, immediate human injuries in the downwind fallout area might have been low or nonexistent. But in the absence of proper evacuation procedures, long-term health damage could have been significant for thousands of people. The disappearance of the villages in the northeast (downwind) corridor may well be due to the fallout from the explosion; other villages to the east may also have been "erased." However, the missing villages in the southeastern corridor along the Techa River can no longer be attributed to the 1958 event.

The Oak Ridge report's conclusion bears repeating since it is an indictment of Soviet secrecy and how such secrecy can affect even non-Soviet victims:

> It seems apparent that the Soviet nuclear program has had to contend with severe environmental contamination involving reactor-generated fission products. . . . However, the reluctance to provide detailed information about the nature of the source, site, and so on, coupled with the probable existence of more research, documented but internal to the Soviet Union, limits the usefulness of the experiences gained by Soviet scientists. . . . We urge the Soviet scientific community to share all pertinent information with others concerned with achieving the safe development of nuclear energy. Soviet experience gained during the application of remedial measures on an unparalleled scale following this accident is clearly unique and would be invaluable to the world nuclear community.

Since human radiation casualties almost certainly occurred at Kyshtym, both associated with this 1958 accident, then with others in the same region over the years, knowledge of the Soviet experience in diagnosing and treating them could have saved lives during similar, lesser accidents in the West. Menaker described a special "Med-city" near Chelyabinsk where radiation cases (including his own mother and his wife, who both died there) were examined and treated. Medvedev later noted that the kinds of medical data available to the Soviets included several unique reports on radiation effects. After some accident in the late 1950s (possibly the 1958 event), two leading Soviet doctors were in charge of medical teams working in special hospitals in Sverdlovsk and Chelyabinsk. They were A. I. Burnazyan, the deputy minister of health of the USSR, and Professor G. D. Baisogolov, an expert on radiology and radiation sickness. Baisogolov prepared a special report describing eleven cases of acute radiation sickness, but the report was never released; Medvedev later tracked it down through a series of citations to it in other Soviet reports.

Dr. Burnazyan, who had been intimately involved in the medical treatment of the 1958 victims, apparently came to some conclusions of his own about nuclear plants and large population centers. In a 1975 paper on medical radiology, he sincerely advised that: "A nuclear power station, as far as possible, should be located in an area of low population with good natural ventilation toward the leeward side with respect to populated areas. The hydrological conditions of the area should be assessed, to eliminate the possibility of radioactive materials entering ground water." What he saw at Kyshtym may have impelled him to these conclusions. But despite these experiences, large reactors were later emplaced close to Voronezh, Gorkiy, Odessa, Kharkov, Bilibinsk, Leningrad, and Kiev, at a place called Chernobyl.

The official Soviet silence on the stories of the Urals nuclear disaster(s) is eloquent testimony to the continuing sensitivity of the subject. One curt off-the-record comment—that "the event described by Medvedev did not occur"—can hardly be considered a blanket denial since the most recent reconstructions vary somewhat from Medvedev's original scenario. Radio commentator Vladimir Posner's 1986 assurance that the catastrophe could not have happened because he had never heard of it also cannot be regarded as authoritative. In private, and after several drinks, some leading Soviet nuclear power officials have gone as far as saying it wasn't their fault. "The events at Kyshtym had nothing to do with the civilian power plant program," they have earnestly (and probably truthfully) told their Western colleagues.

This heritage of nuclear disasters over many decades remained a tightly guarded Soviet state secret. If there were safety lessons to be learned, the West had to learn them independently, at cost in time, treasure, and human lives. The secrecy surrounding the Urals nuclear accident(s) arguably had Western victims, too.

14

NUCLEAR
GULAG

QUESTION: Is it dangerous to remember in the USSR?

ANSWER: I do not believe so, but I am not sure that my opinion is shared.

—*Yuriy N. Afanasyev, appointed director of
USSR Institute of History and Archives, 1986*

When the defecting Soviet nuclear scientist Mikhail Klochko described how Soviet authorities "spared neither material expenses nor human lives" in their push for nuclear weapons, he made estimates of the human casualties of the program. Writing in Western publications in the early 1980s, Klochko provided long lists of names of nuclear workers who died prematurely, arguably from radiation exposure. He described research facilities, including ones he worked at, where even the simplest safety precautions (such as adequate ventilation, functional drains, and clean face masks) were ignored despite pleas by informed workers and specialists. Extrapolating figures he believed to be valid, he arrived at an estimate of an incredible

50,000 to 100,000 premature deaths among nuclear weapons workers in the first decade of the program alone.

Klochko then turned to one of the most gruesome aspects of the Soviet nuclear industry, the wanton use of slave labor, the so-called *zeks* of Solzhenitsyn's *Gulag Archipelago*. Klochko wrote: "The path from the uranium mines to the test grounds is paved with corpses. During the first decade of the bomb's development, inmates of Soviet concentration camps did the lion's share of that work. The camps neglected even the most elementary safety arrangements. Radiation sickness was a complementary mishap to the many accidents in mines and on the production line." Other authorities such as Zhores Medvedev concur that the use of forced labor in the Soviet nuclear industry, at least in the Stalin years, was widespread.

These tens of thousands of victims have remained almost completely anonymous. Solzhenitsyn has recounted the story of one of them, a former *zek* (political prisoner) named Chebotarev who had been a worker at one of the atomic projects in the late 1940s. When his group was "released," they were deemed too dangerous to return to society (they knew too many state secrets), so they were sent off to the Kolyma goldfields in Siberia. Most died there, but Chebotarev outlived Stalin and in 1956 was able to return home.

Among the thousands of pages in Solzhenitsyn's *Gulag Archipelago*, his treatment of the Stalinist slave labor camp empire, only a few paragraphs discuss the Soviet nuclear industry and the role of forced labor in it. He listed the projects he knew of: "Moscow-10," "Tura-38," "Sverdlovsk-39," and "Chelyabinsk-40." In the late 1940s tens of thousands of prisoners "were engaged in separating uranium-radium ores, and construction was proceeding according to Kurchatov's plans, and the construction chief was Lieutenant General Tkachenko, who was subordinate only to Stalin and Beriya." Solzhenitsyn acknowledged having only the most sketchy knowledge of this aspect of the gulag history. "How can one really keep up with all this and describe it?" he asked rhetorically. "Chapters and chapters are necessary!" Later in a long list of prisoner construction projects he mentioned a few nuclear projects: "Construction of nearly all the centers of the nuclear industry; mining of radioactive elements (uranium and radium—near Chelyabinsk, Sverdlovsk, and Tura); work on isotope separation and enrichment plants (1945–1948); radium mining in Ukhta. . . ."

The Los Alamos study on the 1950s Urals nuclear waste disaster(s) had also cast light on the use of forced labor for dangerous work and the subsequent high death rates among the workers. In the early 1960s one dry lake bed near Kyshtym, which had been used as a waste dump, had to be covered over with dirt because winds were dispersing the radioactive dust over wide areas. "Information indicates that they used volunteer prisoners to dump truckloads of sand on top of the contaminated soil," the report said. "The truck drivers were referred to as 'death people' or 'death squad.' They were prisoners with 10- to 15-year sentences whose time in prison would be reduced through their volunteering for this duty. They lived in special barracks, and it was thought they would probably die there."

Menaker's account of the disaster period also described the use of prisoner labor. When the serious contamination of the Techa River was discovered, the laborers who erected the barbed-wire fences for 100 miles on both sides of the river were from two nearby camps. They were bused in every day and were guarded by MVD troops wearing special protective garb; naturally the prisoners had no such gear. "At the finish of the work at the river," noted Menaker, "the zeks from the Chelyabinsk and Balandinskiy camps were sent somewhere else. In place of them new zeks arrived in these camps."

Official Soviet attitudes of carelessness toward the dangers of radioactivity may be partially based on the belief that many of those most in danger didn't warrant protection.

Avraham Shifrin's catalog of Soviet prison camps, which was prepared in Israel in the late 1970s and published in book form in 1981, suggested that the use of forced labor in the Soviet nuclear industry was still going on many years later, even if possibly at a somewhat reduced scale. His book included a special section on death camps, and radiation poisoning was the leading cause of death among prisoners incarcerated "for life" at these penal facilities. The purpose was to serve Soviet state military security needs. Simultaneously it had the effect of disposing of prisoners it could be inconvenient to formally sentence to death.

How trustworthy is Shifrin's material? Specialists in USSR

human rights abuses generally consider him a reliable chronicler of testimony received from informants. His main weakness seems to be not recognizing that most labor camps have only a transitory existence and that many of his reports refer to facilities which no longer exist. The net effect is for his depiction of the scope of "current" gulag facilities to be exaggerated.

The main nuclear weapons facilities employing slave labor in the 1970s, wrote Shifrin, were at a warhead plant at Chelyabinsk 40 and at Kyshtym, both mentioned by Solzhenitsyn. The Chelyabinsk facility is forty kilometers southeast of the main city, where 2,000 prisoners were kept in Camp YaV-48/6. The Kyshtym facility is a uranium enrichment plant where 2,500 prisoners in the strict-regime camp number YaV-48/7 processed uranium. There was another nuclear warhead plant at Novosibirsk, in the innocuously named *khimkontsentrat* ("chemoconcentrate") and *khimapparat* ("chemo-apparatus") plants in the Dzherzhinskiy district of the northern section of the city; about 1,000 prisoners from Camp number 91/8, a strict-regime facility, worked there. At the Mangyshlak Peninsula on the Caspian Sea there was nuclear reactor work and more uranium enrichment. Many of these facilities are doubtlessly still in operation in the late 1980s, but whether they are now staffed with free, salaried labor or still use prisoners cannot be determined.

Shifrin located other nuclear fuel enrichment facilities on the basis of credible firsthand accounts. Two were at Olga Bay and at Shamor Bay (on the Sea of Japan), a "zone of deadly radioactivity" where 10,000 prisoners in four strict-regime camps work (see below). Two more were at Cape Medvezhiy (on Novaya Zemlya island, a major nuclear bomb test zone in the Arctic Ocean) and at the nearby Vaygach Island. One was east of Frunze, where 2,500 prisoners worked in a strict-regime camp; others were at Zeravshan, Bekabad, and Leninabad (northern Tadzhikstan)—"the high level of radiation in the area constitutes a serious health hazard" to 10,000 prison workers in camps number UYa-64/2, /4, /6, /8, /9, and /37, who wind up being transferred to a camp hospital in Nukus to die of leukemia.

The reference to leukemia is probably medically incorrect because that disease takes a long time to develop. More likely the continuous exposure to high levels of radiation would induce bone marrow collapse in the workers, leading to death. As a blood disease, it might easily be confused with "leukemia" by careless medical personnel.

Shifrin also had reports of radioactive processing facilities throughout Soviet Central Asia, at Margilan, at Fergana (2,500 prisoners), at Leninsk (Uzbekistan), at Rudnyy and at Aksu in Kazakhstan. At Aksu "the entire region is exposed to a high-level of radiation." Other sites were at Groznyy (in the Chechen-Ingush ASSR, north of the Caucasus), at Totma and near Vologda at Cherepovets (about 5,000 prisoners).

Shifrin received a deposition from one "A.K.," a former military physician stationed at the military hospital in Vladivostok. His duties included inspecting the living conditions of military personnel at the uranium mines about 100 miles north along the coast.

As a member of a team of three military physicians, I inspected the military camps in the vicinity of Olga Bay, Kavalerovo, and Shamor Bay in order to determine whether the servicemen stationed here were exposed to radioactive contamination. Their camps were not in the contamination zones; we could not therefore establish any danger to the soldiers or officers. We were, however, able to establish deadly radiation in the uranium mine areas. I inspected the labor camps and saw that the barracks were located within the radiation zone. I asked the officer who accompanied us, "How do the prisoners and guards here live?" His answer was merely to shrug his shoulders. I realized immediately that I had touched upon a dangerous subject. I became silent.

"I.M." used to work at Sotsgorod, near Leninabad in northern Tadzhikstan, near the uranium mining complex. He wrote to Shifrin:

The fatality rate of the prisoners is high. Even high pay cannot lure volunteers to work here. In order to attract volunteers, the state had declared in 1975 that every employee . . . could build his own house with cost-free building stone and cement. The offer was accepted by many; many good homes were constructed as a result. As it happened, the building material for the foundations of the houses consisted of tailings that had been extracted from the uranium mine shafts. Thus exposed to heavy doses of radioactive contamination, the occupants of the houses fell ill by the hundreds and had to be treated in special hospitals.

Shifrin's book also mentions the location of numerous uranium mines, both open-pit and underground. There was one at Achinsk (near Krasnoyarsk), with 2,500 men working at a nearby enrichment facility in the Glinozemnyi plant, and there was a major open-pit mine at Borovoye in Kazakhstan, where "although a large health resort is located in this very vicinity, the government has characteristically refrained from warning holiday guests against the dangerous radiation." Near Kyshtovka north of Novosibirsk were several especially harsh-regime camps, including an open-pit uranium mine: "The prisoners are sent into the pits to mine uranium ore and die only after a few months of work in them. . . . Prisoners convicted of insurrection or sentenced to death are among those who are sent here."

Other open-pit mines in Kazakhstan were located at Karagayly (at the end of a 120-mile railway line from Karaganda) and at Tselinograd—"the entire work area is exposed to radiation." There was one at the western edge of the USSR, in the vicinity of Rakhov in Transcarpathia, where "the surrounding area is exposed to radiation." Underground uranium mines were also located north of Zhitomir in the Ukraine, near the small towns of Cholovka and Novaya Borovaya (2,000 prisoners in a camp about a mile from the train station). Shifrin has reports of mines at Zhyoltiye Vody ("Yellow Waters"), near Dnepropetrovsk, at Almalyk (Kazakhstan), near Kokand and Andizhan (Uzbekistan), at Sovetabad and Asht (Tadzhikstan)— "area exposed to high-level radiation"—at Oymyakon (in the Yakutsk area of Siberia), and at Lermontov, near Stavropol, Gorbachev's home district.

The Lermontov uranium mine facilities were actually photographed by a Western news crew in 1985. Although the mines were closed about 1972 and large new apartment complexes are now located near their site, the camp walls still exist and the gates are still locked.

Producer Geoffrey Seed was working on a program for the Channel 4 London television station, subsequently broadcast in mid-1986 as *The Nuclear Gulag.* His researchers had tracked down a man who used to live near a slave labor uranium mine in the Beshtau Mountains south of Lermontov. The Russian, named Aleksandr Khakhulin ("Chachulin" in the Germanic transliteration when he emigrated to West Germany), told a British camera crew what he and a friend named Myshastiy had found out about the facility.

Khakhulin related that countless thousands of prisoners died in the nearby mines. Trainloads of carriages, maybe fifty at a time, brought new prisoners; departing trainloads consisted of one or two full carriages. He estimated that the 4,000 or 5,000 prisoners were replaced every two or three months for many years. "They were indifferent to the fate of the people who worked at the mines," Khakhulin told the interviewers. "Apparently the prisoners were condemned from the very beginning to slow death."

Work teams brought bodies out of the camp every night and dumped them down abandoned mine shafts. Before the workers took the bodies out of the compound, they verified the prisoners' deaths by bashing their skulls in with hammers. "There were no coffins or boxes," Khakhulin bitterly complained. "There were no marks of respect."

A friend of Khakhulin's had been a prisoner at the camp and had actually been released shortly before his death. "He was like skin and bones, like an electric pole," the Russian recounted. On his face and skin were spots and bruises, with a strange dark blue color and irregular shapes (probably hematomas from skin exposure to radioactive dust). Myshastiy, his friend, used to have "fantastic hair," but when he got out, it was all gone. "His cheeks and head were absolutely hairless."

These were typical symptoms of radiation poisoning, although Khakhulin would have had no way of knowing it. The skin blotches would have been slow subcutaneous bleeding resulting from a low blood platelet count caused by "bone marrow depression." Radiation killed the tissue inside the bones which manufactured cellular components of the blood, such as platelets, red cells with hemoglobin, and white blood cells to fight infection. Although Western medicine has not considered long-duration radiation exposures as a realistic situation, there are some data which can help estimate Myshastiy's exposure. The human body can tolerate up to 300 rem per year without any bone marrow damage, but a much higher exposure would likely have led to gastrointestinal collapse instead of bone marrow collapse as a cause of death; this puts an upper limit of perhaps 1,000 rem. Had Myshastiy or any of his fellow prisoners avoided short-term death from bone marrow collapse, their life expectancies in the face of leukemia and other cancers would not have exceeded several years to a decade.

One particularly chilling aspect of dying of radiation poisoning in the Beshtau Mountains was that medical specialists came out from Moscow to do research on the doomed prisoners. Some dying prisoners were especially isolated for these unspecified experiments; eventually they all died, too, and presumably were thoroughly autopsied.

Medical research on dying prisoners was confirmed by another former inmate also interviewed by the British news crew. Herman Hartfeld had been a Baptist minister sentenced in the 1960s to five years for religious activity. He spent a year and a half in uranium processing in Kazakhstan and spoke with bitterness about the "clinic" in Karaganda where sick prisoners were sent, never to return. Free workers from there, male nurses, sometimes came to Hartfeld's camp to perform simple medical chores, and they told the prisoners about various drug experiments.

Hartfeld had been at the mine at Aksu mentioned by Shifrin and at a nearby processing plant at Zholymbet. At the mine workers were exposed to dust and to dangerous chemicals and grew weaker and weaker. "They were exhausted, very tired, they couldn't even move or walk, many experienced a lot of pain—they became so thin they looked like shadows of persons," Hartfeld told the British interviewers. "I was often called to some prisoners who were dying," Hartfeld recalled. "They wanted moral help, and were aware they were dying." Suicides were frequent, mostly by hanging. One group of six or seven men used explosives in a mine shaft to blow themselves up together.

Hartfeld heard of a prisoner uprising at the Zeravshan uranium mine in the late 1960s, caused by the hideous, hopeless conditions. Strikers had erected barricades, but troops (either army or KGB) moved in. "Some prisoners went out and surrendered; nevertheless they were shot down," Hartfeld recounted. About 300 men were killed, and many more wounded.

At Zholymbet, Hartfeld worked inside a processing factory with about 500 to 600 other prisoners, again without any protective gear. On one occasion there was an explosion in an adjacent room, killing some prisoners; the rest were rushed outside "because of very dangerous radiation." But they were soon back at work.

Testimony such as Khakhulin's and Hartfeld's is eminently credible because it corroborates material from Shifrin and is itself supported by other accounts. Émigré Konstantin Simis had been a defense lawyer in the Soviet Union before he came to America; one of his clients had escaped the death penalty only to be sent to a uranium mine. Reflected Simis: "Radiation performed the same sentence in six months, a year, a year and a half—the sentence is the same."

It cannot be determined how much of this is still going on and how many Soviet labor camp inmates continue to die in the uranium mines and processing plants. Another imprisoned Baptist minister reportedly died at the Shevchenko uranium mine as late as 1983. Since many of these accounts took a decade or two to come out, the lack of many recent reports cannot be interpreted as being due to a lack of real inmates. The human toll of the Soviet nuclear industry, both for peaceful and military purposes, may be obscenely high; at Aksu and Zeravshan and Lermontov there may well be mass graves for tens of thousands of the individual victims described statistically en masse by Klochko.

15

MISCELLANEOUS NUCLEAR ACCIDENTS

We have no accidents which would give rise to anxiety among people and set them against the development of nuclear power engineering.

—*Andronik Petrosyants, chairman of the USSR's State Committee for the Utilization of Atomic Energy, 1979*

When faced with having to confess their own technological failures, Soviet spokesmen often used to fall back on the "Negroes in the South" gambit, a pathetically clumsy attempt to redirect the attention of the conversation in progress. A somewhat less unsophisticated modern gimmick is to catalog allegedly similar technological failures in the West.

But such catalogs are often highly exaggerated, if not counterfeit. Western observers would be startled to learn that Soviet experts actually believe people died during the Three Mile Island (TMI) nuclear power plant accident or that Soviet military experts have concluded that the loss of the submarine *Thresher* was due to the accidental detonation of one of its nuclear-armed torpedoes. And in 1986 a big Soviet media fuss was made over a West European "power plant accident" at what turned out to be (but was not explicitly described as) a *solar* power plant.

Furthermore, like must be compared with like. The commonly listed Western nuclear accidents are of such small scale that they would never, even under *glasnost*, be disclosed in the USSR. As for the biggest disasters, such as the 1958 Urals contamination, there are no Western equivalents anywhere.

Whatever had been happening to the nuclear industry in the Kyshtym area of the Urals was not unique to that region of the Soviet Union. Elsewhere in the nuclear industry, accidents were also occurring. Under the working conditions which have been described in the last two chapters, the occurrence of frequent major nuclear accidents at industrial facilities in the USSR must be seen as highly plausible, even unavoidable. One Soviet nuclear scientist confided to a Western counterpart that five of the first nine Soviet nuclear reactors had suffered major fires. Zhores Medvedev noted reliable accounts of another major accident in 1958 at Troitsk, south of Chelyabinsk, where other reactors are located. More recent events, while rarer, also preceded Chernobyl.

A 1974 rumor spoke of a major failure at the showcase nuclear reactor complex at Shevchenko on the Mangyshlak Peninsula. A "large fire" was alleged to have struck in July, something serious enough to be detected by American reconnaissance satellites. The chairman of the Soviet Union's State Committee for Atomic Energy emphatically denied that anything untoward had happened. "[It's] an invention and obviously pursues some other aims," complained Dr. Andronik Petrosyants. "It is evidently of benefit to some people to try to do damage to cooperation, and set public opinion against cooperation by inventing 'explosions.' " Yet at about the same time another Soviet scientist visiting London readily admitted that three of the plant's six reactors had been taken out of service because of serious problems in their sodium-to-water heat exchangers; his answer was so forthright, detailed, and internally consistent that most reporters readily accepted his description of the problem(s).

Early in 1980 a different account appeared of another nuclear disaster near Sverdlovsk. According to a private Soviet source, a bad fire had broken out a year previously in the sodium-to-water heat exchanger at a power reactor at Beloyars-kiy, sixty miles outside the city. While the fire raged out of control, trains and buses were assembled to evacuate the residents of the nearby settlement of Zarechnaya. Several firemen were killed before the fire was brought under control. It was later determined that the shift on duty that New Year's Eve had been drunk.

Some sort of accident seems likely at the Atommash ("Atomic Machine") plant, near Volgodonsk, in 1983. *Pravda* later denounced the local management when it "failed to ensure the accident-free exploitation of engineering communications." The management was censured in the weekly political meeting in mid-July; a top Politburo member, Vladimir Dolgikh, visited the site soon afterward. But no details of any accident or casualties ever appeared.

A newspaper in Copenhagen, Denmark, published an intriguing story on November 11, 1976:

> There are more and more indications [goes the translation prepared by the U.S. embassy there] that the strong earthquake believed to have taken place two weeks ago in the Gulf of Finland in reality was a nuclear arms explosion in the subterranean Soviet naval base in Tallinn, Estonia. Some days after the "jolt," increased radioactivity has reportedly been observed in Finland, according to SVENSKA DAG-BLADET [Stockholm]. Rather vague statements have been made on this point, but today at least some circles believe that it was really a nuclear arms explosion. To this a striking radioactivity has been noted in the part of the Soviet Union in question after the event, which is interpreted to mean that something unusual has happened. That radioactivity has not increased more significantly can, if the theory that a nuclear arms accident has occurred is correct, simply mean that it has been in connection with a subterranean plant. This would naturally limit the fallout. In this connection it is also noted, SVENSKA DAGBLADET states, that no comment has appeared from the Soviet side.

Further accounts are unavailable, so the speculation must remain unconfirmed; the occurrence of an accidental nuclear weapons detonation, however, must be regarded as highly implausible.

The Pentagon term for an accident involving nuclear weapons is a "broken arrow." It might be a bomb accidentally dropped off an aircraft or going down with a crashed aircraft; it might be an exploded ICBM, as happened in Arkansas in 1980. News of the Soviet analogs of such accidents is extremely unlikely to leak out, but several available stories might be related to Soviet "broken arrows."

According to Sovietologist John Prados, two people were killed by the USSR's second H-bomb test in November 1955. A soldier was fatally injured when he was thrown to the ground by the concussion, and a little girl in a nearby settlement was crushed by a falling wooden beam.

An alleged accident at the Semipalatinsk nuclear testing zone was reported by one Soviet émigré. The unidentified informant had heard (between May 1975 and November 1976) from some "extended-service NCOs" who had served at the Semiyarka airfield (north of Lake Balkhash) that a "nuclear accident" in 1972 or 1973 had killed an entire company of soldiers (about 100 men) who were responsible for maintaining the test facilities. The explosion had been tremendous enough to cause panic at a garrison located fifteen miles from the testing ground and five miles from Semiyarka. The troops there, fearing radiation, ran off into the surrounding desert but were eventually rounded up by security forces.

A similar incident was referred to in a recent American book on U.S. intelligence operations. It reported that the KGB's full control of all nuclear weapons operations was modified following a "near disaster" during a test sometime in the mid-1960s. In their highly sanitized account ("Any more details wouldn't have gotten past the censors," one explained), the authors (two former intelligence analysts) referred to the incident as a "bureaucratic nuclear accident." During a routine nuclear test detonation KGB officials had "ordered" the device to be fired despite objections from the technical experts. Appropriate safeguards were not in place, and human casualties—deaths and injuries—resulted. The scandal led to a restructuring of weapons control policy, giving scientific and technical personnel a larger say. "Technical competence as well as ideological purity" was henceforth to be required of the KGB officers in charge of such operations.

On May 24, 1983, a "very serious" explosion reportedly occurred at a Soviet military base in Czechoslovakia. The location was Turnov, north of Prague in the mountains near the Polish border. Residents of the area noticed a shock wave and ground tremor at the time and saw local officials taking radiation measurements soon afterward. The explosion, which reportedly killed thirty to sixty Soviet soldiers, may have involved a short-range surface-to-surface missile. The reports of radiation monitoring (which went on for two months after the blast) may indicate that a tactical nuclear weapon could have been installed on the missile.

Early in 1987 anti-Soviet sources within Estonia smuggled out a detailed account which sounds like another nuclear weapons handling accident. Reportedly a Soviet missile base near Keila was suddenly evacuated completely, but all weapons and other equipment were left behind. After several days all sheep in the area died. A forest ranger living nearby developed a mysterious blood disease which required two complete blood transfusions; also, all his hair fell out. He and his family were told not to drink their well water but were provided with a tank truck for use. No corroborative radioactive winds were noted in Scandinavia, but low-level dispersals need not leave such traces.

Soviet accidents in the handling of nuclear weapons are occurring, by statistical argument alone. That nuclear weapons have been lost aboard submarines is known because the United States has retrieved some of them. Similar accidents with aircraft, missiles, and other delivery and storage systems are bound to occur, but in the very strictest secrecy.

Another Soviet army weapons accident supposedly occurred in the late summer of 1979. It involved no fatalities, but some sort of field training exercise or test of a Soviet bacteriological weapon got out of hand. There is a twenty- by forty-mile zone in central Slovakia that is regularly used as a training zone for Soviet paratroops. Some weapon is said to have discharged accidentally, leading to military casualties so numerous that existing army facilities were saturated and cases were sent to nearby civilian hospitals in Poprad and Spisská Nová Ves. There were also "several thousand" civilian cases, as winds bore the virus outside the training ground. The disease was described by Czech sources as a new form of infectious hepatitis, evidently intended not as a killer but as an incapacitator. This rumor, while intriguing, may be subject to several prosaic explanations when (and if) exaggerations and gossip can ever be filtered out of the available accounts.

At unofficial East-West disarmament seminars around the world, Soviet spokesmen exploit such secrecy to denounce reports of American nuclear weapons mishaps as proof of the danger of accidental nuclear war. When asked about analogous Soviet incidents, some Russians just deny any (and get laughed at) while others resort to the familiar refrain of "I am not qualified to comment in that specialty." When asked about the two greatest lost Soviet nuclear weapons incidents which happened overseas, they also refuse comment. One incident in the mid-Pacific involved nuclear warheads lost off a sunken submarine which was subsequently largely recovered by the CIA, and the other involved nuclear weapons aboard a Soviet submarine which ran aground inside Swedish territorial waters. The two incidents were major Soviet disasters, in terms of lives lost (in the former case), in diplomatic loss of face (in the latter case), and in intelligence gains for the West.

The loss of a Soviet submarine on April 11, 1968, led to a major intelligence coup for the United States. It could also have led to a serious international confrontation.

An internal explosion aboard a Golf II-class missile boat resulted in its sinking with all hands (about seventy men) in three miles of water 750 miles northwest of Hawaii. Underwater listening devices operated by the U.S. Navy heard the implosions as the submarine was crushed. Soon afterward American robot submersibles located the wreck and took detailed photographs. The Soviets, too, looked for it, but they never found it.

The U.S. government subsequently spent half a billion dollars to attempt to retrieve the code machines and thermonuclear warheads from the submarine. The whole story was recounted in Roy Varner and Wayne Collier's book *A Matter of Risk*. The giant Hughes *Glomar Explorer* ship, built under cover of a seafloor mining vessel, lowered a claw device and grabbed the sub in August 1974, but during the raising of the system most of the sub broke free and fell back to the bottom (one of the nuclear-tipped missiles slid out of the conning tower as the horrified operators on the surface watched helplessly). The recovered nose section of the sub had about a third of the interior compartments squeezed into it, and the contents were studied carefully. Although the megaton-size missile warheads were lost, smaller nuclear warheads for torpedoes were recovered.

In terms of technology, American specialists were amazed and appalled. The boat's workmanship was primitive, with the welding uneven and pitted. Hatch covers were crudely built, and one compartment was reinforced with wooden beams. Another section was full of a few tons of lead weights which were evidently manually moved back and forth to trim the sub's center of gravity during maneuvers.

In human terms, the finds were equally striking. One officer's logbook provided key information on cryptographic procedures, but more common in the crew quarters was typical maritime reading material: letters from home, maintenance manuals, and pornography.

The recovered section was scattered with body fragments (from at least six individuals, maybe more). These were carefully collected (they along with the rest of the debris were radioactive) and ultimately were solemnly buried at sea. The ceremony, in Russian and English, was videotaped in case the Soviets ever chose to make a fuss.

To this day the Soviets have not publicly uttered a peep about the whole affair. There were always some legal questions about whether the submarine remained Soviet government property, since the occasional presence of fishing trawlers in the area might be construed as evidence the Soviets did not consider it "abandoned." In terms of precedents, however, the Soviets had set one in 1919 when they sank a British submarine, the *L-55,* off Kronshtadt and later raised it and commissioned it into the Soviet Navy. Consequently, the international law aspects were at least obscure, if not fully supportive of the CIA project.

Rumors persist to this day that the "partial recovery" story is only a cover for an actual full recovery of all the sought hardware. Varner's reconstruction, however, appears to be the authentic one. That does not mean, though, that the target hardware was not recovered later. Although President Gerald Ford canceled a second retrieval attempt in 1975 in recognition of U.S./USSR détente, such motivations would hardly have weighed heavily with subsequent administrations. Add to this the fact that the sub's second fall to the floor may have left it broken piñatalike on the bottom, with the sought-for intelligence treasures no longer sequestered away behind solid steel hulls, and the possibility then must be considered that somebody later returned with advanced small-scale robot submersibles (like the ones which scouted the *Titanic* at a similar depth) to rummage among the wreckage and pick up the hardware for which so much money had been spent. Other knowledgeable sources insist that since 1975 the Soviets have permanently stationed a ship over the submarine's resting place, and this has prevented any subsequent American recovery operation.

Following disclosure of the project in 1975, stories of similar, earlier recoveries appeared. On March 19 NBC-TV newsman Ford Rowan reported on three specific cases, according to published newspaper accounts:

> NBC said that about three years ago American and British forces recovered electronic gear from a Russian plane that had crashed in the North Sea. About four years ago, the TV network said, American naval forces retrieved electronic eavesdropping equipment from a small Soviet vessel that sank in the Sea of Japan. About five years ago, the report continued, American military forces recovered a nuclear weapon from a Russian plane that had crashed in the Sea of Japan.

The file on Soviet "broken arrows" is evidently far from empty.

A Soviet submarine doesn't have to sink, burn, or lose its nuclear weapons to suffer a disaster. A Soviet submarine captain, Gushin, proved that on October 27, 1981, near the Swedish naval base at Karlskrona, at the southeast tip of that country, on the Baltic Sea. In the case of the nuclear-armed Whiskey-class patrol sub *U-137,* all the submarine had to do was sit on the rocks in a small cove deep within Swedish territorial waters, be stared at, and give off measurable radiation from its torpedo tubes.

The submarine had run aground in a channel near a cove named Gåsefjarden ("Goose Bay"), where the Swedish Navy tests new underwater equipment. Gåsefjarden is marked as a Swedish military restricted zone, ENTRY PROHIBITED TO ALIENS. About a month earlier the Swedish Navy had issued a warning to mariners that "hazardous operations" of an unspecified (but "very interesting," according to one Swedish observer) nature would be going on there the week that the Russians later happened to arrive.

The channel where *U-137* actually went aground has a direct but narrow entrance, about 600 feet wide, from the open sea. To get to where it got, the sub had to have made a steady and perfectly aligned 3-mile run up the channel, a well-nigh impossible feat without operating navigational instruments (the Soviets later claimed that all navigation equipment had failed). The passage into the channel had a maximum depth of 20 feet, while Whiskey-class subs even when fully surfaced draw upwards of 16 feet. This is not much room for error.

The submarine had gotten stuck about 8:00 P.M., running aground at a speed of at least seven knots; Western naval experts are baffled by such a speed in such tight waters and theorize the sub may have been trying to turn around for an exit. The sub had spent the whole night trying to get free. Villagers three miles away in the fishing town of Hastholmen heard the sub's engines racing and called the Swedish naval authorities by telephone. Early the following morning a patrol boat eased its way into the foggy channel and found the submarine, apparently deserted. The Swedes went aboard.

As a Swedish officer walked toward the conning tower, he was suddenly confronted by three sleepless and very haggard Soviet submarine officers. In broken German they engaged in a bizarre conversation.

SWEDE: "No, you are not in Poland."

RUSSIAN: "All of our navigation equipment is out of order."

SWEDE: "You cannot have a tow until you explain why you are here."

RUSSIAN: "We thought we were on the other side of the Baltic."

SWEDE: "You passed near the Utklippan lighthouse, did you not see it?"

RUSSIAN: "No, what we saw was a fishing boat."

Russian-speaking Swedish officers soon arrived and expanded the range of the conversation topics. For ten days they discussed the Russian "navigation error" and eventually compiled four distinctly different stories, each of them resulting in the submarine's winding up at locations scores of miles from its actual position. Documents offered for inspection were useless. The submarine's equipment reportedly consisted of an inertial system, a Decca radio, a high-frequency radio direction finder, a gyro compass, a magnetic compass, and a pit log (speed indicator); depending on the explanations, everything but the last item had broken, although the Swedes were never allowed to verify this. The submarine's actual predicament contradicted every one of the Soviet explanations.

For the first four days the submarine remained on the rocks (much to the anxiety of its officers), and for some reason its power plant was fully shut down; there was no heat, no means of cooking, no active ventilation. On the fourth day a wind came up and began to rub the boat against the rocks; the second-in-command (the captain was conferring aboard a nearby Swedish ship) radioed for help and fired flares. Swedish tugs pulled the sub off the rocks and took it to a safer anchorage, farther up the channel from the open sea.

The submarine's officers seemed to be a special lot. The boat's captain was Lieutenant Commander Anatoliy Gushin; the political officer was identified as Lieutenant Vasiliy Besedir; an official observer, who really seemed to be in charge, was Captain First Rank Yosef Avtsukyevich (he claimed to be "a visiting expert.") The presence of the other high-ranking Soviet officers (and possibly more whom the Swedes never saw) certainly supported the hypothesis that the sub had been on a special mission.

Just outside Sweden's twelve-mile limit sat a Kashin-class destroyer with the first deputy commander of Baltic submarines, Vice Admiral Aleksey M. Kalinin, aboard. Nearby was assembled his fleet of a Kilden-class destroyer, two Nanuchka-class missile corvettes, five salvage vessels, and an unknown number (more than one, it turned out) of submarines. The threatening nature of this display was too overt to miss.

Meanwhile, the Swedes kept a close surveillance—and discovered a surprise. Radiation levels around the torpedo tubes were exceptionally high, too high to be merely leftover traces of the former presence of nuclear munitions. Some observers concluded that the Soviets had nuclear weapons of some sort aboard the sub and that for safety reasons (perhaps some sort of leak?) they were stashed in the torpedo tubes. Another theory was that the weapons were torpedoes, with nuclear warheads, possibly hidden in the tubes in anticipation of a Swedish search.

Prime Minister Thorbjorn Falldin expressed "indignation" over the discovery. "The violation was bad enough," he told a press conference. "But worse is the fact that the submarine most likely carried nuclear warheads, according to our investigation." The Soviets did not at first deny Sweden's charge. Their official reply merely noted that "the submarine carries, as do all naval vessels at sea, the necessary weapons and ammunition." They also tried to brush off the complaint as immaterial and irrelevant: "This has nothing to do with the circumstances surrounding the unintentional intrusion by the submarine into Sweden's territorial waters."

Within a few days, however, Moscow spokesmen were denouncing the nuclear weapons story as "inventions evidently intended for ignoramuses." Complaints were part of an anti-Soviet plot: "The question arises, why and who should need to dramatize such an ordinary, routine incident at sea."

Then TASS, without mentioning the submarine at all, began trumpeting general accusations that Sweden was allowing NATO members, particularly the United States, to use its territory to spy on the USSR. "It makes it possible to listen in to areas deep in Soviet territory, determine the location of military bases, control and communications centers, and monitor the flights of aircraft."

In rejecting Sweden's protests, Moscow asserted that international law granted a Soviet warship immunity from any foreign power and that under normal practice, Sweden had no right to hold the boat but was entitled only to demand it leave its territorial waters. It was a curious interpretation.

Ultimately the submarine was allowed to proceed out to sea under its own power, escorted by Swedish warships. Part of the deal was that the Soviets had agreed to pay all Swedish expenses during the confrontation. In late December the defense staff in Stockholm sent a memo to the government giving a figure equivalent to $960,000 for the cost of all salvage and surveillance operations. A few months later the Swedish government handed the Soviets a bill for about a third of the original estimate, and in May the Soviets agreed to pay, as promised.

The Soviet submarine captain paid the price, too. Gushin reportedly soon disappeared into a Soviet prison camp with a relatively light three-year sentence.

The first reactor meltdown at sea may have occurred in 1966 or 1967, aboard the nuclear-powered icebreaker *Lenin*. It is believed to have rendered the ship unusable for several years. According to one CIA report, "A nuclear reactor . . . melted in a sudden catastrophic accident. The exact number of casualties . . . was believed to be between 27 and 30 people." A 1982 U.S. Navy report also referred to the *Lenin*'s having "suffered a reactor casualty." The ship's three old reactors were ultimately replaced with two new ones. The location of the accident is unknown. It could have been in port but more probably was at sea in the Arctic. The Soviets never said a word.

Soviet nuclear ships and submarines don't just irradiate their crews; they zap anybody near their waste products, too. In 1985 a former Soviet Estonian engineer told Swedish radio that there were very dangerous nuclear waste dumps at a site nine miles south of Tallinn, in Estonia. "Nobody in the West can imagine the carelessness with which they handle radioactive waste," he said. The waste, mainly from the nuclear submarine base at Paldiski, was stored in a simple concrete bunker staffed with unskilled workers. According to Reuters from Stockholm, "Waste was brought to the site in an ordinary minibus and there were no instruments to measure radiation." At least one driver reportedly had died of radiation poisoning during the previous ten years.

Russian émigré Avraham Shifrin, working in Israel with a group called the Research Center for Prisons, PsychPrisons, and Forced-Labor Concentration Camps of the USSR, has compiled data on death camps for condemned prisoners. One of the leading locations of these camps is maintenance depots for nuclear submarines, where such work as "cleaning nozzles" (presumably coolant water intakes and exhausts) is done by convicts expected to die. Shifrin listed the following nuclear facilities where there are attached prison camps: Paldiski Bay, Estonia; Severodvinsk, Arkhangelsk Region; Rakushka Bay, Primorsk Territory; and Tarya Bay, Kamchatka Region. Of the last facility, he wrote:

At Tarya bay, there is a strict-regime camp for 400 to 500 prisoners assigned to repair and construction duties at the atomic-powered submarine base next to it. The prisoners are also made to clean the nozzles of the submarines without being given any kind of protective clothing. As a result, they become contaminated and eventually die of leukemia. This is an extermination camp. Here there is no firing squad and no court that pronounces death sentences.

One apparently doesn't have to go far from home to suffer radiation accidents in the USSR. In fact, one account from Chelyabinsk demonstrated that even one's home isn't safe. Menaker's description of the 1958 Urals disaster included an anecdote about factory workers at a city plant which did weapons work. At one point workers in several of the workshops were given radiation dosimeters to keep track of accidental contamination. The small pencillike devices would light a bulb if high radiation levels were detected. One of the workmen brought one dosimeter home to show his family, and the bulb lit, probably because of local contamination from the Kyshtym nuclear waste accident. Soon this story had spread throughout the city. Menaker mocked the official "wise" reaction: "They took back all the 'pencils' . . . " and installed immobile radiation sensors in the workshops.

Radiation from the Kyshtym disaster had other ways of spreading. In examining the disaster's impact on regional wildlife, Zhores Medvedev in London noted that some migrating birds could have been particularly badly affected by eating fish, insects, and plants from the contaminated regions. Birds from those regions of the Urals regularly winter over in the Nile Valley, the Greek and Yugoslav islands, and other areas of Iran, Turkey, and North Africa. It is therefore certainly possible that isolated incidents of low-level radiation poisoning occurred when radioactive birds were killed and eaten in these foreign countries. Nobody noticed, but then nobody had any reason to check the radioactivity of their locally snared dinners.

Some other interesting reports of Soviet radiation releases beyond the USSR borders remain unexplained. Since the Chernobyl catastrophe of 1986 (next chapter) broke secrecy through just such an indicator, these earlier analogs should not be forgotten.

* * *

In 1977 the Swedish scientist Dr. Lars Erik de Geer of the National Defense Research Institute reported on five occurences (at approximately monthly intervals) of anomalously high radioisotope concentration in winds from the USSR. The radionuclides neptunium 239 and molybdenum 99, plus fission products iodine 131 and barium 140, were in the samples; de Geer believed that "the material arrived in Sweden by way of southern Finland or western USSR and Baltic Sea." The isotope mixture is consistent with neither typical bomb tests nor reactor leaks. No closer sources, such as anywhere in Scandinavia, seemed possible because of the geographically widespread collection of similar samples.

Again, in December 1983, an increase in radioactivity in Sweden was connected with a big leak from a Soviet underground nuclear test. That effect, called "venting," is forbidden by the Limited Test Ban Treaty of 1963, although by some counts there have been more than thirty occasions when Soviet nuclear debris has escaped from underground chambers and ultimately crossed out of the USSR territory in detectable (but not dangerous) amounts. U.S. intelligence agencies are not at all displeased by such accidents, since they allow high-flying USAF aircraft to "sniff" the isotopes and provide insight into the construction and operation of the actual Soviet bomb; the practical value may explain the lack of official U.S. government protests.

Swedish scientists later thought that the December 1983 radiation (and two further events in the middle of the next two winters) were from "a possible accident." Said de Geer: "The radiation from fallout we received in Sweden was very slight on each of those occasions, only about one millionth as intense as what we have had from the Chernobyl accident [that is, only several times as much as the TMI release]. But the composition of the fallout was what made us strongly suspect there had been releases of radioactive material from power plant accidents." The latest of the clouds, in February 1985, had been tracked back to the general vicinity of Chernobyl. "We don't say it was coming from the same plant, just the same general vicinity."

Even after the 1986 Chernobyl disaster had become known to the world by news borne on the winds, similar "news" could be overlooked or stonewalled by the Soviets. In particular, in mid-March of the following year increased radioactivity of winds from the USSR prompted speculation throughout Europe that another (although smaller) nuclear power plant accident had occurred in Russia.

On April 13, 1987, a spokesman for the West German Federal Environment Ministry's Institute for Atmospheric Radioactivity told the press that a simultaneous radiation rise had been noted in Finland, southern Sweden, Germany, Switzerland, and Austria (France and Norway also reported noticing increases). Traces of isotopes iodine 131, xenon 133, and xenon 135 were several times normal. "The experts are all saying it was almost certainly a nuclear power accident," noted Heinz-Joerg Haury of the government-financed Institute for Radioactivity and Environmental Research in Munich. Tommy Godaas, chief inspector of the Swedish National Radiation Protection Agency, suggested that while "an accidental minor reactor leak was possible, it might as well have been a deliberately increased emission while cleaning a reactor."

The Soviets denied it all. "Wrong speculation," a Foreign Ministry spokesman told the West German ambassador in Moscow. "Pure invention," a Soviet official told the news media. "Malignant provocation," TASS responded. The Soviets insisted that their new network of monitoring stations had detected nothing out of the ordinary; if the winds moving westward were radioactive, they became that after crossing the Soviet border—thus asserted the official Soviet position.

As with so many earlier incidents, the ultimate authenticity of this latest report of a covered-up Soviet nuclear accident was left where it started, blowing in the wind.

16

THE CHERNOBYL SYNDROME

Probably your side was overreacting and ours was under-reacting. But in our country we don't want to demoralize people. If we are treating a patient for cancer, we never tell them they have it; we don't want them to give up hope. In this regard we treat the population as children.

—*Soviet embassy official in Washington commenting on Chernobyl coverage*

At 1:23 A.M. on Saturday, April 26, 1986, the worst nuclear accident on record—but not the worst in history—began. Sometime later, news, often in highly distorted form, began to filter out. These distortions were sometimes innocent and sometimes not.

Two explosions shook the building housing reactor number four at the Chernobyl power plant fifty miles north of Kiev, scattering fragments of the reactor over the entire neighborhood. Flames rose to 100 feet in the air. A heavily radioactive plume rose into the sky and was caught by the wind from the southeast. Over the next ten days, as radioactive fumes continued to stream out of the ruins, several million times as much radiation escaped as had from Three Mile Island in 1979 in Pennsylvania—more on par with a large open-air nuclear weapons explosion. The winds carried the radioactive particles to the northwest, first across the Ukraine, Lithuania, Latvia, then to Poland, Sweden, Norway, and later, when the winds shifted, to Germany, the Netherlands, and Belgium. After the initial blasts a continuing graphite fire poured more radioactive contamination into the atmosphere.

Plant operators notified Moscow officials within hours, by early Saturday morning, although they still did not completely grasp the scope of the disaster. Emergency medical and administrative teams were flown in later the same day, and these specialists soon determined that local authorities had grossly underestimated the danger of the event. Central government agencies in Moscow had preliminary reports from their own people by Sunday, but no information was given to TASS to release to the public. Western embassies were not notified until the radiation reached Sweden the following day, Monday.

By midafternoon Sunday, the day after the explosion, the decision was made to evacuate the nearby small town of Pripyat (a mile and a half from the reactor). The process took only three hours. Officials later said the one-day delay was due to a local lack of appreciation of the situation, but as it turned out, the delay probably saved lives. On Saturday the initial radiation from the explosion was dropping, and that radiation was not contaminating the town of Pripyat; because of wind direction, it was falling on many of the evacuation routes. By Sunday the graphite fire had caused radiation levels to rise dramatically, and the winds had changed, dumping more of the fallout on the town but less on the evacuation routes.

The evacuation of Pripyat was executed in a special manner. Fearing mob panic, the authorities did not direct residents to central marshaling points but had buses pick them up in front of their apartment buildings. One evacuee explained the calmness in traditional Soviet terms: "There was no panic because everyone knows our country will not leave us in a disaster or in trouble." This citizen had never read of a single case in which the government violated its social contract with its citizens, so he assumed, as he was supposed to, that there was none.

The reactor burned for days. By May 10 the best the Soviets could boast of was that "emission of radioactive substances has practically stopped." Actually emission rates went up briefly a week after the accident, when insulating material dumped on the reactor from helicopters made it overheat. These changes were written on the winds reaching Europe and only afterward were confirmed by TASS dispatches. As the weeks went by, helicopter shuttles dumped hundreds of tons of material onto the reactor. Eventually a massive "sepulcher" was constructed to seal in the ruins.

Ultimately about 100,000 people were evacuated from the area around the accident, and 18,000 of them were sent to clinics for intensive screening. At the same time 5,000 doctors and nurses from across the Soviet Union came in to survey the population of the nearby regions and set up a medical register of all evacuees for health monitoring over the remainder of their lives. About 200 monitoring stations were established to keep watch on the contamination boundaries.

Children of evacuees were sent to Black Sea youth camps, often so quickly that it then took weeks to find out where their parents had been relocated. Many children were seriously depressed, according to camp doctors; some "thought they were doomed." Folk remedies made things worse; local medical officials advised against getting too much sun, fearing the ultraviolet rays would worsen any earlier radiation doses. The result was extreme sadness. "They thought they would not be allowed to be in the sun forever after," a camp doctor noted sadly.

The chasm between East and West had been highlighted during the Chernobyl disaster and its aftermath. The West first heard of the disaster not from the Russians but from the Swedes, two days after it had happened. Alarm and then outrage were expressed by all the free world at the gross social irresponsibility the USSR displayed at not reporting what was perceived as a huge health problem.

Responding to charges that they had been slow to inform other countries of the nuclear contamination, Soviet spokesmen angrily rejected the grounds for any complaints with evasions. Speaking on American television, one official claimed that since government offices were closed over the weekend, there really had been nobody to talk to. When asked why the USSR had not informed other European countries about radiation levels,

Georgi Arbatov responded: "Our scientists are not able to get data on the radiation level in Scotland, Wales, northern Norway or Japan for the simple reason that they are far removed from the USSR." In other words, Arbatov asserted that Soviet scientists had no idea that once the radiation had crossed their border, it wouldn't vanish completely.

Later the excuses changed. "As soon as we received reliable initial information it was made available to the Soviet people and sent through diplomatic channels to the governments of foreign countries," Gorbachev said in a speech two weeks after the incident. The key word was "reliable." The Soviet government possessed—and sat on—preliminary assessments for at least a day and a half before anyone outside the country suspected anything.

Gorbachev's May 14 speech also attacked the motives of Western critics. He told the Soviet public:

> Generally speaking, we faced a veritable mountain of lies, most dishonest and malicious lies.... As to the "lack" of information, over which a special campaign, a political campaign, has been launched, it is an invention. The following confirms this. It took U.S. authorities ten days to inform their own Congress and months to inform the world community about the tragedy that took place at Three Mile Island nuclear power plant in 1979. All this enables one to judge who approaches in what way the matter of informing their own people and foreign countries.

The Soviet leader was leaning on a basic fallacy: The American government was not the operator of the TMI plant, and its owners did talk without delay. Press sites were immediately set up, and reporters were able to interrogate officials. Gorbachev, if poorly informed, may have believed—and wanted the Soviet public to believe—that all news of TMI was withheld for ten days since the government (which in the USSR monopolizes news releases) said nothing. As for the responsibility of officially informing the rest of the world, Gorbachev's alleged parallel also collapses since TMI radiation did not measurably go beyond U.S. borders—even as the news circled the world within hours.

(This myth that the United States kept TMI secret became a key tenet of Soviet damage-limitation-by-counterattack propaganda. Andrey Illesh, a deputy editor of *Izvestiya*, wrote: "It took ten days for information to reach Congress about what happened; other countries learned about the accident after two months." Illesh didn't even check his *own* newspaper's back files: The accident was reported there within two days!)

Reporting on a personal meeting with Gorbachev, the eighty-seven-year-old international businessman Armand Hammer recalled that the Soviet leader "felt their misfortune was being used as a propaganda point. He was also upset with the Reagan and [Secretary of State George] Shultz criticism of the Chernobyl secrecy. 'What are they trying to do to me?' he said. 'Create a breach between me and the Russian people?' " Gorbachev's anger, charitably based on a profound ignorance of Western information control practices, may have been genuine, but it's hard to defend such misperceptions being promulgated throughout the official Soviet media.

Leading "America watcher" Georgi Arbatov, who knew better, joined the chorus: "The unscrupulous tendentiousness of the Western press and of some Western governments surrounding the accident in Chernobyl demonstrates once again how certain circles strive to discredit the USSR, to shake confidence in it and to describe it as an unreliable partner. And all this is being done to justify their own policy of stepping up the arms race." Complained author Y. Lvov in *Soviet Union:* "The initiators of this immoral campaign of whipping up fear, hysteria and malevolence at the expense of another's misfortune are not in the least concerned with either the actual situation or the fate of people. They are obsessed by one thing only: finding a chance to cast aspersions on the USSR. . . ." A letter from Boris Yunker of Moscow, published in *Moscow News* on June 15, complained: "As Soviet people, we are outraged at the immoral anti-Soviet campaign launched by the Western propaganda agencies in connection with the nuclear accident in Chernobyl. Not only press reports, television and radio broadcasts but also public addresses by political leaders are permeated with hatred of this country."

Some Western press reports did turn out to be grossly in error. In the absence of trustworthy spokesmen and their own on-site reporters, the Western news media had grabbed for any reports within reach. Some were wildly exaggerated and were soon disproved. But they were "typical" USSR public rumors, and they were genuine in the sense that many Soviet people believed them.

A puzzling radio transmission, allegedly from near Chernobyl, was picked up late Tuesday night by Dutch ham operator Annis Kofman. In heavily accented English, a strained voice reported there were "many hundreds" dead and wounded. "We heard heavy explosions—you can't imagine what's happening here with all the death and fire—there are not one but two reactors melted down—exploded and are burning—thousands and thousands of people are moving, taking their children and cattle to the south." (The part about the children and the cattle being moved south turned out to be true.) The man concluded: "I heard many dead can't be removed because of the radiation. . . . This is a real disaster. Please tell the world to help us." Although there was no way to verify the actual point of origin of the call (admittedly it could have been a macabre prank), Kofman believed it was authentic and was consistent with other "real rumors."

United Press International had received information via a telephone call from a known source in Kiev that 2,000 people had been killed, and it reported the claim—with a caveat about it being unconfirmed—for news clients worldwide. The source was a Russian woman long known to the agency as accurate. She was particularly known for her reliable contacts with medical authorities. She was first called on Monday when the Swedes broke the radiation story and was able to provide information later confirmed: Kiev buses were being sent to assist in the evacuation, troops were being deployed, and military aircraft were operating over the area (all this was later found to be true). The following day, during a second telephone conversation, she reported that 80 people had been killed immediately at the explosion site and some 2,000 more had died on their way to hospitals: "The whole October Hospital in Kiev is packed with people who suffer from radiation sickness." Bodies were being disposed of carefully: "The people were not buried in ordinary cemeteries but in the village of Pirogov, where radioactive wastes are usually buried." UPI distributed the report with the warning that it was based on a single source and unconfirmed.

Following the Tuesday conversation, UPI could no longer

reach its source. Such calls were typically difficult since even though the USSR has direct-dial long-distance services, Western news agencies must place their calls through an operator. Presumably the sensitive source had called at a public phone, but it's generally believed that those are also routinely tapped and traced. What happened to her is unknown.

The rumor of 2,000 dead was not anywhere near true, but it was "authentic" in the sense that people all over Kiev really did believe it, in the absence of credible information from the government. Multiple sources were available to confirm this. Zenon Snylyk, editor of the daily Ukrainian-language newspaper *Svoboda* ("Freedom") in Jersey City, New Jersey, listened in on two brief phone conversations between Ukrainian-Americans and relatives in Kiev on Tuesday night, April 29 (Wednesday morning in Kiev). One man's uncle estimated that between 10,000 and 15,000 people had died. "He was able to walk around the city and saw a number of people, heavily bandaged, unloaded from trucks and buses in hospitals and other makeshift facilities," Snylyk told the *New York Times*.

This particular report led directly to the sensational front-page headline of the *New York Post* on May 2: MASS GRAVE—15,000 REPORTED BURIED IN NUKE DISPOSAL SITE. Outraged Moscow officials held up copies of this on Soviet television to show the mendacity of the capitalist press. Yet tourists returning to Moscow, or telephoned in Kiev, were also reporting widespread death toll estimates as high as 500. The Soviet government acted as if it believed the rumors were fabricated in the West, when in fact, as these examples prove, the rumors grew in the USSR itself and crossed the borders outbound. The first people to disbelieve Moscow's own statements were Moscow's subjects, and they didn't need any foreign instigation to do so.

A few weeks later *Pravda* acknowledged the existence of the rumors: "Maybe in the beginning, the Kievans had not received full information on the things that were taking place. Hence the foundation for various rumors, helped along by foreign radio stations." Even months afterward local newspapers were denouncing rumors. "Gossiping tongues are worse than guns," chided *Sovietskaya Belorussiya* as it debunked readers' fears.

More than a year later Soviet medical officials began to admit in print that reports of mass panic had been accurate. Writing in the restricted-circulation magazine *Argumenty i Fakty* in June 1987, Professor V. Knizhnikov, of the USSR Health Ministry's national commission on radiobiological defense, described a "mass phobia" in the local population. It was a fear, he wrote, "which is first and foremost the result of lack of objective information and poor training of doctors in radiation medicine" (even a year later Soviet physicians were recommending the wearing of sunglasses to reduce the effects of harmful radiation; the local population was more confident of a high-proof cocktail of vodka and Ukrainian wines). As a result of such phobias, Knizhnikov admitted, there were many dangerous late-term abortions and there were cases of malnutrition among children, primarily rickets when parents withheld all milk. The radiation expert concluded, "Silence and the absence of objective and precise scientific evaluation in our press [are] not only contrary to the course of glasnost, but [are] very harmful."

Several important observations must be made at this point, and they reinforce Knizhnikov's evaluations of the situation. Soviet secrecy was the nation's own worst enemy. First, the Soviets could have forestalled the worldwide promulgation of these rumors within a few hours by the simple expedient of flying a small team of Western journalists to Kiev and letting them drive around the city (for example, visiting the hospitals). Instead, they inexplicably expected the Western press to "follow orders" the way the Soviet press did. Secondly, gross exaggeration of casualties is a feature of Soviet rumors that the reader has encountered numerous times in earlier chapters, and it seems to be based less on deliberately lying than on classical oral dramatization of "forbidden knowledge," plus the misinterpretation of actual events, such as the evacuation of the hospital at Pripyat and the arrival of hundreds of routine patients at Kiev hospitals.

Amid all the rumors the "official" death toll eventually climbed to just above thirty. Two had died the first night (one man's body was never found). A dozen of the firemen who rushed to the scene eventually died (their sacrifice was made more tragic by the fact that they really didn't stem the radiation hemorrhage from the unquenchable reactor ruins, although their efforts may have facilitated the work of men who later did), along with an equal number of plant workers. One of the doctors treating the early flow of casualties also was fatally contaminated.

Meanwhile, some American officials unwisely took the early rumors of a vast slaughter at face value. Kenneth Adelman, director of the Arms Control and Disarmament Agency, termed Soviet claims of only two initial deaths as "frankly preposterous." Secretary of State Shultz announced his belief that fatalities were "far in excess" of that figure. Senator Patrick Leahy (Democrat from Vermont) of the Senate Intelligence Committee, said the accident "goes beyond even the worst nightmares of nuclear scientists." These men must have been basing their estimates on their evaluations of traditional Soviet methods of dealing with previous disasters (which was to cover up and downplay anything negative) rather than on any hard facts from Chernobyl.

Former Secretary of Defense James Schlesinger, who also had once headed the Atomic Energy Commission, estimated that immediate casualties were probably in the "tens"—one of the most accurate of all the approximations at that time. Martin Walker, Moscow correspondent for the *Guardian* in England, had the most realistic view: "The only way that 2000 people could have died at Chernobyl would have been through the kind of explosion that seismic stations around the globe would have recorded."

The Soviet press counterattacked in its own traditional pattern of xenophobia. Some American statesmen were reacting with "outright malice" and "a surge of joy," complained journalist Mikhail Ozerov in the newspaper *Sovietskaya Rossiya*. "Soviet people are heroically combating the disaster, risking their lives, even dying, but across the ocean people are rubbing their hands with glee, saying, that is fine, that serves them right, let us take advantage of this." But there were no accounts of public glee over the Chernobyl disaster anywhere in the West; at worst there was a sense of "poetic justice," especially concerning an article about the Chernobyl power plant in *Soviet Life* the previous February which had boasted of its near-perfect safety. And those with long, unforgiving memories remembered the post-Three Mile Island words of Academy of Sciences head Professor Aleksandrov, who smugly had declaimed, "This accident can only happen in a capitalistic society where they put profits ahead of safety." (Aleksandrov, a party hack, had been forced on the academy by Brezhnev; he resigned soon after Chernobyl.)

The Western media's desperate search for details and particularly for video material led to a major embarrassment for American television network news. In Rome an enterprising French tourist posed as an agent for a Yugoslav tourist who had been "only eight miles from the Chernobyl plant on the day after the disaster." Actually the hoaxer had taken some film of smoking factories in Trieste, Yugoslavia, which he successfully peddled to American news agencies. NBC and ABC each agreed to pay $11,000 for use of the film; CBS was apparently saved from humiliation by a communications failure, although it, too, was eager for the film. The scenes were broadcast on Monday, May 5, but two days later the anchormen publicly apologized. "We were had," Tom Brokaw of NBC told viewers. "We were badly misled," complained Peter Jennings of ABC. The Soviet media accused the networks of a deliberate fraud.

Excuses and explanations were quick to appear for such excesses. "If the Russians had simply given us the knowledge that we had the right to expect, it wouldn't have happened," asserted Stephen Hess, a media expert at the Brookings Institute. Noted columnist Drew Middleton: "By stifling the news the Soviet government encourages rumor. . . . In a police state, gossip thrives on censorship." *Newsweek* offered a good explanation: "For all the frenzy, the press was just obeying a natural law: journalism abhors a vacuum." This is all true in principle, but it's a poor excuse for haste and lack of caution in some reporting.

The Soviets did resort to some standard propaganda formulas in dealing with the story. From the very beginning, less than an hour after their initial brief admission of trouble on Monday, April 28, they launched their counteroffensive. "The accident at the Chernobyl atomic power station is the first one in the Soviet Union," TASS asserted. "Similar accidents happened on several occasions in other countries. In the United States, 2,300 accidents, breakdowns and other faults were registered in 1979 alone. . . ." (Radio Moscow science correspondent Boris Belitzky soon raised that 1979 figure to 20,000, with "hundreds of them rated as particularly serious.") Gorbachev himself continued this falsification in his speech on May 14, when he claimed: "For the first time ever we encountered in reality such a sinister force as nuclear energy that has escaped control." For those Westerners concerned about Chernobyl, Georgi Arbatov demanded self-righteously, "Don't they know about the dozens of accidents during the operations of military nuclear technologies, including the two cases involving U.S. submarines?" (Arbatov's intention was clearly to imply deceptively that there had been no Soviet equivalent accidents.)

Such deceptions were intended for more than just the domestic market. *Soviet Life,* the leading USSR propaganda monthly for foreign readers, insisted falsely: "Doctors had previously known about radiation sickness only from lectures and textbooks." And when Dr. Michael McCally, treasurer of International Physicians for the Prevention of Nuclear War, wrote of his experiences at one of the hospitals treating the injured, he ignored the entire existence of earlier Soviet radiation accident victims. "The inescapable image was of Hiroshima and Nagasaki," he lamented. "My only experience of people with burned faces, no hair, and bruise marks from bleeding in their skin had been from medical textbook pictures of the Hiroshima bombing victims." Such ignorance was the result of the deliberate Soviet secrecy policy over many years.

Genrik Borovik, a noted Soviet television commentator, responded to Western coverage of Chernobyl with such outrageous "facts" as that the deaths of John Wayne and his whole film crew had been due to fallout from an atomic test in Nevada and that the United States had maliciously exaggerated Chernobyl fallout in Greece so that the local U.S. Air Force base could buy cheap vegetables. Other Soviet commentators suggested that radiation detected in Italy had really come from a West German nuclear accident. Borovik continued: "While the Chernobyl accident is by far the most untoward occurrence in nuclear facilities in the Soviet Union, given their high safety margin, it seems there have been numerous accidents of this kind in the West."

Among the Soviet population, two conflicting currents ran powerfully. While some were all too eager to accept and embellish the "worst case" rumors, others—at least in front of Westerners—put on brave faces of unconcern. Speaking to American reporters in Baku a few days after the explosion, an ostensibly typical "comrade in the street" named Yuriy Zhavavov waved a copy of *Pravda* and proclaimed, "This is enough for us—everything seems to be under control." A student listening to music in an outdoor café was also unconcerned. "Soviet science is very good, very accurate," asserted Misha Yegorov to the Americans. "It is very rare there is a problem." In Moscow the typical man-in-the-street reaction to questions about the "nuclear accident" was to ask, "You mean the one in the United States?"

There was initial Western skepticism that the full story would ever come out (a not unreasonable expectation considering previous Soviet behavior). A week after the disaster some commentators were cynical. "Those who expect anything like full disclosure of the facts of the accident and its effects on the Soviet Union will wait in vain," warned Drew Middleton. "There will be a thorough investigation by the central government. But there will be no detailed reconstruction of what went wrong and who is to blame. For what went wrong went wrong in the Soviet Union, where things do not go wrong."

But the cynics were wrong for once. In astonishing detail the story began to come out. The Soviets may have had an array of motivations, both internal and external, but to the West they appeared to give in to unrelenting pressure for candid information because their image and credibility were becoming badly eroded throughout the world. They told how the accident had happened and how the people had died.

The initial official Soviet explanation for the explosion itself was that it had occurred inexplicably during a "routine shutdown." But by late summer a complete and detailed chronology of the catastrophe had been prepared for release to the International Atomic Energy Agency (IAEA) meeting August 25–29 in Vienna. The leader of the Soviet delegation was academician Valeriy A. Legasov, and he expressed initial uneasiness that he was being forced to play an unprecedented role, one with which the Soviets had scant experience: "We are sharing not our successful experiments with nuclear icebreakers or an encounter with Halley's Comet, but a painful experience, which was a great tragedy." Nevertheless, before 600 nuclear experts from sixty-two countries, the Soviet team made its presentation. "Explicit, vivid, and chilling," commented one observer.

Despite the detailed chronology of "what" and "when," the Soviets were not specific on "why." Noted one Western observer: "The mystery remains that so many apparently well-trained people should hit on the precise blend of indiscretions that would make an apparently safe reactor blow up." The best answer the Soviets could give did not address the operators' reasoning. "The defect of the system was that the designers did not foresee the awkward and silly actions by the operators," Legasov had noted. The operators had deliberately violated six safety rules, a contingency that the reactor's designers understandably could have overlooked.

Operator blunders were greatly compounded by the poor design of the reactor, noted American nuclear safety expert Richard Wilson. "The [Chernobyl types of] reactors have the worst shut-down capability of any commercial reactor in the world," he wrote. The reactor's inherent instability constituted an "atrocious" design fault. The Russians evidently know this but still refuse to admit it because of foreign commercial deals for such reactors. At a meeting of the Soviet Academy of Sciences later that fall, Legasov reportedly confessed: "I did not lie at Vienna, but I did not tell the whole truth. . . ," presumably about the bad design features of the reactor.

As the nuclear power system lost cooling water (to steam, for example), the power increased. In the final seconds the reaction rate skyrocketed from a tenth full-rated power to more than 100 times normal. A surge to a million megawatts of thermal energy created a physical shock in the material, pulverizing the uranium oxide fuel rods and flashing the remaining water to superheated steam. The 1,000-ton concrete lid of the reactor vessel went right through the roof of the containment building.

Within seconds, air and steam reacted with superhot zirconium metal fragments, producing hydrogen, which viciously exploded, showering the building and surrounding area with blazing core material, setting several dozen fires. At this point the 100-ton graphite core caught fire.

This is what awaited the emergency personnel who began to arrive within minutes. It was death incarnate for many of them.

Within the first thirty-six hours 350 people were treated at hospitals. The level of exposure was estimated by the speed of the onset of radiation poisoning symptoms, such as vomiting, headache, and fever, and later by blood tests. Treatment was hampered by serious thermal burns. Also, many people had been exposed only partially, on one side of their bodies or on their arms and torsos.

Of the 20 people who had received whole-body doses of what was considered a "fatal" amount, within six weeks 17 of them were dead. Those with the highest dosages probably died of gastrointestinal collapse, causing severe vomiting, diarrhea, and dehydration. Those with lesser dosages died of bone marrow collapse, which causes hemorrhaging from lack of clotting factors and destruction of oxygen-carrying hemoglobin. Altogether, some 300 people received serious doses of radiation. Of these treated, all but 2 were plant workers or firemen; the exceptions were 2 residents of Pripyat who had been cycling or walking through badly contaminated areas before authorities had roped them off. If they survived the first few months, chances are these victims walked away with only an elevated chance of getting radiation-induced cancer some years later.

Western estimates of long-range casualties range into tens of thousands of "excess" cancer deaths, although more cautious estimates seem to vary between 2,000 and 10,000 over the next seventy years (i.e., until the last babies from Chernobyl have died of "old age," there will be deaths caused by the disaster). To put this in perspective, it means an increase in natural cancer rates of from a fraction of 1 percent to several percents. Out of every several hundred cancer deaths until past the middle of the next century, one to ten would not have happened without the disaster, but the determination of which ones is impossible. For their part, evidently recalling the initial baseless report of thousands dead, the Soviets denounced such speculation as "rumors." Thousands didn't die in one day but will over a period of years as a direct result of Chernobyl. In comparison, the "excess deaths" (mostly from lung cancers) to be expected from the operation of coal-fired plants operating to replace the lost Chernobyl electricity are approximately the same, if not more.

"Extra" deaths could also be expected in Western Europe, according to sober projections. Richard Wilson estimated the eventual number to be "hundreds," or several per year for decades. They would not be randomly scattered; regions in which rainfall brought the fallout to earth received contamination up to ten times higher than nearby dry regions. In

Konstanz in southern Germany, for example, a spring thunderstorm drenched the city with radioactive rain on April 30; the result may be from 25 to 45 additional cancer deaths over the next several decades in the city of 100,000.

"Openness" was clearly a tactical response to the unprecedented situation, and there were occasions when Western observers suspected recidivism.

On May 23, while the reactor was being "safed," and out of sight of Western journalists, a second fire broke out in the ruins of the reactor building. It was not disclosed at the time. Some fuel oil tanks still in the building were endangered ("We won't talk about what would have happened if these [tanks] had got into trouble," a later Soviet newspaper account delicately stated), and teams of firemen had to be sent inside in shifts to avoid accumulating dangerous radiation doses. Noted fire fighter Nikolay Bocharnikov: "We received respirators, flashlights and radiation meters, and entered the empty hall." Their dosimeters "went right off the scale," the fireman later told a reporter for *Leninskoye Znamya*. The fire broke out before dawn and took all day to extinguish—and two more months to burn through layers of official secrecy.

Meanwhile, in mid-June several Finnish monitoring stations picked up a radiation burst four times higher than that from Chernobyl, which lasted several hours. Winds were from the southwest; but the Soviets never explained it, and the Finns, unlike the Swedes the previous April, didn't make a fuss.

Why the unprecedented openness, despite its selectivity? The expectations that the Russians would cling to tight-lipped type were confounded by a novel candor. But the suspicion remains that if the radiation had not been detected beyond their borders, they might have said nothing.

What the Soviets wanted to tell the world was that it could never happen again. Armen Abagyan, director of Moscow's Nuclear Power Station Institute, called post-Chernobyl hardware and procedural modifications an "absolute guarantee" against a repetition. In response to some skeptical mutterings of Western journalists, he went on to proclaim: "These reactors are situated in our country, where our children and grandchildren are going to live. Do you really think we will allow the operation of reactors that can repeat the same story?"

The public availability of nonmilitary satellite photographs was also credited with prompting full disclosure. "I don't think there's any question about it," asserted Charles Z. Wick, director of the United States Information Agency. "Their previous nuclear disaster [in 1958] was kept quiet. Now satellite technology caught them red-handed, and it couldn't be covered up." Concluded Wick: "This is the end of the Soviet monopoly on telling people what they want to tell them."

One other thing has been left undisclosed. "What has happened to the operators?" Abagyan was asked in Vienna by a Western reporter.

"They have been punished," he replied forcefully.

"How?" was the follow-up question.

Abagyan hesitated, then answered to the best of his abilities: "That is not a field in which I am an expert."

CONCLUSION

It is true that a view, a behavior existed according to which nothing bad could be written about the Soviet Union. The world could not learn of any mistake because an unfavorable picture would then evolve about the Soviet Union in the eyes of the world public. Now, on the other hand, we name our mistakes, our problems, and it surprised many that through this a much more nuanced and favorable picture of the Soviet Union has developed. This proved to us that frankness and openness is worth much more than the most perfect but falsely colored picture.

—Nikolay Shishlin, CPSU Central Committee Information Department, interview on Radio Budapest, April 22, 1987

The Chernobyl disaster came to symbolize the eventual victory of openness over reflexive secrecy. But reflexes tell a system's true characteristics more accurately than do morning-after thoughts and stratagems. There has yet to be a Soviet disaster announced in progress, as true *glasnost* should require (the next falling nuclear satellite may afford an opportunity). The limits of *glasnost* have been sharply demarcated by the official handling of news of disasters; "openness" is broad, indeed, but not universal by any means, and it is shallow, very shallow.

Typical recent news stories suggest that by and large *glasnost* remains mainly a public relations stratagem, not a fundamental new doctrine. Early in 1987 TASS gave official figures confirming what Western experts had known for years about falling Soviet life expectancy—but only to point out that Gorbachev's new antialcoholism campaign had resulted in a reversal of the hitherto secret downward trend. And when *Izvestiya* discussed fire deaths in mid-1987 (admitting for the first time that about 8,000 Soviet citizens die in fires every year), it was also aiming at particular segments of the unresponsive consumer industry with the horrifying disclosure that over the past five years more than 900 Soviet citizens had been killed by fires caused by defective television sets. Such "openness" would be more trust-worthy if the facts weren't so "useful" to Gorbachev.

If secrecy was a trait grafted onto Russian culture by the Soviet regime, there might also be grounds for optimism in imagining that political decisions could engender fundamental changes in national attitudes toward "openness." But as observ-ers have noted for centuries, secrecy is a deep-seated Russian characteristic. The Marquis de Cousine recorded an incident in St. Petersburg a century and a half ago, when a large boat on a picnic cruise to the Peterhof Palace was sunk by a sudden storm. Hundreds died, but nothing was ever reported in the newspapers; instead, police just arrived at the houses of the dead, boarded them up, and shipped off all their belongings. Centuries earlier, similar incidents were observed by foreign visitors; centuries from now, one may wonder how much will have changed.

Richard Longworth, formerly the Moscow correspondent for UPI, recently described the predicament of contemporary Western journalists in Russia this way:

> Article 65 of the Soviet criminal code forbids an unauthorized person to possess a state secret. But what exactly is a secret? This is much less clear. After some time in the Soviet Union, the only solid conclusion a correspondent can reach is that a secret is whatever the state chooses to hold confidential or declines to make public—no limits, no rules. How many pedestrians were killed by vehicles in Moscow in 1985? What is the death rate for Soviet males in the age group 26–34? How many persons were hospitalized from frostbite in Nizhne Angarsk in the most recent year for which medical statistics are available? When will the Baikal–Amur Mainline be completed?

Longworth recalled an exchange with an official of Aeroflot at the inauguration of Tu-144 passenger service to Alma Ata in 1976. A Western correspondent asked the obvious question: "How many planes do you have for the service?" The Aeroflot officials gave what for them was the obvious (and safe) answer: "Enough." The true answer was "four," but why (beyond reflex) the Soviets should be unwilling to give it remains obscure.

Since the West cannot wait for the Soviets to move themselves all the way to full openness, we must still take the major initiatives of investigations. Subsequently the Soviet media often respond, sometimes in astonishing detail and candor. But this openness traditionally is a reaction to a stimulus of publication of initial data in the Western press.

Because it deals so intimately with a fundamental feature of Soviet life, this book should better have been written in the Soviet Union by a Soviet author with credentials of unquestionable patriotism. But this was impossible for a number of reasons, not least of which is that the mere possession—much less the publication—of most of this information would be a clear-cut violation of existing Soviet law, *glasnost* or no *glasnost*. Any Soviet citizen who said the things this book has said would be branded a criminal, a madman, a spy, or worse. And he or she would be punished accordingly.

That's the greatest tragedy, since its victims suffer terminal truth deprivation. The Western drive to decipher and document these Soviet disasters, performed for whatever primary motivations, ultimately will most benefit ordinary Soviets themselves. Since they've been the ones to pay the hideous human costs of these disasters, it's only fair that they get something valuable in return: truth.

NOTES AND ACKNOWLEDGMENTS

Beyond specific help on individual topics, a number of people provided me with general advice and a wide variety of source material. Deserving special appreciation are Curtis Peebles, Joe Rowe, Henry Palka, Leonid Vladimirov, Thornton Page, Peter Fiechter (of the Swiss Re Insurance Company, Zurich), Judy Thornton, and Vera Rich.

Special library assistance is acknowledged from the Lunar and Planetary Institute; the Freeman Library in Clear Lake City, Texas; the Fondren Library at Rice University; and the University of Houston at Clear Lake; also the Soviet Interview Project in Champaign, Illinois, and the Delphic Associates in Falls Church, Virginia.

INTRODUCTION

The Bukovsky quotation is from "How the Soviets Break News: Selectively and Dishonestly," Henrik Bering-Jensen, "Insight," *Washington Times*, June 2, 1986, pp. 11–13.

The Atkov interview occurred in Houston, Texas, in March 1986. Accounts of the Vasyutin orbital medevac are from contemporary press accounts, plus private sources. The NASA "medical checklist" for the Skylab space station was furnished by Dr. Daniel Woodard.

The Jiri Kotas and N. G. Palgunov quotations are also from the Bering-Jensen article, 1986.

Klochko's list was published in "Victims of Stalin's A-Bomb," *New Scientist* (June 23, 1983), pp. 845–49.

Kaiser's list was in his book *Russia* (New York: Simon and Schuster, 1984).

The *Sunday Times* list was published on January 5, 1986 (Louise Branson, "How Kremlin Keeps Editor in Line"), p. 1.

1. ANTHRAX IN SVERDLOVSK

The epigraph is from Vivian Wyatt's article "Anthrax in the Air" in the "Comment" section of *New Scientist* (March 27, 1980), p. 986.

U.S. government reports include *Soviet Biological Warfare Activities*, a report of the Subcommittee on Oversight, Permanent Select Committee on Intelligence, U.S. House of Representatives, five pages, June 1980 (Washington, D.C.: Government Printing Office, 1980), and *Soviet Biological Warfare Threat*, a Defense Intelligence Agency report released in late 1986. Eloquent pro-weapon argumentation was made by the U.S. State Department's deputy assistant for negotiations policy, Douglas J. Feith, before the Subcommittee on Oversight and Evaluation of the House Permanent Select Committee on Intelligence, August 8, 1986, published in *Defense Issues*, vol. 1, no. 60, American Forces Information Service, from the Office of the Assistant Secretary of Defense (Public Affairs), Washington, D.C. See also "Biological Weapons: Outlawed but Not Gone," letter by Douglas J. Feith, *New York Times*, October 8, 1986. Soviet accounts are drawn from the *Daily Report—Soviet Union* of the Foreign Broadcast Information Service (hereafter FBIS-SU), particularly these lengthy translations: June 13, 1980, pp. A6–7; July 2, 1980, pp. A4–6; August 8, 1980, pp. AA7–9; August 12, 1980, pp. AA7–10; October 1, 1980, pp. "annex 2–4"; January 23, 1981, p. A9. In the Western public press the incident was widely reported throughout 1980. Articles in *Science* included: Constance Holden, "What Is Siberian Ulcer Doing in Sverdlovsk?" (April 4, 1980); R. Jeffrey Smith, "Soviet Anthrax Explanation Is Debunked" (July 18, 1980); Nicholes Wade, "Death in Sverdlovsk: A Critical Diagnosis" (September 26, 1980), pp. 101–02. *New Scientist* (London) took a highly skeptical position from the beginning and published several important articles: Zhores Medvedev, "The Great Russian Germ Warfare Fiasco" (July 31, 1980), pp. 360–61; Vivian Wyatt, "Anthrax: Recipe for a Blunt Weapon" (September 4, 1980), pp. 721–22. See also Vera Rich, "Incident at Military Village 19," *Nature* (March 27, 1980), p. 294, and David Satter, "Support for Soviet Explanation of Anthrax Outbreak," London *Financial Times* (June 10, 1980). Many of the quotations from the 1980 classified U.S. government report come from a contemporary column by Rowland Evans and Robert Novak. The best available account of how American analysts grappled with this puzzle is found in Leslie Gelb's article, "Keeping an Eye on Russia," *New York Times Magazine* (November 29, 1981), pp. 31–33 ff.; Gelb conducted dozens of interviews with current and former U.S. officials and with independent experts.

Later discussion of the incident included: Raymond A. Zilinskas, "Anthrax in Sverdlovsk?," *Bulletin of the Atomic Scientists* (June/July 1983), pp. 24–27, and letters in October 1983 (p. 63) and November 1983 (pp. 61–62); William Kucewicz, "Accident Prone and Asking for Calamity," *Wall Street Journal*, May 3, 1984; *New Scientist* (October 25, 1984), p. 40, in which former editor Bernard Dixon attacked the pro-Pentagon motivations of proponents of the weapons theory; Meselson's quotation from " 'Shameful' War of Words on Yellow Rain," *New Scientist* (June 5, 1986), p. 25.

It didn't help the credibility of Moscow's case that Soviet propagandists took their own liberties with the Western accounts they quoted to back up their claims of innocence. Where Wyatt wrote that "the evidence suggests a form of anthrax that could come from handling contaminated food," author V. Uvarov's *Izvestiya* article "The Falsifiers Not Relenting" (August 6, 1980, p. 5, FBIS-SU, August 8, p. AA7), quotes him as saying, "ALL the data ATTEST TO a form of anthrax which can be caused by contaminated foodstuffs." Where Wyatt had said that newspaper articles were "a wise move if there had been an outbreak of the disease and the authorities wanted to warn people . . . of the danger," Mishin's article (*Literaturnaya Gazeta*, August 6, 1980, p. 9, FBIS-SU, August 12, pp. AA7–9) altered it to be an absolute and unconditional assertion "that [newspaper publication] means that the authorities wanted above all to warn the population of the danger."

A Russian domestic broadcast on January 22, 1981 (FBIS-SU, January 23, 1981, p. A9), quoted "the [American] scientific magazine *Science*" as having surveyed various specialists and concluding that the accusations were fantasy and that "that which is regarded by us as precise evidence in actual fact emanates from exceedingly murky and unreliable sources." The actual quotation seems to have been that "the sources of the State Department's information about the alleged incident remain obscure," a passage written (by Constance Holden) in late March 1980, immediately after the first reports, and subsequently subject to amendment by more detailed data. Searches of all American magazines with *Science* or *Scientific* in their titles showed nothing any closer to the Russian radio's quotation.

Such patent misrepresentations of Western expert testimony harmed the credibility of the Soviet case, at least among those with the ability to do independent research and with the freedom to believe or not to believe on the basis of merit, not coercion.

The 1986 developments were described in David Dickson, "Soviets Discuss Sverdlovsk," *Science* (October 10, 1986), p. 144. Details of the actual anthrax outbreak came through private sources.

2. Accidents on Ice

A general survey of Soviet Antarctic activities can be found in Barney Brewster, *Antarctica: Wilderness at Risk* (Wellington, New Zealand: Friends of the Earth, 1982), and in the *Polar Regions—Atlas*, National Foreign Assessment Center, CIA, May 1978 (reprint November 1981), National Technical Information Service, Washington, D.C.

Russian exploration of Antarctica goes back to the beginning of European and American voyages to that region, when Admiral Fabian Bellingshausen of the czarist navy circled the continent from 1820 to 1822. His two ships were the *Vostok* and the *Mirniy*, and his deputy commander was a naval officer named M. P. Lazarev; a century and a half later the names of both commanders and both ships were assigned to the Soviet scientific bases which came to ring the continent's coastline.

For today's expeditions, supplies come annually from Leningrad in three or four ships, on six-week sea voyages. The Soviet reliance on ships rather than airlifts results in a larger winter population than that of other nations; many Soviet scientists must wait out the winter in place before beginning summer activities.

Air transport has been improved in recent years. In 1980 a new compressed-snow runway suitable for heavy wheeled aircraft was completed at Molodezhnaya. For priority passengers and cargo, a twenty-four-hour flight from Leningrad via Aden to Maputo (Mozambique) and on to Molodezhnaya (the main Soviet base) replaced the long sea voyage. Because of severe climate, routine airborne operations can be run only from November through February, at which time all aircraft are pulled out of the continent and returned to their home airfields. However, American aircraft based in Christchurch, New Zealand, perform midwinter resupply drops at various stations, including the South Pole itself, and have on occasion conducted emergency medical evacuations.

The Soviet bases ring the continent's coastline, where ships could approach near enough to off-load supplies by tractor, sled, or helicopter. Running around the continent's rim from the Bellingshausen base on the northern tip of the Antarctic Peninsula clockwise, the bases are: Druzhnaya, 40W; Novolazarevskaya, 12E; Molodezhnaya, the Soviet headquarters, 45E; Mirniy, 93E; Dobrovolski (formerly Oazis), 101E; and Leningradskaya, 159E.

A general discussion of life at the Vostok station can be found in Dr. Robert B. Flint, Jr., "With the 19th Soviet Antarctic Expedition (SAE) at Vostok Station, 1973–1975," *Antarctic Journal* (November/December 1975), pp. 287–92.

Specific references to the 1982 Vostok fire are found in the Soviet newspaper *Trud* (March 10, 1983, p. 4); in Neonila Yampolskaya, "Vello Park and His Peaks," *Soviet Life* (September 1984), pp. 10–15; in "Vostok's Ordeal by Fire and Ice," *Antarctic* (June 1983), pp. 71–72; and in *Man's Potential—Seven Portraits* (Moscow: Progress Publishers, 1985) in English, in which Chapter 3, "The Polar Station," was written by the veteran polar journalist Vasiliy Peskov (the chapter header epigraph comes from p. 50, ibid.). Details also came from interviews with officials of the National Science Foundation (Washington, D.C.). "We became aware of it only after the fact," an NSF spokesman told me in 1986. "They never notified any other treaty parties at the time; they didn't advise anyone of their difficulties; they didn't request assistance."

The January 1979 medevac from Molodezhnaya was described in VXE-6 records and in the *Deepfreeze '79* report prepared by COMNAVSUPP for Antarctica and provided by Lieutenant Commander Art Kilpatrick, USN, of the National Science Foundation. Noted the official VXE-6 history for that season: "The rescue effort [was] faced with a critical fuel factor. . . . [It] involved VXE-6 aviators, crewmen, and medical personnel in a venture into previously untried antarctic locations and terminated in one of the longest flights in Operation Deep Freeze history—over [6,400 miles]. Above all, the rescue effort attested to the spirit of international cooperation in antarctic exploration." Invaluable material also came from the files of R. K. Eunson, editor of the *Otago Daily Times* in Dunedin, New Zealand.

The February 1986 Il-14 crash was described in *Polar Geography and Geology* (January to March 1986), pp. 84–85. The Soviet press references were *Izvestiya*, March 24, and *Pravda*, March 28.

The story of the 1986 misadventures with Druzhnaya base on the Filchner Ice Shelf is compiled from contemporary Western and Soviet accounts.

Part of the Soviet problem seems to be a reflexive fear of Western spies, even in Antarctica. The irony of the possibility of Soviet officials' considering visiting American scientists to be spies was that it was widely believed by the Americans that many of the visiting Soviet exchange personnel really were intelligence agents (voicing that suspicion was discouraged by NSF officials). In 1978 and 1979 an alleged Soviet "geologist" at McMurdo Sound astounded and amused his American associates with his naive ignorance of geology. A few years later a Russian visitor at the South Pole station who had arrived with 60 pounds of personal effects tried to ship 500 pounds home when he left (when his crates were opened, they were found to be full of photocopies of practically every repair and maintenance manual at the base, made on the base's own copying machine). Experienced Antarctic researchers have little concern for Soviet sensitivity on such issues.

Special thanks to Guy Guthridge, Brian Shoemaker, John Schutt, Everett Gibson, and John Annexstad, and to *amerikanskiye vostochniki* Michael Fancher, Edward Grew, Rex Hanson, Arthur Ford, and Robert Flint, who shared their experiences and impressions of life at the Vostok station, and to Ms. Kim Fletcher of the Stanford University Radio-Science Laboratory, who helped me track some of them down.

3. The Bloody Border

The official Soviet version of the July 1980 incident was published in the April 6, 1986, issue of *Krasnaya Zvezda*, in an article by Colonel A. Andryushkov entitled "I'm Going for Ram" [excellent translation by Dr. Michael Launer]. The rest of the material came from contemporary press accounts and from contemporary transcripts of the FBIS daily reports for the Soviet Union, for Latin America, and for Africa/Middle East. The inside details of the arms deal were spelled out in "Crash Reveals Israel's Arms Deal with Iran," *London Sunday Times*, July 26, 1981, "Insight," pp. 1–2. For details of CL-44 operations I am indebted to Captain Harold Ewing; the characteristics of the particular aircraft lost on this flight was described to me by Canadair spokesman E. A. Rankin. No cooperation at all was received from the Argentine government or from Transporte Aéreo Río Platense officials in Buenos Aires.

Vegin's story appeared in *Biblioteka Yunogo Patriota* ("Library of a Young Patriot"), a series devoted to stories "on the homeland, on deeds, and on honor," published in 1973 by the Ministry of Defense in 65,000 copies, quoted in David R. Jones, "Soviet Concepts of Security: Reflections on KAL Flight 007," *Air University Review* (January 1987), pp. 29–39. Yeliseyev's story appears in Colonel General S. Golubev, "*Zadacha Gosudarstvennoy Vazhnosti* [Tasks of National Importance]," *Aviatsiya i Kosmonavtika* (January 1984), p. 2. The 1978 Iranian helicopter incident was briefly noted in the *Times* of

London ("Pilots 'Ignored' Soviet Order," July 18 dispatch from Moscow, printed July 19 on p. 9), but all details of the incident come from contemporary Iranian newspaper articles provided by a private source.

The Italian pilot Benito Niolu's comments about the dangers of flying the Iran-USSR border were published in Reuters dispatch from Rome, "Alitalia Pilot Fears Attack by Soviet Jet," *Times* of London, March 5, 1984, p. 6.

The 1984 Baltic Sea incident is recounted from contemporary Swedish and Soviet press accounts as translated by FBIS.

Earlier incidents along the Soviet border have been culled from contemporary press accounts and from Lennart Berns, "Soviet and Warsaw Pact Air Incidents," *Jane's Defence Weekly* (January 12, 1985). The late 1970s Baltic Sea case of Soviet mistaken identity of an RC-135 for a B-52 was reported in Seymour Hersh, *The Target Is Destroyed* (New York: Random House, 1986), p. 10.

The July 1960 RB-47 Barents Sea incident is described from contemporary press accounts plus *Khrushchev Remembers: The Last Testament*, tr. and ed. Strobe Talbott (Boston: Little, Brown, 1974), p. 448, and *The Penkovsky Papers* (New York: Avon Books, 1965), p. 355. Two of six crewmen survived and were captured.

The 1978 KAL 902 incident was described in Anthony Paul, "Shot Down Over Russia! The Mysterious Saga of Flight 902," *Reader's Digest* (1978), pp. 138–144; the intercepted Soviet conversations were described in Hersh, op. cit., pp. 11–15.

The 1976 Japanese Neptune attack is described ibid., p. 12.

The 1983 KAL 007 tragedy has an extensive literature, much of it garbage. Contemporary press accounts and FBIS transcripts provided the foundation for significant further research.

The spy flight ravings of David Pearson of Yale (in the *Nation*), R. W. Johnson of Oxford (in *Shootdown: Flight 007 and the American Connection* [New York: Viking, 1986]), Oliver Clubb of the University of Syracuse (in *KAL Flight 007: The Hidden Story* [Sag Harbor, N.Y.: Permanent Press, 1985]), Sugwon Kang of Oneonta College (in the *Bulletin of Concerned Asian Scholars*), Conn Hallinan of the U.S. Peace Council, Akio Takahashi (in *The President's Crime*), and the pseudonymous "P. Q. Mann" (*Defense Attaché*) are pure crackpottery.

The 1983 *Rainbow Warrior* invasion of the USSR is reconstructed from contemporary press accounts, from FBIS transcripts, and from a Greenpeace documentary film on the incident.

The 1986 lost Kuwaiti plane story is in the FBIS-SU, October 30, 1986, p. H1, and November 4, 1986, p. H1.

4. MILITARY DISASTERS

The epigraph is from FBIS-SU, May 19, 1987, p. A8. The Salang Tunnel disaster is described from contemporary press accounts and FBIS transcripts. TASS carried a brief account from Kabul, mentioning "loss of life," on November 18, documented in FBIS-SU, November 19, p. D1. Comments attributed to "Paghmani" were in "Afghan Tunnel Inferno," *Soldier of Fortune*

(April 1983), pp. 28, 86–88, which is accompanied by Bill Guthrie, "Tunnel Theories." The Soviet account was in V. Sukhodolskiy, "Salang," *Krasnaya Zvezda*, January 14, 1984, p. 3; an earlier general description was in A. Poltavskiy, "Red Army's Perils Along Afghanistan's Salang Pass Highway," *Krasnaya Zvezda*, December 25, 1983, p. 1.

The Severomorsk ammunition dump disaster was first mentioned in *Jane's Defence Weekly* (July 10 and July 14, 1984), reported in FBIS-SU, July 19, 1984, p. A2, plus regular contemporary news clippings, July 1984. The theory of how the accident happened was in S.V.C., "What Happened at Severomorsk?," *Review of the News*, weekly publication of the John Birch Society (September 12, 1984), p. 48.

Turetsky's account of safety concerns at the Northern Fleet missile test range is found in his memoir, *The Introduction of Missile Systems into the Soviet Navy (1945–1962)* (Falls Church, Va.: Delphic Associates, 1983).

The Belenko jet fighter crash vignette appeared in John Barron, *MiG Pilot* (New York: McGraw-Hill, 1980), p. 106. Other crash accounts are from contemporary press clippings and from *Flight International*'s annual survey of military aviation safety. The 1976 Newfoundland crash is mentioned in "Reconnaissance Aircraft Lost," datedlined Washington, in the *Times* of London, August 6, 1976, p. 6. The December 1983 East German crash was from an Agence France Presse (AFP) report from Berlin, December 24, 1983, quoting the West Berlin newspaper *Berliner Morgenpost* of that same date, cited in FBIS-SU for January 3, 1984, p. F1. The 1984 Kabul crash was described in an AFP report dated October 30, cited in FBIS-SU, October 30, 1984, p. D2. The April 1984 crash that killed Fedotov and Zaytsev is mentioned in *Pravda*, April 19, 1984, p. 6. The official Soviet story of the posthumous awards was in *Krasnaya Zvezda*, January 19, 1985, p. 5. The July 1985 Baltic Sea crash was described in "Soviet SU-15 Crashes Following Intercept over Baltic," *Aviation Week* (July 15, 1985), p. 24; the Norwegian Sea crash later that same month was described in "Soviet YAK-36 Forger Pilot Ejects Safely in Norwegian Sea," *Aviation Week* (September 9, 1985), pp. 67–68 (six photographs). The 1986 test laser fire is described in Michael R. Gordon, "U.S. Aides Report Soviet Lost Airborne Laser Lab in a Fire," *New York Times*, August 24, 1986, p. 18.

Khrushchev's account of the Mya-4 bomber problems is from *Khrushchev Remembers*, loc. cit.

The 1974 Black Sea naval explosion is described in Drew Middleton, "Soviet Destroyer Is Reported Sunk," *New York Times*, September 27, 1974, p. 7, and "Soviet Destroyer Reported Blown Up in Black Sea," *Times* of London, September 27, 1974, p. 1; further details were provided by Norman Polmar, personal communication. The 1984 Kresta-class smoke (and fire?) was described in London's Press Association wire service, March 14, 1984, quoted in FBIS-SU, March 15, 1984, p. V1. Another Soviet warship suffered major damage (and an unknown number of dead and injured) when it rammed the Soviet freighter *Kaptan Soraka* in the Sea of Marmara (Ankara Radio, May 14, 1986), FBIS-SU, May 15, 1986, p. G2.

The December 1984 Russian drone landing in Finland is described from contemporary press accounts (*Facts on File*, 1985, 5E2), as is the September

1986 missile hitting China by accident (specifically, a Reuters dispatch from Washington dated September 16). The Soviet denial was noted by AFP from Moscow, FBIS-SU, September 19, p. B1.

The 1976 pilot defection attempt account is from Barron, op. cit., pp. 88–89; the two soldiers' account is on p. 104. The account of the Northern Fleet mutinies is based on an interview with Dmitriy Mikheyev. The 1975 *Storozhevoy* mutiny was reconstructed from contemporary press accounts (in particular, Lars Perrson, "Soviet Mutiny," *London Sunday Times*, May 16, 1976, p. 6), and from the research of Gregory Young (Lieutenant Commander, USN), as described in press accounts (e.g., Associated Press [AP], "Thesis Reveals Details of Soviet Mutiny," clipping from *Houston Post*, February 7, 1985, p. 6B) and personal interviews.

The 1987 Polish missile accident was reported in Western wire services from Warsaw and published in various U.S. newspapers on May 20. The account quoted a "Rev. Jan Skiba"; the accident had occurred the previous Monday.

5. SUBMARINES

The cited survey article is Jan S. Breemer, "Soviet Submarine Accidents— Background & Chronology," *NAVY International* (May 1986), pp. 309–12.

Turetsky's narrative is found in his memoir, op. cit.

To appreciate the catalog of disasters in the rest of this chapter, a "score card" of submarine types is necessary.

In the early 1960s several submarines were designed or modified to carry the SS-N-4 (Sark) missile. This was a surface-launched missile with poor accuracy, a 400-mile range, and a hefty one-megaton warhead. Turetsky recalls that even the Soviets had only low to medium confidence in it. Zulu-class diesel subs got two missile tubes (several were converted), and Golf-class diesel subs had three tubes (twenty-three of this model were built). Hotel-class nuclear subs had three tubes (eight subs were built). After 1963 most Golf and Hotel subs were retrofitted with the SS-N-5 (Serb) missile, which had an underwater launch capability, a range of about 800 miles, and an 800-kiloton nuclear warhead; the Soviets called this system the "R-21 missile," and according to Turetsky, they had only low confidence in it.

Next came the Yankee-class missile subs, carrying sixteen SS-N-6 missiles; they have a range of 1,500 miles, have increased accuracy, and each carries a one-megaton warhead. The first such sub was produced in 1967, and thirty-four were built over the next seven years. In the mid-1970s eighteen Delta-class subs (carrying twelve SS-N-8 missiles with a range of almost 5,000 miles) were built. By 1982 eighteen more of the advanced Delta II and Delta III categories had been launched. The new Delta IV-class missile subs are now being built. In 1980 the first Typhoon class was launched.

The source of the 1966 Polyarny report is a raw, unevaluated CIA DID (Domestic Intelligence Division) report (evidently an interview with a recent Soviet émigré), dated November 23, 1977, and released to the public through a Freedom of Information Act request in 1985. The 1966 report received corroboration when in early 1986 the Soviets were celebrating the twentieth anniversary of their first round-the-world underwater cruise. Accounts in *Pravda* (April 27, 1986, p. 6) described how "a detachment of Soviet nuclear-powered submarines" headed west from "an ice-laden naval base" (presumably Severomorsk) on a dark February night and returned "to the homeland" (though apparently not necessarily the same base) about six weeks later. The detachment commander was identified as A. Sorokin, now a rear admiral; one of the sub commanders was identified as Lev Nikolayevich Stolyarov; the current commander in chief of the Soviet Navy, V. N. Chernavin, took part in the planning of the cruise as chief of staff of a submarine group. This expedition may have been the one referred to by the émigré source. The existence of such a major expedition seems to lend some credibility to the accident report.

The April 11, 1968, loss of a Golf II-class missile sub in the mid-Pacific is discussed in a later chapter dealing with nuclear weapons accidents (the United States recovered some of the submarine's weapons). It is curious to note that no DID reports mentioned this incident; either there had been no Soviet domestic rumors, or (more likely) the relevant CIA reports were never declassified.

The April 11, 1970, sinking is documented in *Naval Nuclear Propulsion Program—1982*, an official U.S. Navy report to Congress, and also in an AP dispatch by Fred S. Hoffman, Washington D.C., June 22, 1984. Liardet's remarks about radiation monitoring of the 1970 sinking site were carried in Tam Dalyell, MP, "Low-Level Risks and a Mystery Sub," *New Scientist* (December 18, 1986), p. 21. For some reason, Dalyell wrote that the sub sank off the Scilly Islands, off Cornwall.

The January 1971 collision is documented in the USNI *Proceedings* (May 1972). The source of the February 1972 incident report is the USNI *Proceedings* (May 1973), and the *Naval Nuclear Propulsion Program—1982*.

The August 28, 1976, collision is documented in contemporary press accounts (e.g., *New York Times*, March 15, 1977, p. 3) and in the USNI *Proceedings* (May 1977).

The October 1978 Sea of Japan tow is reported by the *Times* of London, October 14.

The "late 1970s" Alfa-class meltdown is described by the "Center for Investigative Reporting"; other USN sources do not corroborate this story.

The August 19, 1978, incident off Scotland is documented in the USNI *Proceedings* (May 1979), and in *Naval Nuclear Propulsion Program—1982*.

Breemer's caution is on page 312 of his article.

The August 21, 1980, Sea of Japan breakdown is documented in the USNI *Proceedings* (May 1981), and *Naval Nuclear Propulsion Program—1982*. Details came from contemporary press accounts ("9 on a Soviet Vessel Feared Dead," *New York Times*, August 22, 1980), and particularly the article "Sailors Suffocated," *Times* of London, March 6, 1981, p. 7.

The October 27, 1981, grounding of a Whiskey-class submarine in Swedish territorial waters is described in a subsequent chapter about nuclear weapons mishaps.

The June 1983 sub loss was reported in *Combat Fleets of the World 1984/1985*.

It had first been mentioned in public on August 10, by CBS News in New York, which broadcast an exclusive report that there was almost certainly "substantial loss of life" among the ninety crewmen ("Sub Sinks, Many Dead, CBS Reports," Associated Press, *Houston Post*, August 11, p. 15A). In March 1984, before a closed session of the House Appropriations defense subcommittee, Director of Naval Intelligence Rear Admiral John L. Butts explicitly identified the sub, lost "in salvageable waters," as "Charlie-class" (*Aerospace Daily*, June 25, 1984, pp. 306–7).

The October 31, 1983, incident is documented in *Jane's Defence Weekly*, July 7, 1984, and in contemporary press clippings.

The March 21, 1984, collision is documented in contemporary press clippings and in "Adm. Schoultz Describes Collision of Soviet Sub, Carrier," *Aerospace Daily*, August 17, 1984, pp. 269–70. Contemporary press accounts document the September 1984 Sea of Japan fire and the January 1986 crippled sub in the East China Sea.

The October 1986 missile submarine explosion is documented in contemporary press clippings and in transcripts from the FBIS. The specific account of the Soviet captain refusing pickup is from George C. Wilson, "Soviet Sub Skipper Balked at Rescue," *Washington Post*, October 7, 1986.

6. Disaster Afloat

The Aliyev remarks are from an interview while working on the *Nakhimov* disaster, quoted in a Soviet press account transcribed by FBIS.

The 1982 *Tarasov* disaster is described in contemporary press reports summarized in *Facts on File* (1982), p. 136. Solzhenitsyn's account of the *Dzhurma* tragedy is in *Gulag Archipelago* (New York: Harper & Row, 1973), p. 582. Other sinkings are documented in the annual *Facts on File* volumes.

KOSPAS-SARSAT information is from contemporary press accounts and news releases; data on USSR distress calls are from personal communications from Kare Oyre (Norwegian Mission Control Center), C. Augoyard (French Mission Control Center), and Major Bill Roark, USAF Aerospace Rescue and Recovery Service, Scott Air Force Base, Illinois. The Soviet complaints about the operation of the KOSPAS system appeared in an article by N. Dombkovskiy in *Sovietskaya Rossiya*, August 20, 1987, page 4.

The 1977 *Skulptor Vuchetich* breakdown is documented in Werner Bamberger, "Soviet Ship Is Heading Home After Slow, Slow Crossing," *New York Times*, March 6, 1977, p. 42.

The 1977 Volga River oil tanker explosion is documented in "Volga Tanker Accident," *Times* of London, August 4, 1977, p. 5, and August 11, 1977, p. 6 ("28 Die in Tanker Blast").

The 1983 Volga cruise ship tragedy is documented in Agence France Presse accounts published in the FBIS-SU for June 7 and 8, 1983. The sinking of the *Komsomolets Nakhodki* is mentioned in a Reuters dispatch from Hakodate, Japan, printed in the *New York Times*, February 27, 1981, p. 2. The 1986 New Zealand sinking is based on contemporary press accounts plus FBIS-SU, March 7, 1986, p. E1.

The *Frieda K.* story is recounted in contemporary press clippings and, in highly distorted form, in official TASS releases transcribed in the FBIS daily report.

The myth of the *"Eshghabad* disaster" apeared in "270 Feared Lost in Caspian" (Associated Press report from Teheran, printed in the *Times* of London, July 16, 1957, p. 8). The subsequent denial of the report appeared in the *Times* of London on July 19, p. 9. Records from *Lloyd's* are maintained in the Guildhall Library in London, and they were searched by Miss J. M. Wright (personal communication dated August 19, 1987); a historical expert for *Jane's* also reported no records of the ship's existence (personal communication from Captain J. E. Moore, RN (August 30, 1987).

Information on the *Admiral Nakhimov* disaster comes from contemporary press clippings plus the FBIS-SU, particularly issues of September 2, 3, 5, and 10, November 3, December 15, 17, and 23, and the feature article "Grief, Tears, Kindness" in *Moscow News*. The *Admiral Nakhimov* (named after a hero of the Crimean War) had been built in Germany in 1925 and served as a hospital ship in World War II; the Soviets took possession of it after the war and converted it into a passenger liner on the Black Sea, where it was the flagship of the fleet in the 1950s. It had just been overhauled in Bulgaria the year before. The *Pyotr Vasyov* had been built in Japan in 1981 and purchased only shortly before the accident.

The list of reprimanded officials was impressive: Stanislav A. Lukyanchenko, chief of the Black Sea Shipping Company, expelled from the party and removed from his post; Anatoliy B. Goldobenko, USSR deputy minister of the Maritime Fleet, dismissed from his post and "strictly punished along party lines"; Guzhenko, former minister of the Maritime Fleet, "severe reprimand with endorsement" on party service records; Kuznetsov, chief of the ministry's Main Cadres Administration, "severe reprimand with endorsement" on party service records; Shchegolev, deputy chief of same office, same punishment; B. S. Maynagashev, member of the collegium and chairman of the All-Union Seafaring Association, dismissed from his post and "strictly punished along party lines"; Leontyev, deputy chairman of same association, severely reprimanded; Abukov, chairman of the Central Council for Tourism and Excursions, "reprimand with endorsement" on party service records; Oshcherin, deputy chairman of the Morpasflot ("Sea Passenger Fleet") All-Union Association, "severe reprimand with endorsement" on party service records; Boris A. Yunitsyn, USSR deputy minister of the Maritime Fleet, party proceedings instituted against; Sukhov, chief of the Sea Navigation Inspectorate, "reprimand with endorsement" on party service records.

The *Nakhimov* trial results were reported in *Pravda Ukrainy*, April 1, 1987, translated in FBIS, April 16, 1987, pp. R14–16.

The *Turkmenia* sinking was described in Moscow TASS in English, November 11, 1986, transcribed in FBIS-SU, November 12, 1986, p. R13.

The *Komsomolets Kirgizii* information came from contemporary press accounts, plus Viktor Loshak, "The Crew Battled to the End," *Moscow News*, 1987, No. 12, p. 4.

The 1987 rescue story is from a TASS dispatch transcribed in FBIS-SU, June 3, 1987, p. A5.

7. On Land . . .

The Shishlin quotation is taken from FBIS-SU, May 8, 1987, p. R19.

The Moscow fire street scene (September 3, 1976) is documented in "Muscovites Stay Cool About City Centre Blaze," *Times* of London, September 4, 1976, p. 4.

The February 25, 1977, Hotel Rossiya fire is documented in contemporary press accounts, in particular: "6 Die, Many Trapped in Big Moscow Hotel Fire," *Times* of London, February 26, p. 1; "Reporters Protest over Film Ban on Moscow Fire," Reuters and AP accounts, *Times* of London, March 1, p. 7; *Facts on File*, 1977, p. 204; Edmund Stevens, "Fire at Moscow Ministry After Hotel Disaster," *Times* of London, February 28, p. 6. The fire at the Zagorsk Monastery is described in *Izvestiya*, September 30, 1986, p. 6, translated in FBIS-SU, September 30, 1986, p. R17, and in Viktor Loshak, "Fire in Zagorsk," *Moscow News* (October 19, 1986), p. 4. The January 29, 1987, fire report is from contemporary press accounts.

The June 10, 1981, subway fire was reported in "Metro Deaths," *Times* of London, June 12, p. 8; the February 17, 1982, escalator collapse was documented in "Tube Disaster in Moscow," *Times* of London, February 19, p. 1, and February 20, p. 5. The March 30, 1983, subway collision was reported in "Moscow Metro Accident," *Times* of London, April 6, 1983, p. 5, and in "Moscow Denies Metro Accident," April 7, 1983, p. 8.

The January 1977 terrorist bombing was described in numerous press accounts, including: Edmund Stevens, "Six Reported Killed by Moscow Metro Bomb," *Times* of London January 11, p. 1; "Armenians Arrested," *Times* of London, December 1, 1977, p. 7. Emergency medical services were graphically portrayed in Dr. William A. Knaus, M.D., *Inside Soviet Medicine* (Boston: Beacon Press, 1981), pp. 227–29.

The September 1973 bombing in Lenin's tomb was described in Theodore Shabad, "Explosion at Lenin's Tomb Kills Three," *New York Times* news service, September 3, 1973, plus a personal account from a Western eyewitness in the Moskva Hotel. The June 1977 bombing is documented in the *Times* of London, July 8, 1977 p. 6. The February 1981 KGB headquarters bombing was mentioned in Michael Binyon, "Bomb Kills Soldier at KGB Base," *Times* of London, February 10, 1981, p. 1.

Kaiser's comments on auto safety were on page 330 of *Russia*, loc. cit. *Times* of London 1977 items were: "Eight Die at Bus Stop," June 10, p. 11; "Soviet Soldiers Killed," July 12, p. 8; "Dancers Killed," August 11, p. 3; "Crushed to Death," August 26, p. 5. The 1980 bus crash was from the files of the Swiss Re Insurance Corporation. The *Times* of London, February 28, 1983, p. 6, carried "14 Years for Bus Driver," about a jail sentence for careless driving which killed "several" people. The 1987 crash is documented in a Reuters dispatch from Moscow, "8 Die in Soviet Bus Crash," March 2, in *New York Times*, March 3, 1987, p. 5. Total annual fatalities were revealed in *Izvestiya*, June 20, 1987, p. 3; Western wire services carried a summary on the following day.

The August 1977 footbridge collapse is from "10 Killed in Collapse of Railway Bridge," *Times* of London, August 19, 1977, p. 5. The September

1986 bridge collapse in Latvia was mentioned in Western wire services from Moscow.

The April 1975 train disaster is documented in "Crash 'Kills Hundreds,' " *Times* of London, April 8, 1975, p. 6. The 1977 railway blaze is described in "Dining Car Blaze," *Times* of London, November 24, 1977, p. 8. The 1981 Caucasus collision is documented in "Soviet Crash," *Times* of London, June 29, 1981, p. 4. TASS reported the November 6, 1986, train crash in the Ukraine, in Moscow TASS in English, November 12, 1986, transcribed in FBIS-SU, November 14, 1986, p. R6. The results of the accident commission findings, and the punishment of the guilty, were described in "Severely Punished," *Pravda*, December 2, 1986, p. 2, translated in FBIS-SU, December 3, 1986, p. R7. The January 1987 crash is from contemporary Soviet press accounts.

The August 7 crash was reported in Viktor Alexandrov, "Train Collision Gives Rise to Serious Concern," *Moscow News*, #33, August 23–30, 1987, and contemporary Western wire service reports from Moscow.

The December 1984 gas explosion is from contemporary Western press accounts. The January 8, 1987, explosion is documented in "Pravda Notes Karelian ASSR Gas Explosion," FBIS-SU, January 16, 1987, p. R1, translation from *Pravda*, January 13, 1987, p. 6. The January 20 explosion was also from local Soviet press reports, TASS, transcribed in FBIS-SU, January 21, 1987, p. R7.

The March 1972 Minsk factory explosion was reported in *Facts on File*, 1972, p. 258. The 1982 Davidkovo blast is from Agence France Presse dispatches from Moscow, March 5, 9, and 11, 1982, translated in FBIS-SU. The Sterlitamak explosion was mentioned on the editorial page of the *Wall Street Journal*, May 3, 1984. The 1985 Leninsk-Kuznetskiy munitions plant disaster was documented in Martin Walker, "Hundreds Die in Munitions Blast," *Guardian* (London), January 10, 1985, p. 8, and in "Blast Kills Hundreds in Siberia," AFP dispatch from Moscow, *Times* of London, January 9, 1985, p. 5. The 1986 Biysk missile factory explosion was reported in FBIS-SU, April 23, 1986, p. R1, transcript of Vienna ORF Teltext, translated from German, quoting *International Defense Review* in Geneva.

The mid-1986 Ekibastuz power plant disaster was described in Soviet press accounts and a subsequent AP story filed from Moscow on September 20.

Klebanov's drive for mine safety was mentioned in David K. Shipler, "Soviet Workers Tell of Hazards of Complaining," *New York Times*, December 2, 1977. The 1986 Donetsk coal mine explosion was widely reported in contemporary clippings from wire services and from FBIS (December 29, 1986); in particular, "Mine Disaster Blamed on Safety Rule 'Breaches,' " *Izvestiya*, January 11, 1987, p. 6, translated in FBIS, January 16, 1987, p. S1.

The 1987 Chaykino mine explosion was documented in Soviet media accounts in FBIS-SU transcripts of TASS stories, May 27, 1987, pp. R10–11, and June 3, p. R11.

8. DISASTERS IN THE AIR

There are no authoritative lists of Soviet aviation disasters. Inquiries to Soviet agencies went unanswered. However, reports filter out via Western journalists and when non-Soviets are involved. *Flight International* publishes an annual review of civil aviation flight safety, including: 1969, on January 15, 1970; 1970, on January 21, 1971; 1971, on January 20, 1972; 1972, on January 18, 1973; 1973, on January 17, 1974; 1976, on January 22, 1977; 1977, on January 21, 1978; 1980, in the January 24, 1981, issue; 1981, in the January 23, 1982, issue; 1983, in the January 28, 1984, issue; 1984, in the January 26, 1985, issue.

Hedrick Smith's account of this tragic story of the missing student is recounted in *The Russians* (New York: Ballantine Books, 1976), pp. 461–62. Kaiser's use of the same story is on page 217 of his book. The case in which a man was put off the plane at Novosibirsk for drunkenness, and thus survived, was on January 13, 1977. Kaiser's interview with Kirilova was reported on page 64 of his book.

Concern over problems with Soviet aircraft safety goes way back, despite what Soviet newspapers wrote. It constitutes a theme of the two major memoirs from the 1960s, those of Khrushchev and Penkovskiy. The former Soviet leader wrote: "At that time [1959], there was a problem with our own helicopters. They weren't too reliable, and we had quite a few accidents with them. I used to fly in Soviet-made helicopters sometimes, but it wasn't recommended for me to do so." (*Khrushchev Remembers*, loc. cit., p. 371.) Penkovskiy, too, particularly mentioned helicopter safety problems. In his papers is this account: "In May 1961, near Odessa, practice firing of combat missiles was being conducted. On May 17 a group of Soviet generals including General Kolakchi, Chief of Combat Training of the General Staff; General Perevertkin, Deputy Chairman of the KGB; General Goffe, Varentsov's deputy; General Morozov, Chief of the Operations Directorate of the Odessa Military District; and others were flying to the proving grounds near the city of Nikolayev in a helicopter belonging to Lieutenant General Babadzhanyan, Commander of the Odessa Military District. While they were already over the proving grounds, one of the large rotor blades broke loose, and the helicopter crashed into the ground. Everybody including the crew was killed. All bodies were mangled terribly, and the relatives were not even allowed to see them. Soviet newspaper accounts of this tragedy merely said they died in an air accident. . . . There were also other accidents involving this same type of helicopter. Here is a striking example of effrontery and deceit! After that, how can one trust the statements of the central Party organ and the government, which always claim that they say nothing but the truth!" (*Penkovskiy Papers*, loc. cit., pp. 326–27.)

February 17, 1966: *Facts on File*, 1966, p. 152.

August 26, 1969: *Flight International*, annual review.

July 18, 1970: *Flight International*, annual review.

December 13, 1970: *Facts on File*, 1971, p. 80.

December 19, 1970: *Flight International*, annual review.

August 11, 1971: *Flight International*, annual review.

September 16, 1971: *Flight International*, annual review.

October 13, 1971: Swiss Re Insurance data base.

May 18, 1972: *Flight International*, annual review.

This assessment of the best of Soviet flight crew procedures is found in

Jerry terHorst and Joe Albertazzi, *The Flying White House* (New York: Coward, McCann, Geoghegan, 1979). Albertazzi was captain of the presidential airplane in the late 1960s and early 1970s.

October 3, 1972: *Flight International*, annual review.

October 13, 1972: *New York Times*, March 15, 1980.

November 28, 1972: *Flight International*, annual review.

February 19, 1973: *Flight International*, annual review.

March 3, 1973: *Flight International*, annual review.

May 7, 1973: Vladislav Krasnov, *Soviet Defectors* (Stanford, Calif.: Hoover Institution Press, Stanford University, 1986), p. 218.

June 30, 1973: *Flight International*, annual review.

October 13, 1973: *Flight Internationl*, annual review.

December 8, 1973: *Flight International*, annual review.

December 15, 1973: *Flight International*, annual review.

Aeroflot and public reaction to the series of air disasters is described in AP and UPI dispatches, "Aeroflot Admits Safety Problem," *Times* of London, December 28, 1973, p. 5. The deicing fluid story is from private sources.

April 27, 1974: *New York Times*, April 28, 1974, p. 1.

January 16, 1975: *Flight International*, annual review.

July 25, 1975: *Flight Internationl*, annual review.

September 3, 1975: *New York Times*, September 4, 1975, p. 2.

January 3, 1976: AFP bureau, Moscow, and *New York Times*, January 15, 1976, p. 8.

March 5, 1976: *New York Times*, March 10, 1976, p. 2.

June 1, 1976: *New York Times*, June 4, p. 6 and June 5, p. 4.

September 6, 1976: *Flight International*, annual review.

November 28, 1976: *New York Times*, November 30, p. 12, and December 1, 1976, p. 7.

ICAO safety statistics are from *Flight International*.

January 13, 1977: *New York Times*, January 23, 1977, p. 9.

February 15, 1977: *Times* of London, February 21, 1977, p. 5.

May 27, 1977: *New York Times*, May 28, 1977, p. 3, and May 29, 1977, p. 7.

Il-62 disasters: Following the crash of a LOT Il-62 with members of the U.S. Olympic boxing team, the *New York Times* (March 15, 1980, p. 5) carried a UPI article entitled "Il-62's Involved in Other Crashes." The "Chinese connection" story is from private sources.

March 17, 1979: Western news sources, Moscow.

August 11, 1979: *Flight International*, annual review.

June 5, 1980: Swiss Re Insurance data bank.

June 12, 1980: *Flight International*, annual review.

July 7, 1980: *New York Times*, July 18, 1980, p. 5.

February 7, 1981: *New York Times*, February 14, p. 4.

July 6, 1982: *Times* of London, July 7, 1980, p. 4.

September 30, 1982: *Flight International*, annual review.

August 30, 1983: *Flight International*, annual review.

August 5, 1984: *Flight International*, annual review.

October 15, 1984: *Flight International*, annual review, and Western news sources, Moscow.

February 1, 1985: *Sovietskaya Belorussiya*, February 3, 1985, p. 1.

May 3, 1985: AFP, May 7, 1985, in FBIS-SU, May 7, p. V1.

July 10, 1985: Tashkent, *Pravda Vostoka*, July 13, 1985, p. 1, translated in FBIS-SU, August 21, p. R1.

October 13, 1985: AFP, October 15, in FBIS-SU, November 6, p. R9.

October 16, 1986: *New York Times*, October 18, 1986, p. 2.

December 12, 1986: Contemporary clippings, including TASS.

ICAO figures on Soviet flight safety statistics are in *Flight International*, January 31, 1978, p. 186.

Vladimir Gerasimov, "On the Trail of Accidents: The Price of Truth," *Pravda*, June 15, 1987, p. 4. The October 20, 1986, crash is documented in "Blinds Go Up on Lowered Blinds," anon., *Flight International*, July 18, 1987, p. 8.

The politicization of the October 1986 crash of Samora Machel's jet in South Africa is documented in: "The Catastrophe of the Mozambique Aircraft: An Eye-Witness's Account," TASS International Service in Russian, November 13, 1986, translated/transcribed in FBIS-SU, November 14, 1986, p. J1; Moscow Radio Peace and Progress, unattributed commentary discussing causes of crash, October 24, 1986, in English, transcribed in FBIS-SU, October 28, 1986, p. J2; interview with Ivan Vasin, Moscow TASS in English, November 12, 1986, cited in FBIS-SU, November 13, 1986, p. CC1.

The earlier Mozambique crash was described in *Flight International*, October 25, 1986, p. 3.

The official South African commission's findings were well summarized in *Wall Street Journal*, July 1, 1987.

9. SUPERPROJECTS

The *Maxim Gorkiy* aircraft catastrophe story is from *Khrushchev Remembers*, loc. cit., p. 38, and "Out of the Past," *Aerospace America* (May 1985), p. 111.

A good overview of the Tu-144 project can be found in contemporary press accounts and in sections of Kenneth Owen, *Concorde—New Shape in the Sky* (London: Jane's, 1982), pp. 155–57, and *Jane's All the World's Aircraft*, especially the 1973 edition.

The Greville Wynne story (his autobiography, *A Man from Odessa*, was published in London in 1981) was told to the BBC television program *Newswatch*. He claimed that the false data might have contributed to a Russo-French tragedy in 1973, when a Tu-144 crashed into a Paris suburb. But that seems farfetched since pilot error is a much more realistic verdict (see below). See Henry Stanhope, "Russia 'Duped' over Concorde," *Times* of London, October 2, 1981, p. 3.

The design of the 1973 version (Paris Air Show) is critiqued in "*Tupolev: Ses 'Moustaches' Étaient Trop Longues et Fragiles*" ("Tu: Its 'mustaches' were too long and fragile"), *Science et Vie* (August 1973), pp. 44–47. Firsthand accounts of the accident are from private sources.

The subsequent chronology of the aircraft's fall from glory is given in: "Russians Term Tu-144 Flights Start of Supersonic Service," *Aviation Week* (January 5, 1976), p. 25; "All Quiet on the Concordeski Front," *New Scientist* (November 25, 1976), p. 429; "Concordeski into Service," *New Scientist* (November 3, 1977), p. 273; "Problems Pare Soviet Tu-144 Flight Service," *Aviation Week* (November 28, 1977), p. 2; "A Shaky Lift-off for 'Concorde-ski,' " *Business Week* (December 12, 1977), p. 58; "Moscow Suspends Flights of Supersonic Airliner," *Times* of London, September 15, 1978, p. 6; Roger Eglin, "Why Russia's Concordeski Was a Drag," *Sunday Times* of London, September 17, 1978, p. 10; AP dispatch from Moscow, by Seth Mydans, November 1, 1978, *New York Times* news service; "Technical Aid Sought for Tu-144," *Aviation Week* (December 4, 1978), pp. 26–27; "Russia Explains Tests on Supersonic Plane," *Times* of London, January 23, 1981, p. 4; Richard Owen, "Russia Grounds Its Ill-starred Concordeski," *Times* of London, August 10, 1984, p. 5.

The Zelenchuk Observatory's facilities are described in Siegfried Marx and Werner Pfau, *Observatories of the World* (New York: van Nostrand Reinhold, 1982). Freeman Dyson's personal observations are in "Astronomy in a Private Sphere," *The American Scholar* (Spring 1984), pp. 174–75. Another personal memoir is A. G. David Philip, "Observing with the Soviet Union's 6-Meter Telescope," *Astronomy* (September 1983), pp. 26–28; see also David H. Smith, "Six-Meter Views of M33 [a nearby galaxy]," *Sky & Telescope* (August 1987), pp. 140–41, which shows high-quality photographic results ("It seems as though the world's largest telescope is useful for something after all"). Personal communications from Dr. Anthony Fairall provided additional details.

The full argumentation about Soviet manned moon plans is found in my book *Red Star in Orbit* (New York: Random House, 1981).

The history of Soviet Mars probes is found in Nicholas Johnson, *Handbook of Soviet Lunar and Planetary Probes* (San Diego: Univelt, 1982), and in Saunders Kramer, "A Retrospective Look at the Soviet Union's Efforts to Explore Mars," in *The Case for Mars* (San Diego: Univelt, 1982), pp. 269–80.

10. Dead Cosmonauts

The epigraph is from the series of articles by Yaroslav Golovanov in *Izvestiya*, April 2, 3, 4, 5, 6, 1986; this one was from April 3, p. 6.

The photograph of Leonov with my book came from Arthur C. Clarke. The "missing cosmonaut mystery" was described in my book *Red Star in Orbit*; additional photographs were published in my book *Outer Space Mysteries* (Virginia Beach, Va.: Donning, 1982). The original publication of the Sochi Six photograph was in *Spaceflight* (1973), and the side-by-side comparison of the before/after forgery was first published in *Spaceflight* (1974).

Nelyubov's fate was described in *Izvestiya*, April 5, 1986, p. 3. Leonov's lies (to Dutch journalist Peter Smolders) are found in "Those Missing Cosmonauts," *Spaceflight* (March 1975), pp. 172–74. Bondarenko's death was described in *Izvestiya*, April 3, 1986, p. 6, and was the subject of a UPI story by Jack Redden in Moscow, April 4. Tiktin's mention of the name Boychenko occurred in *Posev* (October 1982), p. 46 ff.; Golyakhovsky's detailed account of the cosmonaut's death agonies was in *Russian Doctor* (New York: St. Martin's Press, 1984), pp. 130–33. One interesting aspect was that Golyakhovsky had recalled that the event had occurred in the winter of 1960–1961, but more toward the beginning (later he discounted this error as a bad guess based on the weather). His error in remembering the date of the cosmonaut's death is paralleled in other verbal testimony by Soviet émigrés, in which the dates of long-remembered disasters can be greatly in error. He also misremembered another character's name, hearing "Seryegin" and almost two decades later remembering "Sergeyev"; this type of error, too, seems to happen with some regularity.

My articles debunking the "dead cosmonaut" rumors appeared in *Aerospace Historian* (December 1973) and in longer form in "Phantoms of Space," *Space World* (January 1975), pp. 6–16.

Shonin's book was *Samiye Perviye*, "The Very First Ones," Mashinostroyenie (Moscow, 1977). He first gave the first names of the missing eight cosmonauts.

Versions of the Sochi photographs appeared in:

All six, Yevgeniy Ryabchikov, *Russians in Space* (New York: Doubleday, 1971).

Minus Grigoriy, M. Vasilyeva, ed., *Shagi K Zvezdam* (Moscow: Molodaya Gvardiya, 1972), p. 58.

Golovanov's attack on me was in *Izvestiya*, April 3, 1986, p. 6. The Novosti English-language bulletin was issued on May 4. Later that year, Izvestiya Publishers released Golovanov's *Kosmonavt N. 1*, and on page 40 he had completely rewritten the attacks on me into kisses.

The Ogden/Ilyushin story (April 1961) is recounted in my article "Phantoms of Space," *Space World* (January 1975).

Shatalov's admission that "six or eight" cosmonauts had died in training was made to an American astronaut, who told me within a few days of the conversation. The Tokov story came from other NASA personnel.

Michael Cassutt received his intriguing CIA letter on March 23, 1987; he received the DIA document (dated June 13, 1967) shortly afterward.

Khrushchev's comments on the release of space accident reports are from *Khrushchev Remembers*, loc. cit.

A detailed description of Komarov's spaceflight death is in *Red Star in Orbit*. Additional new details have come from Victor Yevsikov, *Re-Entry Technology and the Soviet Space Program (Some Personal Observations)* (Reston, Va.: Delphic Associates, December 1982), and from private interviews.

Gagarin's death was described in contemporary press accounts, but in 1987 the Soviets finally released the official accident report.

The deaths of the Soyuz 11 trio and the 1975 Soyuz launch abort were described in *Red Star in Orbit*.

The Soviet space candor blitz of 1983 was documented in *Krasnaya Zvezda* on: January 29, p. 4; April 2, p. 4; April 12, p. 4; April 13, p. 4; and August 9, p. 4. The *Literaturnaya Gazeta* article on the Soyuz 23 splashdown was published on January 25, 1984, p. 10.

11. Exploding Rockets

The Khrushchev quotation is from *Khrushchev Remembers*, loc, cit., p. 46.

The American general's interview in question was with Danny Graham at the offices of *High Frontier*. Although the photos themselves are still classified, launch records confirmed that the general's disclosure was consistent with actual spy satellite flight schedules. In public these satellites were called "Discoverer satellites." The reconnaissance hardware was called "KH-4," a "keyhole" in the sky to peep in on the Russians. One such American "spysat" had been launched on October 26, 1961, only hours after the Soviet catastrophe. But the booster had failed. The next launch had occurred on November 12, and a film capsule had been successfully recovered a few days later. Quite possibly this one contained the photographs the general had referred to. If so, the photos would have been taken only three weeks after the explosion. Another three-day reconnaissance mission ended successfully on December 10, but then a string of booster and satellite problems prevented the retrieval of any additional spysat pictures until the following June. Scorch marks probably would have been gone by then.

The Nedelin catastrophe constituted an entire chapter in *Red Star in Orbit*. Penkovskiy's reference was on pp. 325–26 of *The Penkovskiy Papers*; Khrushchev's comments were in *Khrushchev Remembers, The Last Testament*, p. 51 ff; Zhores Medvedev's account was in *New Scientist* (1976). Tiktin's article providing further crucial data was in *Posev* (October 1982), p. 46 ff. Medvedev's letter with corroborating information had been sent to me on June 25, 1977, but the significance of the passage in question had not been recognized.

Blyadskiy rot! is an equivalent of the Americanism *son of a bitch!*; it actually designates "born of a whore."

Titov's lie about no Soviet space failures in that period was published in *Aviatsiya i Kosmonavtika* (September 1985), translated by the author. Khrushchev's comments had been on page 122 of the second volume of his memoirs.

Curtis Peebles wrote his report, "Soviet Launch Losses," for *Spaceflight* (April 1987), pp. 163–66. These formerly secret American data had been contained in a special CIA report prepared in mid-1964 for Bill Moyers, then White House press secretary. The cover note, dated June 1, 1964, read simply: "Here is the CIA forecast of Soviet Space Spectaculars in Balance of 1964 which was requested in your name by Hays Redmon. . . . [signed] Bromley Smith." It was prepared jointly by the CIA's Directorate of Science and Technology and the Directorate of Intelligence. The document, one of millions in the Lyndon B. Johnson Library, was approved for public release on March 11, 1985. Although the text mainly addressed expected future activities, the document also included a chart labeled "Soviet Space Probes," with little boxes indicating "Success," "Partial Success," and "Failure" arrayed along a time line from late 1957 through mid-1964. It is this chart which Peebles analyzed for his own report to the British Interplanetary Society's magazine. See also Phillip S. Clark, *Soviet Launch Failures, 1957–1985* (London: privately published, 1986), 49 pages.

The 1960 unmanned Vostok failures were described in *Izvestiya*, April 6, 1986, p. 3, and later in the pamphlet form of the same Golovanov material

(p. 48). Vladimirov's reference to the same incident had been made in his book *The Russian Space Bluff* (New York: Dial Press, 1971), p. 88.

The failure of the Soviet's Saturn V booster in the 1969–1971 period is detailed in studies by Charles Patrick Vick, "The Soviet G-1-e Manned Lunar Landing Programme Booster," *Journal of the British Interplanetary Society*, vol. 38, pp. 11–18, 1985. The new Energiya booster is described in my article "Soviets Tell All (?) About New Booster," *Aerospace America* (July 1987).

The September 26, 1983, on-pad Soyuz fire-explosion is recounted in contemporary Western wire service and newsmagazine accounts, particularly in *Aviation Week* (December 12, 1983). For a detailed treatment, see "Drama of Soyuz T-10A," in my book *The New Race for Space* (Harrisburg, Pa.: Stackpole Publishers, 1984). The Soviets officially acknowledged the incident only in early 1987; see, for example, *Krasnaya Zvezda*, May 30, 1987.

The UFO panics in Russia sparked by secret Soviet space and missile activity are described in various articles and books of mine. The 1977 "jellyfish" over Petrozavodsk is the subject of a chapter in *Outer Space Mysteries*, loc. cit. The 1967 UFO flap is described in the USSR Academy of Sciences report, Gindilis, Karteshev, et al., "Observations of Anomalous Atmospheric Phenomena—A Statistical Analysis," and is debunked in my two-part article published in the *MUFON UFO Journal* (1985). The June 14, 1980, flap was described in my article in *Fate* (January 1984).

The June 21, 1985, illegal satellite foul-up was described in "Mysterious Soviet Space Launch," *Wall Street Journal* (January 24, 1986), and later in "Soviet Space Booster Progress," *Aerospace America* (March 1987); nobody at the United Nations or the U.S. State Department has expressed any concerns about the treaty violation despite my repeated written inquiries.

Original Proton rocket statistical summaries were given in an interview with Poletayev, *Moscow News* (August 31, 1986), p. 10. Launch-by-launch descriptions were subsequently released at the International Astronautical Federation convention in Austria in October. The interview, Theo Pirard with Aleksandr Dunayev, is quoted courtesy of Space Information Center, Pepinster, Belgium. The foolish boast of "35 straight" successes was made in an interview in *Izvestiya* published December 12, 1986. The subsequent two launch failures are documented in contemporary Western media and via private sources.

12. REACTORS FROM THE SKY

The Soviet RORSAT program is well described in Curtis Peebles's book *Battle for Space* (New York: Beaufort Books, 1983).

The recovery operations which followed the Kosmos 954 fall in 1978 are described in *Operation Morning Light*, Department of Energy, Las Vegas, Nevada, 1978, Washington D.C.: Government Printing Office and in C. A. Morrison, *Voyage into the Unknown: The Search and Recovery of Cosmos 954* (Stittsville, Ont.: Canada's Wings Press, 1982).

The reconstruction is also based on contemporary press clippings and on Soviet material from the FBIS. In particular, this account was very useful: "Kosmos-954 May Have Been in Collision," Moscow TASS, February 4, 1978.

The rerun of the debacle, Kosmos 1402 in 1983, was documented from the popular press, in particular these articles: editorial, "Russian Roulette, Global Style," *New York Times*, January 9, 1983, p. 22E; Craig Covault, "Soviet Nuclear Spacecraft Poses Reentry Danger," *Aviation Week* (January 10, 1983), pp. 18–19; Oleg Belotserkovskiy, "Kosmos-1402: Why Nuclear Reactors on Satellites Present No Danger," *Pravda*, January 16, 1983, p. 3; John Noble Wilford, "Russian Satellite Falls Harmlessly over Indian Ocean," *New York Times*, January 24, 1983, p. 1.

General dangers of current orbiting reactors are discussed in "Radioactive Space Debris Study Cities Hazards to Satellites, Earth," *Aviation Week* (September 22, 1986), pp. 19–20. One Soviet denunciation of falling American nuclear satellites is Yuriy Zhukov, "Nuclear Reactors for SDI," *Pravda*, November 12, 1986, p. 6.

13. THE URALS DISASTER

The Powers U-2 incident in 1960 is described in detail in Michael R. Beschloss, *Mayday: Eisenhower, Khrushchev, and the U-2 Affair* (New York: Harper & Row, 1986).

The early years of Soviet nuclear weapons development are described in Peter Kelly, "How the USSR Broke into the Nuclear Club," *New Scientist* (May 8, 1986) pp. 32–35.

The earliest Western mention of the "Urals disaster" was in the July 29, 1958, issue of *Argentinisches Tageblatt* (published for the German community in Argentina), reported in the August 1958 issue of the Argentine government's *Boletín Informativo—Comisión Nacional de Energía Atómica*, pp. 10–11.

The initial round of public debate, sparked by the article by Medvedev ("Two Decades of Dissidence," *New Scientist*, London [November 4, 1976], pp. 264–67), included such useful pieces as Sarah White, "CIA Confirms Medvedev's Disaster Claim," *New Scientist* (December 1, 1977), p. 547.

Subsequent debate was chronicled in: Lee Torrey, "Experts Go Critical over Soviet Nuclear Disaster," *New Scientist* (July 26, 1979), pp. 267–68; Sarah White, "More Soviet Fallout," *New Scientist* (August 2, 1979), p. 361; Zhores Medvedev, "Nuclear Disaster in the Urals," *New Scientist* (October 11, 1979), pp. 115–17; W. Stratton et al., "Are Portions of the Urals Really Contaminated?," *Science* (October 26, 1979), pp. 423–25.

Medvedev's book is *Nuclear Disaster in the Urals* (New York: W. W. Norton, 1979). Its publication was followed by further discussion, such as: anon., "The Wasteful Truth About the Soviet Nuclear Disaster," *New Scientist* (January 10, 1980), p. 61; Richard Pollock, "The Siberian Coverup: Why Did U.S. Officials Keep Silent About a Nuclear Catastrophe for 20 Years?," *Critical Mass* (April 1980), p. 4; John R. Trabalka et al., "Analysis of the 1957–1958 Soviet Nuclear Accident," *Science* (July 18, 1980), pp. 345–53; Colin Norman, "Soviet Radwaste Spill Confirmed," *Science* (April 16, 1982), p. 274; Deborah Shapley, "Soviet Radio-Catastrophe: Another Theory," *Nature* (April 22, 1982), pp. 696–97; John Trabalka et al., "Radioactivity in the Urals," letters, (p. 198) and Zhores Medvedev, (p. 200), *Science* (July 16, 1982).

Further useful sources include: Frank L. Parker, "Search of the Russian

Scientific Literature for the Descriptions of the Medical Consequences of the Kyshtym 'Accident,' " Environmental and Water Resources Engineering, Vanderbilt University, Nashville, Tenn., March 1983; Colin Norman, "The Kyshtym Mystery (contd.)," *Science* (July 8, 1983), p. 138; "Shuttle Photographs Nuclear Accident Site," *Aviation Week* (October 15, 1984); F. Morgan, *Kyshtym Revisited*, Atomic Weapons Research Establishment Report No. 0 24/84, Aldermaston, Berkshire, Great Britain, August 1985; Zhores Medvedev, "Ecological Aspects of the Chernobyl Nuclear Plant Disaster," *Trends in Ecology and Evaluation (TREE)* (July 1986), pp. 23–25.

The Menaker account is from *Posev* (August 1983), pp. 45–49, and to the best of my research was never noticed in any English-language publication (translation is by this author). Perspectives on this and other still-obscure aspects of the disaster(s) were enhanced by personal communications with John Trabalka, Frank Parker, Richard Wilson, Stuart Nachtwey, and others.

A curious feature of the nuclear disaster(s) in the Urals and the history of nuclear unsafety in the Soviet weapons programs is that neither of the famous memoirs covering the period of the 1950s and early 1960s, Penkovskiy's and Khrushchev's, mentions anything at all about such subjects.

For Khrushchev's material, a satisfactory explanation may rest with the obvious fact that the material had been edited both in Khrushchev's own mind and by the agency which transported the tapes to the West. Jerrold Schecter, in his introduction to the second volume, explicitly mentions this: "There was evidence, from comparison of tapes and transcripts, that some controversial material had been removed before it reached the West. . . . There are still omissions in this volume, sometimes marked by gaps in the tapes, sometimes by Khrushchev's own reluctance to discuss a subject in detail. . . . Actual gaps in the tapes are caused by those working with Khrushchev who thought the material might be compromising to them or to Khrushchev himself. There is careful avoidance of certain matters [such as] details about the first Soviet atomic bomb. To have published such details would have subjected Khrushchev and his heirs to charges of disloyalty and violation of the laws governing state secrets." (*Khrushchev Remembers*, loc. cit., pp. xiv and xviii.)

Khrushchev may have actually given public testimony about the Kyshtym disaster when in 1958 he announced a nuclear test moratorium. If the weapons-grade plutonium industry had been crippled by a major accident, it could have used a year or two to get back on its feet again. The moratorium ended in a few months.

The Kyshtym disaster was just the kind of thing that Oleg Penkovskiy, who hated what the Soviet system was doing to his beloved Mother Russia, would have wanted to complain about. His material covers the period through 1962, when he was arrested. But no mention of such nuclear disasters appears in his memoirs. At least the version of his memoirs released by the CIA in 1965 omits any mention of the event, whatever may have been in the original material he sent out prior to his arrest. The published version is believed to have been heavily edited at the CIA, both to excise certain categories of data and to add several counterfeit sections. It's impossible to tell what was—or wasn't—in the original.

14. NUCLEAR GULAG

Solzhenitsyn's account is in *The Gulag Archipelago* (New York: Harper & Row, 1974), pp. 407 and 592–93.

The other material is derived from Mikhail Klochko, "Victims of Stalin's A-Bomb," *New Scientist* (June 23, 1983), pp. 845–49; from Avraham Shifrin, *The First Guidebook to Prisons and Concentration Camps of the Soviet Union*, Stephanus ed. (Switzerland: Uhldingen/Seewis, 1980), and from the television documentary *The Nuclear Gulag*, Twenty Twenty Television London, produced by Geoffrey Seed, telecast on July 12, 1986. Additional material came from Menaker (in *Posev* [August 1983]) and from Los Alamos reports on the Kyshtym disaster.

Significant effort was spent in evaluating and calibrating the sources of this horrifying material. Features such as plausibility and consistency were analyzed, and external corroboration was sought. For example, a formerly classified document released by the CIA in 1986 corroborates some of Shifrin's material on the existence of particular nuclear facilities and the level of radioactive contamination there. The document, released without an origination date, was so highly censored it was rendered useless but was still intriguing. It read: "Chelyabinsk-40 was located approximately 50 km from Chelyabinsk-70 and was rumored to have been involved with nuclear weapons in some capacity. Some officers, who may have served in C-40 and were later transferred to C-70, described an explosion accident that occurred at C-40 approximately 5 to 10 years prior to Source's arrival at C-70 [year not given]. There was no information on the cause of the explosion but there were reports that it was powerful and that trees were levelled in a large area. In conversations among enlisted men, C-70 was referred to as a 'clean' city as opposed to C-40 which was referred to as a radioactively 'contaminated' city. Source thought that atomic explosives may have been produced at C-40." Such independent material significantly enhances the credibility of the otherwise incredible reports relayed by Shifrin and Seed.

15. MISCELLANEOUS NUCLEAR ACCIDENTS

The string of pre-Chernobyl nuclear plant accidents are documented in: unnamed Soviet correspondent, "Soviet Breeder Reactor Accident," *Nature* (March 8, 1974), p. 95; same author, "Soviet Reactor Accident: Official," *Nature* (April 5, 1974), p. 468; Vera Rich, "Fire Threatened Fast Reactor Cooling System, Says Unofficial Report," *Nature* (January 31, 1980), p. 420 (the source of the Petrosyants epigraph); Vera Rich, "Soviet Nuclear Energy: Accident at Construction Plant," *Nature* (July 28, 1983), p. 301; Vera Rich, "Teething Trouble Persists," *Nature* (March 15, 1984).

Many of the declassified CIA reports on these items were obtained by David E. Kaplan of the Center for Investigative Reporting, and they contributed to his articles such as "Was Chernobyl an Isolated Incident?," *San Francisco Chronicle*, November 12, 1986, pp. A1, 7.

There are several accounts of fatalities during Soviet thermonuclear weapons tests. The H-bomb test fatalities were reported by John Prados, *The*

Soviet Estimate (New York: Dial, 1981), p. 23. The mid-1960s accident was documented in William R. Corson and Robert T. Crowley, *The New KGB: Engine of Soviet Power* (New York: William Morrow, 1985), p. 249, and interviews with both authors. The early 1970s accident is reported in an émigré interview conducted by the CIA's DID and later declassified.

The 1983 Turnov explosion is documented in the *Kurier,* of Vienna, January 14, 1984, p. 3, reported in FBIS-SU, January 17, 1984, p. F1; the 1987 Estonian story comes from "Mischievous Soviets," *Insight,* May 4, 1987, p. 36. The Czech plague story was reported by Vera Rich in *Nature* (March 27, 1980).

The loss and recovery of the Golf II-class submarine in the mid-Pacific are well described in Roy Varner and Wayne Collier, *A Matter of Risk* (New York: Random House, 1978). Key elements of the story have been independently verified with private sources.

The embarrassing grounding of a nuclear-armed submarine in Swedish territorial waters is reconstructed from contemporary press accounts, particularly the following: Frank J. Prial, "Sweden Releases Soviet Sub; Finds Signs of Nuclear Arms," *New York Times,* November 6, 1981, p. 1; Michael Binyon, "Russia Uses Spy Claim to Justify Sub Incident," *Times* of London, November 11, 1981, p. 8; Serge Schmemann, "Soviet Rejects Swedish Protest in Submarine Affair," *New York Times,* November 12, 1981, p. 12.

An excellent overview of the incident is provided by Julian S. Lake, "Whiskey on the Rocks," *Defense Electronics* (January 1982), pp. 23–28. Even years later the Soviets continued to plead innocent incompetence. In mid-1984, in response to a new article in *Jane's Fighting Ships,* TASS political news analyst Vladimir Vashedchenko wrote: "As far as the instance with Soviet submarine 137, which, on a routine training cruise in the Baltic Sea in October 1981, ran off her course as a result of a disrepair of navigation instruments and found itself in Sweden's territorial waters, the Soviet government then expressed its regret to the government of Sweden and clarified that it was an unintentional incident and that it in no way affected Sweden's security interests."

The disaster on the nuclear icebreaker *Lenin* is documented in two declassified CIA Intelligence Information Reports, one dated May 7, 1970, entitled "Nuclear Accident and Predicted Down Time for Nuclear Icebreaker 'Lenin,' " and the other, dated June 9, 1970, with a deleted title.

Military-generated nuclear waste leaks in Estonia are reported in Reuters, from Stockholm, "Russian Nuclear Waste Dump Leaks," *Times* of London, August 30, 1985, p. 6. The nuclear submarine "death duty" for condemned prisoners is described in Shifrin, op. cit.

Menaker's story of the domestic radiation alarms in Chelyabinsk is in *Posev* (August 1983), p. 49. Other sources (Sarah White, "Soviets Worried About Nuclear Power Too," *New Scientist* [November 8, 1979], pp. 419–20) have reported on dangerously high radiation levels in portions of the Volga River where nuclear industrial waste is dumped carelessly. Medvedev's account of radioactive birds is from his book *Nuclear Disaster in the Urals,* loc. cit.

Swedish detection of radiation on winds from Russia in 1977 is documented in Wendy Barnaby, "Soviet Beams over Sweden?," *Nature* (December 15, 1977), pp. 551–52. Later incidents are reported in "Soviet Radiation," *Times* of London, December 22, 1982, p. 6, and in Malcolm W. Browne, "Swede Reports Data Suggest Previous Russian Accidents," *New York Times*, May 7, 1986, p. 9.

Some radioactive winds need not be from power plant accidents. Soviet underground nuclear explosions frequently punch through to the surface and inject fallout into the atmosphere (Quentin Crommelin and David S. Sullivan, *Soviet Military Supremacy* [Los Angeles, University of Southern California Press, 1985], estimated there had been more than thirty such ventings in the past several decades). Since it occasionally occurs with American tests, too, and since analysis of the radioactive isotope ratios provides American nuclear experts with first-rate intelligence on Soviet weapons technology, the U.S. government has not objected too strenuously to the Soviet habit.

The 1987 radioactive winds story is documented in an Associated Press wire story, "Radiation Increases Are Detected in Europe," *New York Times*, April 15, 1987, and in Debora MacKenzie, "Mystery Radiation Stalks Europe," *New Scientist* (April 23, 1987), p. 23. Other accounts are provided in FBIS-SU, April 17, 1987, pp. R19–20.

16. THE CHERNOBYL SYNDROME

The source of the epigraph is a Soviet embassy official identified as "Mike De'Revyanko [Derevyanko?]" in William Allmans' article "Chernobyl: An Overreaction?," *Science 86* (July/August 1986), p. 11.

The basic chronology is derived from contemporary press clippings, plus in particular: Richard Wilson, "What Really Went Wrong?," *Nature* (September 4, 1986), pp. 29–30; Vladimir Kyucharyants, "Chernobyl—Tragedy of Six Errors," *Moscow News* (issue unknown, 1986), pp. 3, 6; "Chronology of a Catastrophe," *Nature* (September 4, 1986), pp. 26–27; Walter C. Patterson, "Chernobyl—the Official Story," *Bulletin of the Atomic Scientists* (November 1986), pp. 34–36; and Bennett Ramberg, "Learning from Chernobyl," *Foreign Affairs* (June 1987), pp. 304–22.

The Soviet "heroic" version is described in Y. Lvov, "Chernobyl: A Chronicle of Heroism," *Soviet Union* (August 1986), p. 54, and in Pyotr Avanesov, "Accident," *Soviet Life* (September 1986), pp. 34–41.

The vivid descriptions about the impact on evacuated children is in Felicity Barringer, "From Children of Chernobyl, Tales of Flight and New Fears," *New York Times*, June 5, 1986, p. 1.

Two different versions of Gorbachev's speech were printed in *Soviet Life* (July 1986, p. 38) and *Soviet Union* (July 1986, p. 2), both official Soviet English-language propaganda magazines. The nastiest comments about lies and TMI were omitted from *Soviet Life*, which is primarily distributed in the United States; *Soviet Union*, which is for English-language readers elsewhere in the world, traditionally carries more viciously anti-American material. Armand Hammer's account of Gorbachev's feelings, in Charlotte Curtis, "The Soviet Connection," *New York Times*, May 27, 1986, p. 6.

See Andrey Illesh, *Chernobyl: A Russian Journalist's Eyewitness Account* (New York: Richardson & Steirman, 1987). His TMI cover-up fraud is on page 194, where he also maintains there were no previous Soviet nuclear accidents.

Soviet complaints about Western reactions are typified by Mikhail Ozerov, "Exploiting Misfortune," *Sovietskaya Rossiya*, May 18, 1986, p. 5, translated in FBIS-SU, May 21, 1986, p. A5 (criticism of Adelman), and interview with Georgi Arbatov, "Human Misfortune Mustn't Serve to Fan Hate," *Moscow News* (May 25, 1986), p. 5.

The nature of the exaggerated fears is explored in: William A. Dorman and Daniel Hirsch, "The U.S. Media's Slant," pp. 54–56, and "Nuclear Deception: Soviet Information Policy," pp. 32–36, *Bulletin of the Atomic Scientists* (August/September 1986); Sara Rimer, "New York's Ukrainians Await Word," *New York Times*, May 1, 1986, p. 10. Western media performance was analyzed in Richard Smyser, "TMI to Chernobyl: What Have We Learned?," *Science Writers* (December 1986), pp. 1–5. Soviet concerns about radiation effects were reported in a November 25, 1986, AFP dispatch from Moscow, transcribed in FBIS-SU, November 26, pp. R8–9. Knizhnikov discussed the "mass panic" in an article described in the *Times* of London, June 18, 1987, p. 7. A week earlier correspondent Christopher Walker had filed a story from the scene, "An Eerie Silence in the Shadow of Chernobyl," *Times* of London, June 10, pp. 1, 28.

The view of Soviet public attitudes is from Gina Thomas and Peter Adams, "Soviet People Seem to Find Little to Fear," *Orlando Sentinel* news service in *Houston Chronicle*, May 4, 1986, pp. 1, 29. McCally's remarks were in his article "Hospital Number Six: a First-hand Report," *Bulletin of the Atomic Scientists* (August/September 1986), pp. 10–12.

Soviet propaganda counterattack was exemplified by Moscow World Service in English, "Commentators Discuss Use of Nuclear Power," May 11, 1986, FBIS-SU, May 15, 1986, pp. U1–U4.

The Soviet performance at the Vienna conference was described in John Maddox, "Soviet Frankness Creates Sense of Solidarity," *Nature* (September 4, 1986), p. 3, and "Search for Extra Safety," *Nature* (September 4, 1986), p. 25. Valuable insights (including the private Legasov comment) are in Richard Wilson, "A Visit to Chernobyl," *Science* (June 26, 1987), pp. 1636–40. Aleksandrov's ideological comments are from Wilson; another idiotic statement by Aleksandrov is: "The fuss over the construction of nuclear energy plants in the United States has nothing to do with safety; the real reason is that the development of large nuclear power stations could endanger the profits of the fuel-producing monopolies," quoted in Marshall Goldman, "Keeping the Cold War out of Chernobyl," *Technology Review* (July 1986), pp. 18–19.

The Charles Wick quotations from Irvin Molotsky, "Chernobyl and the 'Global Village,'" *New York Times*, May 8, 1986. The Abagyan quotation is from Michael S. Serrill, "'We Are Still Not Satisfied'—Doubt and Mistrust Prevail as Scientists Discuss Chernobyl," *Time* (September 8, 1986), p. 46.

CONCLUSION

The epigraph is from FBIS-SU, May 8, 1987, p. R18.

The Longworth quotation is from Richard C. Longworth, "Reporting from

Moscow: Then and Now," *Bulletin of the Atomic Scientists* (December 1986), pp. 20–23.

Official disclosure of falling life expectancy was in an article by L. Ivchenko (interviewing Vladimir Guryev, deputy head of the USSR Central Statistical Administration) in *Izvestiya*, February 8, 1987, p. 4, and further details were in a TASS English-language dispatch released on February 10, 1987, transcribed in FBIS-SU, February 10, p. R15. Yet even such a source has been accused of deception: Mark D'Anastasio, "Soviets Are Said to Practice Deception to Show Their Economy Is Improving," *Wall Street Journal*, May 14, 1987.

The account of fire deaths appeared in A. Illesh, "Lost in Fire," *Izvestiya*, July 17, 1987, and in Viktor Grigoryev, "Not a Natural Calamity: The Cost of Fire," *Moscow News*, no. 26, July 5–12, 1987, p. 12.

APPENDIX 1:
LOCATIONS

This is a listing of most of the places mentioned in this book and their precise locations. Spelling and latitude/longitude from *The Times Atlas of the World,* 7th ed. (London: John Bartholomew & Son, 1985).

	N lat E long		N lat E long
Achinsk	56.20 090.33	Chita	52.03 113.35
Aksu (Kazakhstan)	52.31 072.00	Cholovka	North of Zhitomir
Alma Ata	43.19 076.55	Chukotsk Sea	65 180
Almalyk	40.50 069.40	Davidkovo	Moscow suburb
Andizhan	40.40 072.12	Dolon	41.47 075.42
Araks River	39 046	Domodedovo Airport	55.25 037.46
Argayash	Near Kyshtym	Donetsk	48.00 037.50
Asanova	Near Kyshtym	Druzhnaya Base	−77.56 −40.22
Ashkhabad	37.58 058.24	Ekibastuz	51.50 075.10
Asht	40.38 070.20	Fergana	40.23 071.19
Bagaryak	Near Kyshtym	Frunze	42.53 074.46
Barents Sea	70 040	Gagra	43.21 040.16
Batumi	41.37 041.36	Gåsefjarden	56.20 015.50
Bekabad	40.38 071.11	Gorkiy	56.20 044.02
Belokataiski	Near Kyshtym	Groznyy (Chechen-	
Beloyarskiy	56.47 061.28	Ingush)	43.21 045.42
Biysk	52.35 085.16	Irkutsk	52.18 104.15
Bobruysk	53.08 029.10	Kaliningrad	54.40 020.30
Borovoye	53.07 070.20	Kamchatka Peninsula	55 160
Boyevka	Near Kyshtym	Kamenskaya	48.21 040.19
Bratsk	56.20 101.82	Karaganda	49.53 073.07
Brest	52.08 023.40	Karagayly	49.20 075.41
Brodokalmak	Near Kyshtym	Karshi	38.53 065.45
Chaykino	Near Donetsk	Kasli	55.54 060.45
Chelyabinsk	55.12 061.25	Kavalerovo	44.19 135.08
Cherepovets	59.09 037.50	Keila	59.18 024.29
Chernobyl	51.17 030.15	Kem	64.58 034.39

	N lat	E long
Khabarovsk	48.32	135.08
Kharkov	50.00	036.15
Kiev	50.25	030.30
Kirovograd	48.31	032.15
Kishinyov	47.00	028.50
Kokand	40.33	070.55
Kola Peninsula	68	035
Kondopoga	62.12	034.17
Koristovka	Near Kirovograd	
Krasnodar	45.02	039.00
Kuibyshev	53.12	050.09
Kuptovikh	Near Kyshtym	
Kyshtovka	56.35	076.34
Kyshtym	55.43	060.32
Leninabad	40.14	069.40
Leninsk (Uzbekistan)	40.37	072.15
Leninsk-Kuznetskiy	54.44	086.13
Lermontov	44.05	043.00
Lvov	49.50	024.00
Mangyshlak Peninsula	44	051
Margilan	40.35	071.45
Medvezhiy, Cape		
Metlino	Near Kyshtym	
Miasskoye	Near Kyshtym	
Mineralniye Vodiy	44.14	043.10
Minsk	53.51	027.30
Mirniy Base	−66.55	093.02
Molodezhnaya Base	−67.67	045.85
Moskva	55.45	037.42
Murmansk	68.59	033.08
Novaya Borovaya	North of Zhitomir	
Novorossiysk	44.44	037.46
Novosibirsk	55.04	083.05
Nukus	42.28	059.07
Olga Bay	44	135
Omsk	55.00	073.22
Oymyakon	63.30	142.44
Paldiski	59.22	024.08
Petrovka	Near Kyshtym	
Petrovskiy	Near Chelyabinsk	
Poti	42.11	041.41
Rakhov	48.02	024.10
Rakushka Bay	Far East	
Ramenskoye	55.61	038.22
Riga	56.53	024.08
Rudnyy	53.00	063.05
Russkaya Karabolka	Near Kyshtym	

	N lat	E long
Salang Tunnel	35	068
Samarkand	39.40	066.57
Semipalatinsk	50.26	080.16
Semiyarka	50.74	078.54
Severodvinsk	64.35	039.50
Severomorsk	69.05	033.30
Shamor Bay	44	135
Sheremetyevo Airport	Near Moscow	
Shevchenko	43.37	051.11
Simferopol	44.57	034.05
Sochi	43.35	039.46
Sonkovo	57.50	037.22
Sotsgorod	Near Leninabad	
Sovetabad	40.50	072.58
Sterlitamak	53.85	057.40
Sverdlovsk	56.52	060.35
Syktyvkar	61.42	050.45
Tallinn	59.22	024.48
Tarya Bay	Kamchatka	
Tashkent	41.16	069.13
Tbilisi	41.43	044.48
Techa River	Near Kyshtym	
Techa-Brod	Near Kyshtym	
Totma	59.59	042.44
Troitsk	54.08	061.33
Tselinograd	51.10	071.28
Tyubuk	Near Kyshtym	
Tyuratam Spaceport	46	064
Ufa	55.46	060.08
Ulyanovsk	54.19	048.22
Vaygach Island	70.28	058.59
Verkhneuralsk	53.52	059.14
Vilnius	54.40	025.19
Vnukovo Airport	55.36	037.22
Vorkuta	67.27	064.00
Vostok II Base	−78.47	106.80
Yasinovataya	48.06	037.54
Yerevan	40.10	044.31
Yugo-Koneva	Near Kyshtym	
Zagorsk	56.20	038.10
Zarechnaya	56.03	097.29
Zelenchukskaya	43.53	041.36
Zeravshan	39.10	068.39
Zheltiye Vodiy	48.21	033.31
Zhitomir	50.30	028.81
Zholymbet	Near Aksu	
Zvyozdniy Gorodok	Northeast of Moscow	

APPENDIX 2:
DISASTER CHRONOLOGY

This is a summary by date of the disasters discussed in this book.

1935 May 18	*Maxim Gorkiy* crash kills 48.
1950 April 8	USN plane destroyed, Baltic, 10 killed.
1952 June 13	Swedish C-47 destroyed, 8 killed.
1952 June 16	Swedish rescue plane shot down.
1952 October 7	RB-29 destroyed, Sea of Japan, 8 killed.
1953 July 29	RB-29 destroyed, Sea of Japan, 16 killed.
1954 November 7	RB-29 destroyed, Sea of Japan, 1 killed.
1955 June 23	USN aircraft attacked, Bering Sea, by mistake.
1957 May 15	First Soviet ICBM launch, explodes.
1958 ???	Troitsk reactor, major fire.
1958 February?	Kyshtym nuclear disaster.
1958 February	Sputnik 3A launch failure.
1958 June 22	Moon shot fails.
1958 September 24	Moon shot fails.
1958 December 4	Moon shot fails.
1959 June 18	Moon shot fails.
1960 April 15	Moon shot fails
1960 July 1	RB-47 shot, Barents Sea, 4 killed.
1960 July 22	Unmanned Vostok rocket fails.
1960 October 10	Mars rocket fails.
1960 October 14	Mars rocket fails.
1960 October 24	Nedelin catastrophe kills dozens.
1960 December 4	Unmanned Vostok burns up.

1960 December 22   Unmanned Vostok rocket fails.

1961 ???   Missile test sub lost with all hands.
1961   Nuclear contamination, sub off England.
1961 March 23   Cosmonaut killed in fire.

1962 October 24   Mars rocket disintegrates over United States.

Mid-1960s   Nuclear test accident, many dead.

1966   Major nuclear contamination, sub.
1966 Approx.   Reactor meltdown, icebreaker *Lenin,* 30 killed.
1966 February 17   Tu-114 crash, Moscow, 48 die.
1966 February 18   Ex-cosmonaut Nelyubov suicide (?).
1966 December 31   Fishing fleet refrigerator ship sinks, Alaska, 50 killed.

1967 February 28   Fish-processing ship sinks, Denmark, 57 killed.
1967 April 24   Space crash kills cosmonaut Komarov.
1967 Summer   Ukrainian-Caucasus pseudo-UFO panic.

1968 Approx.   Sub lost with all hands, off Severomorsk.
1968 Approx.   Uranium mine *zek* uprising, 300 killed.
1968 March 24   Air crash kills Gagarin.
1968 April   Off-course test moon ship falls in China.
1968 April 11   Sub sinks, Pacific; United States later finds.

1969 January   Space nuclear reactor in pad explosion.
1969 March 23   Trawler sinks off North Carolina, 25 drown.
1969 July 4   Superbooster explodes on pad.
1969 July   Moon robot crashes.
1969 August 26   Il-18 crash, Moscow, 16 dead.
1969 September   Moon shot fails.
1969 October   Moon shot fails.

1970 February 6   Proton rocket explodes.
1970 April 11   Sub sinks off Spain, many dead.
1970 May   Nuclear sub scuttled off Faeroe Islands.
1970 July 18   An-22 vanishes, 23 die.
1970 August   Proton rocket fails.
1970 December 13   Air crash, Leningrad, kills 90.
1970 December 19   An-22 crash, India, kills 17.

1971 January   Collision cuts off nose of sub, ?? killed.
1971 May   Proton rocket fails.
1971 June   Superbooster explodes in flight.
1971 June 30   Three cosmonauts die on return to earth.
1971 August 11   Air crash reported, Irkutsk, kills 97.
1971 September 16   Tu-134 crash, Kiev, 49 killed.
1971 November 27   Mars probe crashes.
1971 December 2   Mars probe crashes.

1972 February   Off Newfoundland, sub taken in tow, ?? killed.
1972 March 11   Minsk factory blast kills 100.

1972 May 18	Air crash, Kharkov, kills 108.
1972 July 30	Proton rocket fails.
1972 October 3	Air crash, Sochi, kills 100.
1972 October 14	Worst Soviet air crash kills 176, Moscow.
1972 November 22	Superbooster explodes in flight.
1972 November 28	Japan Airlines DC-8 crashes in Moscow, 42 killed.
1972 December	Off United States in Atlantic, sub radiation leak.
1973	Nuclear test at Semipalatinsk kills dozens.
1973 February 19	Air crash, Prague, kills 66.
1973 March 3	Il-18 crash, Moscow, kills 25.
1973 April 25	Space nuclear reactor lands near Hawaii.
1973 May 7	Midair explosion kills 100.
1973 June 3	Tu-144 crash, Paris, kills 9.
1973 June 30	Tu-134 crash, Amman, kills 9.
1973 September 1	Lenin's tomb bomb kills 3.
1973 October 13	Air crash, 28 killed.
1973 December 9	Air crash, Moscow, kills 13.
1973 December 16	Lithuania air crash kills all aboard.
1974 February 10	Probe misses Mars.
1974 March 9	Mars probe crashes.
1974 March 12	Mars probe crashes.
1974 April 27	Leningrad air crash kills 118.
1974 July	Fire at nuclear plant, Shevchenko.
1974 August 31	Destroyer *Otvazhniy* blows up, 200 dead.
1975	Defecting aircraft shot down, Black Sea.
1975 January 16	Air crash, Laos, 12 killed.
1975 April ?	Train crash kills 40–100, Lithuania.
1975 April 5	Soyuz launch abort, crashes in mountains.
1975 July 25	Batumi air crash kills 28.
1975 September 3	Crew member suicide over Atlantic, Aeroflot.
1975 October 16	Proton moon probe fails.
1975 November 7	*Storozhevoy* mutiny, dozens die.
1976 January 3	Moscow air crash kills 87.
1976 March 5	Armenia air crash kills 120.
1976 April 2	Sea of Japan, Japanese plane attacked.
1976 June 1	Africa air crash kills 46.
1976 August 5	Tu-95 crashes off Newfoundland.
1976 August 28	Sub hits U.S. warship in Mediterranean.
1976 September 3	Major downtown Moscow fire.
1976 September 6	Sochi air crash kills 90.
1976 October	Nuclear accident (?) near Tallinn.
1976 October	Fire aboard nuclear sub kills several.
1976 October 15	Cosmonauts splashdown accident.
1976 November 28	Moscow air crash kills 72.
Late 1970s	Alfa-class sub reactor meltdown.

1977	Nuclear leak on sub, many crew evacuated.
1977 ???	Fire on express train kills 4.
1977 January 8	Moscow subway explosion kills 7.
1977 January 13	Alma Ata air crash kills 90.
1977 February 15	Air crash kills about 100.
1977 February 25	Hotel Rossiya fire kills 20–40.
1977 May 27	Havana air crash kills 68.
1977 June 9	Truck accident kills 8.
1977 June 11	Hotel bombing, no deaths.
1977 July 9	Truck-bus collision kills 15.
1977 August	Caucasus road crash kills 8.
1977 August	Proton rocket fails.
1977 August 1	Volga barge explosion kills 28.
1977 August 18	Footbridge collapse kills 10.
1977 August 25	Car kills 8 pedestrians.
1977 September 20	Petrozavodsk UFO panic
1977 Late	Radiation detected on Soviet wind.
1978 January	Kosmos 954 nuclear reactor hits Canada.
1978 January 2	Plane crash, Antarctica, 3 killed.
1978 April 20	Korean airliner shot at, 2 killed.
1978 May	Tu-144 crash kills 2
1978 May 27	Proton rocket fails.
1978 June 21	Iranian helicopter shot down at border.
1978 August 17	Proton rocket fails.
1978 August 19	Sub taken in tow off Scotland.
1978 October 13	Sub taken in tow in Sea of Japan.
1978 October 17	Proton rocket fails.
1979 March 17	Moscow air crash kills 90.
1979 April	Anthrax outbreak in Sverdlovsk.
1979 April 13	Two cosmonauts almost stranded in space.
1979 August 11	Midair collision, 173 killed over Ukraine.
1979 December 31	Fire at nuclear power plant, several dead.
1980 March 3	Bus accident kills 21.
1980 June 5	Air crash kills 110.
1980 June 12	Air crash kills all aboard Yak-40.
1980 June 14	Moscow pseudo-UFO panic.
1980 July 7	Alma Ata air crash kills 163.
1980 August 21	North Pacific sub fire kills 9.
1981 February 7	Leningrad air crash kills 70.
1981 February 16	Bomb near KGB HQ kills 1.
1981 February 26	Freighter sinks off Japan, 38 die.
1981 May 15	Moscow pseudo-UFO panic.
1981 June 10	Moscow subway fire kills 7.
1981 June 24	Caucasus train crash kills 70.
1981 July 18	Lost Argentine airliner destroyed, 4 die.
1981 September	Baltic sub accident.

1981 October 27	"Whiskey on rocks" in Sweden.
1982 January 8	Radio factory blast kills 50.
1982 January 23	Krasnoyarsk air crash kills 150.
1982 February 16	Freighter sinks off Newfoundland.
1982 February 17	Moscow subway accident kills 32.
1982 March 4	Moscow munitions factory blast kills dozens.
1982 April 12	Fire destroys generators, Vostok base.
1982 July 6	Moscow air crash kills 90.
1982 July 23	Proton rocket fails.
1982 September 30	Luxembourg air crash kills 7.
1982 November 3	Salang Tunnel fire kills 1,000.
1982 December 24	Proton rocket fails.
1983 January 23	Body of Kosmos 1402 burns up over Indian Ocean.
1983 February	Core of Kosmos 1402 burns up over South Pacific.
1983 March 30	Moscow subway collision kills some.
1983 April	Rendezvous abort, Soyuz T-8.
1983 May 24	Czech explosion kills 30–60 soldiers.
1983 June ?	Sub sinks, North Pacific, all killed.
1983 June ?	Major accident, Atommash nuclear plant.
1983 June 5	Volga, cruise ship hits bridge, 170 die.
1983 August 30	Alma Ata air crash kills all on Tu-134.
1983 September ?	Fuel leak cripples space station.
1983 September 1	Korean airliner shot down, 269 die.
1983 September 26	Soyuz explodes on pad.
1983 October 31	Sub snared in U.S. equipment, North Atlantic.
1983 December ?	Dolon Airfield, arsenal blows up.
1983 December	Radiation on winds from USSR.
1983 December 24	Soviet bomber seen to crash, East Germany.
1984 March 21	Sub rammed by U.S. aircraft carrier.
1984 May 13	Severomorsk ammo dump blast kills 200.
1984 May 15	Bobruysk ammo dump explodes.
1984 June 25	Schwerin ammo dump blast kills 100.
1984 August 5	India air crash kills 3.
1984 August 9	Swedish airliner chased by Soviet jet.
1984 August 31	Destroyer blows up, Black Sea, 200 killed.
1984 September 20	Sea of Japan, sub accident.
1984 September 21	Strait of Gibraltar, sub hits freighter.
1984 October 15	Omsk air crash kills 150.
1984 October 28	Kabul plane crash kills 240 soldiers.
1984 December ?	Ammo plant blast kills hundreds.
1984 December 2	Tbilisi gas explosion kills 100.
1984 December 28	Off-course missile lands in Norway.
1985 February	Short circuit cripples space station.
1985 February	Radiation on winds from USSR.
1985 February 1	Minsk air crash kills 80.
1985 February 18	Tu-95 crashes into sea off Cam Ranh Bay.

1985 May 3	Midair collision kills 80.
1985 May 16	Helicopter crash, Sea of Japan.
1985 June 21	Rocket failure violates UN registration requirement.
1985 July 7	Fighter seen to fall into sea, off Sweden.
1985 July 10	Uzbek air crash kills all aboard.
1985 July 21	Fighter seen to fall into sea, off Norway.
1985 October 13	Poti air crash kills 12.
1985 November	Soyuz mission aborted, cosmonaut ill.
1986 January	Sub taken in tow, East China Sea.
1986 January ?	Ammo plant blast kills many.
1986 February ?	Plane crash, Antarctica, 6 dead.
1986 February 16	Passenger ship sinks off New Zealand.
1986 April 26	Chernobyl reactor explodes.
1986 May 23	Second Chernobyl fire.
1986 June 1?	Airborne laser lab burns, some killed.
1986 Mid-June	Radiation on winds from USSR.
1986 August 31	Cruise ship sinks, Black Sea, 400 die.
1986 September 11	Off-course missile hits China.
1986 September 20	Bridge collapse kills 10.
1986 September 28	Fire at Zagorsk Monastery kills 5.
1986 October	Urals air crash kills 2.
1986 October 6	Missile sub explosion kills 3, sub sinks.
1986 October 16	Air crash kills 2.
1986 October 19	Mozambique air crash kills 37.
1986 October 20	Tu-134 crash kills "many," Kuibyshev.
1986 November 6	Ukraine train crash kills many.
1986 November 11	Fire on liner kills 2, Sea of Japan.
1986 December	Donetsk mine blast kills 7.
1986 December 12	Berlin air crash kills 69.
1987 Early	Estonia weapons accident.
1987 January ?	Train accident kills 2.
1987 January 8	Gas explosion kills 3.
1987 January 20	Gas explosion kills 3.
1987 January 29	Hotel Rossiya fire kills 1.
1987 January 30	Proton rocket fails.
1987 March 2	Caucasus truck accident kills 8.
1987 March 14	Freighter sinks off New Jersey, all saved.
1987 Mid-March	Radiation on winds from USSR.
1987 April	Proton rocket fails.
1987 May	Fighter drops missile on Poland, 1 killed.
1987 August 7	Train crash kills up to 80, Kamenskaya.

INDEX

ABOUT THE AUTHOR

JAMES OBERG works in the space shuttle program in Houston, specializing in Mission Control activities during manned orbital rendezvous operations. As an aerospace engineer, he has received numerous honors from the American Institute of Aeronautics and Astronautics and other aerospace professional societies. Beyond his day-to-day spaceflight duties, Oberg has been a student of Soviet aerospace technology since before *Sputnik,* and is a recognized free world authority on Soviet space activities. He has written eight books and hundreds of magazine articles on the past, present, and future of space exploration around the world, and he frequently appears on national news programs and in newspapers and magazines and wire services as an expert commentator. Oberg's widely publicized "sleuthing" into official USSR government space secrets has often prompted the Soviet news media to release hitherto classified information about undisclosed rocket bases, unacknowledged cosmonaut fatalities, falling satellites, and similar secretive topics. Born in New York City, Oberg now lives on Soaring Hawk Ranch in rural Galveston County, Texas, with his wife (and often coauthor) Alcestis ("Cooky"), their young sons Gregory and John, and numerous dogs, cats, and horses.